P9-AQI-816

The 9/11 Encyclopedia

THE 9/11
ENCYCLOPEDIA

VOLUME 1

Stephen E. Atkins

Praeger Security International
Westport, Connecticut • London

Library of Congress Cataloging-in-Publication Data
Atkins, Stephen E.
  The 9/11 encyclopedia / Stephen E. Atkins.
    p. cm.
  Includes bibliographical references and index.
  ISBN-13: 978-0-275-99431-0 ((set) : alk. paper)
  ISBN-13: 978-0-275-99432-7 ((vol. 1) : alk. paper)
  ISBN-13: 978-0-275-99433-4 ((vol. 2) : alk. paper)
  1. September 11 Terrorist Attacks, 2001—Encyclopedias. 2. September 11 Terrorist
Attacks, 2001—Influence—Encyclopedias. I. Title: Nine eleven encyclopedia. II. Title.
  HV6432.7.A85 2008
  973.931—dc22   2008004185

British Library Cataloguing in Publication Data is available.

Library of Congress Catalog Card Number: 2008004185
ISBN-13: 978-0-275-99431-0 (set)
       978-0-275-99432-7 (vol. 1)
       978-0-275-99433-4 (vol. 2)

First published in 2008

Praeger Security International, 88 Post Road West, Westport, CT 06881
An imprint of Greenwood Publishing Group, Inc.
www.praeger.com

Printed in the United States of America

The paper used in this book complies with the
Permanent Paper Standard issued by the National
Information Standards Organization (Z39.48-1984).

10 9 8 7 6 5 4 3 2 1

Contents

List of Entries   vii

List of Primary Documents   xi

Guide to Related Topics   xv

Volume 1

Preface   xix

Encyclopedia   1

Volume 2

Chronology of Events Surrounding 9/11   xix

Primary Documents   327

Annotated Bibliography   547

Index   567

List of Entries

Abdel Rahman, Sheikh Omar
Able Danger
Abouhalima, Mahmud
African Embassy Bombings
Alec Station
American Airlines Flight 11
American Airlines Flight 77
American Society of Civil Engineers
  Report
Argenbright Security Company
Atef, Mohammad
Atta, Mohamed el-Amir Awad
  el-Sayed
Azzam, Sheikh Abdullah Yussuf

Bahaji, Said
Beamer, Todd Morgan
Biggart, William
Bingham, Mark Kendall
Bin Laden, Osama
Bin al-Shibh, Ramzi
Bucca, Ronald
Burlingame, Charles Frank "Chic" III
Burnett, Thomas Edward
Bush, George W.
Bush Administration

Cantor Fitzgerald
Casualties of September 11
Central Intelligence Agency
Chomsky, Noam
Churchill, Ward
Clarke, Richard A.
Cleanup Operations at Ground Zero
Clinton Administration
Conspiracy Theories
Counterterrorism Center

Dahl, Jason Matthew
DCA
Department of Design and
  Construction
Disaster Mortuary Operation
  Response Team
Dog Rescue and Recovery Teams
Downey, Ray Matthew

Economic Impact of September 11

Fadl, Jamal al-
Fahrenheit 9/11
Families of Victims of September 11
Family Assistance Center
Family Steering Committee

Federal Aviation Administration (FAA)
Federal Bureau of Investigation (FBI)
Federal Emergency Management
    Agency (FEMA)
Feehan, William M. "Bill"
Fetzer, James H.
Fire House 40/35
Firefighters at Ground Zero
Firefighter Riot on November 2,
    2001
Floyd, Nancy
Foreign Intelligence Surveillance
    Act of 1978
Freedom Tower
Freeh, Louis
Fresh Kills Landfill

Ganci, Peter J. "Pete"
Giuliani, Rudolph William Louis
    "Rudy" III
Giuliani Time (Documentary)
Glick, Jeremy
Goss, Porter J.
Graham, Daniel Robert "Bob"
Griffin, David Ray
Guantánamo Bay Detainment Camp

Hage, Wadih el-
Hamburg Cell
Hamburg Cell (TV Movie)
Hamdani, Mohammad Salman
Hamilton, Lee H.
Hanjour, Hani Saleh Husan
Hazmi, Nawaf bin Muhammad
    Salim al-
Homer, LeRoy Wilton Jr.

Ielpi, Lee
Immigration and Naturalization
    Services (INS)

Jarrah, Ziad Samir
Jersey Girls

Joint Terrorism Task Force
Jones, Steven E.
Judge, Mychal
Justification for the September 11
    Suicide Mission

Kean, Thomas Howard
Kerik, Bernard Bailey
Kifah Refugee Center, al-
Kuala Lumpur Meeting

Levin, Neil David
Lewin, Daniel M.

Marrs, Jim
Mazza, Kathy
Merino, Yamel
Meyssan, Thierry
Mihdhar, Khalid al-
Millennium Plots
Mohamed, Ali Abdel Saoud
Mohammed, Khalid Sheikh
Motassadeq, Mounir el-
Moussaoui, Zacarias
Murad, Abdul Hakim Ali Hashim

National Commission on Terrorist
    Attacks upon the United States
National Security Agency (NSA)
Naudet Documentary on 9/11
New York City Landmarks Bombing
    Conspiracy
New York City Police Department
    (NYPD)
Nineteen Martyrs
North American Aerospace Defense
    Command (NORAD)
Nosair, El Sayyid

Office of Emergency Management
    (OEM)
Ogonowski, John
Olson, Barbara

O'Neill, John
Ong, Betty Ann
Operation Bojinka
Occupational Safety and Heath
    Agency (OSHA)

The Path to 9/11 (TV Miniseries)
Pavel Hlava Video
Pentagon Attack
Phoenix Memo
Pilot Training for September 11
Port Authority of New York and
    New Jersey
Predator

Qaeda, al-
Quds Mosque, al-

Rendition
Rescorla, Cyril Richard (Rick)
Ressam, Ahmed
Rowley, Coleen

Samit, Harry
Saracini, Victor J.
Scheuer, Michael
Scholars for 9/11 Truth
Senate Select Committee on
    Intelligence and the House
    Permanent Select Committee on
    Intelligence Joint Inquiry into the
    Terrorist Attacks of September 11
Shehhi, Marwan Yousef Muhammed
    Rashid Lekrab al- (1978–2001)

Smith, Moira
Swift Project

Taliban
Tenet, George
TIPOFF
Transportation Security
    Administration

United Airlines Flight 93
United Airlines Flight 175
United 93 (Film)
USA PATRIOT Act

Victims' Compensation Fund
Von Essen, Thomas

Wag the Dog (Movie)
The Wall
Weldon, Curtis "Curt"
World Trade Center
World Trade Center, September 11
World Trade Center (Movie)
World Trade Center Bombing
    (1993)

Yousef, Ramzi Ahmed

Zadroga, James
Zammar, Muhammad Heydar
Zawahiri, Ayman al-
Zubaydah, Abu

List of Primary Documents

Document 1: Letter Justifying the Bombing of the World Trade Center (February 7, 1993)

Document 2: Osama bin Laden's Declaration of Jihad (August 23, 1996)

Document 3: Declaration of World Islamic Front (February 23, 1998)

Document 4: Communiqué of the World Islamic Front (1998)

Document 5: Al-Qaeda Training Camps in Afghanistan in 2000

Document 6: Al-Qaeda's Instructions on Living in the Western World While on a Mission

Document 7: Martyr's Blood

Document 8: Memorandum from Richard A. Clarke for Condoleezza Rice Informing Her about the al-Qaeda Network (January 25, 2001)

Document 9: Letter from Brian F. Sullivan, Retired FAA Special Agent, to U.S. Senator John Kerry (May 7, 2001)

Document 10: Letter from Michael Canavan, Associate Administrator for Civil Aviation Security, to FAA Security Managers (May 30, 2001)

Document 11: Presidential Daily Briefing (August 6, 2001)

Document 12: Brian Sullivan's E-mail to Michael Canavan, FAA Associate Administrator for Civil Aviation Security, about Aviation Security (August 16, 2001)

Document 13: Mohamed Atta's Letter of Advice for Hijackers (September 2001)

Document 14: Oral Testimony from Survivors of the World Trade Center

Document 15: Pentagon Attack

Document 16: United Airlines Flight 93

Document 17: Dog Handlers at Ground Zero

Document 18: President George W. Bush's Address to the Nation (September 11, 2001)

Document 19: Interview with Mullah Omar Muhammad (September 21, 2001)

Document 20: Environmental Protection Agency's Press Release (September 13, 2001)

Document 21: Statements by Federal Emergency Management Agency on

Its Response to the Terrorist Attacks on the World Trade Center in New York City and the Pentagon before the United States Senate's Committee on Environment and Public Works (October 16, 2001)

Document 22: *Dawn* Interview with Osama bin Laden (November 10, 2001)

Document 23: Bin Laden's Homage to the Nineteen Students (December 26, 2001)

Document 24: White House Declaration on the Humane Treatment of Al-Qaeda and Taliban Detainees (February 7, 2002)

Document 25: Testimony of Dr. W. Gene Corley on Behalf of the American Society of Civil Engineers before the Subcommittee on Environment, Technology and Standards and Subcommittee on Research of the U.S. House of Representatives Committee on Science (May 1, 2002)

Document 26: Report by Eleanor Hill from the Joint Inquiry Staff Statement on the Intelligence on the Possible Terrorist Use of Airplanes (September 18, 2002)

Document 27: Report by Eleanor Hill from the Joint Inquiry Staff on the Intelligence Community's Knowledge of the September 11 Hijackers Prior to September 11, 2001 (September 20, 2002)

Document 28: Statement of Special Agent of the Federal Bureau of Investigation (September 20, 2002)

Document 29: Report of the Joint Inquiry by Eleanor Hill on the FBI's Handling of the Phoenix Electronic Communication (September 23, 2002)

Document 30: Report of the Joint Inquiry Staff by Eleanor Hill on the FBI Investigation of Zacarias Moussaoui (September 24, 2002)

Document 31: Testimony of Richard A. Clark Before the National Commission on Terrorist Attacks Upon the United States (March 24, 2004)

Document 32: Testimony of Mary Fetchet, Founding Director, Voices of September 11th, on the Need for Reform in a Hearing of the Senate's Committee on Government Affairs (August 17, 2004)

Document 33: Assessment of the FBI on Pre-9/11 Intelligence (August 18, 2004)

Document 34: Testimony by Lee Hamilton, Vice Chairman of the 9/11 Commission, before the House of Representatives' Financial Services Committee (August 22, 2004)

Document 35: The Aviation Security System and the 9/11 Attacks (2004)

Document 36: Letter from Brian F. Sullivan to Thomas Kean, Chairman of the National Commission on Terrorist Attacks Upon the United States (2004)

Document 37: Comments of Representative Maxine Waters (D-CA) on Saudi Financial Support for Al-Qaeda before the House of Representatives' Financial Services Committee (August 22, 2004)

Document 38: Curt Weldon's Testimony about Able Danger (September 20, 2005)

Document 39: Essay by Ward Churchill (September 11, 2001)

Document 40: Selected Excerpts from the Testimony of FBI Agent Harry Samit in the Zacarias Moussaoui Trial (March 9, 2006)

Document 41: Testimony of the
American Red Cross before the
Management, Integration, and
Oversight Subcommittee of the
House Homeland Security
Committee (July 12, 2006)

Document 42: Confession of Khalid
Sheikh Mohammed at the
Combatant Status Review Tribunal
at Guantánamo Detention Camp
(March 10, 2007)

Guide to Related Topics

Airline Flights
American Airlines Flight 11
American Airlines Flight 77
United Airlines Flight 93
United Airlines Flight 175

Airport Security
Argenbright Security Company
TIPOFF
Transportation Security
    Administration

American Intelligence Efforts
Able Danger
Central Intelligence Agency
Counterterrorism Center
National Security Agency (NSA)
Phoenix Memo
Scheuer, Michael
The Wall

American Political Leadership
Bush, George W.
Bush Administration
Clinton Administration
Clarke, Richard A.
Tenet, George
Weldon, Curtis

Centers of Terrorist Planning
Kifah Refugee Center, al-
Kuala Lumpur Meeting
Quds Mosque, al-

Counterterrorism
Foreign Intelligence Surveillance
    Act of 1978
Joint Terrorism Task Force
Predator
Rendition
USA PATRIOT Act

Critics of U.S. Policy before 9/11
Chomsky, Noam
Churchill, Ward

Economic Aftermath
Cantor Fitzgerald
Economic Impact of September 11
Swift Project

Families of 9/11
Families of Victims of
    September 11
Family Assistance Center
Family Steering Committee
Ielpi, Lee

Jersey Girls
Victims' Compensation Fund

FBI Agents
Floyd, Nancy
Freeh, Louis
Rowley, Coleen
Samit, Harry

Fighting Terrorism
Guantánamo Bay Detainment Camp

Firefighters
Fire House 40/35
Firefighters at Ground Zero
Firefighter Riot on November 2, 2001

Government Agencies
Federal Aviation Administration (FAA)
Federal Bureau of Investigation (FBI)
Federal Emergency Management Agency (FEMA)
Immigration and Naturalization Services (INS)
North American Aerospace Defense Command (NORAD)
Occupational Safety and Heath Agency (OSHA)

Ground Zero
Casualties of September 11
Cleanup Operations at Ground Zero
Department of Design and Construction
Disaster Mortuary Operation Response Team
Dog Rescue and Recovery Teams
Fresh Kills Landfill
Zadroga, James

Jihad Supporters
Azzam, Sheikh Abdullah Yussuf

Joint Committee on Intelligence
Goss, Porter J.
Graham, Daniel Robert "Bob"
Senate Select Committee on Intelligence and the House Permanent Select Committee on Intelligence Joint Inquiry into the Terrorist Attacks of September 11

Movies and Documentaries
Fahrenheit 9/11
Giuliani Time (Documentary)
Hamburg Cell (TV Movie)
Naudet Documentary on 9/11
Pavel Hlava Video
United 93
Wag the Dog
World Trade Center

New York City Officials and Agencies
Giuliani, Rudolf William Louis "Rudy" III
Kerik, Bernard Bailey
New York City Police Department
Office of Emergency Management (OEM)
Port Authority of New York and New Jersey
Von Essen, Thomas

9/11 Commission
Hamilton, Lee H.
Kean, Thomas Howard
National Commission on Terrorist Attacks upon the United States

9/11 Conspiracy Theories
Conspiracy Theories

Fetzer, James H.
Griffin, David Ray
Jones, Steven E.
Marrs, Jim
Meyssan, Thierry
Scholars for 9/11 Truth

9/11 Hijackers
Atta, Mohamed el-Amir Awad
  el-Sayed
Hamburg Cell
Hanjour, Hani Saleh Husan
Hazmi, Nawaf bin Muhammad
  Salim al-
Jarrah, Ziad Samir
Justification for the September 11
  Suicide Mission
Mihdhar, Khalid, al-
Nineteen Martyrs
Pilot Training for September 11
Shehhi, Marwan Yousef
  Muhammed Rashid Lekrab al-

9/11 Hijacking Supporters
Bahaji, Said
Bin al-Shibh, Ramzi
Taliban

Al-Qaeda Leadership
Atef, Mohammad
Bin Laden, Osama
Mohammed, Khalid Sheikh
Qaeda, al-
Zawahiri, Ayman al-
Zubaydah, Abu

Al-Qaeda Operatives
Fadl, Jamal al-
Hage, Wadih el-
Mohamed, Ali Abdel Saoud
Motassadeq, Mounir
Moussaoui, Zacarias

Murad, Abdul Hakim Ali Hashim
Nosair, El Sayyid
Ressam, Ahmed
Zammar, Muhammad Heydar

Pentagon
Pentagon Attack

Reconstruction Efforts
Freedom Tower

Structural Reports
American Society of Civil Engineers
  Report

Support Efforts after 9/11
DCA

Terrorist Acts and Plans
African Embassy Bombings
Millennium Plots
New York City Landmarks
  Bombing Conspiracy
Operation Bojinka

**Victims of 9/11—American
Airlines Flight 11**
Lewin, Daniel M.
Ogonowski, John
Ong, Betty Ann

**Victims of 9/11—American
Airlines Flight 77**
Burlingame, Charles Frank "Chic"
  III
Olson, Barbara

**Victims of 9/11—United Airlines
Flight 93**
Beamer, Todd Morgan
Bingham, Mark Kendall
Burnett, Thomas Edward
Dahl, Jason Matthew

Glick, Jeremy
Homer, LeRoy Wilton Jr.

Victims of 9/11—United Airlines Flight 175
Saracini, Victor J.

Victims of 9/11—World Trade Center Complex
Biggart, William
Bucca, Ronald
Downey, Ray Matthew
Feehan, William M. "Bill"
Ganci, Peter J. "Pete"
Hamdani, Mohammad Salman
Judge, Mychal
Levin, Neil David

Mazza, Kathy
Merino, Yamel
Rescorla, Cyril Richard "Rick"
Smith, Moira

World Trade Center Bombing (1993)
Abdel Rahman, Sheikh Omar
Abouhalima, Mahmud
World Trade Center Bombing (1993)
Yousef, Ramzi Ahmed

World Trade Center Complex
World Trade Center
World Trade Center, September 11

Preface

Few events in American history have rivaled the September 11, 2001, attacks for impact on American society. Before that date most Americans had a hazy idea that the U.S. government was engaged in a war against terrorism, but there was little concern as long as terrorism was only a threat abroad. As the sole remaining superpower, the United States had few enemies that constituted a present danger to the American mainland. The collapse of the Soviet Union had ensured this. Although the United States and its government's policies were not universally beloved in the international community, Americans felt safe behind its two oceans. This all changed on that fateful day of September 11. Much as December 7, 1941, was a day that transformed the history of the United States, September 11, 2001, has become a date that is a watershed in American history.

Little did most Americans realize that Islamist extremists had considered themselves at war against the United States for more than thirty years. Americans had been targets abroad of kidnappings and assassinations. The most obvious case was the killing of 241 marines in Beirut, Lebanon, by Hezbollah during the Reagan administration. Eighteen American servicemen were killed in a single incident in Somalia during the Clinton administration. There were other attacks against Americans in Saudi Arabia, in Yemen, and in Africa. Representatives of the U.S. government had long been targets. American diplomats were not immune from assassination—the U.S. ambassador to Sudan, Cleo A. Noel Jr., and his chargé d'affaires, George C. Moore, had been assassinated in 1973.

One thing that characterized early terrorism was that much of it was state sponsored, so pressure could be applied by the United States against regimes aiding terrorists. This pressure worked particularly well against Libya and its mercurial leader, Muammar al-Qaddafi. With other states pressure was less successful, Iran being the most noticeable failure. Even the Palestine Liberation Organization (PLO) responded to pressure. But in the last twenty years a new brand of terrorism espoused by Islamic fundamentalists, or Islamists, has made its appearance. Adherents to this religious ideology have operated in independent nongovernmental organizations, making it more difficult for counterterrorism forces to isolate and overcome. The most obvious example has been Osama bin Laden and al-Qaeda.

Osama bin Laden's hostility toward the United States began during the Afghan-Soviet war in the late 1980s. This hostility intensified as American troops were based on the soil of Saudi Arabia beginning with the 1991 Gulf War. He issued two documents declaring war on the United States—one in 1996 and another in 1998. But none of al-Qaeda's early acts of terror took place on American soil. Most experts on terrorism, including CIA intelligence analysts, knew that it was only a matter of time before there was an al-Qaeda operation on American soil, but none of them could pinpoint an actual date or act. The fact that the terrorists devised a plan to use commercial aircraft as guided missiles surprised everybody in the intelligence and political community. Although there were hints of al-Qaeda interest in using aircraft as a weapon in the mid-1990s, this information was never acted upon. In a comedy of errors and lost chances, the agencies of the U.S. government did little to prevent the September 11 plot from succeeding. All of this lack of attention to Islamist terrorism changed on September 11.

There has been a lack of objective resources available on the events surrounding September 11, 2001. Most objective have been inquiries by Congress, the 9/11 Commission, and a handful of journalists. They have pointed out major deficiencies in how government agencies handled intelligence about al-Qaeda operations prior to September 11, 2001. Besides establishing weakness, the inquiries have been most interested in reforming the American intelligence community so that there will be no future September 11ths. Despite these lengthy inquiries, questions still arise on how the September 11 plot was carried out so successfully.

Several noteworthy books have appeared on Osama bin Laden, al-Qaeda, and the hijackers, and they have been able to fill in some of the gaps of information about the September 11 attacks and the U.S. government's reaction. Less trustworthy books have also appeared, questioning the accepted facts. A growing industry of books has been published trying to debunk the official positions on the events of September 11. Conspiracy theories have proliferated at a lively rate. In the last few years these books have overshadowed the few accounts of the events of the day that reflect well on the victims of that day.

Opinions vary on who was responsible for the September 11 attacks, and the debate is growing. There are five major theories, with the debate extending from the extreme right to the extreme left with variations in the middle.

1. Official Position of the U.S. Government: No one was responsible because there was no credible evidence available that such an attack would take place. American intelligence knew something was up with al-Qaeda, but no one envisaged such an attack on American soil.

2. 9/11 Commission Thesis: The members of the 9/11 Commission and its *9/11 Final Report* believed that the plot should have been discovered except for intelligence failures—in the Bush and Clinton administrations, the CIA, the FBI, the FAA, and other government agencies—to cooperate and find out about terrorist operations both in the United States and abroad. September 11 was preventable, but systemic failures in the U.S. government allowed it to happen.

3. Systemic Bungling Thesis: The actions of the U.S. government were negligent before September 11 because of turf wars between agencies, bureaucratic bungling, and over-dependence on lawyer's rulings prevalent in

the U.S. government. There was also a cozy relationship between aviation regulators and the airline industry, as well as interference from politicians over the years on ways to improve aviation safety. Those responsible for the bureaucratic bungling and sometimes deceitful conduct have never been held accountable, and in many cases received post–September 11 promotions.

4. They Allowed It to Happen Thesis: There is the belief in certain circles that the Bush administration knew about the September 11 plot and allowed it to happen so that there would be a plausible excuse to expand American military might in the Middle East. The special target would be Iraq, but the Taliban in Afghanistan was also a prime candidate for removal. This thesis has been especially popular with the American and international extreme left. They blame everything on the neoconservatives surrounding President George W. Bush. These left-wing adherents also believe that it was allowed to create an opportunity for the Bush administration to weaken American civil liberties.

5. They Made It Happen Thesis: This thesis abandons the role of Osama bin Laden and al-Qaeda for the September 11 attacks and places all the blame on the U.S. government. In the eyes of these conspiracy theorists, agents of the U.S. government carried out the attacks in a methodical manner in the pursuit of President George W. Bush's objectives on foreign and domestic policies. Believers of this thesis have concocted various schemes of how the U.S. government carried out the attacks that verge on the incredible.

The events of September 11 have produced a mass of data. This two-volume work is an attempt to bring some order to an otherwise undifferentiated mass of conflicting information. The A-to-Z section of this set contains entries on people and events leading up to September 11, what actually took place on September 11, and the aftermath of September 11. This means that the participants in the September 11 plot are covered in some depth. The sequence of events on the day itself are covered in detail in various citations. Finally, the reasons why American intelligence and law enforcement agencies were unable to prevent September 11 are covered in considerable depth. Also of interest are the various conspiracy theories that have emerged in the last five years. The goal is to present to the reader a comprehensive look at all aspects of September 11 so that it can be understood in its context.

This work is intended to be as inclusive as possible. In total, there will be 158 entries, a lengthy chronology of events surrounding September 11, 42 primary documents, and an annotated bibliography. Each entry ranges from around 300 words to nearly 3,000 words, with the average entry being around 850 words. Each entry has suggested readings for further research. As a convenience there is a cross reference to the document that covers come of the same material as the entry.

A note needs to be made of spelling of Arabic names and groups. I have been uniform in the spelling of names, but other forms appear in the documents and in the quotes. In the course of the book, Osama bin Laden is also transliterated into Usama bin Ladin, or in another variation Osama bin Ladin. This is also true of al-Qaeda, which is referred to as al Qaeda, al Qaida, or al-Qida in other sources. Regarding alphabetization of the encyclopedia, for individuals or groups with names prefixed by *al-* or *el-* those prefixes are ignored. In other words, Jamal al-Fadl is alphabetized in the text and the List of Entries as "Fadl, Jamal al-," and the entry appears in the "F" section.

Normally, I dedicate a book to an individual or a group of individuals. This encyclopedia I dedicate to the victims and families of September 11, 2001. They became victims of a war that they had no part in. Let us hope that another September 11 will never happen.

The 9/11 Encyclopedia

A

Abdel Rahman, Sheikh Omar (1938–)

Sheikh Omar Abdel Rahman is the spiritual leader of radical Islamists' war against the United States. His reputation as a religious leader and his renowned militancy have made him influential among many Muslims, to whom he issued two fatwas, or religious rulings, that justified war against the United States. His band of Islamist militants participated in the 1993 World Trade Center bombing. American authorities were eventually able to tie him to another plot to blow up facilities in New York City, sentencing him to life in solitary confinement without parole.

Abdel Rahman has spent most of his life as an Islamist militant. He was born on May 3, 1938, in the small village of al-Gamalia in the Nile Delta region of Egypt. When he was ten months old, he lost his eyesight, probably because of diabetes. After demonstrating early scholastic ability by memorizing the Koran at age 11, he was sent to an Islamic boarding school. He excelled there, and his academic achievements allowed him to enter Cairo University's School of Theology. There, and later, at the prestigious University of al-Azhar, Abdel Rahman earned degrees in Islamic jurisprudence. At al-Azhar, he was a good, though not brilliant, student, finding it an excellent place to establish contacts with others in agreement about the need for an Islamist state in Egypt. Abdel Rahman's compatriots shared the same agenda—an Islamic society created unilaterally and, if necessary, forcefully. One of Abdel Rahman's compatriots at al-Azhar was Abdullah Azzam.

Soon after leaving university, Abdel Rahman, who had become a religious scholar with a militant Islamist agenda, started preaching against the secular regime of Egyptian President Gamal Abdel Nasser. In 1965 he preached at a small mosque on the outskirts of Fayoum about sixty miles south of Cairo, but his attacks against Nasser's regime led to his dismissal from his religious teaching post in 1969. This setback only intensified his hatred of Nasser and his regime. He then found work teaching at a girls' school south of Cairo, in Assiut. Perturbed by his mounting attacks, Egyptian authorities arrested him in 1970, and he spent eight months in Citadel Prison. After his release, Abdel Rahman was awarded a post as professor of theology at the University of Assiut, but, still under police surveillance, he decided to go into exile in Saudi Arabia.

Abdel Rahman helped launch the terrorist group Islamic Group (al-Gama'a Islamiyya) in 1976 with the goal of overthrowing the Sadat regime and establishing a theocratic Islamic state. This group began carrying out terrorist attacks in Egypt, and Abdel Rahman returned from exile in 1980. He was arrested a month before the assassination of President Anwar Sadat in October 1981. Because members of the Islamic Group had participated in the assassination, Abdel Rahman was tried for conspiracy to overthrow the Egyptian government; but, because the evidence was circumstantial, he was acquitted. He promptly sued the state for torturing him in prison, a suit eventually settled for $10,000. Despite his acquittal, the Egyptian government kept him under house arrest for the next six years, in 1985 allowing him to make a pilgrimage to Mecca. After his release from house arrest, Abdel Rahman's attacks on the Mubarak government continued, but gradually he turned his attention to preaching against the Soviets in Afghanistan. By this time Abdel Rahman had become, according to T. Bowyer Bell's *Murders on the Nile*, famous throughout the Middle East as the "spiritual mentor of the righteous gunmen of the new jihad."

Sheikh Omar Abdel Rahman's Concept of Terrorism

No, if those who have the right to have something are terrorists then we are terrorists. And we welcome being terrorists. And we do not deny this charge to ourselves. And the Koran makes it, terrorism, among the means to perform jihad for the sake of Allah, which is to terrorize the enemies of God . . . who are our enemies too.

Quoted in Daniel Benjamin and Steven Simon, *The Age of Sacred Terror* (New York: Random House, 2004), pp. 15–16.

After Abdel Rahman's release from house arrest, he made a visit to Afghanistan, where Abdullah Azzam introduced him to Osama bin Laden. Bin Laden held him in high respect for his spirituality.

Although Abdel Rahman had achieved recognition as one of the leading Islamist scholars in the international Islamist movement, he faced difficulty in Egypt. A movement among other leaders of the Islamic Group tried to replace him because of his blindness. This attack did not prevent him from issuing a fatwa legitimizing the murder of Coptic Christians. Fearful of losing influence in the Islamic Group in Egypt, and finding the political atmosphere in Egypt too oppressive, Abdel Rahman moved to Sudan in April 1990. After bin Laden left Sudan, two of Abdel Rahman's sons went to Afghanistan to work with al-Qaeda.

Abdel Rahman decided to relocate to the United States, where recruits and money were available to advance the Islamist cause. Despite his reputation as a sponsor of terrorism, he obtained a visa in Khartoum without problem, arriving in the United States in July of 1990. In the United States, he found loyal supporters, but he also ran into dissidents, some of whom were unhappy with Mustafa Shalabi. At first Abdel Rahman supported Shalabi, but then the two disagreed over how to use the money they raised. Shalabi insisted that the funds go to Afghanistan to build an Islamist state there, but Abdel Rahman wished to finance efforts to overthrow the Mubarak regime. This disagreement ended with the murder of Shalabi. His murder case has never been solved. Shalabi's removal left Abdel Rahman in charge, and, in March 1991, Abdel Rahman received a permanent residence visa from the United States.

Abdel Rahman lived on the edge of several conspiracies. Several of his most militant supporters participated in the 1993 bombing plot that tried to bring down the Twin Towers of the World Trade Center complex in New York City.

American authorities questioned him, but his involvement was mostly circumstantial. He claimed to have known Ramzi Yousef only briefly. His role in the plot to bomb other New York landmarks, however, was more pronounced, and he was arrested in August of 1993. American authorities charged him with a seditious conspiracy to wage a terrorist war against the United States. In January 1996 a New York City court sentenced him to life imprisonment in solitary confinement without chance of parole. Since then, Abdel Rahman has been held in a variety of maximum-security prisons in Missouri and Minnesota. Even in prison, however, he has been charged with directing activities of his followers through his lawyer and translators. In 1998, he had a fatwa smuggled out of prison urging his followers to cut all ties with the United States and wage war against it. This fatwa gave religious justification for the September 11 attacks. His lawyer received a jail sentence for passing on information to Abdel Rahman's followers.

Abdel Rahman is still regarded as one of the leading figures in the Islamist movement. Although he had no role whatsoever in the planning for September 11, or knowledge of it beforehand, his religious rulings offered justification for it. His association with Abdullah Azzam, Ayman al-Zawahiri, and, more indirectly, Osama bin Laden, helped produce the atmosphere that led to September 11.

See Also
Azzam, Sheikh Abdullah Yussuf; Bin Laden, Osama; New York City Landmarks Bombing Conspiracy; World Trade Center Bombing (1993); Yousef, Ramzi Ahmed; Zawahiri, Ayman al-

Suggested Reading
J. Bowyer Bell, *Murders on the Nile: The World Trade Center and Global Terror* (San Francisco: Encounter Books, 2003); Daniel Benjamin and Steven Simon, *The Age of Sacred Terror* (New York: Random House, 2004); Peter Lange, *1000 Years for Revenge: International Terrorism and the FBI* (New York: ReganBooks, 2003).

> **Fatwa of the Prisoner Sheikh Doctor Omar Abdel Rahman**
>
> America is in the process of eliminating the ulema (clergy) who are speaking the truth. And America has suggested to its clients in Saudi to imprison Sheikh Safar al Hawali and Sheikh Salman al Awdah, and all the others who speak the truth . . . . And the Koran has made a decree upon these Jews and Christians, which we have forgotten or allowed to be forgotten: Allah said, "If they could, they will continue to kill you until they make you run away from your religion." And so all Muslims everywhere. Cut off all relations with [the Americans, Christians, and Jews], tear them to pieces, destroy their economies, burn their corporations, destroy their peace, sink their ships, shoot down their planes and kill them on air, sea, and land. And kill them wherever you may find them, ambush them, take them hostage, and destroy their observatories. Kill these Infidels. Until they witness your harshness. Fight them, and God will torture them through your hands, and he will disgrace them and make you victorious over them, and the national of the believers is on the verge of creation, and the rage will go from them. Your brother Omar Abdel Rahman from inside American prisons.
>
> Quoted in Peter L. Bergen, *The Osama bin Laden I Know: An Oral History of al Qaeda's Leader* (New York: Free Press, 2006), pp. 204–205.

Able Danger
Able Danger was a highly secret military intelligence program whose leaders have claimed to have identified Mohamed Atta and three other members of the September 11 plot well before September 11, 2001. General Hugh Shelton, the

chairman of the Joint Chiefs of Staff, issued a directive in early October 1999 to establish an intelligence program under the command of the U.S. Special Operations Command (SOCOM) to be directed specifically against al-Qaeda and its operatives. The commander of Able Danger was Navy Captain Scott Philpott, who commanded a unit of twenty military intelligence specialists and a support staff. The chief analyst of Able Danger was Dr. Eileen Priesser.

The purpose of Able Danger was to identify al-Qaeda members and neutralize them before they could initiate operations against the United States, much like a military version of the CIA's Alec Station. The data-mining center was at the Land Information Warfare Activity (LIWA)/Information Dominance Center at Fort Belvoir, Virginia. In the summer of 2000, the LIWA was transferred to Garland, Texas.

Members of this unit began intelligence operations seeking to identify al-Qaeda operatives both in the United States and abroad. Its computer analysts set up a complex computer analysis system that searched public databases and the Internet for possible terrorist cells. One of the terrorist cells so identified contained the name of Mohamed Atta and three others who were later implicated in the September 11 plot. Atta's name, as well as the others', was supposedly placed on a chart of al-Qaeda operatives.

Lieutenant Colonel Anthony Shaffer, a reserve officer attached to the Pentagon, and Able Danger's liaison with the Defense Intelligence Agency (DIA), as well as others, decided to inform the FBI about the threat posed by the al-Qaeda operatives. Three potential meetings with the FBI were postponed because of opposition from military lawyers in the Pentagon. The apparent reason for the opposition from the U.S. Special Operations Command of the Department of Defense (DOD) was fear of controversy that might arise if it was made public that a military intelligence unit had violated the privacy of civilians legally residing in the United States. Another possible reason was that the lawyers believed the program might be violating the Posse Comitatus Act of using the military against civilians.

The leaders of Able Danger then decided to work their way up the military chain of command. In January 2001, the leadership of Able Danger briefed General Hugh Shelton, still the chairman of the Joint Chiefs of Staff, on its findings. Shortly afterward, the Able Danger unit was disbanded, its operations ceasing in April 2001. DOD lawyers had determined that the activities of Able Danger violated President Reagan's Executive Order 12333, intended to prevent the Pentagon from storing data about U.S. citizens. A direct order came from the DOD to destroy the database; 2.4 terabytes of information about possible al-Qaeda terrorist activities were destroyed in the summer of 2001. A chart identifying four hijackers, including Mohamed Atta, was produced by Able Danger and presented to the Deputy National Security Advisor, Jim Steinberg, but nothing came of it.

Able Danger was a military secret until its story surfaced shortly after the National Commission on Terrorist Attacks Upon the United States, or the 9/11 Commission, issued its report, which stated categorically that the U.S. government had no prior knowledge about the conspiracy that led to the September 11 attacks. Keith Phucas, a reporter for the *Times Herald* (Norristown, Pennsylvania), broke the story of Able Danger on June 19, 2005, in an article entitled "Missed Chance on Way to 9/11."

When the story about Able Danger became public, it erupted into a political controversy. On June 27, 2005, Representative Curt Weldon (R-PA) and the vice

chairman of the House Armed Services and House Homeland Security committees brought the Able Danger issue to the national limelight. In a speech before
the House of Representatives, Weldon accused the U.S. government of negligence
in its failure to heed the information gathered by Able Danger.

Despite some lapses of information (and a tendency to blame
the Clinton administration for
the lapse), Weldon summarized
many of the features of Able
Danger without disclosing its
nature as a secret military intelligence initiative run from within
the Department of Defense.
Weldon also disclosed that the
information about Able Danger
had been reported to the staff of
the 9/11 Commission.

Members of the 9/11 Com-
mission responded to these
charges with a series of denials.
Lee H. Hamilton, former Vice
Chair of the 9/11 Commission,
admitted learning about the
Able Danger program but
denied hearing anything credible about a possible identification of Atta or other skyjackers

> **Congressman Weldon's Remarks before the House of Representatives**
>
> Mr. Speaker, I rise because information has come to my attention over the past several months that is very dis-turbing. I have learned that, in fact, one of our Federal agencies had, in fact, identified the major New York cell of Mohamed Atta prior to 9/11; and I have learned, Mr. Speaker, that in September of 2000, that Federal agency actually was prepared to bring the FBI in and pre-pared to work with the FBI to take down the cell that Mohamed Atta was involved in New York City, along with two of the other terrorists. I have also learned, Mr. Speaker, that when that recommendation was dis-cussed within that Federal agency, the lawyers in the administration at that time said, "You cannot pursue con-tact with the FBI against that cell. Mohamed Atta is in the U.S. on a green card, and we are fearful of the fallout from the Waco incident." So we did not allow that Federal agency to proceed.
>
> *Congressional Record—House* June 27, 2005. 109th Congress. 1st Session. HRH5244.

in the 9/11 plot. This argument contradicted the testimony of Shaffer that he had
communicated Able Danger's findings about Atta in a meeting with the commission's executive director, Philip Zelikov, at Bagram Air Base, Afghanistan, in late
2003. Leaders of the commission then requested and obtained information about
Able Danger from the DOD, but there had been nothing about Atta in the information provided. They also admitted that Navy Captain Philpott had mentioned
something about Atta only days before the final report came out.

This denial of prior knowledge by members of the 9/11 Commission drew the
attention of Lieutenant Colonel Shaffer. In an interview on August 15, 2005,
Shaffer told the story of Able Danger, and he indicated that he had been at the
"point of near insubordination" over the refusal to pursue the information about
Atta. Furthermore, Shaffer insisted that he had talked to the staff of the 9/11
investigation in October 2003, in Afghanistan, where his next tour of duty had
taken him. Captain Philpott and civilian contractor J. D. Smith confirmed Shaffer's
claim about Able Danger's knowing about Atta.

The controversy has continued because the participants have felt left out of the
investigation of the events surrounding September 11. Many of them have placed
their careers in jeopardy by countering the government's version. Colonel Shaffer
had his security clearance pulled by the Defense Intelligence Agency (DIA) and his
personal records of Able Danger destroyed. In September 2006 the DOD's
Inspector General issued a report denying that Able Danger had identified Atta by

calling the testimony of witnesses inconsistent. Weldon criticized the report and investigation as incomplete. Although Weldon was an effective spokesperson in Congress who kept the story alive, his loss of office in the 2006 election deprived him of that important forum. Nevertheless, the last word has not been said about Able Danger and about whether information about Atta and others was stored in a government database.

See Also
Atta, Mohamed el-Amir Awad el-Sayed; Clinton Administration; Hamilton, Lee H.; National Commission on Terrorist Attacks upon the United States; Weldon, Curtis

See Document
Document #38

Suggested Reading
Peter Lance, *Triple Cross: How Bin Laden's Master Spy Penetrated the CIA, the Green Berets, and the FBI—and Why Patrick Fitzgerald Failed to Stop Him* (New York: ReganBooks, 2006); Andrew C. McCarthy, "It's Time to Investigate Able Danger and the 9/11 Commission," *National Review* (December 8, 2005), p. 1; James Rosen, "Able Danger Operatives Sue Pentagon," *News Tribune* [Tacoma, WA] (March 4, 2006), p. 6; James Rosen, "A 9/11 Tip-Off: Fact or Fancy?: Debate Still Swirls Around Claim That Secret Military Program ID'd Hijackers a Year before Attacks," *Sacramento Bee* (November 24, 2005), p. A1; Philip Shenon, "Officer Says Military Blocked Sharing of Files on Terrorists," *New York Times* (August 17, 2005), p. 12; Philip Shenon, "Report Rejects Claim That 9/11 Terrorists Were Identified before Attacks," *New York Times* (September 22, 2006), p. A15.

Abouhalima, Mahmud (1959–)

Mahmud Abouhalima was one of the principal conspirators in the 1993 World Trade Center bombing. He was a devoted follower of the militant Islamist imam Sheikh Omar Abdel Rahman, serving as his guide and driver. When Ramzi Yousef took charge of the plot to bomb the World Trade Center, Abouhalima, his friend, became his chief assistant.

Abouhalima never fit into any community he lived in until he became an Islamist. Born in 1959 in the small town of Kafr Dawar, about fifteen miles south of Alexandria, Egypt, he was unhappy about his lack of career prospects in Egypt and left school early, immigrating to Munich, West Germany. There he lived among fellow Arabs, working first as a dishwasher and later in the meat department of a grocery store. Although he disliked Germany, he married a German woman. When his German visa expired, Abouhalima decided to move his family to the United States.

Abouhalima and his wife arrived in the United States in 1986. Soon after arriving in New York City, he found a job as a taxicab driver. His career as a cabbie had its ups and downs. Because he drove his taxi without license or registration, Abouhalima was often in trouble with police because of traffic violations. His most common offense was running red lights, but his income allowed him to live in Brooklyn with his wife and four children.

Abouhalima became a convert to the extremist theology of Islamists while in the United States. He left New York City in the late 1980s to travel to Afghanistan to fight against the Soviets. Besides gaining combat experience, he received a strong dose of Islamist propaganda that culminated in his conversion. While there, he became friendly with expert bomb maker Ramzi Yousef.

Abouhalima returned to the United States, determined to carry the religious fight to the secular West.

The arrival of Abdel Rahman in July 1990 gave Abouhalima a spiritual mentor. Most of Abouhalima's nonwork activities revolved around the al-Farouq Mosque and the al-Kifah Refugee Center. Abouhalima became Abdel Rahman's principal guide and driver. When the militants began to plan terrorist operations, Abouhalima participated in discussions and volunteered his services. When El Sayyid Nosair decided to assassinate the Israeli extremist Meir Kahane, Abouhalima was to provide his escape transportation. However, a mistake kept Abouhalima and his transportation from arriving. Nosair shot Kahane and tried to escape but was wounded in the throat and captured. Abouhalima's role in this conspiracy was never discovered by the police until much later.

Abouhalima played a major role in the 1993 World Trade Center bombing, helping Yousef build the bomb. On February 23, 1993, Abouhalima drove a car escorting the bomb van. After the terrorists parked the Ryder van in the underground garage of the World Trade Center, Abouhalima and the others awaited the results of the explosion but were disappointed when the North Tower failed to collapse and fall into the South Tower. The day after the bombing, Abouhalima flew to Saudi Arabia. After a brief stay, he decided to visit family in Egypt but, on entering the country in March of 1993, was arrested and turned over to Egyptian interrogators. Abouhalima soon confessed to his role in the World Trade Center bombing.

Egyptian authorities turned Abouhalima over to American authorities for trial. Despite evidence of a large terrorist conspiracy, Abouhalima and his fellow plotters were tried as criminals rather than as national security concerns or an intelligence matter, in keeping with FBI policy. After five months of testimony, Abouhalima was found guilty on all counts on March 4, 1994. Abouhalima and his three co-defendants received a sentence of 240 years that he is now serving at a maximum-security federal prison. Unfortunately, this bombing was only the first salvo in a continuing war by Islamist terrorists against the United States.

See Also
Abdel Rahman, Sheikh Omar; Kifah Refugee Center, al-; Nosair, el Sayyid; World Trade Center Bombing (1993); Yousef, Ramzi Ahmed

Suggested Reading
J. Bowyer Bell, *Murders on the Nile: The World Trade Center and Global Terrorism* (San Francisco: Encounter Books, 2003); Simon Reeve, *The New Jackals: Ramzi Yousef, Osama Bin Laden and the Future of Terrorism* (Boston: Northeastern University Press, 1999).

African Embassy Bombings
The biggest and most lethal al-Qaeda operation against the United States before September 11, 2001, was the 1998 embassy bombings in Africa. As early as 1993, Osama bin Laden had his military commanders study the feasibility of a major terrorist act in Africa. The Egyptian American soldier, Ali Mohamed, scouted out targets in Nairobi, Kenya, for al-Qaeda. Mohamed surveyed American, British, French, and Israeli embassies as potential targets and reported to bin Laden that the best target was the American embassy in Nairobi. Bin Laden, then living in Khartoum, Sudan, agreed in a personal report. Reluctant at that time to approve a bombing mission in Africa with retaliation so close at hand, he kept the operation under advisement.

Several years later, bin Laden decided to give permission to carry out the bombings of the American embassies in Nairobi, Kenya, and Dar es Salaam, Tanzania. In the meantime, al-Qaeda operatives assisted the Saudi group Hezbollah al-Hijaz in carrying out the bombing of the Khobar Towers on June 25, 1996, in Dhahran, Saudi Arabia, killing nineteen American servicemen and wounding hundreds of others. Bin Laden denied direct participation, but his statement was disbelieved by American authorities. After issuing his declaration of jihad in 1998 against Americans for occupying sacred Saudi soil, bin Laden proceeded with preparations for the African embassy bombings as previously planned.

Al-Qaeda prepared methodically. Early in 1995, agents had been sent to Kenya and Tanzania to establish cells there. The mastermind of the operation was Abdullah Ahmed Abdullah. Mohamed Odeh arrived in Mombasa, Kenya, where he set up a fishing business as a cover. To maintain further cover, he married a Kenyan woman. He was soon followed by al-Qaeda's military commander, Abu Ubaidal al-Banshiri, who died in a ferry accident on Lake Victoria in the spring of 1996. His successor was Haroun Fazil, who stayed with bin Laden's former secretary, Wadih el-Hage. Fazil rented a villa in Nairobi, where the bomb was assembled, and a Nissan truck was purchased to carry the bomb.

One of the two men selected for martyrdom in Nairobi was Mohamed Rashed al-Owhali. Al-Owhali was born in 1977 in Liverpool, England, but he never cared for English life. In 1996, he traveled to Afghanistan where he underwent al-Qaeda training and was selected for a martyrdom mission in Nairobi, Kenya. Al-Owhali arrived in Nairobi on August 2, 1998, just five days before the mission. Al-Qaeda's Egyptian bomb expert, Abdel Rahman, had already built the bomb. Leaders of the Kenyan cell were already leaving for Afghanistan at the time of his arrival. Al-Owhali soon met his fellow martyr, a Saudi named Azzam. On August 5, 1998, they scouted out the embassy target.

The Nairobi bombing was scheduled for Friday, August 7, 1998. The explosion was timed to take place before 11:00 a.m. when observant Muslims would be at prayer. Azzam was to be the driver, and al-Owhali's job was to persuade the guards to let them close to the embassy. Unable to persuade the gate guard, he threw a homemade stun grenade and ran away before exploding the bomb. The bomb, which was large, exploded at 10:30 a.m. on a workday, producing horrible casualties.

The Nairobi embassy building sustained considerable damage. Prudence Bushnell, the American ambassador to Kenya, had previously cabled and written Madeleine Albright, then Secretary of State, and the State Department about the vulnerability of the embassy in its location on a busy thoroughfare in the middle of Nairobi, close to the street. Twelve Americans and two hundred one Kenyans were killed. Four thousand others were wounded—some seriously.

Nine minutes after the Nairobi bombing, a bomb exploded at the American Embassy in Dar es Salaam, Tanzania. Less is known about this operation; indeed, what little is known comes from a low-level al-Qaeda operative, Khalfan Khamis Mohamed, who was trained in an al-Qaeda training camp and was then sent back to his home in Dar es Salaam. An al-Qaeda leader approached him several years later to help find a place to build a bomb and a way to transport it to the target. Al-Qaeda's Egyptian bomb expert, Abdel Rahman, built this bomb also. Mohamed's sole responsibility was to guide the bomb's driver, Hamden Khalif

Allah Awad—also called Ahmed the German—to the target, leaving before the bomb went off. The bomb exploded at exactly 10:39 a.m.

The bombing at the Dar es Salaam embassy caused less damage and fewer casualties than the Nairobi bombing. Because the embassy was better protected, the bomb did less structural damage to the embassy. No Americans were killed, but eleven Tanzanians died—most of them Muslims.

American intelligence had been following an al-Qaeda cell in Kenya for over a year before the bombings. But agents were caught by surprise by the plot—an astounding thing in light of the warning of an Egyptian defector from al-Qaeda, Mustafa Mahmoud Said Ahmed, who informed Nairobi embassy intelligence officers of a plot to bomb the embassy, using stun grenades to allow a truck loaded with a bomb close to the embassy. This warning was given nine months before the bombing, but nothing was done by the American agents to guard against such an event.

One of the leaders of the African bombing plot, Odeh, was arrested in the Karachi Airport when returning from Africa. Odeh was detained because of discrepancies in his passport, but soon Pakistani officials suspected him of participation in the African embassy bombings. They turned Odeh over to Pakistani intelligence, and he soon confessed to his role in the bombings. Another member of the plot, Khalfan Khamis Mohamed, was arrested in Cape Town, South Africa, in October 1999.

Another break for American intelligence was the arrest of al-Owhali while receiving medical treatment for injuries sustained at the bombing. His wounds were all in his back, causing speculation that he had been running away from the bomb explosion. Kenyan officials arrested him on August 12, 1998, and immediately turned him over to American intelligence officials. It took only a few days for al-Owhali to confess to his role in the Nairobi embassy bombing.

Once it was established that the African embassy bombings were an al-Qaeda operation, President William Clinton authorized retaliatory attacks on alleged al-Qaeda targets in Afghanistan and Sudan. Tomahawk cruise missiles were fired with limited effect at six al-Qaeda base camps around Khost, Afghanistan, and at an alleged chemical-weapons al-Shifa plant in Khartoum, Sudan. Al-Qaeda leaders had been expecting retaliation and made preparations, but an addition warning about the date gleaned from Pakistani intelligence made certain that damage to al-Qaeda would be minimal. The death toll at the Khost was lessened further because two of the cruise missiles failed to explode.

At the time of the missile attacks, the movie *Wag the Dog* portrayed a president who started a war to mitigate the effects of a sex scandal. Critics of the Clinton administration seized upon the theme of this movie and accused him of misjudgments in his fight against terror. This criticism seemed to make Clinton less aggressive in his operations against bin Laden and al-Qaeda during the remainder of his administration.

Those arrested in Kenya, Pakistan, and Tanzania were extradited to the United States for trial as terrorists. Four members of the African embassy bombing plot—Wadih el-Hage, Mohamed Rashed Daoud al-Owhali, Khalfan Khamis Mohamed, and Mohammed Saddiq Odeh—were tried before a Manhattan federal court beginning February 5, 2001. Odeh and Mohamed faced the death sentence, but Odeh and El-Hage faced life in prison. A jury of seven women and five men declared the men guilty in May 2001. At a July 2001 death penalty hearing, however, the jury refused to bow to prosecutors' demands for death sentences for Odeh and Mohammed. All four men were sentenced to life imprisonment without parole on October 18, 2001, only weeks after the September 11 attacks. Jurors later explained that they didn't want to risk portraying Odeh and Mohamed as martyrs.

See Also

Bin Laden, Osama; Clinton Administration; Qaeda, al-; *Wag the Dog*

Suggested Reading

Peter L. Bergen, *Holy War; Inside the Secret World of Osama bin Laden* (New York: Free Press, 2001); Benjamin Weiser, "Going on Trial: U.S. Accusations of a Global Plot; Embassy Bombings Case," *New York Times* (February 4, 2001), p. 29; Benjamin Weiser, "A Jury Torn and Fearful in 2001 Terrorism Trial," *New York Times* (January 5, 2003), p. 1.

Alec Station

Alec Station was the U.S. government–sanctioned CIA program designed to hunt down, capture, or kill Osama bin Laden. Two members of the Clinton administration, Tony Lake (the National Security Advisor) and Richard Clarke (the National Coordinator for Counterterrorism) met in late 1995 with the head of the CIA's Counterterrorism Center to discuss the need for a unit to concentrate solely on Osama bin Laden. Soon afterward, the director of the CIA, George Tenet, approved just such a unit. The plan called for Alec Station to run only a couple of years before merging completely with the Counterterrorism Center, but as bin Laden became a greater and greater threat, Alec Station continued its operations for more than a decade.

When the CIA began Alec Station, on January 8, 1996, bin Laden was mostly known as a financier of terrorism. Soon afterward, it became apparent that bin Laden had declared open warfare against the United States and its allies, and the campaign against bin Laden was stepped up. Mike Scheuer, a veteran CIA agent, was placed in charge of the program when it was founded; although the formal title of the program was the Usama Bin Laden Issue Station (UBL), it soon took the name Alec Station, after Scheuer's adopted Korean son, Alec. Alec Station functioned as a subunit of the CIA's Counterterrorist Center (CTC). Sponsors of this program set it up as an interagency unit running agents from both the CIA and the FBI. The plan was for this unit to fuse intelligence disciplines into one office—including operations, analysis, signals intercepts, overhead photography, and covert action. As the unit developed, its strength lay in analysis. It started out as a small unit with a staff of only about fifteen analysts, mostly young women. It was not considered a choice assignment. Alec Station was a low-profile operation and was at first housed outside Langley until it moved to the CTC.

By 1998 Scheuer was convinced that bin Laden posed an ongoing danger to the United States, but he had difficulty convincing his superiors—partly because of his difficult personality, which managed to alienate even those who agreed with him. After Scheuer learned that bin Laden had attempted to acquire nuclear materials, he had difficulty making his superiors accept the information and use it to inform others in the government. Scheuer believed that bin Laden constituted a clear and present danger, and he became increasingly frustrated by the lack of action taken toward bin Laden.

Scheuer also had difficulties with the FBI. Although Alec Station had been set up as an interagency operation, the FBI often refused to share information with the CIA. The most notorious member of the FBI in this regard was John O'Neill, the FBI's top counterterrorism expert. O'Neill possessed a notebook captured from an al-Qaeda operative that he refused to turn over to Alec Station for a year. In another instance, an FBI agent was caught raiding CIA files with the intent of taking their contents back to the FBI. Scheuer has claimed that Alec Station sent 700 to 800 requests for information to the FBI but never received answers to any of them.

Alec Station planned to capture bin Laden after he moved to Afghanistan in May 1996. For the first time, the CIA knew where bin Laden and his family lived—in the Tarnak Farm compound twelve miles outside Kandahar. Beginning in 1997, plans were made with Afghan tribal leaders to kidnap bin Laden and take him to an Arab country or the United States for trial. The CIA even staged four rehearsals for the operation in late 1997 and early 1998. Then, on May 29, 1998, George Tenet, the head of the CIA, called off the operation. Scheuer's reaction was swift. He complained that the CIA had enough intelligence against bin Laden and al-Qaeda to eliminate both, and he couldn't understand why the U.S. government had failed to take the chance to do so. The Clinton administration responded that it feared collateral damage and any negative publicity that might follow a less-than-perfect operation.

It was only after the bombings, on August 7, 1998, of the two U.S. embassies in East Africa that the attention of the Clinton administration was redirected toward bin Laden in the August 20, 1998, attack on an al-Qaeda Afghanistan training camp near Khost and on the al-Shifa pharmaceutical plant in Khartoum, in which seventy-nine Tomahawk cruise missiles were fired from U.S. Navy ships in the Arabian Sea. However, warnings from Pakistani sources made certain that bin Laden escaped the missiles, and the Sudanese plant proved a harmless pharmaceutical plant. Several other plans were made to either capture or kill bin Laden, but they were cancelled each time because of one difficulty or another. Most cancellations were caused by a lack of confidence in intelligence sources and information.

The most promising opportunity was in February 1999. CIA agents learned that bin Laden was going to join a number of sheikhs from the United Arab Emirates at a desert hunting camp in Helmand Province, Afghanistan. Satellite pictures identified the camp on February 9. CIA operatives confirmed bin Laden's presence and requested a missile strike. Over the next several days, the Clinton administration debated a missile strike without deciding before learning that members of the United Arab Emirates royal family were also present at this camp. Because of foreign policy complications with the U.A.E. (a provider of gas and oil supplies), nothing happened, and Scheuer was furious. His e-mails expressing his unhappiness traveled around government circles.

Tenet removed Scheuer from his position as head of Alec Station in the spring of 1999. Scheuer's inability to work with superiors and the FBI led to his dismissal. His critics intimated that he had become dysfunctional because of his vendetta against Osama bin Laden. CIA analysts at Alec Station blamed John O'Neill for the firing of Scheuer because the dispute had reached the level of the agency heads of the CIA and FBI—Tenet and Freeh. Scheuer's replacement was a key assistant on Tenet's staff and a Middle East specialist, but he lacked Scheuer's drive. By this time, Alec Station had grown from twelve analysts to twenty-five. Most of these analysts were women, something that hurt their credibility in the male-dominated CIA. There was a feeling in the Counterterrorist Center that others in the CIA ridiculed members of the Alec Station for their zeal in tracing the actions of bin Laden.

The status of Alec Station became more precarious after September 11. Some of the criticism directed against the CIA for failing to uncover the September 11 plot descended on Alec Station, and Scheuer reappeared as a senior analyst at the Station after September 11. Members of the Alec Station adamantly insisted that little, if any, connection existed between Saddam Hussein and al-Qaeda, something they communicated to Tenet. However, this stance made them enemies in the Bush administration, which wanted the CIA to provide justification for the invasion of Iraq and the overthrow of Hussein. Those in the CIA who opposed the invasion became enemies. Personnel were transferred out of Alec Station until only twelve analysts remained. Scheuer protested this action, resigning from the CIA on November 12, 2004. Not long afterward, the CIA disbanded the Station entirely.

See Also
Bin Laden, Osama; Central Intelligence Agency; Federal Bureau of Investigation; Freeh, Louis; O'Neill, John; Tenet, George

Suggested Reading
Steve Coll, *Ghost Wars: The Secret History of the CIA, Afghanistan, and Bin Laden, From the Soviet Invasion to September 10, 2001* (New York: Penguin Books, 2004); George Tenet and Bill Harlow, *At the Center of the Storm: My Years at the CIA* (New York: HarperCollins, 2007); Lawrence Wright, *The Looming Tower: Al-Qaeda and the Road to 9/11* (New York: Knopf, 2006); Ned Zeman, et al., "The Path to 9/11: Lost Warnings and Fatal Error," *Vanity Fair*, 531 (November 2004), p. 326.

Al-Fadl, Jamal.   *See* Fadl, Jamal al-

Al-Hazmi, Nawaf.   *See* Hazmi, Nawaf bin Muhammad Salim al-

Al-Kifah Service Center.   *See* Kifah Refugee Center al-

Al-Mihdhar, Khalid.   *See* Mihdhar, Khalid al-

Al-Qaeda.   *See* Qaeda, al-

Al-Quds Mosque.   *See* Quds Mosque al-

Al-Shehhi, Marwan.   *See* Shehhi, Marwan Yousef Muhammed Rashid Lekrab al-

Al-Shibh, Ramzi bin.   *See* Bin al-Shibh, Ramzi

Al-Zawahiri, Ayman.   *See* Zawahiri, Ayman al-

American Airlines Flight 11
American Airlines Flight 11 was a Boeing 767-223ER that was the first aircraft to crash into the North Tower of the World Trade Center complex in New York City on September 11, 2001. The pilot of the aircraft was John Ogonowski, a fifty-two-year-old Vietnam veteran from Massachusetts, and its First Officer was Thomas McGuinness. Flight 11 departed from Boston's Logan International Airport

nearly 14 minutes late, at 7:59 a.m., bound for Los Angeles International Airport. It carried slightly more than half its capacity of 181—81 passengers and a crew of 11—and had a full load of 23,980 gallons of aviation fuel at takeoff, which was routine.

The leader of the terrorist team, and its designated pilot on board Flight 11, was Mohamed Atta. Atta and other members of the hijack team Satam al-Suqami, Waleed al-Shehri, Wail al-Shehri, and Abdul Aziz al-Omari had bought first-class seats, which research conducted on other flights convinced them gave them the best opportunity to seize the cockpit and gain control of the aircraft. Two of the hijackers sat near the cockpit and two near the passenger section. Atta sat in 8D, whence he could command both teams.

The hijackers had little trouble passing through checkpoint security. American Airlines' security checkpoints at Logan International Airport were operated by a private company, Globe Security, which operated these checkpoints under a contract with American Airlines. Because American Airlines' desire was for passengers to be harassed at checkpoints as little as possible, the hijackers had no difficulty in passing through the checkpoints carrying box cutters and mace.

Instructions had been given by al-Qaeda trainers to the hijackers to seize the aircraft by force within 15 minutes of takeoff. Around 8:14, they did so, killing two attendants and a passenger, Daniel Lewin, immediately. Lewin, formerly an officer in the elite Sayeret Matkal unit of the Israeli military, was seen as a threat. The hijackers, who had apparently identified him as a potential air marshal, killed him as soon as possible. To allay suspicions, the hijackers lulled the passengers and crew into a false sense of hope by giving the impression that the plane would land safely and that the passengers would be used as hostages, a successful tactic of hijackers in the past.

Air traffic controllers received information from the cockpit via Ogonowski's radio, over which they heard a conversation between the pilot and a hijacker in the cockpit that made it evident that a hijacking was in progress. More ominously, they also learned from a hijacker's comment about plans to seize control of other aircraft. This information was the first indication of a plot to hijack numerous aircraft in flight.

The first concrete information about the hijacking came from Betty Ong, a stewardess on Fight 11, who contacted the American Airlines Flight Center in Fort Worth, Texas, and related that two flight attendants had been stabbed and that another was on oxygen. A passenger, she said, had been killed, and the hijackers had gained access to the cockpit, using some type of mace-like spray to neutralize the crew.

Once the hijackers gained control of the aircraft, they took precautions to control the passengers, securing the first class section by intimidation, mace and pepper spray, and threats to detonate a bomb. The rest of the passengers, in coach, were led to believe a medical emergency had occurred in the first class section. The hijackers also told the passengers that the aircraft was returning to the airport. Another attendant, Madeleine Sweeney, contacted authorities and confirmed Ong's earlier message to the American Flight Services Office in Boston. She reestablished communication and was in fact on the line when the aircraft approached the North Tower of the World Trade Center. By the time the passengers realized what was happening, it was too late to do anything about it. Many hurriedly called their loved ones and said goodbye either by talking with them or by leaving messages.

The aircraft crashed at about 378 miles per hour between the ninety-fourth and ninety-eighth floors of the North Tower. The crew, passengers, and hijackers all died instantly from the force of the explosion and the fire that accompanied it. The force of the explosion alone shattered the aluminum wings and fuselage of the air-craft into pieces the size of a human fist.

The impact of the crash and the prolonged burning of aviation fuel weakened the structure of the North Tower, trapping those people above the ninety-eighth floor, who had no chance of escape. Those threatened by fire and smoke began to jump from the building. The North Tower collapsed on itself shortly after the South Tower fell.

See Also
Atta, Mohamed el-Amir Awad el-Sayed; Lewin, Daniel M.; Ogonowski, John; Ong, Betty Ann; World Trade Center, September 11

Suggested Reading
Stefan Aust et al., *Inside 9–11: What Really Happened* (New York: St. Martin's Press, 2001); Richard Bernstein, *Out of the Blue: The Story of September 11, 2001, from Jihad to Ground Zero* (New York: Times Books, 2002); Olga Craig, "At 8:46 AM, the World Changed in a Moment," *Sunday Telegraph* [London] (September 16, 2001), p. 14; 9/11 Commission, *The 9/11 Commission Report: Final Report of the National Commission on Terrorist Attacks Upon the United States* (New York: Norton, 2004); Susan B. Trento and Joseph J. Trento, *Unsafe at Any Altitude: Failed Terrorism Investigations, Scapegoating 9/11, and the Shocking Truth About Aviation Security Today* (Hanover, NH: Steerforth Press, 2006).

American Airlines Flight 77

American Airlines Flight 77, a Boeing 757-223, was the third aircraft seized by hijackers on September 11, 2001. It left Dulles International Airport, near Washington, D.C., at 8:20 a.m., bound for Los Angeles International Airport with fifty-eight passengers and a crew of six. The pilot was Charles Burlingame and the First Officer David Charlebois. Because of problems at the security gate, the flight was ten minutes late taking off. The security checkpoint at Dulles International Airport was operated by Argenbright Security under a contract with United Airlines. Passenger screeners at Dulles International Airport were 87 percent foreign-born and mostly Muslim. Three of the hijackers failed the metal detector test, but, after passing hand-wand screening, were permitted to enter the aircraft. There was no indication that any of them were carrying prohibited weapons.

The five-person terrorist team was led by Hani Hanjour, who was also the team's designated pilot. Other members of his team were Nawaf al-Hazmi, Salem al-Hazmi, Khalid al-Mihdhar, and Majed Moqued, who had all bought first-class tickets to gain better access to the aircraft's cockpit. The hijackers used knives and box-cutters to gain control of the cockpit sometime between 8:51 and 8:54 a.m., after which Hanjour, the designated pilot, turned the aircraft around and headed for Washington, D.C. Like the hijackers of American Airlines Flight 11, the hijackers of Flight 77 calmed passengers by convincing them that the plane would land, after which they would be used as hostages.

Although by this time it was known that other aircraft had been seized and turned into flying bombs, authorities in Washington, D.C., were slow to respond.

Two passengers, Renee May and Barbara K. Olson, the wife of the United States Solicitor General, Theodore Olson, made phone calls reporting the hijacking. Olson made two calls to her husband, giving him details of the hijacking. He told her the news of the two aircraft crashing into the World Trade Center.

By this time the Dulles air controllers were aware of an approaching unauthorized aircraft coming at high speed toward Washington, D.C. They had been able to obtain a visual confirmation from a military transport, a C-141, as the hijacked aircraft headed toward the Pentagon. Between 9:37 and 9:40 a.m., Flight 77 crashed at 530 miles per hour into the ground at the base of the west side of the Pentagon, killing all passengers. Although much of the crash site contained recently renovated, unoccupied offices, the explosion and the resulting collapse of parts of the five-story building killed 125 people. The explosion did its greatest damage to the three outer rings of the Pentagon, but the two inner rings sustained damage as well.

Eyewitness Account of Pentagon Attack by Terry Morin from Federal Office Building #2 Parking Lot

I can't remember exactly what I was thinking about at that moment, but I started to hear an increasingly loud rumbling behind me and to my left. . . . One to two seconds later the airliner came into my field of view. By that time the noise was absolutely deafening. I instantly had a very bad feeling about this but things were happening very quickly. The aircraft was essentially right over the top of me and the outer portion of the FOB (flight path parallel the outer edge of the FOB). Everything was shaking and vibrating, including the ground. I estimate that the aircraft was no more than 100 feet above me (30 to 50 feet above the FOB) in a slight nose-down attitude. The plane had a silver body with red and blue stripes down the fuselage. I believed at the time that it belonged to American Airlines, but I couldn't be sure. It looked like a 737 and I so reported to authorities.

Within second the plane cleared the 8th Wing of BMDO and was heading directly towards the Pentagon. Engines were at a steady, high-pitched whine, indicating to me that the throttles were steady and full. I estimated the aircraft speed at between 350 and 400 knots. The flight path appeared to be deliberate, smooth, and controlled. . . . I could only see the tail of the aircraft. The tail was barely visible when I saw the flash and subsequent fireball rise approximately 200 feet above the Pentagon. . . . At once there was a huge cloud of black smoke that rose several hundred feet up. Elapsed time from hearing the initial noise to when I saw the impact flash was between 12 and 15 seconds.

Quoted in Accounts of Survivors at Tools for Coping with Life's Stressors (http://www.coping.org/911/survivor/pentagon.htm).

See Also
Burlingame, Charles Frank "Chic" III; Hazmi, Nawaf bin Muhammad Salim al-; Mihdhar, Khalid al-; Olson, Barbara; Pentagon Attack

Suggested Reading
Stefan Aust et al., *Inside 9–11: What Really Happened* (New York: St. Martin's Press, 2001); Richard Bernstein, *Out of the Blue: The Story of September 11, 2001, from Jihad to Ground Zero* (New York: Times Books, 2002); 9/11 Commission, *The 9/11 Commission Report: Final Report of the National Commission on Terrorist Attacks Upon the United States* (New

York: Norton, 2004); Susan B. Trento and Joseph J. Trento, *Unsafe at Any Altitude: Failed Terrorism Investigations, Scapegoating 9/11, and the Shocking Truth About Aviation Security Today* (Hanover, NH: Steerforth Press, 2006).

American Society of Civil Engineers Report

A committee of the American Society of Civil Engineers (ASCE) issued a report in the late spring of 2002 concerning the reasons for the collapse of the buildings of the World Trade Center complex on September 11. ASCE was founded in 1852 and is the oldest organization of its type in existence—and one of the most prestigious. After receiving a $1 million grant from the Federal Emergency Management Agency (FEMA), a twenty-two member committee was formed that contained specialists on metallurgy, fire, structural dynamics, and other relevant fields. Some of the biggest names in civil engineering participated in this study.

The chair of the ASCE committee was W. Gene Corley, senior vice president of an engineering research facility north of Chicago, whose PhD is in civil engineering. Corley had been the leader of the official engineering review of the 1995 Oklahoma City bombing of the Alfred P. Murrah Federal Building. He had a reputation as a fair and independent investigator of building failures.

The final report of the ASCE committee was never intended to definitively analyze the entire situation but rather to understand how and why the buildings at the World Trade Center collapsed. Other pertinent issues, such as crowded stairwells and lack of egress for those above the damaged areas, were not included in the scope of the investigation. The investigators visited the World Trade Center complex site, but they found it too chaotic for normal surveying of materials. Even an examination of the steel proved disappointing. Instead, the investigators used known facts and computer simulations.

The investigators soon learned that the Twin Towers had been designed for lightness and efficiency—not for strength. The towers were essentially 1,362-foot-tall tubes. The architects had designed the buildings to withstand winds of 150 miles per hour, and the decision to anchor them in bedrock gave them even more strength. There was some give in the building, and in strong winds people noticed some sway. Most of the support columns and elevators were in the middle of the building. The floors were built on thin steel trusses covered in concrete. The total weight of each tower, discounting people, furniture, and equipment, was around 600,000 tons.

The investigators came to understand the dynamics of the collapse of the South Tower best. It was relatively easy to calculate the force of impact of a Boeing 767 fully loaded with aviation fuel. The hijacker pilot, Marwan al-Shehhi, crashed the Boeing 767 at a speed of nearly 590 miles per hour into the south side of the South Tower, three-fourths of the way up the building. Because of its speed, the aircraft penetrated deeply into the building, severing as many as half the columns in the central core. The building might have survived except for the fire fueled by the aviation fuel. ASCE's final report claims that the South Tower would have remained intact even with the aviation fuel fire if the fire had not reached flammable material, such as furniture and paper, that intensified it, spreading it to six different floors. Molten aluminum began to flow down the building.

The investigators noted that the fire began to degrade the strength of the steel. Although the report ignored the issue, detractors had long charged that the fireproofing of the Twin Towers' steel was inferior. The fire burned at about 1,500 degrees. Structural steel begins to weaken at 300 degrees and at 1,100 degrees loses half its strength.

The fire could not be stopped. The building's sprinkler system was destroyed in the crash and would not have been powerful enough to put out such a fire anyway. Firefighters were eager but lacked equipment and a water supply sufficient to put out such a disastrous high-rise fire.

Fifty-six minutes after the aircraft crashed into the South Tower, it collapsed, beginning with the southeast corner of the eightieth floor, whose collapse triggered the progressive collapse of the entire east side of the building. As supports gave way, the collapse began to accelerate. The upper sections fell east and south, damaging the Bankers Trust Building, and the lower sections fell north and west, damaging the Marriott Hotel.

The investigators knew less, however, about the collapse of the North Tower. The Boeing 767 that hit it traveled about 100 miles per hour slower than the one that crashed into the South Tower and severely damaged thirty-six of the sixty-one columns on the north face of the building. Damage was done to all three stairways, and the sprinkler system was knocked out. Parts of the aircraft blew through the building. A massive fire broke out, fueled first by aviation fuel and then by the furniture and paper contained in the offices. Because the aircraft hit high in the building, it bore a lighter load as the fire degraded the steel on the four floors. After nearly two hours of high-temperature fires, the building finally collapsed for the same reasons as the South Tower.

The other buildings in the World Trade Center complex also suffered severe enough damage that they also collapsed. Most mysterious was the burning and eventual collapse that evening of Seven World Trade Center. This building was situated away from the Twin Towers but caught fire nonetheless. Eyewitnesses report that the fuel oil storage unit caught fire at the base of the building. By this time the firefighters were so demoralized by their losses from the collapse of the Twin Towers that the leadership of the New York Fire Department (NYFD) refused to risk any more men. Building Seven collapsed from the bottom by early evening. A probable contributing cause was a fuel storage unit just outside the building, which caught fire. The fire intensified fed by furniture and paper in the building until the structure, undermined, collapsed.

The final report explained the process that contributed to the collapse of the buildings at the World Trade Center complex but left room for further study. Despite earlier criticism of the architectural design and the building materials to build the World Trade Center complex, the committee defended the construction of the buildings while expressing concern about the centralized columns and stairways and recommending that new structures be capable of withstanding the type of airliner crash experienced on September 11.

See Also
Firefighters at Ground Zero; World Trade Center

See Document
Document #25

Suggested Reading
David Bianculli, "NOVA: Why the Towers Fell," *Daily News* [New York] (April 30, 2002), p. 91; William Langewiesche, *American Ground: Unbuilding the World Trade Center* (New York: North Point Press, 2002).

Argenbright Security Company

An economic and political casualty of the September attacks was the Argenbright Security Company. Before that date it was the largest and most successful of the private security companies employed by American commercial airlines. Frank Argenbright had founded the company and made it successful before selling it to the British Securicor for $175 million, after which he remained associated with the company in a gradually diminishing role before his replacement in the summer of 2001.

Argenbright Security manned the security screening stations at Dulles International Airport in Arlington, Virginia. Because it had difficulty finding security screeners, most of its screeners were foreign-born Muslims. Turnover among personnel was high. Despite these difficulties, the screeners at Dulles had a good track record of catching those trying to take forbidden items through airport security. On September 11 the hijackers of American Airlines Flight 77 passed the security screeners only with difficulty. They were challenged over their baggage but had nothing on them that violated FAA rules.

After September 11, Argenbright Security became a convenient scapegoat. Government agents descended on Dulles and closed down the airport. They then began to interview everybody at the airport. Employees of Argenbright Security received special scrutiny. Teams of officials wanted Argenbright employees to confess to violations of FAA rules. Some of the employees disappeared into government hands, never to reappear at Dulles. Many were deported and others lost their jobs in the aftermath of the investigations. The government needed a scapegoat, and Argenbright Security was available. Information about alleged deficiencies began to be leaked to the media.

Efforts to Make the Screeners the Scapegoat for the Events of September 11

For Nelson [Ed Nelson—administrator for Argenbright Security at Dulles International Airport] nothing the FBI and INS agents were asking his people made sense. "They were not asking about the hijackers—they were focusing in on what my screeners might have done wrong. It was as if they were working off a script," he says.

According to FBI agents assigned to Dulles that day, who agreed to speak only if their names and office assignments were not published, that is precisely what they were given by supervisors at several Washington-area FBI offices. The orders came from headquarters through the local Washington-area FBI field offices and the Joint Task Force on Terrorism. The teams of agents were told to "get the screeners to admit they had violated FAA recommended procedures," one of the FBI supervisors says.

Susan B. Trento and Joseph J. Trento, *Unsafe at Any Altitude: Failed Terrorism Investigations, Scapegoating 9/11, and the Shocking Truth about Aviation Security Today* (Hanover, NH: Steerforth Press, 2006), p. 36.

An earlier brush with the authorities in 1999 made Argenbright Security susceptible to scapegoating. An employee had been arrested for drug possession in January 1999, leading to an investigation by the Philadelphia FAA security staff. A screening text revealed that some of the employees had not received mandatory training. A subsequent investigation revealed that a supervisor had falsified records, and he ended up in jail. This black mark made the Philadelphia FAA suspicious of Argenbright Security and its screening procedures, suspicions that resurfaced after September 11.

Argenbright Security and other private security companies were unable to survive the aftermath of September 11. Despite some efforts by Republican congressmen to preserve the private security system, Congress passed legislation creating the Transportation Security Administration (TSA), a bill that President Bush signed into law. Almost all employees of the private security companies were excluded from employment with the new organization.

See Also
American Airlines Flight 77

See Document
Document #35

Suggested Reading
Susan B. Trento and Joseph J. Trento, *Unsafe at Any Altitude: Failed Terrorism Investigations, Scapegoating 9/11, and the Shocking Truth about Aviation Security Today* (Hanover, NH: Steerforth Press, 2006).

Atef, Mohammad (1944–2001)

Mohammad Atef was al-Qaeda's head of military operations during the planning and implementation of the September 11 operation. At that time Atef was number three in the al-Qaeda hierarchy, behind Osama bin Laden and Ayman al-Zawahiri. Atef made decisions about the events of September 11 from the beginning, assisting Khalid Sheikh Mohammed in the final stages of the plot.

Atef converted to Islamist extremism early in his career. Born in 1944 in Menoufya, Egypt, in the Nile Delta, about thirty-five miles north of Cairo, he was named Sobhi Abu Sitta. After graduating from high school, he served his required two years of military service in the Egyptian Army. Reports that Atef was a policeman in Egypt have been denied by the Egyptian government, but nearly all sources state that he was. In the late 1970s, Atef joined an Egyptian terrorist organization, the Egyptian Islamic Jihad. Evidently a low-ranking member, he didn't meet with its leader, al-Zawahiri, while both were in Egypt. Despite his involvement in this group, he escaped arrest after the crackdown on extremists that followed the assassination of President Anwar Sadat in 1981. In 1983 Atef left Egypt for Afghanistan to fight with the mujahideen against Soviet forces, where he first met al-Zawahiri, who then introduced him to bin Laden. Atef and bin Laden became close friends. Atef also became acquainted with Abdullah Azzam and admired him greatly, but in the subsequent battle between Azzam and al-Zawahiri for bin Laden's support, Atef supported al-Zawahiri. In 1999 Egyptian authorities sentenced Atef to a seven-year prison term in absentia for his membership in the Egyptian Islam Jihad, but Atef never returned to Egypt.

Atef's close personal relationship with bin Laden made him an important member of al-Qaeda. When bin Laden founded al-Qaeda, Atef was a charter member. Ubaidah al-Banshiri was al-Qaeda's head of military operations, and Atef assisted him. He was active in organizing Somali resistance to American military presence in 1992, but some evidence suggests that his stay there was not entirely successful. Atef also served as bin Laden's chief of personal security. Al-Banshiri's death in a boat accident in Africa allowed Atef to replace him in 1996. From then until his death in 2001, Atef was in charge of military operations for al-Qaeda. All military operation came under his oversight, but he always remained subordinate to bin Laden even after bin Laden's eldest son married one of Atef's daughters in January 2001.

> **Mohammad Atef's Explanation of the Attack on the USS Cole**
>
> I will tell you one thing. We did [the USS] Cole [attack] and we wanted [the] United States to react. And if they reacted, [we thought,] they are going to invade Afghanistan and that's what we want. We want them to come to our country, and then we know that they would have bases in Pakistan, in Uzbekistan, Kazakhstan. And they are going to hit Afghanistan from these countries. And then we will start holy war against the Americans, exactly like [we did against the] Soviets.
>
> Quoted in Peter L. Bergen, *The Osama bin Laden I Know: An Oral History of al Qaeda's Leader* (New York: Free Press, 2006), p. 255.

Atef was aware of the September 11 plot from its beginning. Khalid Sheikh Mohammed outlined the plan to bin Laden and Atef as early as 1996. Bin Laden finally agreed on the basics of the plot in 1998. It was Atef's job to search al-Qaeda's training camps for suitable candidates for a martyrdom mission that required operatives to live unnoticed in America. Once the members of the Hamburg Cell were picked and recruited by bin Laden, Atef explained to Mohamed Atta, Ramzi bin al-Shibh, Ziad Jarrah, and Marwan al-Shehhi the outlines of the plot.

Al-Qaeda avoided having its leaders at a single site except for particularly special occasions, a policy prompted by fears of American assassination of al-Qaeda's leaders. Bin Laden announced that in case of his death or capture, Atef would succeed him as head of al-Qaeda. Once the United States began military operations against the Taliban and al-Qaeda in Afghanistan, it became even more important for al-Qaeda's leaders to be at separate locations. Atef was at a gathering in Kabul on November 18, 2001, when a Predator unmanned aerial vehicle fired Hellfire missiles, killing Atef and those with him—something for which the United States had been offering a $5 million reward. The loss of Atef was a blow to al-Qaeda, but he was soon replaced as military commander by Abu Zubaydah.

See Also

Atta, Mohamed el-Amir Awad el-Sayed; Bin Laden, Osama; Bin al-Shibh, Ramzi; Jarrah, Ziad Samir; Hamburg Cell; Qaeda, al-; Shehhi, Marwan Yousef Muhammed Rashid Lekrab al-

Suggested Reading

Khaled Dawoud, "Mohammed Atef; Egyptian Militant Who Rose to the Top of the al-Qaida Hierarchy," *Guardian* [London] (November 19, 2001), p. 1; MATP, "Iron Fist Reaches from Far Side of the Globe," *Australian* [Sydney] (November 19, 2001), p. 8.

Atta, Mohamed el-Amir Awad el-Sayed (1968–2001)

Mohamed Atta was the commander of the al-Qaeda team that hijacked four American commercial aircraft and used them as guided missiles on September 11, 2001. He had been recruited by al-Qaeda for this mission after being trained by al-Qaeda trainers. Only the most highly motivated individuals were selected for martyrdom missions, and Atta met this requirement.

Atta had a strict family upbringing. He was born on September 1, 1968, in the village of Kafr el-Sheikh in the Egyptian delta. His father was a middle-class lawyer with ties to the fundamentalist Muslim Brotherhood. Atta's family moved to the Abdin District of Cairo in 1978 when Atta was ten. His father, who had a dominating personality, insisted that his children study, not play. Atta's family life allowed him few friends. After attending a local high school, he enrolled in the Cairo University in 1986. As usual in the Egyptian system, Atta's admittance to the university was based on his exam scores, and he was assigned to a specialty— the architecture section of the engineering department. At his graduation in 1990, his grades were not good enough to admit him to graduate school. On the recommendation of his father, he then planned to study town planning in Germany. In the meantime, he worked for a Cairo engineering firm. After learning German at the Goethe Institute in Cairo, Atta traveled to Hamburg, Germany, in July 1992 to begin studying town planning. He applied first to study architecture at the University of Applied Science but, after being turned down, migrated to the Technical University of Hamburg-Harburg to study the preservation of the Islamic quarters of medieval cities in the Middle East. During his coursework, Atta interacted very little with fellow students, earning a reputation as a loner. His classmates also noted his strong religious orientation. He traveled to Turkey and Syria in 1994 to study old Muslim quarters. After receiving a German grant, Atta and two fellow students visited Egypt to study the old section of Cairo that was called the Islamic City. They were appalled at what the Egyptian government was doing to this old part of the city. Up to this point his life, Atta appeared to be an academic preparing for a career as a teacher at a university.

In 1995, however, he became active in Muslim extremist politics. After a pilgrimage to Mecca, he initiated contact with al-Qaeda recruiters. Atta was just the type of individual that al-Qaeda recruiters were looking for—intelligent and dedicated. After his return to Hamburg to continue his studies, he attended the al-Quds Mosque, where his final recruitment to radical Islam took place. There Atta met radical clerics who steered him toward an al-Qaeda recruiter. Muhammad Zammar, a Syrian recruiter for al-Qaeda, convinced Atta to join al-Qaeda. Several of his friends, Ramzi bin al-Shibh, Marwan al-Shehhi, and Ziad Jarrah, also joined al-Qaeda. Atta became the leader of the so-called Hamburg Cell of radical Islamists.

In 1998 Atta left for Kandahar, Afghanistan, to receive military and terrorist training at the al-Qaeda training camp at Khaldan. He so distinguished himself during the training that al-Qaeda leaders decided to recruit him for a future suicide mission. Atta ranked high in all the attributes of an al-Qaeda operative—intelligence, religious devotion, patience, and willingness to sacrifice. Atta, Jarrah, and al-Shehhi met and talked with Osama bin Laden in Kandahar. Bin Laden asked them to pledge loyalty to him and accept a suicide mission. They agreed, and Mohammed Atef, al-Qaeda's military chief, briefed them on the general outlines of the September 11 operation. Then Atta and the others were sent back to Germany to finish their academic training.

Difference in Orientation between Mohamed Atta and Ramzi Bin al-Shibh

Although Amir [Mohamed Atta] and Omar [Ramzi Bin al-Shibh] seemed to agree on many things, they had different emphases. Omar was motivated more by religious belief, and Amir by politics. With Amir, it was always hate when it came to the Jews. He was very emotional about the political issues, while Omar was emotional about the religion. Amir saw a worldwide conspiracy at work, bolstered by the Americans, but run always by Jews. He blamed Jews for almost every wrong imaginable.

Terry McDermott, *Perfect Soldiers: The Hijackers: Who They Were, Why They Did It* (New York: HarperCollins, 2005), p. 67.

Atta was a complex individual deeply affected psychologically. He had puritanical and authoritarian views towards women and, despite having two sisters and a reportedly normal relationship with his mother, believed women and sexual intercourse were polluting. Only once, in Syria, did a woman attract him—but he complained that the Palestinian woman was too forward. Atta also held strong anti-American views, disturbed by the Americanization of Egyptian society.

After he finished his degree in 1999, al-Qaeda's leaders assigned him his martyrdom mission in the United States, a mission planned by Khalid Sheikh Mohammed. Atta arrived in the United States on June 2, 2000. His orders placed him in charge of a large cell, but he, Jarrah, and al-Shehhi were the only members of his cell who knew the details of his mission. Several times Atta flew back and forth between the United States and Germany and Spain to coordinate the mission. Members of his cell arrived in the United States at various times. Atta and key members of the cell received orders to take pilot lessons to fly large commercial aircraft.

Most of Atta's time was spent in pilot lessons in Florida. Before he could qualify for training on large commercial aircraft, Atta had to learn to fly small planes. Most of his flying instruction took place at Huffman Aviation in Sarasota, Florida. He had an attitude problem that hurt his relations with his instructors, but it did not prevent him from earning his small aircraft license in December 2000. Next, he began to use simulators and manuals to train himself to fly large commercial aircraft.

Atta gathered most of the members of his cell together in Florida for the first time in early June 2001. He organized the cell into four teams, each of which included a trained pilot. Throughout the summer of 2001, each team rode as passengers on test flights in which they studied the efficiency of airline security and strategized about the best time to highjack an aircraft. They discovered that airline security was weakest at Boston's Logan International Airport and decided that the best days for hijacking were Tuesdays. They decided that first-class seats would give them better access to cockpits. Although the teams tried to remain inconspicuous, the Hollywood actor James Woods reported suspicious behavior by one of the teams on a flight. He reported his suspicions to the pilot and a flight attendant, who passed them on to the FAA, but nothing came of his report. Atta selected two airlines—American Airlines and United Airlines—that flew Boeing 757s and 767s, aircraft used for long flights that thus held the most aviation fuel. Furthermore, these aircraft were equipped with up-to-date avionics, making them easier to fly.

Atta called for a leadership meeting in Las Vegas, Nevada, in late June 2001. Atta, Ziad Jarrah, Hani Hanjour, and Nawaf al-Hazmi stayed at the EconoLodge Motel in Las Vegas, where they completed plans for the September 11 operation. Atta and Jarrah used a local Cyberzone Internet Café to send e-mails to al-Qaeda leaders abroad.

Atta then traveled to Spain via Zurich, Switzerland, to update his handlers on his final plans and receive last minute instructions. He met with al-Qaeda representatives in the resort town of Salou on July 8, 2001, receiving his final authorization for the September 11 mission. Atta was given final authority to determine the targets and date of the operation. Several times bin Laden had attempted to push the plan forward, but Atta had refused to carry out the mission before he was ready and was backed by Khalid Sheikh Mohammad in this. Atta flew back to the United States, and, despite an expired visa, had no trouble getting past the INS agents at the airport.

Atta issued final instructions about the mission on the night of September 10. One-way tickets for flights on September 11 had been bought with credit cards in late August. Atta had made arrangements to have the cell's excess funds transferred back to al-Qaeda on September 4. He traveled to Portland, Maine, with Abdul Aziz al-Omari where they stayed at the Comfort Inn in South Portland. They caught a 5:45 a.m. flight out of Portland International Airport, but Atta's luggage arrived too late to make American Airlines Flight 11 from Logan International Airport. At 7:45 a.m., Atta and al-Omari boarded American Airlines Flight 11. Soon afterward, Atta phoned Marwan al-Shehhi, on board United Airlines Flight 175—also at Logan International Airport—to make sure everything was on schedule.

Mohamed Atta is shown in this photo released Wednesday, September 12, 2001, by the State of Florida Division of Motor Vehicles. (AP IMAGES.)

Atta commanded the first team. Approximately fifteen minutes after takeoff, his team seized control of the aircraft using box openers as weapons. Atta redirected the aircraft toward New York City and the World Trade Center complex, where it crashed into the North Tower of the New York Trade Center at about 8:45 a.m. Other members of the team carried out their attacks successfully except for one flight lost in Pennsylvania.

See Also
American Airlines Flight 11; bin al-Shibh, Ramzi; Hamburg Cell; Jarrah, Ziad Samir; Mohammed, Khalid Sheikh; Qaeda, al-; Quds Mosque, al-; Shehhi, Marwan Yousef Muhammed Rashid Lekrab al-; World Trade Center, September 11

See Document
Document #13

Suggested Reading
Terry McDermott, *Perfect Soldiers: The Hijackers: Who They Were, Why They Did It* (New York: HarperCollins, 2005); Yosri Fouda and Nick Fielding, *Masterminds of Terror: The Truth Behind the Most Devastating Terrorist Attack the World Has Ever Seen* (New York: Arcade Publishing, 2003); John Miller, Michael Stone, and Chris Mitchell, *The Cell: Inside the 9/11 Plot, and Why the FBI and CIA Failed to Stop It* (New York: Hyperion, 2002); Marc Sageman, *Understanding Terror Networks* (Philadelphia: University of Pennsylvania Press, 2004).

Azzam, Sheikh Abdullah Yussuf (1941–1989)
Sheikh Abdullah Yussuf Azzam was one of the spiritual leaders of the international radical Islamist movement. His ideas of jihad inspired the September 11, 2001, terrorists. Before his death, he traveled around Europe, the Middle East, and the United States advocating religious warfare against the West.

A Palestinian by birth, Azzam devoted his life to building the Islamist movement. He was born in 1941 in the small village of Selat al-Harithis, near Jenin,

Palestine. Most of his early schooling took place in Jordanian religious schools. After graduating from Khadorri College, he taught in the village of Adder in South Jordan. In the early 1960s, he attended the Sharia College of Damascus. Azzam fought with the Palestinians in the Six Day War in 1967 but left the Palestinian resistance movement because he considered it "a political cause insufficiently rooted in Islam." In 1967 he moved to Egypt, where he worked toward a master's degree in Islamic Law at Cairo's famous al-Azhar University. Among his acquaintances was Omar Abdul Rahman, with whom he often talked about the creation of an Islamist state. After graduation, Azzam taught for a couple years before returning to al-Azhar University to study for a PhD in Islamic jurisprudence. Azzam received his doctorate in 1971, after which he took a teaching job at the University of Jordan. In 1980 he was dismissed from the university because of his activity with the Palestinian movement. He found a job leading prayers at the school mosque at King Abdul Aziz University in Jeddah, Saudi Arabia. Among his students at King Abdul Aziz University was Osama bin Laden. Azzam refused to return to Palestine because of his continued unhappiness with the secularism of the Palestine Liberation Organization (PLO). Later, when his views crystallized, he helped start Hamas in December 1987 to serve as a counterweight to the PLO.

Azzam was a proponent of the use of holy war, or jihad, to liberate the Muslim world from what he considered the tyranny of the secular West. He wanted to reestablish the Caliphate by any means possible. J. Bowyer Bell described Azzam's tactics as use of "jihad and the rifle alone; no negotiations, no conferences, no dialogues." Azzam taught this doctrine of jihad at every turn at King Abdul Aziz University. Although his teachings made the Saudi government nervous, it left him alone. After the invasion of Afghanistan by the Soviet Army in 1979, Azzam decided to place his Islamist doctrine and himself at the service of the Afghan fighters. At the same time, Saudi authorities expelled him from his teaching post. In November 1981 he found a position teaching Arabic and the Koran at the International Islamic University in Islamabad, Pakistan, but he soon found the war in Afghanistan more important than his teaching.

Azzam moved to Peshawar, Pakistan, to organize the mujahideen fighters in their operations against the Soviets. He traveled throughout the Arab world—and even Europe and the United States—recruiting fighters and raising money. His former student, bin Laden, who was also in Pakistan, began working with him. They founded the Mujahideen Services Bureau (MSB) in 1984, Azzam providing the inspiration and theology and bin Laden the funding (from his personal fortune). It was also in 1984 that Azzam issued a fatwa making it obligatory for every able-bodied Muslim to fight against the Soviets in Afghanistan. Azzam made frequent trips into Afghanistan to preach global jihad, but he avoided the fighting. His sermons and other discourses reached most of the 16,000 to 20,000 Afghan War veterans. He also made several trips to the United State looking for money and recruits for the war. While in the United States, he established branches of the MSB. Both abroad and in Pakistan he constantly preached the necessity of jihad, expressing himself best in his own works explaining his doctrine of jihad.

Azzam's ideas became more radical as the war in Afghanistan progressed. He became convinced of a conspiracy on the part of Pakistan and the United States to weaken the Islamist cause. In 1987 he conceptualized an Islamist vanguard, or al-Qaeda al-Sulbah (the Solid Base) to carry the creation of a purified Islamist society. It was this concept of an Islamist base organization that Osama bin Laden later developed into al-Qaeda.

Azzam and bin Laden's relationship deteriorated because they disagreed over the strategy of exporting terror. Azzam first wanted to concentrate on building an Islamist society in Afghanistan. He opposed launching a terrorist campaign against Arab regimes before consolidating affairs in Afghanistan and Pakistan. Azzam was not adverse to the idea of rolling back Christian encroachment on for-

---

Azzam's Position on Jihad

Sheikh Azzam's fatwas, which are still widely quoted in the responses of today's radical ulama, call for continuous jihad "until all of Mankind worships Allah." He did not, however, stop at determining jihad as the primary means for achieving Allah's rule; jihad became a moral goal in itself. In his preaching and writing he reiterated, "A few moments spent in jihad in the Path of Allah is worth more than seventy years spent in praying at home." Waging jihad was, for Azzam and his followers, a way to imitate the Prophet and his Companions by reenacting the events of the seventh century—belief, emigration from infidel society (the hijrah of the Prophet from Mecca), and finally jihad for spreading Islam. The implicit goal, in Sheikh Azzam's view, was reestablishing the caliphate through jihad (ultimately offensive jihad) until Islam holds sway over the world.

Shmuel Bar, *Warrant for Terror: The Fatwas of Radical Islam and the Duty to Jihad* (Lanham, MD: Rowman & Littlefield, 2006), p. 39.

---

merly Muslim lands, but he opposed internal Muslim infighting. In contrast, bin Laden aimed to liberate the Muslim community everywhere—including in Muslim countries. Al-Zawahiri, who was even more radical in his views than bin Laden, used his close contacts with bin Laden to undermine Azzam. This open disagreement between Azzam and bin Laden led bin Laden to break with Azzam in 1987, something partly caused by Azzam's increasing closeness with Ahmad Shah Massoud. Azzam believed that Massoud was a possible future leader of an Islamic Afghanistan. Bin Laden and al-Zawahiri violently disagreed with Azzam over this. Azzam's career ended abruptly on November 24, 1989, when a bomb exploded under his car in Peshawar, killing him, two of his sons, and a companion. He was killed shortly after a meeting where he had been forced to justify his spending on Islamist operations. At first, suspicion centered on Pakistani security forces as the killers, but there is no satisfactory evidence of who planted the bomb—although the person who benefited most was al-Zawahiri. Regardless of the intent of the assassins, Azzam's stature in the Islamist movement remains strong because his backers have continued to advance his cause.

See Also
Abdel Rahman, Sheikh Omar; bin Laden, Osama; Qaeda, al-; Zawahiri, Ayman al-

Suggested Reading
J. Bowyer Bell, *Murders on the Nile: The World Trade Center and Global Terror* (San Francisco: Encounter Books, 2003); Rohan Gunaratna, *Inside Al Qaeda: Global Network of Terror* (New York: Columbia University Press, 2002); Marc Sageman, *Understanding Terror Networks* (Philadelphia: University of Pennsylvania Press, 2004); Lawrence Wright, *The Looming Tower: Al-Qaeda and the Road to 9/11* (New York: Knopf, 2006).

B

Bahaji, Said (1975–)

Said Bahaji was an active member of the Hamburg Cell, and served as its administrative secretary. This role gave him access to all the planning for the September 11 conspiracy. He also served as a conduit between the Hamburg Cell and al-Qaeda.

Bahaji was a product of mixed cultures. He was born on July 15, 1975, at Haselunne, Lower Saxony, Germany. His father was Moroccan and his mother German. The father ran discotheques in Germany, but was never successful. Bahaji lived in Germany until age nine, when the family moved to Meknès, Morocco, where his father became a farmer. In Meknès Bahaji attended the local school. After graduation he returned to Hamburg, Germany, to continue his education. With a desire to study electronics, Bahaji enrolled in an electrical engineering program at the Technical University of Hamburg-Harburg (TUHH) in 1996. He became an excellent computer programmer. Because Bahaji was a German citizen, he had a military obligation to fulfill. He served with the 72nd Tank and Rifle Battalion in Hamburg's Fischbek district, although his tour of duty ended with a military discharge after five months because of asthma and allergies. Bahaji married a Turkish woman in 1999, and they had a son.

Bahaji held pro-Western views until he began attending the al-Quds Mosque. Mounir el-Motassadeq introduced him to Mohamed Atta and Ramzi bin al-Shibh. Within weeks of this introduction, Bahaji began making militant Islamist remarks. Shortly after meeting Atta and bin al-Shibh, Bahaji decided to share an apartment with them at 54 Marienstrasse. They soon formed what came to be known as the Hamburg Cell. Each member of the cell had a job. Bahaji's job was as administrative secretary, paying bills and handling the cell's administrative duties. His computer skills were invaluable. He made certain that the cell's bills were paid on time to attract as little attention as possible. Bahaji was never considered a candidate for the September 11 plot team, but continued to conduct support activities from Hamburg. He was in frequent contact with the leaders of the September 11 conspiracy, providing them with money and with instructions from their al-Qaeda contacts.

Preparing for the backlash of September 11, bin Laden ordered al-Qaeda personnel to destroy records and return to his protection in Afghanistan. Responding to these orders, Bahaji left Germany on September 4, 2001, for Afghanistan. His whereabouts since then are unknown. His mission to supply logistical support for the Hamburg Cell had been successful.

Personality of Bahaji

Bahaji was an electrical engineering student at TUHH and an able computer programmer, according to his bosses at a company where he worked part-time. In many ways, he was a typical computer nerd—an autodidact, as one man describes him—who seemed more at ease at a keyboard than in social situations.

Terry McDermott, *Perfect Soldiers: The Hijackers: Who They Were, Why They Did It* (New York: HarperCollins, 2005), p. 64.

See Also

Atta, Mohamed el-Amir Awad el-Sayed; Hamburg Cell; Quds Mosque, al-

Suggested Reading

Terry McDermott, *Perfect Soldiers: The 9/11 Hijackers: Who They Were, Why They Did It* (New York: HarperCollins, 2005).

Beamer, Todd Morgan (1968–2001)

Todd Beamer was on United Airlines Flight 93 on September 11, 2001, and was one of the passengers who attempted to regain control of the aircraft from the hijackers. Beamer and others burst into the cockpit and contested the hijackers for control of the plane. The fact that the attempt to regain control of the cockpit was unsuccessful does not detract from the effort. Beamer and his fellow passengers kept the hijackers from crashing the airliner into a Washington, D.C., building—probably the U.S. Capitol.

Beamer has been described by his wife as an ordinary man. He was born on November 24, 1968, in Flushing, Michigan, near Flint. His father worked for several large corporations, and the family moved several times, ending up in Chicago. Beamer attended a private elementary school in Glen Ellyn—Wheaton Christian Grammar School. For three years he went to Wheaton Christian High School, until his father was transferred to California. In his senior year Beamer attended Los Gatos High School in Los Gatos, California, where he was a starter on the basketball and baseball teams. After graduation from high school, he entered California State University–Fresno, but the aftereffects of a car wreck and his inability to make the nationally ranked baseball team as a walk-on led him to transfer to Wheaton College in Wheaton, Illinois, where he did become a member of the baseball team. After graduating from college with a business degree, he started work on an MBA at DePaul University, which he earned in 1993. He found a job as an account manager for the Oracle Corporation, and over the next eight years he made steady progress up the corporate hierarchy. He worked long hours, and his job required constant travel. On May 14, 1994, Beamer married Lisa Brosious. By September 2001 he and his wife had two young sons and she was five months pregnant. They had just returned from an Oracle Company–sponsored vacation in Rome.

Beamer took United Airlines Flight 93 on September 11 because he had an important business meeting in San Francisco with high-level representatives of Sony Corporation. Beamer wanted an early morning flight in order to keep his 1:00 p.m. appointment in San Francisco.

Beamer has become one of the more famous of those who tried to regain control of UAL Flight 93. Soon after the hijackers seized control of the plane at 9:45 a.m. Beamer contacted Lisa Jefferson, the GTE Airfone operator, to inform her that the aircraft had been hijacked. He reported that one passenger had been killed, and that a flight attendant had told him the pilot and copilot had been forced from the cockpit and may have been wounded. From the other passengers Beamer had learned that the hijackers were on a suicide mission. When hijacker Ziad Jarrah turned the aircraft around, Beamer and the others decided to try to regain control by attacking the hijackers. He teamed with Mark Bingham, Thomas Burnett, Jeremy Glick, and others to fight for control of the airliner. Beamer was under no illusions, and he told the Airfone operator that he knew he was going to die and asked her to pray with him. First they recited the Lord's Prayer. Then they recited the 23rd Psalm, and other passengers joined in the prayer. He also asked the operator to relay a message to his wife and their two sons: "Tell her I love her and the boys." Beamer was still on the phone with Lisa Jefferson when his last audible words were heard: "Are you guys ready? Let's roll." By this time all of the hijackers had retreated into the cockpit area. The passengers had coffeepots full of hot water prepared by the flight attendants to use as weapons, and they took a cart of food trays to crash into the cockpit area. A struggle ensued, with the hijackers close to being overpowered. To keep from losing control of the aircraft, hijacker Jarrah crashed it into the ground near Shanksville, Pennsylvania. Beamer has since become famous for the expression, "Let's roll," which became the battle cry of soldiers fighting al-Qaeda in Afghanistan.

Beamer has received several honors since his death. School authorities named a high school in Federal Way, Washington, after him: Todd Beamer High School. His name was given to a post office in Cranbury, New Jersey. His college, Wheaton College, named their student center the Todd M. Beamer Student Center. Finally, his wife, Lisa, wrote a book with coauthor Ken Abraham titled *Let's Roll!: Ordinary People, Extraordinary Courage.* She also established a nonprofit foundation in his name in October 2001—The Todd M. Beamer Foundation—to help the families of victims of September 11 with young children.

Comments about Todd Beamer by His Wife Concerning His Last Moments

The information confirmed to me that Todd was "who he was" right to the very end of his life. It was a tremendous comfort to know that in his last moments, his faith in God remained strong, and his love for us, his family, was at the forefront of his thoughts. I was glad to know that Todd felt he had some control of his destiny, that he might be able to effect change even to the end. The words "Let's roll" were especially significant to me. Just hearing that made me smile, partially because it was "so Todd," but also because it showed he felt he could still do something positive in the midst of a crisis situation.

Lisa Beamer and Ken Abraham, *Let's Roll! Ordinary People, Extraordinary Courage* (Wheaton, IL: Tyndale House Publishers, 2002), p. 187.

See Also

Bingham, Mark Kendall; Burnett, Thomas Edward; Glick, Jeremy; United Airlines Flight 93

See Document

Document #16

Suggested Reading
Lisa Beamer and Ken Abraham, *Ordinary People, Extraordinary Courage* (Wheaton, IL: Tyndale House Publishers, 2002); David Flores, "Heroism of Ex-Athletes on Flight 93 Inspiring," *San Antonio Express-News* (September 10, 2002), p. 7C; Lisa Jefferson and Felicia Middlebrooks, *Called: "Hello, My Name Is Mrs. Jefferson. I Understand Your Plane Is Being Hijacked?"—9:45 AM, Flight 93. September 11, 2001* (Chicago: Northfield Publishing, 2006); Jack Kelly, "Flight 93 Uprising Saved Countless Lives in Capital," *Pittsburgh Post-Gazette* (June 18, 2004), p. A1; Charles Lane, Don Phillips, and David Snyder, "A Sky Filled with Chaos, Uncertainty and True Heroism," *Washington Post* (September 17, 2001), p. A3; Jeer Longman, *Among the Heroes: United Flight 93 and the Passengers and Crew Who Fought Back* (New York: HarperCollins, 2002); Jim McKinnon, "The Phone Line from Flight 93 Was Still Open When a GTE Operator Heard Todd Beamer Say: 'Are You Guys Ready? Let's Roll,'" *Pittsburgh Post-Gazette* (September 16, 2001), p. A1.

Biggart, William (1947–2001)

William Biggart was a working photojournalist covering the World Trade Center attack on September 11 when he was killed by the collapse of the North Tower. He was walking his dog with his wife when he first heard about an aircraft crashing into a building in the World Trade Center complex. Biggart immediately grabbed his cameras and dashed to cover the action two miles away.

Biggart had always wanted to be a photojournalist. He was born on July 20, 1947, in the West sector of Berlin, Germany. His father was in the U.S. Army stationed in West Berlin. He was the second of twelve children in an Irish American family. At the early age of fourteen, Biggart acquired a camera and began working as an apprentice to commercial photographers. Becoming a freelance photojournalist with a small independent agency, he traveled around the world taking pictures at trouble spots. His photographs of the Israeli-Palestinian conflict, Wounded Knee incident, and the collapse of the Berlin Wall gave him a reputation for covering international affairs. His photographs appeared in all sorts of publications. Some of his most famous photographs were of Gerry Adams, the leader of the Irish Republican Army. His access to Adams had been helped by the fact that he held American and Irish citizenship.

Biggart arrived at the World Trade Center complex on September 11 and started taking pictures. He talked briefly on his cell phone with his wife Wendy shortly after the collapse of the South Tower. Part of his reputation as a photojournalist was getting close to the action. He was working beside the firemen when the North Tower collapsed on top of him.

Biggart's body was found in the debris on Saturday, September 15, 2001. Recovery workers found him next to several firefighters. They also located his three cameras, two camera bags, his notes, and his press credentials. In the camera were 290 images (seven rolls of film and 150 digital images). His last shot was taken at the very minute (10:28 a.m.) that the North Tower collapsed.

See Also
World Trade Center, September 11

See Document
Document #18

Suggested Reading
Newseum, Cathy Trost, and Alicia C. Shepard, *Running toward Danger: Stories Behind the Breaking News of 9/11* (Lanham, MD: Rowman and Littlefield, 2002); Conor O'Clery,

"Bill Biggart, an Irish-American, Was the Only Journalist to Be Killed in the Collapse of the World Trade Centre Towers," *Irish Times* [Dublin] (December 23, 2001), p. 62.

Bingham, Mark Kendall (1970–2001)

Mark Bingham was one of the passengers on United Airlines Flight 93 who attempted to regain control of the cockpit of the aircraft on September 11, 2001. Bingham was an athlete and had played on several national championship rugby teams at the University of California–Berkeley. He was also a mainstay of the San Francisco Fog, a rugby union team. His teammates described him as brave and competitive. Bingham was also gay, and he been made into the icon of the gay community.

Bingham had an active youth. He was born on May 22, 1970, in Phoenix, Arizona. His mother, Alice Hoglan, had married at 19 and divorced at 21, while she was a student at Brigham Young University. Soon after her divorce she moved to Miami, Florida, to be close to her family. Hoglan moved from town to town before ending up in Monterey, California, in 1980. For most of this period she was out of work, until finding a job as a secretary for a legal firm. She moved with her son to Redwood Estates, near Los Gatos, California. Later, Bingham's mother became a United Airlines flight attendant. He attended Los Gatos High School, where as a junior he began playing rugby. A good student, he gained admittance to the University of California–Berkeley. He enjoyed college life, joining a fraternity and playing rugby. At six foot five and weighing 225 pounds, he was not only an impressive looking rugby player, but also aggressive and fast for his size. He helped the university win two rugby national championships. In his senior year he was captain of his rugby team. He was also elected president of the Chi Psi fraternity. Bingham kept his sexual orientation a secret until just weeks before his graduation.

After graduation from the university, Bingham entered the world of business. At first he found a job with the high-tech public relations firm Alexander Communications. His promotions were rapid, taking him from intern to senior account manager in less than a year and a half. In 1997 Bingham left Alexander Communications for a high-profile job at another high-tech public relations firm, Burson-Mastellar, but stayed for only about a year before accepting another position at 3Com Corporation's mobile communications division. Unhappy with corporate hierarchy, he started his own public relations firm, the Bingham Group, representing clients in the Silicon Valley. His business prospered, and he traveled frequently. By the summer of 2001, however, his business had dropped sharply because of the dot-com bust, and he was beginning to consider other business options.

Bingham had always been more interested in business than politics, but he held libertarian political views. He was conservative on economic matters and liberal on social matters. The politician to whom he was most oriented was Senator John McCain (R-AZ), and he had worked on McCain's 2000 presidential bid.

Bingham almost missed his flight on September 11, 2001. He was visiting a friend, Matt Hall, in Denville, New Jersey, and he overslept. His reason for returning to San Francisco was to be an usher at a fraternity brother's wedding. Rushing to the Newark International Airport, he barely made United Airlines Flight 93. He was the last passenger to board. Soon after the aircraft took off, the four hijackers seized control of the cockpit. Ziad Jarrah became the pilot after the pilot and copi-lot had been killed or rendered unconscious. With the other passengers, Bingham was herded to the back of the plane. He contacted his mother via the GTE Air-fone and explained the situation. From cell phone calls, news spread of the other hijacked aircraft and of their suicide missions. Armed with this knowledge, several of the male passengers, including Bingham, decided to go down fighting. Bing-ham teamed with Todd Beamer, Thomas Burnett, Jeremy Glick, and others in planning an attempt to regain control of the airliner. In the meantime the hijack-ers had retreated to the cockpit area. The passengers charged the cockpit with a food tray container and broke into the cockpit area. They struggled with the hijackers. Rather than lose control of the aircraft, hijacker Jarrah crashed the airliner into the ground. There were no survivors. Bing-ham, along with the other pas-sengers, became instant heroes for having prevented another crash in the Washington, D.C., area—probably into the U.S. Capitol or the White House.

Bingham's mother has become his biggest champion. She ended her twenty-year career as United Airlines flight attendant with bitterness, which she has expressed in unambigu-ous terms (see sidebar).

> **Reaction to Bingham's Death by His Mother**
>
> Yes, I'm mad, and I'm determined to stay mad. . . . Peo-ple ask me, do you want closure? And I tell them no. I want to go to my grave tortured by the events of Sep-tember 11. I want to spend the rest of my life speaking out. I'm mad at the airlines and the airline lobbies that have held up safety programs, mad at the regulatory agen-cies in the United States that have allowed the circum-stances of 9/11 to play out the way they did. I also want to speak out on the ignorance surrounding gay and les-bian issues, for the importance of patriotism in its proper sense and for the importance of healing the rift we have with Arab countries.
>
> Quoted in Jane Ganahl, "Two years Later: A Steely Resolve, Born of Anguish; Alice Hoglan, Mother of Flight 93 Hero, Turns Focus on Airlines, Gay Acceptance," *San Francisco Chronicle* (September 10, 2003), p. D1.

The Hoglan family and friends have set up a scholarship—the Mark Bingham Leadership Fund—at the University of California–Berkeley that awards scholarships of between $8,000 and $10,000 each year. An annual rugby tournament was named for Bingham—the Mark Kendall Bingham Memorial Tournament. Singer Melissa Etheridge dedicated the song "Tuesday Morning" to Bingham's memory in 2004.

See Also
Beamer, Todd Morgan; Burnett, Thomas Edward; Glick, Jeremy; Jarrah, Ziad; United Air-lines Flight 93

See Document
Document #16

Suggested Reading
Jon Barrett, *Mark Bingham; Hero of Flight 93* (Los Angeles, CA: Advocate Books, 2002); Lisa Beamer and Ken Abraham, *Let's Roll; Ordinary People, Extraordinary Courage* (Wheaton, IL: Tyndale House Publishers, 2002); Christopher Heredia, "Proud Mom of Hero," *San Francisco Chronicle* (June 28, 2002), p. A19; Evelyn Nieves, "Passenger on Jet: Gay Hero or Hero Who Was Gay," *New York Times* (January 16, 2002), A12; Doug Saunders, "A Hero for All Times," *Globe and Mail* [Canada] (February 16, 2002), p. F3; James Sullivan, "Gay Rugby Tournament to Honor Mark Bingham," *San Francisco Chronicle* (June 23, 2002), p. 49.

Bin Laden, Osama (1957–)

Besides status as the most notorious terrorist leader in the world, Osama bin Laden's approval of the plan for the September 11 attacks has made him America's public enemy number one. He was born on July 30, 1957, in the Malazz neighborhood of Riyadh, Saudi Arabia, into a wealthy Saudi family. His father, Muhammad bin Oud bin Laden, was from Yemen, and he became fabulously wealthy because of his close contacts with the Saudi regime. He won construction contracts, beginning with road contracts and culminating in the contract to restore and reconstruct the holy sites in Mecca and Medina. He was also strongly anti-Israel.

Bin Laden was part of a large extended family. He was the only son of his father's fourth wife. His mother was from Damascus, Syria, and was never one of his father's favorite wives, leading to a divorce. Altogether the father had twenty-one wives and reportedly had fifty-four children, of which twenty-four were sons. Bin Laden was the seventeenth son, and members of the family have advanced the theory that his position on the fringe of the family rankled him. Bin Laden's family moved several times in Saudi Arabia and ended up in Jeddah, where he attended Jeddah's best school—al-Thagr. Standards were high at this Western-style school, which several sons of Saudi royalty also attended. Even as a boy bin Laden showed such a strong religious streak that it alarmed his family. Bin Laden also had some familiarity with the West through vacations in Sweden and attendance at a summer class studying English at Oxford University. His father died in the crash of his Cessna aircraft in 1967, leaving an estate of around $11 billion. Bin Laden's inheritance has been described as between $40 million and $50 million. At age seventeen he married a cousin of his mother's, who was fourteen. Beginning in 1977, bin Laden studied economics and management in the Management and Economics School at King Abdul Aziz University in Jeddah. Bin Laden was a mediocre student, in part because he neglected his studies to work for the family construction firm. He left school in 1979, and there is considerable disagreement among scholars regarding whether or not he graduated. His initial interest after leaving school was to become involved in the bin Laden family businesses, but he was blocked by his older brothers. By the late 1990s the Saudi Binladen Group (SBG) employed 37,000 people and was worth around $5 billion.

As a youngster bin Laden had a solid religious training as a Sunni Muslim but beginning around 1973 he became even more religious. One of his first actions was making contact with the fundamentalist Muslim Brotherhood. There is evidence that he joined the Muslim Brotherhood while in high school. He later admitted that his first interaction with the Muslim Brotherhood was in 1973. At the university, he took courses taught by Muhammad Qutb, the brother of the famous martyred Islamist writer Sayyid Qutb, and he had contact with the advocate of jihad Sheikh Abdullah Yussuf Azzam. Furthermore, two events radicalized bin Laden even more. First was the seizure of the Grand Mosque in Mecca by a group of Islamists under the command of Juhayman ibn-Muhammad-ibn-Sayf al-Taibi. The religious faith and the martyrdom of these Islamists impressed bin Laden. Next, and ultimately more significant, was the Soviet Union's invasion of Afghanistan in late 1979.

Bin Laden's participation in the Afghan-Soviet War was a turning point in his life. His immediate reaction was to go to Afghanistan and join in the fighting. In

1979 he made a quick visit to Pakistan to meet with Afghan leaders Burhanuddin Rabbani and Abdul Rasool Sayyaf. Bin Laden returned to Saudi Arabia, but began planning to help in Afghanistan. He was one of the estimated 10,000 Saudis to flock to the Afghan war. In contrast to most, however, he brought construction machinery with him when he came—bulldozers, loaders, dump trucks, and equipment for building trenches. Soon after arriving in Pakistan, he learned that his organizational skills were needed more than his skill in combat.

In Pakistan bin Laden renewed his association with Sheikh Abdullah Yussuf Azzam. They had previously met in Jeddah, Saudi Arabia, in summer 1984. Together they formed the Mujahideen Services Bureau (Maktab al-Khidanet, or MAK) in 1984 to recruit and train Afghan fighters. Most of the early expenses of this organization came out of bin Laden's personal finances. Later, funds came from other sources, and in the end several billion dollars flowed through the MAK. Bin Laden used his Saudi contacts in the mid-1980s to bring more heavy construction equipment to protect the Afghans and mujahideen fighters from Soviet artillery and air strikes.

In 1986 bin Laden extended his activities to the battlefield. He joined an Arab mujahideen unit in the field, and participated in the 1987 Battle of the Lion's Den near Jaji. This brief combat experience raised his prestige among Afghan Arab compatriots. Despite his battlefield experience, bin Laden's most significant contribution to the war was in assisting Azzam in radicalizing the Afghan Arab fighters. Bin Laden also met with Ahmed Shah Massoud, the best military leader among the Afghans, but he had closer ties with Gulbuddin Hekmatyar and Abdul Rasool Sayyaf.

By 1987 bin Laden's relationship with Azzam became strained over differences of jihad strategy. Bin Laden had developed ties with Ayman al-Zawahiri, the former head of the Egyptian Islamic Jihad and an open enemy of Azzam. By 1988 bin Laden had broken with Azzam and sided with al-Zawahiri and his Egyptians. Azzam's mysterious assassination on November 24, 1989, cleared the way for bin Laden to play an even greater role in Islamist politics. Although bin Laden had adopted Azzam's argument in favor of a holy war against the enemies of Islam, he differed from his mentor in his belief that it should be extended to an international holy war to be carried out throughout the world. It was also in fall 1989 that bin Laden first organized the al-Qaeda (the Base) organization. The existence of al-Qaeda was announced at a meeting at which those present were required to sign a loyalty oath (*bayat*).

> **Personality of Osama bin Laden, Described by a Saudi Journalist**
>
> To be honest, the man is likable. He is really nice. You don't see him as somebody who will be the arch-terrorist, who will be the most dangerous man in the world. He doesn't strike you as charismatic. You are with somebody who you feel you knew for maybe ten to fifteen years; you don't feel a stranger when you meet him for the first time. And he doesn't try to impress you. I met a lot of Palestinian leaders. They try to impress you. This man does not try to impress you. Maybe this is his strength. Maybe this is his style. He was extremely natural, very simple, very humble and soft-spoken. You feel he is shy. He doesn't look at you eye to eye. Usually when he talks to you he talks by looking down. His clothes are very, very humble, very simple.
>
> Quoted by Peter L. Bergen, *The Osama bin Laden I Know: An Oral History of al Qaeda's Leader* (New York: Free Press, 2006), pp. 168–169.

After the end of the Afghan-Soviet War, bin Laden returned to Saudi Arabia as a war hero. Both the Saudi regime and the general populace acclaimed him. Shortly after his return to Saudi Arabia he approached Prince Turki al-Faisal, head of Saudi intelligence. Bin Laden offered to use Arab irregulars to overthrow the Marxist government of South Yemen, but Turki turned his offer down. Bin Laden settled down in Jeddah working for his family's construction firm until Iraq invaded Kuwait on August 21, 1990. Bin Laden opposed Saddam Hussein's invasion, and he went to the Saudi government offering to lead a mujahideen army against Saddam. But when the Saudi government opted to accept U.S. troops on Saudi soil to regain Kuwait, bin Laden turned against the Saudi regime. Bin Laden was unalterably opposed to the stationing of U.S. troops on Saudi soil, contending that the presence of non-Muslims on holy ground was a sacrilege. His vocal opposition led the Saudi authorities to place him under house arrest for a period of time.

Bin Laden's opposition to the Persian Gulf War led him to leave Saudi Arabia in 1991. To escape possible retaliation from the Saudi security forces, bin Laden and his family moved first to Pakistan and then to Sudan. Bin Laden had been considering a move to Sudan for several years, and he had been buying property in and around Khartoum. This change had both political and religious implications among Muslims. Husan al-Turabi, an Islamist religious and political leader in Sudan, invited bin Laden and his family to stay in Sudan. Bin Laden moved the bulk of his financial assets to Sudan, and there he established a series of businesses, including a road building company. He acquired a near monopoly of many of Sudan's principal commodity businesses, which ventures only added to his personal fortune.

It was from Sudan that bin Laden launched a propaganda campaign against the Saudi royal family, portraying them as false Muslims. Bin Laden's continuing attacks on the Saudi royal family and religious leadership led to the loss of his Saudi citizenship on April 7, 1994, and to the freezing of his financial assets in Saudi Arabia. This meant bin Laden lost $7 million of his share of the family business. In addition to attacking the Saudi regime, bin Laden made it plain in his publication *Betrayal of Palestine* on December 29, 1994, that he included Israel among the enemies of Islam.

Bin Laden used his secure political base in Sudan to organize the terrorist activities of al-Qaeda (the Base). He had established the outline of this organization in 1989, but in Sudan it became a full-fledged terrorist organization. His goal for al-Qaeda was for it to serve as an incitement to Muslims to join a defensive jihad against the West and against tyrannical secular Muslim regimes, and to help train and lead those Muslims who volunteered to participate in the defensive jihad. He established a training camp for al-Qaeda operatives at Soba, north of Khartoum. In 1992 bin Laden sent advisors and military equipment to Somalia to oppose the American mission there. This mission proved successful for bin Laden and al-Qaeda. The first operations of al-Qaeda were directed against Saudi Arabia and the American forces stationed there. A car bomb exploded in Riyadh on November 13, 1995, killing five Americans and one Saudi and wounding more than sixty others. This attack was followed by a truck bombing at al-Khobar in Dhahran on June 25, 1996, killing nineteen American servicemen and wounding hundreds.

Pressure from the governments of Saudi Arabia and the United States threatened bin Laden's status in Sudan, so he moved his operations to Afghanistan in

This televised image released by Al-Jazeera on October 5, 2001, shows Osama bin Laden (right) and his top lieutenant, Egyptian Ayman al-Zawahiri (left). Al-Jazeera said the scene was believed to capture a celebration of the union of bin Laden's al-Qaeda network and al-Zawahiri's Egyptian Islamic Jihad. (AP IMAGES/Courtesy of Al-Jazeera via APTN.)

May, 1996. The Sudanese government had no choice but to ask bin Laden to leave, much to his displeasure. Bin Laden left Sudan virtually penniless, as the Sudanese government offered him only pennies on the dollar for all of the property he owned in Sudan. Bin Laden has claimed that his $300 million investment in Sudan was lost. There is some evidence that he hid some of his assets in various companies through partial ownerships.

Afghanistan was a natural haven for bin Laden and al-Qaeda because of the victory of the Islamist Taliban and because of bin Laden's personal relationship with the head of the Taliban, Mohammed Omar. They had met in Pakistan during the later stages of the Afghan-Soviet War. There are even reports that bin Laden bought Omar a house in Karachi. Although Taliban leaders welcomed bin Laden as a hero of the Muslim world, they were nervous about his terrorist activities and their reflection on the Taliban regime. Responding to this welcome, bin Laden arranged financing from the Arab world for the Taliban regime. In return, the Taliban government allowed bin Laden to organize a series of training camps in Afghanistan to train a cadre of terrorists to carry out operations worldwide. Cementing this alliance, bin Laden's al-Qaeda forces joined Taliban military units fighting the Northern Alliance Army of General Ahmed Shah Massoud.

Once bin Laden had firmly established his organization in Afghanistan, he started an international campaign against those he considered to be enemies of

Islam. The top target was the United States. On August 23, 1996, he issued a call for jihad against the Americans for their occupation of Saudi Arabian territory. Then in February 1998 he formed the International Islamic Front for Jihad against Jews and Crusaders. Bin Laden followed this up with the announcement on February 23, 1998, of a global jihad against all enemies of Islam. At the top of this list of enemies of Islam is the United States because bin Laden considers the United States to be "the root of all evil—theologically, politically and morally—and the source of all the misfortunes that have befallen the umma (Muslim world)." In a 1998 interview with an American journalist, bin Laden expressed this viewpoint.

Bin Laden is the political head of al-Qaeda and he is responsible for its operations, but there has always been an on-site command that plans and carries out operations. Because al-Qaeda is an umbrella organization, it is extremely decentralized and has as many as thirty separate extremist groups affiliated with it. Bin Laden's role is to coordinate operations without participating in them. After receiving the go-ahead from bin Laden and al-Qaeda's leadership, the on-site commander makes the tactical decisions. Khalid Sheikh Mohammed presented the outline of the plan for the September 11, 2001, operation to bin Laden and the top leaders of al-Qaeda sometime in 1996. Bin Laden approved the plan in principle, but he left the implementation of it to Mohammed and his subordinates. Both bin Laden and Mohammed knew that the failure of the Group Islamique Armé (GIA) to carry out its mission to fly a hijacked aircraft into the Eiffel Tower in December 1994 meant that they needed trained pilots to carry out this mission in the United States.

> **Osama bin Laden's Interpretation of the War between the Islamic World and the West**
>
> I say that there are two sides in the struggle: one side is the global Crusader alliance with the Zionist Jews, led by America, Britain, and Israel, and the other side is the Islamic world. It is not acceptable in such a struggle as this that he [the Crusader] should attack and enter my land and holy sanctuaries, and plunder Muslims' oil, and then when he encounters any resistance from Muslims, to label them terrorist. This is stupidity, or considering others stupid. We believe that it is our legal duty to resist this occupation with all our might, and punish it in the same way as it punishes us.
>
> Quoted by an Al-Jazeera reporter in December 1998. Bruce Lawrence (ed.), *Messages to the World: The Statements of Osama bin Laden* (London: Verso, 2005), p. 73.

It is evident that bin Laden was interested in attacking the United States for economic reasons as much as for political ones. Bin Laden's training in economics and business allowed him to see the total picture. In his homage to the nineteen martyrs, bin Laden justified the September 11 attack by stating that "it is possible to strike the economic base that is the foundation of the military base, so when their economy is depleted they will be too busy with each other to be able to enslave poor peoples."

After his establishing the principles of the plan, the operation proceeded on its own with little or no input from bin Laden. He learned five days before the September 11 attack on what day it would take place. Bin Laden expected a vigorous American response after the end of the attacks in the United Sates, but he counted on the harshness of the response to mobilize Muslims worldwide against the United States and the West. His anticipation of a vigorous U.S. response proved correct, but the rest of his calculations went array. Bin Laden was reluctant to assume any responsibility for September 11, but he did praise the hijackers in the following words.

The collapse of the Taliban to the Northern Alliance with the assistance of the United States was a major setback for bin Laden. Both the ease and the quickness of the Taliban's fall were unexpected. Bin Laden retreated to the mountain complex of Tora Bora, where he stayed until December 10, 2001, before escaping into northwest Pakistan, where there was strong support for him. Evidently he sustained a wound to his left arm in the American bombing of Tora Bora. Despite efforts by American intelligence in the years since the overthrow of the Taliban, searchers have been unable to locate his whereabouts. Most intelligence sources place him somewhere along the Afghanistan-Pakistan border, where he has strong civilian support. Since this border runs approximately 1,500 miles, he could be anywhere along it. Even with reduced capacity to carry out terrorist operations, bin Laden is considered a hero by many Muslims for having stood up to the United States. Muslims not only respect bin Laden, but they love him. He has become a symbol of Muslim resistance to what they consider American imperialism in the Middle East. A positive view of bin Laden is shared by many Muslims. A 2004 Pew Global Attitudes Project opinion poll showed that 65 percent of Pakistanis, 55 percent of Jordanians, and 45 percent of Moroccans view him favorably. There is no indication that these approval ratings have decreased.

By making bin Laden enemy number one, the Americans have elevated his stature in the Muslim world to new heights. As Mick Farren expresses it, "Short of

---

Osama bin Laden's Praise for the 9/11 Hijackers

Those young men did a very great deed, a glorious deed. God rewarded them and we pray that their parents will be proud of them, because they raised Muslims' heads high and taught America a lesson it won't forget, with God's will.

Announced to Al-Jazeera on December 26, 2001. Bruce Lawrence (ed.), *Messages to the World: The Statements of Osama bin Laden* (London: Verso, 2005), p. 153.

Muslim Reactions to Osama bin Laden

The public reaction to Osama in the Muslim world after September 11 has been divided but increasingly sympathetic to him. Opinion polls taken in early 2002 revealed that most Muslims in the Middle East did not believe the 9/11 attacks were carried out by their fellow believers, and chose instead to attribute them to Mossad or the CIA. As the symbol of resistance to the US, bin Laden has become a hero among many Muslim communities, from Pakistan to Indonesia and from Nigeria to Egypt. Osama memorabilia—cassettes, CDs and DVDs of his speeches, to posters, T-shirts, pens, and sweets bearing his imprint and booklets and magazine articles about him—have proliferated. As the authoritarian regimes of the Middle East have prevented their manufacture and distribution, so they have become widely available in South and Southeast Asia. The Osama T-shirts, produced mostly in Pakistan, Thailand and Indonesia, are being sold all over South and Southeast Asia, including countries with small Muslim populations.

Rohan Gunaratna, *Inside al Qaeda: Global Network of Terror* (New York: Columbia University Press, 2002), p. 52.

Osama being captured alive, or exhibited as a very identifiable and well-preserved corpse—in the way Che Guevara's hunters had showed off their trophy—he could, in theory, continue indefinitely as a martyr to the cause." Even in death, and regardless of the means, bin Laden will have accrued enough prestige that his martyrdom will continue to serve as an inspiration throughout the Muslim world.

Popularity of Osama bin Laden, Described by a Saudi Journalist

[The United States] didn't find Osama bin Laden for one reason: Osama bin Laden is a humble man. He can live on a little food. He can live without any luxury, and he is like millions who are in that part of the world in Afghanistan or Pakistan. And also he is loved by the people who move around or among them, wherever they are, whether inside Pakistan or Afghanistan. And I don't believe they will surrender him. He's adored by the people around him. For them, he is not a leader. He is everything. He's the father; he's the brother; he is a leader; he is the imam. He is a good example: a man who sacrificed all his wealth to come and live with them, among them, and to fight for their causes. He is different and he [is] not corrupt and so he represents the pioneers of Muslim early Islamic history—The Prophet Muhammad's companions.

Quoted by Peter L. Bergen, *The Osama bin Laden I Know: An Oral History of al Qaeda's Leader* (New York: Free Press, 2006), pp. 380–381.

See Also

Atta, Mohamed el-Amir Awad el-Sayed; Azzam, Sheikh Abdullah Yussuf; Mohammed, Khalid Sheikh; al-Qaeda; World Trade Center, September 11

See Documents

Document #2; Document #3; Document 22; Document #23

Suggested Reading

Anonymous (Michael Scheuer), *Imperial Hubris: Why the West Is Losing the War on Terror* (Washington, DC: Brassey's, 2004); Abdel Bari Atwan, *The Secret History of al Qaeda* (Berkeley: University of California Press, 2006); Peter L. Bergen, *The Osama bin Laden I Know: An Oral History of al Qaeda's Leader* (New York: Free Press, 2006); Jane Corbin, *Al-Qaeda: The Terror Network that Threatens the World* (New York: Thunder's Mouth Press, 2002); Bruce Lawrence (ed.), *Messages to the World: The Statements of Osama bin Laden* (London: Verso, 2005); Jonathan Randal, *Osama: The Making of a Terrorist* (New York: Knopf, 2004); Adam Robinson, *Bin Laden: Behind the Mask of the Terrorist* (New York: Arcade, 2001).

Bin al-Shibh, Ramzi (1972–)

Ramzi bin al-Shibh was one of the chief planners of the September 11 attacks in the United States. He was an active member of the Hamburg Cell. Frustrated in his inability to obtain a visa to participate in the September 11 attacks, bin al-Shibh stayed in Hamburg, Germany, where he continued to provide logistical support for the conspirators until the eve of the attack.

Bin al-Shibh was a Yemeni. He was born on May 1, 1972, in Ghayl Bawazir, in the province of Hadramaut, Yemen. His father was a merchant. The family moved to the city of Sana'a in northern Yemen when Bin al-Shibh was a small boy. His father died in 1987 when his son was sixteen. Bin al-Shibh was an enthusiastic child, and from the beginning he was more religious than the rest of his family. After finishing his schooling, he began working as a messenger boy at the International Bank of Yemen. For a time he studied at a business school before deciding to leave Yemen. In 1995, he applied for a U.S. visa, but his application was turned down. Determined to leave Yemen, bin al-Shibh then traveled to Germany, where he claimed to be a Sudanese citizen seeking political asylum using the name Ramzi Omar. German authorities were suspicious of his claim for political asylum, and it was initially turned down. Germany received more than 100,000 political asylum seekers annually, most wanting access to Germany's generous welfare system that would guarantee free health care and money for food and lodging almost indefinitely. Bin al-Shibh spent two years at a special camp, the so-called Container Camp, awaiting his appeal. During the period pending the appeal of his asylum claim, he joined the al-Quds Mosque in Hamburg, where he met Mohammed Atta and other Islamist militants. After his appeal was denied by the German government, bin al-Shibh returned to Yemen in 1997. Shortly thereafter, he returned to Germany, this time using his true name. This time bin al-Shibh enrolled in a school in Hamburg, although academic problems led to his expulsion in September 1998.

Bin al-Shibh was an active member of the Hamburg Cell. There he was known by associates as Omar. He roomed with Atta and al-Shehhi beginning in 1998. In summer 1998, bin al-Shibh traveled to Afghanistan for special training at one of al-Qaeda's training camps. He was obviously a top student because leaders of al-Qaeda selected him for a special mission. A fellow recruit testified that bin al-Shibh had extensive contact with bin Laden while in Afghanistan. Along with Atta, Ziad Jarrah, and al-Shehhi, he was recruited by bin Laden for a special martyrdom mission. Mohammed Atef, the military commander of al-Qaeda, gave them a briefing on the outlines of the September 11 plot. After returning to Germany, bin al-Shibh joined with Atta and Marwan al-Shehhi in working at a warehouse packing computers for shipping.

Bin al-Shibh's personality and abilities made him one of the leaders of the Hamburg Cell. He became one of the chief recruiters for the Hamburg Cell because he was better liked and more influential in the Muslim community than Atta. Bin al-Shibh also traveled extensively throughout Germany, and was able to recruit others for the Hamburg Cell.

Bin al-Shibh also served as the cheerleader for the Hamburg Cell. He gathered cassette tapes of jihad activities in Chechnya, Bosnia, and Kosovo and played them all over Hamburg to Muslim audiences. The longer he was active in the cell, the more militant his beliefs became. He believed that the highest attainment in life was to die for the jihad. Only bin al-Shibh's inability to obtain a visa prevented him from joining Mohamed Atta's suicide team on September 11. Four times he sought a visa—three times in Berlin and once in Yemen. Bin al-Shibh was turned down each time because consular officers believed that, being Yemeni, he might be an unlawful immigrant. He even tried using other people's names, but with no luck. Instead, bin al-Shibh provided logistical support and money from Germany. He kept in close contact with Atta, and served as his banker. He also protected the men of the Hamburg Cell by keeping them registered as students. Bin al-Shibh was the only member of the Hamburg Cell to attend the January 2000 Kuala Lumpur meeting where al-Qaeda mid-level operatives discussed future operations.

Another of bin al-Shibh's responsibilities was recruitment.

Bin al-Shibh's Attitude toward Jihad

It is the highest thing to do, to die for the jihad. The mujahideen die peacefully.

They die with a smile on their lips; their dead bodies are soft, while the bodies of the killed infidels are stiff.

Quoted by Terry McDermott, *Perfect Soldiers: The Hijackers: Who They Were, Why They Did It* (New York: HarperCollins, 2005), p. 62.

He recruited Zacarias Moussaoui into al-Qaeda. Bin al-Shibh gave Moussaoui funds for pilot training in the United States. Although Moussaoui was not a part of the Hamburg Cell and the September 11 plot, he was being considered for a future martyrdom mission.

When bin al-Shibh finally learned the date of the attack on the World Trade Center complex, the Pentagon, and the U.S. Capitol or White House in late August 2001, he began to shut down operations in Germany. He was aware the all members and anyone affiliated with the Hamburg Cell would be subject to arrest. In early September bin al-Shibh fled to Pakistan, where he thought he would be safe from American reprisal.

Bin al-Shibh was captured in an apartment complex in Karachi, Pakistan, on September 11, 2002, after a gunfight with Pakistani security forces. On September 16, 2002, the Pakistani government turned bin al-Shibh over to American security officials, who moved him out of Pakistan to a secure interrogation site. Since his arrest, bin al-Shibh has been cooperative in providing intelligence on the nuclear, biological, and chemical capabilities of al-Qaeda, as well as on how the al-Qaeda organization functions. Despite this cooperation, bin al-Shibh has expressed no regrets about his involvement with al-Qaeda; had he not been captured he would still be an active participant. In August 2006, bin al-Shibh was transferred to the

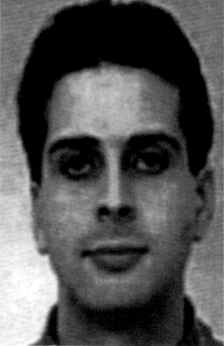

This undated combo shows Ramzi Bin al-Shibh (left) and Said Bahaji (right). Bin al-Shibh and Bahaji along with suspected hijackers al-Shehhi, Atta, and Jarrah—as well as other people as yet unknown—were suspected of "forming a terrorist association in Germany and jointly planning the four attacks in the United States." (AP IMAGES/Winfried Rothermel.)

Guantánamo Bay Detainment Camp with thirteen other high-profile terrorist suspects. The Bush administration announced in March 2007 that he would face a military tribunal as an enemy combatant.

See Also
Atta, Mohamed el-Amir Awad el-Sayed; Guantánamo Bay Detainment Camp; Hamburg Cell; Jarrah, Ziad Samir; Mohammed, Khalid Sheikh; Moussaoui, Zacarias; Qaeda, al-; Shehhi, Marwan Yousef Muhammed Rashid Lekrab al-

Suggested Reading
Yosri Fouda and Nick Fielding, *Masterminds of Terror: The Truth behind the Most Devastating Terrorist Attack the World Has Ever Seen* (New York: Arcade Publishing, 2003); Terry McDermott, *Perfect Soldiers: The Hijackers: Who They Were, Why They Did It* (New York: HarperCollins, 2005); Gerald Posner, *Why America Slept: The Failure to Prevent 9/11* (New York: Ballantine Books, 2003).

Bojinka Operation. *See* Operation Bojinka

Bucca, Ronald (1954–2001)

Ronald Bucca was a fire marshal with the Fire Department of New York City's (FDNY's) Bureau of Fire Investigation. His military intelligence training made him a counterterrorist expert. Bucca's problem was that the Joint Terrorist Task Force (JTTF) had no place for a firefighter despite his expertise. He became convinced that al-Qaeda was a threat to New York City, and his fate was tied to the World Trade Center, where he died fighting a fire on September 11, 2001.

Bucca had two loves: the FDNY and the U.S. Army. He was born in 1954 in New York City. His father was Sicilian, and his mother was Swedish. After high school, Bucca joined the U.S. Army in 1973, serving in the 101st Airborne. He served a tour in South Vietnam as a helicopter door gunner. After leaving active duty, Bucca joined the Fire Department of New York City. He remained in the U.S. Army Reserves, reaching the rank of Special Forces First Sergeant. Bucca was seriously injured in a five-story fall at a fire on September 16, 1986, but made an amazing recovery from a back injury. He resumed his career as a firefighter with the famed Rescue 1 Company. After winning several medals for bravery, he joined the Bureau of Fire Investigators in 1992. His job from then on was to investigate the origins of fires.

Still active as a firefighter, Bucca remained in the U.S.

> **Last Moments of Bucca's Life in the South Tower of the World Trade Center Complex**
>
> Back inside the South Tower, Ronnie Bucca had made it up to the seventy-eighth floor. Radio broadcasts recovered later showed that he had linked with Oriole Palmer, a battalion chief. . . . As the radio broadcasts indicate, Palmer and Bucca actually found a standpipe with water pressure and began fighting the blaze. There were bodies strewn across the seventy-eighth–floor lobby. Between fifty and two hundred people lay dead or dying. Burning jet fuel poured down elevator shafts. . . . At one point Ronnie took off his flame-retardant turnout coat and used it to cover some crash victims huddled in a corner. He returned to the hose, and did his best with Chief Palmer to advance it.
>
> Peter Lance, *1000 years for Revenge: International Terrorism and the FBI—The Untold Story* (New York: ReganBooks, 2003), pp. 417–418.

Army Reserves. In 1999 he transferred to the 242nd Military Intelligence Detachment. Later Bucca transferred to a warrant officer slot in the 3413th Military Intelligence Detachment of the 800th Military Police. In this position, Bucca had access to Top Secret military intelligence. On weekends, he would travel to Washington, D.C., where he studied military intelligence reports on the growing threat of Osama bin Laden and al-Qaeda.

Bucca remained convinced that terrorists would return and attack New York City again. After a tour of duty with a special fire department counterterrorist unit, Bucca resumed his career as a fire marshal investigating fires. On September 11, 2001, he was in his office when the report came in about a plane crashing into the North Tower of the World Trade Center complex. Bucca headed to the scene of the disaster, arriving shortly after the second aircraft hit the South Tower. Although not a member of a fire suppression unit, his first instinct was to the fight the fire. Bucca ran up the stairs to the seventy-eighth floor, where he began fighting the fire alongside Battalion Chief Or[iole] Palmer. They were engaged in fighting the fire when the South Tower collapsed, killing both of them. Bucca's body was found one month later. His fire-retardant coat had been taken off to shield some of the office workers from the fire. He was the first fire marshal to die in action in New York City history.

See Also
Firefighters at Ground Zero; Joint Terrorism Task Force; World Trade Center, September 11

Suggested Reading
Michael Daly, "Cops, Firemen & Miracles," *Daily News* [New York] (August 18, 2002), p. 2; Jim Dwyer and Ford Fessenden, "Lost Voices of Firefighters, Some on the 78th Floor," *New York Times* (August 4, 2002), p. 1; Peter Lance, *1000 years for Revenge: International Terrorism and the FBI* (New York: ReganBooks, 2003).

Burlingame, Charles Frank "Chic" III (1949–2001)

Charles "Chic" Burlingame was the pilot of the American Airlines Flight 77 that crashed into the Pentagon on September 11, 2001. He spent his entire professional life as a pilot, first in the U.S. Navy for eight years and then with American Airlines for seventeen years. Even his marriage was related to flying, as his wife was an American Airlines flight attendant.

Burlingame never considered anything but a flying career. He was born on September 12, 1949, in St. Paul, Minnesota. His father was in the U.S. Air Force, so the family traveled extensively. Most of Burlingame's childhood was spent in England and California. He graduated from Anaheim High School in California. After graduation, he attended the U.S. Naval Academy, where he majored in aeronautical engineering. A member of the class of 1971, Burlingame's first assignment was flying F-4 Phantom jets. He was an honors graduate from the Navy's Top Gun fighter pilot school in Miramar, California. After reaching the rank of captain, Burlingame left active duty in 1979 but remained in the Naval Reserves. He was recalled during the Persian Gulf War to participate as a Navy pilot in 1991. Most of his reserve duty was as a liaison officer in the Pentagon. In 1996 Burlingame retired as a Navy Reserve Captain.

Most of Burlingame's civilian flying career was with American Airlines. Soon after leaving the Navy in 1979, he took a pilot's job with American Airlines. Early in his career with American Airlines he flew regular routes to South America.

When he had achieved enough seniority, Burlingame began to fly routes in the United States. He had a reputation for strict adherence to the rules, and knew the dangers of flying from his experiences landing Navy F-4 Phantom jets. Burlingame had selected the September 11 flight because he and his brother, Brad, had plans to celebrate Burlingame's birthday at an Anaheim Angels baseball game.

The American Airlines Flight 77 on September 11, 2001, was a routine flight from Dulles International Airport to Los Angeles International Airport until the hijackers seized the aircraft. The flight was ten minutes late taking off because of problems at the security gate. Once in flight, the hijackers used knives and box cutters to gain control of the cockpit sometime between 8:51 and 8:54 a.m. In the process of seizing the cockpit, Burlingame was murdered. Hani Hanjour assumed control of the pilot's seat and turned the aircraft around to the Washington, D.C., area. At 9:37:40 a.m. Hanjour crashed the aircraft into the Pentagon.

Bradley Burlingame's office in Los Angeles, full of memorabilia of his brother, Captain Charles Burlingame, who piloted American Airlines Flight 77. The flight was bound for Los Angeles, where Burlingame was to celebrate his fifty-second birthday the next day by going to an Anaheim Angels baseball game with Brad. (AP IMAGES/Krista Niles.)

Burlingame has been honored for his sacrifice on September 11 by burial in Arlington National Cemetery. This honor did not come easily. At first the U.S. Army refused to bury him at Arlington because he had died as a reservist before age sixty. Political pressure from Republican senators and congresspersons led the Secretary of Defense to overturn this decision. Burlingame was buried at Arlington National Cemetery on December 12, 2001, not far from the graves of his parents. Since his death, Burlingame's sister, Debra Burlingame, has been active in September 11 politics. Several times she has clashed with other political figures in the families of September 11 movement by defending the actions of the Bush administration. In 2003 the Burlingame family launched a nonprofit foundation with the goal of providing college scholarships for those wishing to pursue careers as officers in the U.S. armed services.

See Also
American Airlines Flight 77; DCA

Suggested Reading
Anita Huslin, "Family Speaks of Fight 77 Pilot's Mettle," *Washington Post* (September 14, 2001), p. A24; Carol Morello, "Gratitude, Blame at 9/11 Hearings," *Washington Post* (June 18, 2004), p. A7; Tom Murphy, *Reclaiming the Sky: 9/11 and the Untold Story of the Men and Women Who Kept America Flying* (New York: AMACOM, 2007); Steve Vogel, "Siblings of 9/11 Pilot to Help Others Achieve Their Brother's Dream," *Washington Post* (September 25, 2003), p. T23; Josh White, "Honoring a 'True American Patriot,'" *Washington Post* (December 13, 2001), p. B1.

Burnett, Thomas Edward (1963–2001)

Tom Burnett was one of the passengers on United Flight 93 who attempted to retake control of the aircraft on September 11, 2001. The fact that Burnett and his companions did not succeed does not detract from their courage in making the attempt. Burnett was a devoted family man, and his motivation was to survive to return to his family.

Burnett had a typical American upbringing. He was born on May 29, 1963, in Bloomington, Minnesota. His father was a high school English and Literature teacher and a Korean War veteran, and his mother was a real estate agent. He had an older and a younger sister. His family was Catholic and Burnett was raised in that faith. Burnett's entire youth was spent in Bloomington, and he attended Ridgeview Elementary School and Olson Middle School before graduating in 1981 with honors from Thomas Jefferson High School. Burnett played football as a quarterback, and in 1980 his team made it to the state semi-finals. His prowess as a football player led to several scholarship offers from small colleges. Burnett obtained an appointment to the Air Force Academy, but after a few weeks there he decided that a military career was not for him. He then attended Saint John's University in Collegeville, Minnesota, for two years, playing football until a shoulder injury caused him to give up the game. After transferring to the Carlson School of Management at the University of Minnesota, he obtained a BS degree in finance. Burnett was also elected president of the Alpha Kappa Psi fraternity in his senior year.

Shortly after graduation, Burnett entered the business world. His first job was with Calicetek, a manufacturer of dental implants. He became sales director and traveled around the United States and the world beyond. In August 1996 he took a job in California with Thoratec Corporation, a company that builds medical devices, headquartered in Pleasanton, California. Starting at the bottom of the corporate ladder, Burnett worked his way up to vice president of the company, eventually becoming its chief financial officer. During this rise up the hierarchy, he earned an MBA from Pepperdine University.

Burnett's job responsibilities called for him to travel around the country. He had married in April 1992, and he and his wife, Deena, had three daughters. Deena had worked as a flight attendant for Delta Airlines, but retired from her job before the birth of their twin daughters. Traveling was tough on Burnett because he liked family life with his wife and daughters. He also was fond of hunting, fishing, and golfing.

On September 11, 2001, Burnett was returning to California from a business trip to New York City. He had called his parents from the New York Marriott Hotel near Times Square on the night of September 10. Wanting to catch an earlier flight, Burnett rushed to Newark International Airport and caught United Airlines Flight 93. Burnett had reserved a first-class seat. There was a forty-one-minute delay caused by airport congestion.

Nothing about the early flight of United Airlines Flight 93 was out of the ordinary until the hijack team went into action. The team of Ziad Jarrah seized control of the aircraft at approximately 9:28 a.m. Passengers were restricted to the rear of the aircraft. Burnett and others began to make calls to inform authorities that the aircraft had been hijacked. He called his wife at around 9:30 a.m. to tell her of the hijacking. It was a short conversation and Deena had no opportunity to tell him about the other aircraft. He called again and reported that the hijackers had knifed and killed one of the crew. At this time Deena was able to tell him that the other aircraft had been on suicide missions. Burnett relayed the news to the other passengers. In a third conversation Deena told him about the Pentagon crash. In between calls, Burnett and the other passenger began to discuss regaining control of the cockpit. In the fourth conversation with his wife, Burnett told her they were waiting until the aircraft was over a rural area before taking back the plane. He also made it plain that they had no choice. Among others, Burnett, Todd Beamer, Mark Bingham, and Jeremy Glick charged the cockpit. They came close to regaining control of the aircraft, but Jarrah crashed the plane in a field near Shanksville, Pennsylvania, killing everybody aboard.

The news of what the passengers on United Airline Flight 93 had tried to do made them national heroes. Jarrah and his team of hijackers had been prevented from crashing the airliner into the U.S. Capitol, or possibly the White House. When family members later listened to the cockpit tapes, they could hear the desperate struggle. All the bodies were obliterated in the crash, and could be identified only by DNA analysis. Medical technicians were able to find and identify some of Burnett's remains for burial at the Fort Snelling National Cemetery on May 24, 2002. Because he had been accepted to attend the Air Force Academy, Burnett was eligible to be buried at a national cemetery.

Since Burnett's death, his wife has been active in the families of September 11 movement. She was instrumental in the FBI release of the flight records of what happened in the cockpit of United Airlines Flight 93. Knowing that there were unanswered questions, Burnett's wife and parents filed a lawsuit against United Airlines and Argenbright Security Company on August 5, 2001. Then a week later they filed a $1 trillion lawsuit against the financial supporters of terrorist networks. One hundred and fifty defendants were named in this suit, ranging from individuals to charities. Hundreds of others also signed on to this lawsuit. Most of them knew that no

> **Commentary from Tom Burnett's Boss and CEO of Thoratec Corp.**
>
> He'd call it hyperbole, but it's true. Knowing what I know of Tom, I would expect him to die as he lived—with honor, principle, and dignity. He was solidly rooted in the strength of his convictions of right and wrong.
>
> Quoted in Sam McManis, "Passenger's Act of Courage No Surprise," *San Francisco Chronicle* (September 14, 2001), p. A10.

money would be forthcoming, but the families are most interested in exposing the supporters of terrorism. Besides lawsuits, the Burnett family started the Tom Burnett Family Foundation in September 2002, with the goal of educating youth to become active citizens and tomorrow's leaders.

See Also
Beamer, Todd Morgan; Bingham, Mark Kendall; Glick, Jeremy; Jarrah, Ziad Samir; United Airlines Flight 93

See Document
Document #16

Suggested Reading
Lisa Beamer and Ken Abraham, *Let's Roll: Ordinary People, Extraordinary Courage* (Wheaton, IL.: Tyndale House Publishers, 2002); Deena Burnett and Anthony Giombetti, *Fighting Back: Living Life beyond Ourselves* (Altamonte Springs, FL: Advantage Books, 2006); Greg Gordon, "How We've Changed; 9.11.01–9.11.02," *Star Tribune* [Minneapolis] (September 11, 2002), p. 4S; Jere Longman, *Among the Heroes: United Flight 93 and the Passengers and Crew Who Fought Back* (New York: HarperCollins, 2002); Ann McFeatters, "Lawsuit Seeks to Cripple Terrorists' Means to Strike," *Pittsburgh Post-Gazette* (August 16, 2002), p. A1; Sam McManis, "Passenger's Act of Courage No Surprise," *San Francisco Chronicle* (September 14, 2001), p. A10; Bob von Sternberg, "Flight 93 Hero Buried at Fort Snelling," *Star Tribune* [Minneapolis] (May 25, 2002), p. 1A.

Bush, George W. (1946–)

President George W. Bush had been president less than nine months when the events of September 11, 2001, transformed his administration. Bush had won the presidency in one of the closest races in American history in November 2000, but he came into office determined to repudiate the policies of former President William Clinton. President Clinton had pursued an aggressive but lackluster campaign against Osama bin Laden and al-Qaeda. Various efforts had been approved to either assassinate or capture bin Laden, but nothing had come of them. The new Bush administration wanted to reexamine all of Clinton's activities, and members of the Bush administration had priorities that ranged from building a "Star Wars" missile defense shield to fighting domestic crime. Before the attacks, counterterrorism was something of a priority for the Bush administration but was nowhere near the top of the agenda. Several on the administration team had complained openly about overemphasis on bin Laden and al-Qaeda by the Clinton administration. Attorney General Ashcroft made it plain that he wanted to focus attention on organized crime families and on the trade in street drugs. Counterterrorism also assumed a lower priority for the Justice Department and the FBI.

Of the government agencies, only the CIA tried to warn President Bush about the danger of terrorism. George Tenet, the director of the CIA, gave Bush daily intelligence briefings in which he frequently warned Bush about the danger of Osama bin Laden and al-Qaeda. Bush developed a good personal relationship with Tenet, but he listened only, and took no action. In an interview with Bob Woodward after September 11, Bush acknowledged that he knew bin Laden and al-Qaeda were a menace, but that he had felt no sense of urgency before September 11. Bush was waiting for a comprehensive plan that would bring bin Laden to justice, and he was willing to sign off on such a plan.

All of this changed on the morning of September 11. President Bush was in Sarasota, Florida, scheduled to attend a media event at the Emma E. Booker Elementary School in Sarasota, Florida. After an early-morning jog, Bush left for the school. He was in the classroom when American Airlines Flight 11 crashed into the North Tower of the World Trade Center. His chief advisor, Karl Rowe, informed Bush of the crash, but he decided to continue with the program at the elementary school. Bush did contact the White House, where National Security Advisor Condoleezza Rice gave him more details about what was happening in New York City. After consulting with Andrew H. Card, Jr., Chief of Staff, Bush returned to the classroom. Shortly after his advisors learned of the crash into the South Tower they informed Bush. The first crash could have been an accident, but the second meant that the United States was under attack. After contacting Vice President Dick Cheney and the head of the FBI, Robert Mueller, Bush wanted to return to Washington, D.C., although his advisors opposed a return. It was at this time that Bush authorized Vice President Cheney to order the Air Force to shoot down any hijacked commercial aircraft. Advisors began to look for a safe place for the president.

By 9:55 a.m. Air Force One was in the air with President Bush and his entourage. The Vice President suggested that Bush fly to Offutt Air Force Base near Omaha, Nebraska. Offutt Air Force Base was the headquarters of the Strategic Air Command, and had all the facilities necessary for the president to keep up on what was going on. After a brief stop at Barksdale Air Force Base in Louisiana, where Bush made a brief public statement, Air Force One proceeded to Offutt Air Force Base. It arrived at Offutt Air Force Base at 2:50 p.m. After communicating with other government leaders, President Bush insisted, despite opposition from the Secret Service, that he return to Washington, D.C. Winning the argument, Bush and his advisors arrived in Washington, D.C., at 7:00 p.m.

President Bush took charge after September 11. He asserted himself by making it clear that the country was embarking upon a war with few restraints. He focused on results, and put pressure on the CIA and FBI to produce results. His relationship with Tenet became even closer because the CIA was the only agency that had information on Osama bin Laden and al-Qaeda. The CIA had contacts in Afghanistan, whereas the U.S. military had no assets there. By presidential authority the CIA was given complete freedom to conduct covert operations. President Bush was determined to end bin Laden's sanctuary in Afghanistan, even if it meant overthrowing the Taliban regime. Soon American support started flowing to the Northern Alliance.

President Bush had two foreign policy options in his administration after September 11. One was the traditional international diplomacy using the United Nations. Two groups in government supported this option—the U.S. State Department and Colin Powell, and the CIA leadership. The other option was advocated by a small group of neoconservatives whose goal was to use America's preeminent military power to transform the world order—in particular, the Middle East. Vice President Cheney, Assistant Secretary of Defense Paul Wolfowitz, and Chairman of the Defense Policy Advisory Committee Richard Perl were the leaders advancing these views. After much soul-searching, Bush accepted the neoconservative position; the invasion of Iraq was a product of this conversion. Once this decision was made, intelligence operations directed at al-Qaeda and other terrorist groups were redirected toward Iraq. Foreign language experts and special operatives were reassigned, and anti-terrorism intelligence programs were terminated. The main thrust of Bush and the Bush administration was now the overthrow of Saddam Hussein, and the hunt for bin Laden and other al-Qaeda leaders had less urgency.

See Also
Bin Laden, Osama; Bush Administration; Qaeda, al-; Tenet, George

See Documents
Document #11; Document #18; Document #24; Document #31

Suggested Reading
Stefan Aust et al., *Inside 9-11: What Really Happened* (New York: St. Martin's Press, 2001); Ronald Kessler, *The CIA at War: Inside the Secret Campaign Against Terror* (New York: St. Martin's Griffin, 2003); Seymour M. Hersh, *Chain of Command: The Road from 9/11 to Abu Ghraib* (New York: HarperCollins, 2004); James Risen, *State of War: The Secret History of the CIA and the Bush Administration* (New York: Free Press, 2006); Bob Woodward, *Bush at War* (New York: Simon and Schuster, 2002).

Bush Administration

President George W. Bush showed considerable interest in the activities of Osama bin Laden and al-Qaeda during the early days of his administration, but the rest of his administration less so. They had criticized the Clinton administration for its failure to end the al-Qaeda threat, but most high officials in the Bush administration had other priorities. These were missile defense, military reform, China, and Iraq. Most of these priorities were intended to enhance the ambitions of the President Bush and his chief administrators. Even those who knew something about Afghanistan—and they were few indeed—had ties to Pakistan. Pakistan was a supporter of the Taliban, who in turn were protecting bin Laden. Briefings about the importance of terrorism and bin Laden given by the existing Clinton administration to the incoming Bush administration were ignored.

Perhaps the least enthusiastic member of the Bush administration was Attorney General John Ashcroft. Ashcroft had higher priorities for the Department of Justice—guns, drugs, and civil rights. He made counterterrorism a third-tier issue. Requests for increased funding for counterterrorism were turned down. Efforts to talk to Ashcroft about counterterrorism were futile. An FBI request for an increase to its counterterrorism budget by $58 million had been turned down by Ashcroft on September 10, 2001. This proposal had called for 149 new counterterrorism field agents, 200 additional analysts, and 54 extra translators. Ashcroft's refusal to consider counterterrorism as a priority changed dramatically after September 11.

Secretary of Defense Donald Rumsfeld was no more enthusiastic about bin Laden and al-Qaeda than Ashcroft. Rumsfeld had been briefed on counterterrorism activities in the Defense Department by outgoing Secretary of Defense Cohen, but he has since stated that he remembered little of this briefing. Responsibility for counterterrorism in the Defense Department was given to the Assistant Secretary of Defense for Special Operations and Low-Intensity Conflict (SOLIC). This post had not been filled by September 11, 2001. Rumsfeld's major concern upon taking office had been the building of a missile defense system and development of an advanced weapons system. For this reason a request to allocate $800 million more to counterterrorism was turned down by Rumsfeld, and the funds were diverted to missile defense. Counterterrorism was simply not a part of Rumsfeld's agenda. This is also why a weapon useful against al-Qaeda, the Predator unmanned aircraft and its Hellfire missile system, was allowed to languish behind other projects.

Another leading figure in the Bush administration who showed little interest in Osama bin Laden and al-Qaeda prior to September 11 was Condoleezza Rice. In an article in *Foreign Affairs* published before she took office, Rice criticized the Clinton administration for focusing on terrorism rather than on the few great powers whom she considered dangerous to peace. It was her thesis that American power and prestige had been frittered away by the concentration on issues like terrorism. She carried these ideas into her role as National Security Advisor to President Bush. Richard Clarke, the holdover counterterrorism expert, tried to persuade Rice of the danger posed by bin Laden and al-Qaeda in a January 2001 memorandum, but Rice took no action. In a meeting on July 10, 2001, George Tenet, the head of the CIA, warned Rice of the strong likelihood of an al-Qaeda strike against the United States, possibly within the United States. Rice listened to Tenet's arguments, but several times afterward when Tenet brought up the subject she was unable to recall either the meeting or the subject of the meeting. It was only in October 2006 that this meeting and its subject matter surfaced in Bob Woodward's book *State of Denial*. Even then Rice stated that she has difficulty remembering the meeting.

Bush's neoconservative advisors were much more attracted to overthrowing Saddam Hussein in Iraq than to Osama bin Laden and al-Qaeda. Paul Wolfowitz, the deputy secretary of defense, complained that too much attention had been devoted to the activities of bin Laden. In his view, bin Laden was overrated as a threat. Bin Laden was far down on the neoconservatives list of priorities. Only President Bush showed much curiosity about bin Laden and al-Qaeda, ordering intelligence reports sent to him daily about al-Qaeda's activities.

Opposition to Clinton administration policies also extended to economic matters. The previous administration had attempted to control the flow of money to Osama bin Laden. Efforts were made to embarrass those countries with loose banking regulations into tightening them up. More than thirty countries were participating in this effort when the Bush administration assumed office. The Clinton administration had also proposed the creation of the National Terrorist Asset Tracking Center as part of this campaign. Paul O'Neill, the new Secretary of the Treasury, disapproved of any attempt to interfere in the banking industry, even as regards banks and financial institutions that were supporting terrorist activities. Consequently, O'Neill shut down anti–money-laundering operations, and the National Terrorist Asset Tracking Center was dismantled because of lack of funding.

After September 11, 2001, the Bush administration made a complete reversal, and resources now poured into counterintelligence. President Bush gave the CIA complete authority to carry out covert operations against terrorists and terrorist organizations. Once it became apparent that the Taliban regime would not give up Osama bin Laden, an American-sponsored war was unleashed to overthrow it. But soon the earlier desire to overthrow Saddam Hussein in Iraq became paramount, and this diverted the attention of the Bush administration away from bin Laden and al-Qaeda.

See Also

Bin Laden, Osama; Bush, George W.; Clinton Administration; Qaeda, al-

Suggested Reading

David Benjamin and Steven Simon, *The Age of Sacred Terrorism* (New York: Random House, 2002); Steve Coll, *Ghost Wars: The Secret History of the CIA, Afghanistan, and bin Laden—From the Soviet Invasion to September 10, 2001* (New York: Penguin Books, 2004); Timothy Naftali, *Blind Spot: The Secret History of American Counterterrorism* (New York: Basic Books, 2005); James Risen, *State of War: The Secret History of the CIA and the Bush Administration* (New York: Free Press, 2006).

C

Cantor Fitzgerald

The huge financial brokerage firm Cantor Fitzgerald suffered the largest number of casualties of any company in the World Trade Center complex on September 11. About one thousand employees worked for Cantor Fitzgerald on the eve of September 11. The company was housed in the North Tower of the World Trade Center complex between the 101st and 105th floors. Employees for the firm handled transactions worth about $200 billion of securities a day, and in the neighborhood of $30 trillion a year. For all intents and purposes it served as the New York Stock Exchange's handler of bonds. Bernie Cantor had founded the firm, and besides a shrewd businessman he had been a collector of Rodin sculptures. There were some eighty pieces of Rodin's sculpture on display in the North Tower. After Cantor's death, Howard Lutnick became the company's chairman, and he held that position on September 11, 2001.

The September 11 attack on the World Trade Center complex hit Cantor Fitzgerald particularly hard. Shortly after the American Airlines Flight 11 hit the North Tower near the 93rd floor, it became apparent that those on the upper floors had little if any chance of escape. Because the roof was locked and the stairwells were blocked, those in the floors above the 93rd floor had no recourse but to resign themselves to their fate. It became more apparent what their fate would be when the South Tower collapsed. As the fire and smoke threatened them, some began jumping to their deaths rather than burn to death. Some of the jumpers were holding hands as they fell. Others called their loved ones to tell them of the hopelessness of their situation. In the end, Cantor Fitzgerald lost 658 employees, including the brother of the company's chairman. Several of the survivors were badly burnt, and one, Renee Barrett-Arjune, died of burns in October.

The members of Cantor Fitzgerald that survived had luck on their side. Lutnick was taking his young son to his first day of kindergarten. Others were on vacation or preparing for vacations. Some had gone to lower floors on individual tasks, thus saving their lives. Lutnick arrived at the World Trade Center complex at about the time that the South Tower fell, and he ran to save his life like so many others.

In the aftermath of the attack, Cantor Fitzgerald was on the verge of ruin. It had lost nearly two-thirds of its employees, its offices were gone, and its computer system was down. There was pressure to reopen the bond market earlier than the September 17 reopening of the New York Stock Exchange. The decision to reopen the bond market on September 15 threatened to bankrupt Cantor Fitzgerald because its competitors were eager to take away its business. Its only hope was that the London office, which was much smaller than the New York office, could absorb New York office's business as well as conduct its own business. Despite immense difficulties, Cantor Fitzgerald did manage to open its doors on Monday, September 17, saving the firm.

In the meantime, family members of those missing began to show up demanding services. At first they were concerned about finding out what had happened to their loved ones. Then grief took over, rendering family members almost helpless. Grief counselors were called in to help the families cope. Finally, family members reconciled themselves to their loss and began to consider financial matters, such as insurance, death certificates, bonuses, and salaries.

Howard Lutnick's Feelings about September 11

The people I worked with at Cantor were people I respected and liked. I had recruited and promoted them, become part of their lives. We built a place that was bound tightly together. And in many ways the 1993 bombing was the catalyst for that. We emerged from that crisis stronger, closer . . . . Policemen and firemen—as awful as the thought is—begin their days knowing there's a chance they might not make it home at night. Their occupation is built upon bravery, and, by definition, puts them in harm's way. My men and women never told their spouses "Today I'm going to work, and tonight I might not make it out." Because for them, they were just going to the office.

Tom Barbash, *On Top of the World: The Remarkable Story of Howard Lutnick, Cantor Fitzgerald, and the Twin Towers Attack* (London: Headline, 2002), pp. 273–274.

In the aftermath of September 11, Lutnick became a controversial figure. To save his company, he stopped paying salaries for the deceased employees after September 11. In the place of salaries, Lutnick promised the families 25 percent of the profits of Cantor Fitzgerald. The problem was that earning that profit took time, and the national media started attacking Lutnick for financially mistreating the bereaved families. It became especially vicious on Bill O'Reilly's TV show *The O'Reilly Factor* on FOX News. After Lutnick announced his plan to give the 25 percent of profits for the next five years, health insurance for ten years, and $45 million in bonuses for the families, some but not all of the pressure came off. There were still attacks on him from the media. In the end, Lutnick's efforts to assist the families of lost members of Cantor Fitzgerald have proven beneficial. As of June 30, 2004, Cantor Fitzgerald had paid more than $145 million to the families.

Cantor Fitzgerald has also prospered financially. Lutnick decided to concentrate on core issues, and to transform more of his functions to an electronic trading company system, eSpeed. Much of 2002 was spent rebuilding technology and the company's infrastructure. He has also been involved in litigation over attempts of other companies to take over some of his business in the aftermath of September 11.

See Also

World Trade Center, September 11

Suggested Reading
Riva D. Atlas, "Firm That Was Hit Hard on 9/11 Grows Anew," *New York Times* (September 10, 2004), p. C4; Heather Bandur, "Firm Rises from the Ashes; Being 'Ruthless' Helped CEA Rebuild after Tragedy," *Houston Chronicle* (September 15, 2002), p. 2; Tom Barbash, *On Top of the World: The Remarkable Story of Howard Lutnick, Cantor Fitzgerald, and the Twin Towers Attack* (London: Headline, 2002); Diana B. Henriques, "The Bond Trader: From Devastation to Determination," *New York Times* (September 10, 2002), p. C1; Grant Ringshaw, "Counting the Cost at Cantor," *Sunday Telegraph [London]* (September 7, 2003), p. 3.

Casualties of September 11

The explosion of the crashing aircraft, the fire, and the final collapse of the Twin Towers produced massive casualties. The goal of the hijackers was for casualties to be in the hundred thousands range. It was known that there were around 150,000 people at any one time during the day at the World Trade Center complex. This total included people who worked in the complex, around 50,000, and tourists who shopped at the many stores there, about 100,000 daily. The World Trade Center complex was a popular place to visit and shop.

Casualties would have been much higher except for the evacuation supervised by the Fire Department of New York (FDNY) firefighters, New York City and Port Authority police, and security people for the various companies. Their efforts saved countless lives, but it came at a high cost. Collapse of the Twin Towers caught firefighter, police, and Port Authority police by surprise. In the South Tower there were only seconds to respond to a call to evacuate. The North Tower took longer to fall, but communications were so poor that information about the collapse of the South Tower and a recall order was difficult to spread. The FDNY firefighters took the brunt of the casualties with 343. Employees of the Port Authority of New York & New Jersey suffered 74 dead, and the New York City police lost 37.

Only eighteen survivors of the collapse were recovered on September 11, 2001. Rescuers found two policemen early on the first day. Later the same day, sixteen others were found. Twelve firemen, one policeman, and one civilian office worker were saved from the ruins of the North Tower. Finally, late in the day, two Port Authority employees were rescued from the North Tower. There were no survivors from the collapse of the South Tower.

The losses on September 11, 2001, were devastating to all these agencies. All of those looking for

---

Port Authority Police Lieutenant William Keegan Jr. on the Attitude of Those at the Cleanup of Ground Zero

In this place and time we were operating under different rules. Here, this was what success meant. We understood the pain. We took comfort in being able to alleviate it. We felt the suffering. We took solace by ending the suffering of others. The work at Ground Zero was a cause, a righteous cause. There are not many of them anymore. One more person was leaving this place and going home to family, friends, and loved ones, for whatever closure that gave. He was a dead cop, and a dead friend, but those of us at Ground Zero began to glimpse another truth as we worked, one that touched even the hardest cop or operating engineer or firefighter. Could the selfless devotion of so many change part of the evil caused by the worst of us into something reflecting a part of the best of us?

William Keegan Jr., *Closure: The Untold Story of the Ground Zero Recovery Mission* (New York: Touchstone, 2006), p. 114.

remains developed a special attitude toward the fallen. Port Authority police lieutenant William Keegan Jr. described it as a sacred trust that impacted psychologically on those at Ground Zero (see sidebar).

Loss of Paramedics and Emergency Medical Technicians

We lost eight paramedics and EMTs on September 11. What the people in EMS did that day was to go down there to help people, knowing that it was dangerous, knowing that we could die. Janice volunteered to go. I volunteered to go, and a lot of other women volunteered to go. There is a perception that women don't do dangerous things. The truth is that women do do dangerous things. We just do them differently than men do sometimes.

Lieutenant Amy Monroe, Emergency Medical Services Command FDNY, quoted in Susan Hagen and Mary Carouba, *Women at Ground Zero: Stories of Courage and Compassion* (New York: Alpha Books, 2002), p. 143.

The various New York agencies were fiercely protective of the remains of their own fallen. NYFD firefighters, New York City police, and Port Authority police wanted only their representatives to handle the bodies, or body parts. For example, once a firefighter's body was found, the body was placed in a body bag and put on an orange plastic stretcher. An American flag was then placed over the body bag. The firefighters would then have a chaplain lead them in prayer. After acknowledging the sacrifice by saluting the fallen firefighter, six firefighters would carry the stretcher several blocks to the morgue. Along the way people would stop working and take off their hard hats to show respect. The New York City police and Port Authority police treated their fallen comrades in much

The flag-draped body of a victim of the World Trade Center attacks is taken from the rubble by members of the New York City Fire Department on January 10, 2002, in New York. (AP IMAGES/Beth A. Keiser.)

the same way. There has been criticism, however, that civilian remains were not treated with commensurate respect and that their remains were sometimes handled more carelessly.

Early estimates of total casualties at the World Trade Center complex ranged from thousands to as many as tens of thousands. It may be that an accurate figure will never be determined, but as of February 2005 there had been 2,749 death certificates issued by the City of New York as a result of the World Trade Center attack. Of the total of 2,749, it has been determined that 2,117 (77 percent) were males and 632 (23 percent) were females. Only 1,585 (58 percent) had been forensically identified from recovered physical remains when the identification process stopped in February 2005. Median age of the victims was thirty-nine years with the range from two to eighty-five. A total of sixty-two countries were represented among the dead at the World Trade Center complex. Although the overwhelming majority of the dead were American citizens, a significant number of the dead were non-citizens—exactly how many will probably never be known.

Identification of the dead has been difficult. Most of the identifications have been made from body parts, because only 174 whole bodies had been found as of September 11, 2006. By that same date 19,948 body parts had been located and sent to the morgue for identification. More than 800 victims were identified by DNA alone. But even identification by means of DNA was difficult because the high-temperature fire and changes in temperature caused DNA tissues to deteriorate. This fact meant that the doctors had to experiment with ways to preserve tissue for DNA analysis.

The official date for closure on identifying victims of September 11 was in the middle of February 2005. New York City's medical examiner's office began notifying families that they had been unable to identify their loved ones. In an attempt to identify victims in the future, nearly

---

Nature of the Search for Remains

The nature of the search for human remains necessarily underwent changes as the geography of the pile itself did. But a basic template for the process was established early. Normally there were seventy-five firemen on recovery duty at a time, supplemented by equal numbers of police officers from both the city and the Port Authority. They came in on one-month tours, and worked twelve hour shifts according to a schedule that gave them every third day off, resulting in a pattern by which each searcher worked a total of twenty days. Though a few firemen signed on for multiple tours, most did not. This created a visible cycle at the site, between the overeager and incautious searching by teams at the start of their tours and the calmer, more efficient work that was performed later.

William Langewiesche, *American Ground: Unbuilding the World Trade Center* (New York: North Point Press, 2002), pp. 132–133.

Impact on City Morgue

The morgue was at Bellevue Hospital, and it was somewhat of an assembly line because of the number of bodies and body parts coming in. A small truck would come through the barriers, and you'd know that these were new bodies coming in. During the first few days, the bodies were coming in very quickly. They were finding 600 body parts a day—arms, legs, scalps. It was horrendous stuff to see.

Comment of Police Officer Maureen Brown in Susan Hagen and Mary Carouba, *Women at Ground Zero: Stories of Courage and Compassion* (New York: Alpha Books, 2002), p. 172.

10,000 unidentified parts have been freeze-dried and vacuum-sealed for preservation and placed in a memorial. Part of the problem of identification was that fierce fires and pressure from collapsing buildings made it difficult for scientists to extract usable DNA.

See Also
Ielpi, Lee; Von Essen, Thomas; World Trade Center, September 11

See Document
Document #21

Suggested Reading
David Abel, "Effort to ID Sept. 11 Remains Ends," *Boston Globe* (February 24, 2005), p. A2; David W. Ausmus, *In the Midst of Chaos: My 30 Days at Ground Zero* (Victoria, BC [Canada]: Trafford, 2004); William Keegan, *Closure: The Untold Story of the Ground Zero Recovery Mission* (New York: Touchstone Books, 2006); Mike Littwin, "Father of Fallen Firefighter Wages War against Complacency," *Rocky Mountain News* [Denver] (September 11, 2006), p. 25; Shiya Robowsky, "Challenges in Identification: The World Trade Center Dean," in Yael Danieli and Robert L. Dingman (eds.), *On the Ground after September 11: Mental Health Responses and Practical Knowledge Gained* (New York: Haworth Maltreatment and Trauma Press, 2005); Dennis Smith, *Report from Ground Zero* (New York: Viking, 2002); Thomas Von Essen with Matt Murray, *Strong of Heart: Life and Death in the Fire Department of New York City* (New York: ReganBooks, 2002).

Central Intelligence Agency

The Central Intelligence Agency (CIA) record prior to September 11 was emblematic of the pressures placed upon it in a changing world. Its central problem was the transition from the Cold War to international terrorism, and then to stateless terrorism that could strike the United States at any time. Surveillance against terrorism in the continental United States was the responsibility of the FBI, but the CIA had responsibility for international intelligence gathering. In any case, its record was found to be lacking.

The leaders of the CIA had over the years limited human intelligence assets. In the early and mid-1990s the CIA had reduced its human intelligence capability through a reduction of its staff by 20 percent. By the late 1990s the agency lacked the agents, the language skills, and the organizational flexibility to spot a conspiracy in the making. Instead, the CIA depended on intelligence reports from friendly intelligence services and political departments. Even when it had a human intelligence source, the CIA was slow to react to warnings coming from that source. A case in point is that the CIA had an aggressive agent in Germany monitoring the activities of the Hamburg Cell, but no additional resources were placed at his disposal.

Bureaucracy often threatened the efficiency of CIA operations. Its agents were reluctant to share information with the FBI for fear of losing control of the case. Part of this fear was an incompatibility of function between the two institutions. FBI had the task of bringing lawbreakers to justice. They approached a case by accumulating evidence that could stand up in a court of law. CIA agents were less interest in prosecuting than intelligence gathering. They wanted to follow the leads to see where they would go. This meant that the CIA was unwilling to share crucial information because such sharing might compromise intelligence sources.

The decision by John Deutch, director of the CIA from 1995 to 1996, to call for prior approval from CIA headquarters before recruiting any person as an intelligent asset with a criminal or human rights problem, made it difficult for the CIA to recruit intelligence agents. This decision came after a controversy involving the CIA's employment of a paid informant in Guatemala who had been involved in the murders of an American innkeeper and the Guatemalan husband of an American lawyer. Hundreds of paid informants were dismissed from the rolls of the CIA. Almost all of the human intelligence assets in the Middle East were terminated in this purge. This restriction was still in place on September 11, 2001.

The CIA had been monitoring the activities of Osama bin Laden and al-Qaeda through its Counterterrorism Center. CIA agents had been able to recruit thirty Afghans operating under the codeword GE/SENIORS to monitor bin Laden's activities in Afghanistan since 1998. They each received $10,000 a month for this mission. Numerous times during the Clinton administration analysts in the Counterterrorism Center and its Alec Station unit proposed operations to neutralize bin Laden using Afghan agents or missile attacks, but none of these operations received approval. Part of the problem was that bin Laden was so elusive, traveling at irregular times. There was also the fear of collateral damage that would outrage domestic and international public opinion. The Clinton administration became paralyzed by indecision caused by its lack of confidence in CIA intelligence and the ongoing political difficulties of President Clinton's Lewinsky scandal.

George Tenet, who succeeded Deutch, was able to make the transition from the Clinton administration to the Bush administration. He had been constantly warning both administrations about the danger of bin Laden and al-Qaeda. Although the Clinton administration came to recognize the truth of the terrorism threat, the Bush administration was slow to accept it until September 11, 2001. Tenet had been able to establish a good working relationship with President George W. Bush, but he was unable to get him to act quickly on al-Qaeda. After September 11, however, the Bush administration left nothing to chance in fighting against terrorism. According to Seymour Hersh in *Chain of Command*, it unleashed the CIA to undertake covert action against terrorists with no restrictions but deniability for the president. The support for the Northern Alliance led to the overthrow of the Taliban regime in Afghanistan and ended safe sanctuary for bin Laden and the other leaders of al-Qaeda. But bin Laden and most of al-Qaeda's and the Taliban's leaders were able to escape. Part of the reason for the escape was the reluctance of the Bush administration to commit American forces until it was too late.

CIA's Inspector General Summary Report Conclusions on CIS's Efforts against Al-Qaeda

"Agency officers from the top down worked hard" against al-Qaeda but "they did not always work effectively and cooperatively," the investigators concluded. While finding no "silver bullet" or single intelligence lapse that might have prevented the Sept. 11 attacks, the report identified numerous "failures to implement and manage important processes" and "follow through with operations." The report said (George) Tenet bears "ultimate responsibility" for the CIA's lack of a unified, strategic plan for fighting al-Qaeda. The intelligence community "did not have a documented, comprehensive approach" to al-Qaeda, the document said, and Tenet "did not use all of his authorities" to prepare one.

Joby Warrick and Walter Pincus, "CIA Finds Holes in Pre-9/11 Work," *Washington Post* (August 22, 2007), p. A1.

In the middle of the hunt for bin Laden and the wiping out of al-Qaeda's leadership, the Bush administration decided that Saddam Hussein and his weapons of mass destruction were greater threats. Even prior to September 11 it was known in the CIA that the Bush administration was eager to overthrow Saddam Hussein. Their reasoning was that deposing Hussein and establishing a favorable government in Iraq would produce a base of support in the Middle East for the United States, because it was apparent that there was no solution to the Israeli-Palestinian conflict.

Extreme pressure from the neoconservatives in the Bush administration, led by Vice President Dick Cheney, for the CIA to produce intelligence justification to go to war with Iraq resulted in widespread dissatisfaction among CIA analysts. Many of them believed that an Iraqi war would hinder the hunt for bin Laden and other al-Qaeda leaders. They believed that the United States should concentrate exclusively on Afghanistan and the al-Qaeda network. Those analysts who were too vocal with their dissatisfaction were fired, got transferred, or were severely criticized. Despite warnings from these CIA analysts about the lack of concrete intelligence, Tenet assured President Bush and his advisors that Iraq had weapons of mass destruction. The failure to find these weapons of mass destruction ended Bush's confidence in Tenet. In the meantime, the rank-and-file of the CIA had become critics of the Bush administration. They issued a series of intelligence reports that contradicted or were critical of the premises of the Bush administration's occupation of Iraq. Many of these reports were leaked to the news media.

After Tenet's resignation, Bush appointed former Florida congressman Porter Goss to head the CIA. He had worked for the CIA in the 1960s, but most of his knowledge of the CIA came from his seven years as chairman of the House Permanent Select Committee on Intelligence. President Bush gave Goss a mandate to bring the CIA back to Bush's political team. A short time after Goss came into Langley headquarters, senior CIA officials began to leave in droves. In April 2005 the CIA inspector general's report surfaced that presented detailed criticism of the performance of more than a dozen former and current CIA officials. Goss quashed the recommendation that there be accountability boards to recommend personnel actions against those charged in the report. Despite this action, the clash between Goss's team and CIA veterans reached epic proportions. In the long run, however, it was Goss's inability to work with his nominal boss, John Negroponte, the director of national intelligence, that led to his demise. President Bush asked for and received Goss's resignation on May 5, 2006. His successor was U.S. Air Force four-star General Michael Hayden, the former head of the National Security Agency (NSA) and the number two person under Negroponte.

See Also
Alec Station; Counterterrorism Center; Goss, Porter J.; Tenet, George

See Documents
Document #11; Document #27

Suggested Reading
Robert Dreyfuss, "The Yes-Man: President Bush Sent Porter Goss to the CIA to Keep the Agency in Line. What He's Really Doing Is Wrecking It," *American Prospect* (November 2005), p. 18; Tyler Drumheller and Elaine Monaghan, *On the Brink: An Insider's Account of How the White House Compromised American Intelligence* (New York: Carroll and Graf, 2006); Seymour M. Hersh, *Chain of Command: The Road from 9/11 to Abu Ghraib* (New York: HarperCollins, 2004); Joint Inquiry into Intelligence Community Activities before

and after the Terrorist Attacks of September 11, 2001, *Hearings before the Select Committee on Intelligence U.S. Senate and the Permanent Select Committee on Intelligence House of Representatives* (Washington, DC: U.S. Government Printing Office, 2004), 2 vols.; John Miller, Michael Stone, and Chris Mitchell, *The Cell: Inside the 9/11 Plot, and Why the FBI and CIA Failed to Stop It* (New York: Hyperion, 2002); Timothy Naftali, *Blind Spot: The Secret History of American Counterterrorism* (New York: Basic Books, 2005); James Risen, *State of War: The Secret History of the CIA and the Bush Administration* (New York: Free Press, 2006); George Tenet and Bill Harlow, *At the Center of the Storm: My Years at the CIA* (New York: Harper Collins, 2007).

Chomsky, Noam (1928–)

Noam Chomsky has long been an active critic of the U.S. government and its policies, and his views on the events surrounding September 11, 2001, resonate in radical left circles in the United States. A distinguished academic in the field of linguistics, he has devoted much of his career as a self-appointed commentator on the failures of the American government. Chomsky is not an advocate of conspiracy theories, but he has a unique perspective that sometimes gets him into political difficulty. Chomsky belongs to no political party, and his critiques have been equally harsh on both sides of the political spectrum.

Chomsky is the product of an anti-Zionist Jewish background. He was born December 7, 1928, in Philadelphia, Pennsylvania. His father was a Hebrew scholar and a member of the radical labor union International Workers of the World (IWW). Both parents were from Russia: his father was from the Ukraine and his mother from Belarus. Chomsky grew up immersed in Hebrew culture and literature. He attended and then graduated from Central High School in Philadelphia in 1945. That same year he started studying philosophy and linguistics at the University of Pennsylvania. Shortly after graduation from the University of Pennsylvania, he married fellow linguist Carol Schatz. Chomsky continued graduate work in linguistics, receiving his PhD in 1955. During the period from 1951 to 1955 he was a Harvard Junior Fellow working on his dissertation. Soon after graduation, he found a teaching position at the Massachusetts Institute of Technology (MIT). His 1957 book *Syntactic Structures* began to revolutionize the study of linguistics. His growing renown led to his appointment in 1961 as full professor in MIT's department of modern languages and linguistics. In 1966 he received the Ferrari P. Ward Professorship of Modern Languages and Linguistics, which he held until 1976, when he received appointment as institute professor. He remained a professor at MIT until his retirement. He is now a professor emeritus of linguistics at MIT.

Chomsky was famous worldwide for his contributions to theories on linguistics, but he began a lifelong involvement with politics in the 1960s. His first engagement in politics was as a vocal critic of the Vietnam War. After the Vietnam War ended, Chomsky continued his critique of the U.S. government. He asserted that the foreign policy of the United States promoted a double standard by preaching democracy and freedom for all but at the same time supporting and allying itself with nondemocratic and repressive states and political groups. He has also been critical of the American capitalist system and big business. His political views can be loosely defined as a libertarian socialist. Although he is opposed to most wars, Chomsky is not a pacifist: he has stated that he thought World War II was a just war.

In his comments on the September 11 attacks, Chomsky has acknowledged that it was an al-Qaeda operation, but he still questions government actions taken before September 11. He considers September 11 an atrocity, but he is more concerned about the reasons for the attack. He chronicles a series of missteps by the U.S. government in the last thirty years that led to the attack on the United States. It is his contention that the United States is a terrorist state, and it should not be surprising that the American government should be so hated in the Muslim world.

Chomsky warned that the Bush administration would take advantage of the September 11 attacks to embrace an adventurous foreign policy. He was critical of the invasion of Afghanistan, but the invasion of Iraq has brought forth a barrage of articles and talks critical of this action. Chomsky does not defend Saddam Hussein, but he notes that most of the atrocities of Saddam's regime were committed when he was an ally of the United States. Chomsky believes that the United States has overextended itself in a region that is unstable.

> **Chomsky's Response to a Question about the Bush Administration's Role in Orchestrating the September 11 Attacks on October 6, 2006**
>
> I think the Bush administration would have had to be utterly insane to try anything like what is alleged, for their own narrow interests, and do not think that serious evidence has been provided to support claims about actions that would not only be outlandish, for their own interests, but that have no remote historical parallel. The effects, however, are all too clear, namely, what I just mentioned: diverting activism and commitment away from the very serious ongoing crimes of state.
>
> ZNet Blogs, "9-11: Institutional Analysis vs. Conspiracy Theory" (http://blogs.zmag.org/node/2779).

Chomsky frequently agitates right-wing supporters of the Bush administration. They have called him a traitor and a madman. His biographer Robert F. Barsky has commented that Chomsky's ideas have "led people to idolize him, debate about him, arrest him, utter slanderous comments about him, and censor his work." Chomsky responds to his critics in the same way that he addresses his supporters—by careful reasoning and facts. It is interesting to note that in a poll conducted by the British magazine *Prospect* Chomsky was ranked as "the world's greatest intellectual." Chomsky is more modest than this, but he does confess to holding the United States to a higher standard of conduct because it is a free society.

See Also
Conspiracy Theories; World Trade Center, September 11

Suggested Reading
David Barsamian, "The United States Is a Leading Terrorist State," *Monthly Review* 53.6 (November 2001), p. 1; Robert F. Barsky, *Noam Chomsky: A Life of Dissent* (Cambridge, MA: MIT Press, 1997); Robin Blackburn and Oliver Kamm, "For and against Chomsky," *Prospect* [London] (October 20, 2005), p. 1; Noam Chomsky, *9/11* (Seven Stories Press, 2001); Shane Hegarty, "Lighthouse of the Left," *Irish Times* [Dublin] (January 14, 2006), p. 5; Stan Persky, "Who Loves You, Noam Chomsky," *Globe and Mail* [Canada] (February 15, 2003), p. D2.

Churchill, Ward (1947–)

A professional casualty of September 11 has been the radical leftist professor Ward Churchill. His intemperate writings following September 11 produced such a controversy that he has been terminated as a tenured professor at the University of

Colorado at Boulder. He had always been a controversial figure because of his constant left-wing criticism of the policies of the American government and society.

Churchill was born on October 2, 1947, in Elmwood, Illinois. Churchill claims that he was one-sixteenth Cherokee Indian, but there is some doubt about this claim. The Keetoowah Band of Cherokee classified him only as an honorary associate member, not a member of the tribe. After graduation from Elmwood High School in 1965, he was drafted into the United States Army in 1966. His military records show that he was trained as a projectionist and light truck driver, but Churchill has claimed that he went to paratrooper school and served a ten-month tour as a member of a long-range reconnaissance patrol (LRRP). Churchill's claim has never been substantiated. Churchill has also maintained that he worked with the Students for a Democratic Society and the Weather Underground in the late 1960s, but again confirmation has not been forthcoming. What is known is that Churchill attended Sangamon State University (now the University of Illinois at Springfield), where he received a BA and MA in communication. His next known job was as an affirmative action officer at the University of Colorado at Boulder beginning in the late 1970s.

Churchill's academic career has been controversial. He was hired as an associate professor in the department of ethnic studies at the University of Colorado at Boulder in 1990. This appointment was unusual because Churchill did not have a PhD. Nevertheless, he received tenure in 1991; such a rapid granting of tenure was contrary to usual practices. Then he was promoted to professor in 1997. Both in the granting of tenure and the promotion to professor, his credentials as a researcher were examined and not found lacking. He was serving a term as chairman of the ethnic studies department until he resigned under fire in January 2005. Helping these promotions was a prolific publication record on both Indian affairs and American foreign policy.

Churchill was also active in the American Indian Movement (AIM). He became involved with AIM in the mid-1980s. He has served as the co-director of the Denver-based American Indian Movement of Colorado. When some of the chapters broke with the national AIM leadership in 1993, Churchill stayed with the dissidents. Churchill has remained active in AIM, and he has been arrested several times for anti–Columbus Day demonstrations.

Churchill was tolerated as a radical leftist professor at the University of Colorado at Boulder until his essay in September 2001 about the September 11 attacks appeared first on the Internet and then in a print publication. His essay entitled "Some People Push Back: On the Justice of Roosting Chickens" appeared on the Internet in September 2001. In this essay, he charged that the attack on September 11 was a consequence of atrocities committed by Americans in the Middle East. The employees of the Twin Towers and the Pentagon, he wrote, were legitimate targets—those in the Pentagon because they belonged to the American military-industrial complex, and those in the Twin Towers because they were part of "a technocratic corps at the very heart of America's global financial empire." Then he referred to those working in the Twin Towers as "little Eichmanns." The essay continued by attacking the atrocities committed by the U.S. government in the form of collateral damage.

It took time for these writings to filter out, but by 2005 the controversy was in full bloom. People were outraged, and soon Colorado and national politicians began to intervene with calls that Churchill be fired. On February 1, 2005, the

Republican governor of Colorado, Bill Owens, wrote a letter to the College Republicans at the University of Colorado at Boulder calling for Churchill's resignation (see sidebar).

The university administration at the University of Colorado at Boulder took action after receiving this political pressure. After the president of the university

affirmed Churchill's right to academic freedom, the university's Standing Committee on Research Misconduct formed a panel of five members to investigate Churchill's research and publications. Three members of the panel were from the University of Colorado at Boulder, one from the Sandra Day O'Connor College of Law at Arizona State University, and one from the Center for Mexican-American Studies at the University of Texas at Austin. Two were professors of law (one a specialist on criminal law, and the other a specialist on Indian law), one a historian (not on native American subjects), one a sociologist (capital punishment specialist), and one a Mexican American studies specialist. In a 124-page report, they concluded that there was evidence in seven cases of scholarly misconduct that warranted either his firing or suspension of up to five years. The university took this panel's findings and initiated procedures to fire Churchill. His lawyer made it plain that if the University of Colorado at Boulder fired Churchill, there would be a lawsuit.

The panel's findings have not escaped scrutiny. Cathryn Hazouri, executive director of American Civil Liberties Union (ACLU), came to the defense of Churchill with the statement that "death threats, canceling speaking engagements and threats of losing his job are not appropriate responses to Ward Churchill's opinions, even if you believe they are outrageous." The panel's report drew attention to just six pages from Churchill's production of more than twenty books and one hundred articles. There were also complaints that all charges were brought by

---

Letter from Governor Bill Owens Calling on Churchill to Resign as Professor at the University of Colorado (February 1, 2005)

All decent people, whether Republican or Democrat, liberal or conservative, should denounce the views of Ward Churchill. Not only are his writings outrageous and insupportable, they are at odds with the facts of history. The thousands of innocent people—and innocent they were—who were murdered on September 11 were murdered by evil cowards. Indeed, if anyone could possibly be compared to the evildoers of Nazi Germany, it is the terrorists of the 21st century who have an equally repugnant disregard for innocent human life.

No one wants to infringe on Mr. Churchill's right to express himself. But we are not compelled to accept his pro-terrorist views at state taxpayer subsidy nor under the banner of the University of Colorado. Ward Churchill besmirches the University and the excellent teaching, writing and research of its faculty.

Ideas have consequences, and words have meaning. If there is one lesson that we hope that all Coloradans take from this sad case—and especially our students—it is that civility and appropriate conduct are important. Mr. Churchill's views are not simply anti-American. They are at odds with simple decency, and antagonistic to the beliefs and conduct of civilized people around the world. His views are far outside the mainstream of civil discourse and useful academic work.

His resignation as chairman of the Ethnic Studies Department was a good first step. We hope that he will follow this step by resigning his position on the faculty of the University of Colorado.

Letter issued from the Office of the Governor of Colorado.

Interim Chancellor Phil DeStefano, who served as both judge and jury of the case. The American Association of University Professors (AAUP) also concluded that the research misconduct charges might have been politically motivated (see sidebar). There have been concerns expressed by faculty at other universities as well. An open letter to the *New York Times Review of Books* by eleven prominent professors, including Noam Chomsky of MIT and Richard Falk of Princeton University, charged that the actions of the University of Colorado at Boulder constituted a threat to academic freedom.

It is notable how differently the University of Colorado acted in the Ward Churchill case from how Northwestern University has handled the notorious Holocaust denier professor Arthur Butz. Butz has remained controversial, but no panel has ever been established by Northwestern University to study his academic credentials and research on denying the Holocaust.

> **Official Statement of the American Association of University Professors about Ward Churchill**
>
> Freedom of faculty members to express views, however unpopular or distasteful, is an essential condition of an institution of higher learning that is truly free. We deplore threats of violence heaped upon Professor Churchill, and we reject the notion that some viewpoints are so offensive or disturbing that the academic community should not allow them to be heard and debated. Also reprehensible are inflammatory statements by public officials that interfere in the decision of the academic community.
>
> Statement released by the AAUP on February 4, 2005 (http://www.aaup.org/AAUP/newsroom/prarchives/2005/Church.htm).

In the meantime, Churchill has been active on the speaker's circuit. He is quite popular with a large segment of the student population. His difficulties with the University of Colorado at Boulder have made him a martyr in left-wing circles. His fee for speaking has now risen to around $5,000 an appearance.

See Also

World Trade Center, September 11

See Document

Document #29

Suggested Reading

Jennifer Brown, "CU Moves to Fire Churchill," *Denver Post* (June 27, 2006), p. A1; Jennifer Brown, "Panel on Churchill: Fire or Suspend Him; CU Prof Strayed from the Truth," *Denver Post* (May 17, 2006), p. A1; Matt Labash, "The Ward Churchill Notoriety Tour," *Weekly Standard* [Washington, DC] 10.30 (April 25, 2005), p. 1; Michelle Pascucci, "Professor's Essay Sparks Free Speech Debate at Cornell U.," *Cornell Daily Sun* (March 14, 2007), p. 1.

Clarke, Richard A. (1951–)

Richard A. Clarke was the chief counterterrorism advisor on the U.S. National Security Council on September 11, 2001. He was a career specialist in intelligence and counterterrorism. He was one of the few carryovers from the Clinton administration that the Bush administration had retained, but he had difficulty in making the case that al-Qaeda was a major danger to the United States.

His entire career was in government service. He was born in 1951 in Boston, Massachusetts. His father was a blue-collar factory worker at a Boston chocolate factory, and his mother was a nurse. After a divorce, Clarke was raised by his mother. He won a competitive exam to attend the prestigious Boston Latin School, where he graduated in 1969. His undergraduate degree was earned from the University of Pennsylvania in 1972. He then attended the Massachusetts Institute of Technology (MIT), where he earned a degree in management. His first job, beginning in 1973, was with the U.S. Department of Defense as a defense analyst counting Soviet nuclear warheads. After a series of appointments, he was promoted in 1985 to the Assistant Secretary of State for Intelligence in the Reagan administration. By this time Steve Coll asserts that he had earned a reputation as being a "blunt instrument, a bully, and occasionally abusive." He continued to work with the George H. W. Bush administration and helped on security affairs during the 1990–91 Persian Gulf War. In 1992 James Baker, the Secretary of State, fired him for his apparent defense of Israel's transfer of U.S. technology to the People's Republic of China. Clarke then moved to the National Security Council in the White House, where he began to specialize in counterterrorism. Clarke was also held over in the Clinton administration, continuing as a member of the National Security Council from 1992 to 2003.

Clarke's preoccupation was with counterintelligence. Among his contentions was that Osama bin Laden's al-Qaeda was a growing threat to the United States. President Clinton agreed with this assessment, but he was engaged in a series of controversies that distracted him and his administration. Clarke lobbied for a Counterterrorism Security Group to be chaired by a new national security official, the National Coordinator for Infrastructure Protection and Counterterrorism. President Clinton approved this office by signing Presidential Decision Directive 62 on May 22, 1998.

Clarke presided over a working group that included the counterterrorism heads of the CIA, FBI, Joint Chiefs of Staff, and Departments of Defense, Justice, and State. But the National Coordinator for Infrastructure Protection and Counterterrorism had a limited staff of twelve and no budget; moreover, operational decision making could come only from the departments and agencies of the intelligence community. As Clarke has pointed out, he had the "appearance of responsibility for counterterrorism, but none of the tools or authority to get the job done." Nevertheless, Clarke was in the middle of several counterterrorism operations. He was involved in the decision making about the CIA's snatch operation against Osama bin Laden in 1998. An Afghan team was to capture bin Laden at his residence at Tarnak Farms near Kandahar. This raid was called off because there was a lack of confidence that it would succeed by CIA leadership, the White House, and Clarke.

Clarke continued his position on the National Security Council during the early years of the Bush administration. He proposed a plan to combat al-Qaeda that included covert aid to the Afghan leader of the Northern Alliance, Massoud, spy flights of the new Predator, and ways to eliminate bin Laden as a threat to the United States, but there was little enthusiasm for this report by the Bush administration. Becoming frustrated, Clarke decided to resign from government work in November 2001. In the interval, the events of September 11, 2001, transpired, changing the American political landscape. On September 12, President Bush instructed him to try to find evidence that Saddam Hussein was connected to September 11. Clarke sent a report to the White House stating categorically that Hussein had nothing to do with these terrorist attacks, but there is no evidence indicating whether President Bush read the report. The report was sent back to be updated and resubmitted, but nothing came of it.

Clarke left government service in 2003. He then became an outspoken critic of the Bush administration and its policies prior to September 11. This led the White House to engage in a character assassination campaign against him. Clarke testified for twenty hours during the 9/11 Commission hearings. He made national headlines for his apology that the government had failed to prevent the September 11 attacks (see sidebar). In the middle of the 9/11 Commission hearings, Clarke published his book *Against All Enemies: Inside America's War on Terror*, which gives his side of the controversy.

In his book Clarke was especially critical of the Bush administration's invasion of Iraq. Most of his criticism stems from his belief that, by redirecting attention away from bin Laden and al-Qaeda, the Bush administration has allowed al-Qaeda to reconstitute itself into an ongoing threat to the United States. In his eyes the invasion of Afghanistan was so half-hearted in its commitment of American forces that bin Laden and nearly all of the al-Qaeda and Taliban leaders easily escaped. By not committing the necessary resources to rebuild Afghanistan, Clarke wrote, the Bush administration has allowed both al-Qaeda and the Taliban to threaten the pro-American Afghanistan state, all to depose Saddam Hussein.

Clarke's Apology to the Families of the Victims of 9/11 before the 9/11 Commission

I welcome these hearings because of the opportunity that they provide to the American people to better understand why the tragedy of 9/11 happened and what we must do to prevent a recurrence.

I also welcome the hearings because it is finally a forum where I can apologize to the loved ones of the victims of 9/11. To them who are here in the room, to those who are watching on television, your government failed you, those entrusted with protecting you failed you, and I failed you. We tried hard, but that doesn't matter because we failed.

Richard A. Clarke, *Against All Enemies: Inside America's War on Terror* (New York: Free Press, 2004), p. 293.

Former White House counterterrorism advisor Richard Clarke addresses the American Library Association's annual convention in Orlando, Florida, in 2004 while promoting his book *Against All Enemies*. (AP IMAGES/Bruce Weaver.)

See Also
Bush, George W.; Bush Administration; Clinton Administration
See Documents
Document #8; Document #31
Suggested Reading
Daniel Benjamin and Steven Simon, *The Age of Sacred Terror* (New York: Random House, 2002); Richard A. Clarke, *Against All Enemies: Inside America's War on Terror* (New York: Free Press, 2004); Steve Coll, *Ghost Wars: The Secret History of the CIA, Afghanistan, and Bin Laden, From the Soviet Invasion to September 10, 2001* (New York: Penguin Books, 2004); Timothy Naftali, *Blind Spot: The Secret History of American Counterterrorism* (Basic Books, 2005).

Cleanup Operations at Ground Zero

Almost immediately after the attacks on the World Trade Center, cleanup operations started at Ground Zero. The collapse of the Twin Towers meant that there was little chance of survivors, but the effort had to be made. New York Fire Department (NYFD) firefighters, New York City police, Port Authority police, and others from federal agencies began looking for survivors. Only a handful of survivors were found the first day and none thereafter. For the first few days there was chaos as the bucket brigades were ineffectual and barely scratched the surface of the debris. The problem was that the debris from the buildings had fallen into four different sectors that were almost cut off from each other. At first, heavy equipment could not get into the site because of the fallen pedestrian bridge on West Street, so the only debris that was recovered on the first couple of days was by hand.

There was also a cloud of accumulated dust and fumes hanging over the scene of destruction. This air was toxic because, according to the Environmental Protection Agency (EPA), "Ground Zero inhalation tests of ambient air showed WTC dust consisted predominantly (95 percent) of coarse particles and pulverized cement, with glass fibers, asbestos, lead, polycyclic aromatic hydrocarbons (PAHS), polychlorinated biphenyls (PCB), and polychlorinated furans and dioxins." Thousands of police, firefighters, paramedics, and construction workers worked at the site for several months and breathed this air. Many of them began the hacking cough that soon earned the name "the World Trade Center cough."

Search and rescue teams started clearing the site and recovering as many body parts as possible. Four temporary tent morgues were set up on the site at the World Trade Center complex. Later, body parts were taken to a centralized morgue. It was a slow, grueling job recovering bodies and body parts, and it sometimes turned out to be dangerous. Fortunately, there were few major injuries at the site.

Complicating the early days of the rescue and recovery work were calls from family members stating that their loved ones were still alive. Firefighters and police followed up on these calls in the first days after September 11. Then they realized that the calls had been triggered by the backed up communication system. So many cell phone calls had been made on September 11 that the overloaded communication system could not transmit them all. These messages were stored and sent later, when the communication system went back on line. Families then received messages that their loved ones had made before they died on September 11, confusing them and everyone else.

Within days, more than 1,000 construction workers began clearing debris alongside the emergency workers. Four companies participated in the cleanup: Bovis

Company, Turner Construction Company, Tully Construction Company, and Amec Construction Management. They used more than 150 pieces of heavy equipment, including twenty cranes and the Caterpillar 345 Ultra High Excavator for difficult jobs. Work was slow because of frequent interruptions to recover bodies and body parts of victims.

The construction workers received instructions not to be involved in body removal. After ascertaining that there were no bodies or body parts in a particular area, they loaded debris onto semis and dump trucks and took it to a wash and inspection station for inspection by FBI and Secret Service agents and then washed it down. The debris was then hauled down to a pier for loading onto a barge. This barge carried it to the Fishkill Landfill on Staten Island. There the debris was searched again before being added to the landfill.

As the debris removal picked up steam, another serious problem surfaced. In the construction of the World Trade complex, a wall had been built to keep out water from the Hudson River. This wall had been built because half of the sixteen-acre site had extended Manhattan Island 700 feet into the river. The problem was that this wall had been weakened in the collapse of the buildings. This wall had to be reinforced, or Hudson River water would have flooded much of lower Manhattan, causing a catastrophe greater than the World Trade Center attack. So a delicate balance had to be maintained between debris removal and bringing in material to reinforce the wall. This balancing act was successful, so no flooding took place.

Soon after the arrival of the construction workers, a controversy developed over the number of firefighters who were to remain working at Ground Zero. This issue had great importance to the firefighters because they were interested in finding bodies and body parts. The construction workers were more concerned about cleaning up the debris. What made the firefighters particularly assertive about finding any remains was that many of the missing victims were Catholic. Unless there was a body part, the Catholic Church refused to perform a funeral mass.

Ultimately a compromise was worked out, with a significant number of firefighters staying at the World Trade Center site until the last part of the debris was removed in May 2002.

Another significant problem was that decision making for the World Trade Center site was by committee. Representatives from twenty-six federal, state, regional, and city agencies made the major decisions. New York City's Department of Design and Construction had been given overall control of the site, but it had only one representative on the committee. A representative from each agency had an equal vote on decisions, but decisions were not made by majority rule. Some agencies had more clout than others, and this clash of interests and opinions made for chaotic decision making.

Throughout the cleanup the presence of fire made work difficult. These fires were entirely under the pile and the workers rarely saw them. Only when the piles

> **Importance of the Slurry Wall**
>
> The operation to secure the slurry wall lasted nine months, and meanwhile every day at Ground Zero we faced the possibility we could drown if the wall collapsed. It was another reason why security was so tight. We all feared a second terrorist attack. If terrorists breached the slurry wall, they would finish the job they started on 9-11 and destroy New York City itself.
>
> William Keegan Jr., *Closure: The Untold Story of the Ground Zero Recovery Mission* (New York: Touchstone, 2006), p. 11.

were penetrated did the fires' cherry red glow become visible. The fires received their oxygen from tunnels and underground areas, and they burned at a temperature from 1,000 to 1,800 degrees. At times the workers stood in areas where their boots began to melt. Attempts to attack the fires by pouring water on them were ineffective because of the densely packed debris. Water hit the fires and produced steam and smoke, making for two more hazards.

Another hazard of the cleanup was unexploded ammunition. Evidently there had been 1,700 live rounds scattered around World Trade Center Building 6. This ammunition had belonged to the U.S. Customs Service. Although there were no fatalities caused by this loose ammunition, there was one slight injury when a workman set off a round accidentally.

One issue that was unknown by anyone at the site was the gold and silver bullion stored at the World Trade Center complex and owned by Scotiabank. There was $110,000,000 worth of gold bars and $120,000,000 of silver bars in a vault under World Trade Center Building 4. A Port Authority police officer located the vault on October 17, 2001. Scotiabank officials were then notified of the finding of the vault. During a four-day period, all of the gold and silver bars were moved under the authority of the Port Authority police. It took 133 trucks to complete the transfer.

By mid-November a new threat to the site appeared in the form of Freon gas. Underneath the former North Tower was the main chiller plant, which had refrigeration units capable of holding 24,000 pounds of Freon gas. If the units had leaked, the gas would have filled voids in the underground before rising to the surface to kill as many as hundreds of workers. Another danger was that the Freon gas might come into contact with open flames, producing poison gas resembling mustard gas used in World War I. In this case the casualties could be in the thousands. There was also an increasing danger that one of the large construction machines might puncture the Freon gas storage unit. A special team went underground to explore the condition of the chiller plant. This team discovered that the Freon gas had already vented, and the danger had passed without casualties.

One ongoing problem on the cleanup site was the failure of the firefighters, police, and workers to wear their personal protective equipment. This failure was particularly noticeable in the failure to use respirators, despite safety officials' attempts to persuade those working in the debris to wear them. The most stubborn were the firefighters. Their reasoning was that they needed to be able to smell to find the dead bodies. This safety deficiency was reported to the New York City's Department of Design and Construction and to the Committee of twenty-six representatives of the agencies time and again, but nothing was done. The federal Occupational Safety and Health Administration (OSHA) and other safety officials had no authority to enforce safety rules.

The cleanup at Ground Zero officially ended on May 30, 2002, with a ceremony. The "Last Piece of Steel" was to be ceremoniously carried by truck escorted by an honor guard and signaled by the beat of a single drum. In a meeting it was determined that the Port Authority police would guard and be in charge of the "Last Piece of Steel." Plans came from the mayor's office that the honor guard would be composed of fifteen members of each group that had worked at Ground Zero. Those groups interested in the proceedings, however, decided to ignore this limit, and the honor guard consisted of all personnel still working at the site in May 2002. Family members of the victims of September 11 were also invited to participate. The ceremony went off without any difficulty, and crowds lined the way, clapping in rhythm to the drum beat.

Since the end of the cleanup at Ground Zero, numerous workers at the site have been experiencing health problems. The most famous case was the death in January 2006 of New York Police Department Detective James Zadroga, at age thirty-four, from a lung disease directly related to his more than 450 hours working at Ground Zero. Of the approximately 30,000 people who worked at Ground Zero, 12,000 had instituted health claims by 2006. Most of the workers have suffered from pulmonary disease, but cancer has also been a factor. By January 2006 there were reports of the deaths of twenty-two other men, most in their thirties and forties. Another 400 NYPD detectives have also been suffering from health-related problems believed to have been brought on by their work at Ground Zero. In a 2002 survey more than 60 percent of the 1,138 responders reported "lower airway breathing problems," and 74 percent "reported upper airway breathing problems."

Many of the sufferers of the Ground Zero cleanup have resorted to lawsuits. These suits have had little impact on the health of those suffering from respiratory illness, however. Numerous others, potentially intimidated by the legal process, may be suffering in silence. The death toll is rising for those who helped in the cleanup; tumors and lung-scarring diseases have been known to emerge between five and twenty years after a toxic exposure.

See Also
Firefighters at Ground Zero; Ielpi, Lee; Von Essen, Thomas; World Trade Center, September 11; Zadroga, James

See Documents
Document #17; Document #19; Document #25

Suggested Reading
David W. Ausmus, *In the Midst of Chaos: My 30 Days at Ground Zero* (Victoria, BC [Canada]: Trafford, 2004); Gregory A. Butler, *Lost Towers: Inside the World Trade Center Cleanup* (New York: iUniverse, 2006); Daily News Staff, "The Making of a Health Disaster. Officials Failed to Act on Ground Zero Perils," *Daily News* [New York] (July 25, 2006), p. 24; Rosie DiManno, "Toll from 9/11 Climbs, Albeit Too Quietly," *Toronto Star* (January 13, 2006), p. A2; William Keegan Jr., *Closure: The Untold Story of the Ground Zero Recovery Mission* (New York: Touchstone Books, 2006); Robert F. Moore, Thomas Zambito, and Corky Siemaszko, "Stricken 9-11 Heroes in Fight of Their Lives," *Daily News* [New York] (April 16, 2006), p. 16; Rich Schapiro, "WTC Air Doomed Ex-Cop," *Daily News* [New York] (April 12, 2006), p. 7; Dennis Smith, *Report from Ground Zero* (New York: Viking, 2002); Thomas Von Essen with Matt Murray, *Strong of Heart: Life and Death in the Fire Department of New York City* (New York: ReganBooks, 2002).

Clinton Administration
The Clinton administration was no longer in power when the events of September 11, 2001, unfolded, but some of its policies contributed its background. It was during President Clinton's eight years in office that Osama bin Laden and al-Qaeda emerged as a threat to the United States. Bin Laden twice in 1996 and again in 1998 issued declarations of hostilities against the United States. President Clinton had priorities other than terrorism, such as health care, education, NAFTA, gays in the military, instability in Russia, the Israeli-Palestinian conflict, and the policies of rogue states. Early in his administration President Clinton

dealt with foreign policy issues as they became crises: Bosnia, Haiti, and Somalia. Despite these other issues, bin Laden made the Clinton administration pay attention by attacks against Americans around the world.

The lack of attention to terrorism by the Clinton administration led to the weakening of the intelligence capability of the Central Intelligence Agency (CIA), as weak CIA directors were appointed. First, Clinton appointed James Woolsey as the director of the CIA. This appointment was in keeping with Clinton's pattern of keeping his distance from the CIA, which has been described by Steve Coll as "distant, mutually ill-informed, and strangely nonchalant." Woolsey was more interested in scientific and technical programs, particularly spy satellites, than in human intelligence. Consequently, the CIA came to depend on scientific/technical programs and deemphasized human intelligence gathering. It was not all Woolsey's fault; President Clinton only held two semiprivate meeting with Woolsey in his two years as CIA director. The CIA had hindered the FBI on the Aldrich Ames spy case, and this case had long-term negative impact on CIA-FBI relations. Ames, a veteran CIA agent, had been caught spying for the Soviet Union and had betrayed more than 100 CIA agents before being caught in 1994. There had been indicators that Ames was a spy, but the CIA had refused to pass on the information to the FBI. In the course of nearly two years, Woolsey had alienated Clinton, the FBI, Congressional leaders, and the CIA's rank-and-file. He decided to resign on December 26, 1994.

Next, Clinton appointed John Deutch to be director of the CIA. Deutch did not want the job, because he was content in his position as Deputy Secretary of Defense, but Clinton persuaded him to take the job anyway. Even more so than Woolsey, Deutch was a champion of scientific and technical intelligence collection. He belittled the need for human intelligence, and by telling the CIA's analysts his opinion he alienated them. The CIA budget shrank and veteran CIA administrators and analysts were encouraged to retire. Deutch lasted only nineteen controversial months before Clinton fired him.

Several events in 1995 made the Clinton administration aware of the dangers of terrorism. One was the sarin gas attack in the Tokyo subway system by the Aum Shinrikyo sect on March 25, 1995. The vocal anti-Americanism of this sect of 50,000 members worried counterterrorism officials. The next event was the Oklahoma City bombing on April 19, 1995, by Timothy McVeigh and associates. It showed how easily terrorists could acquire bomb-making materials.

The Clinton administration had already introduced the Omnibus Counter-Terrorism Act of 1995 in February, trying to bypass some of the limitations placed on intelligence operations. But even after the Oklahoma bombing, the Republican-controlled House of Representatives refused to bring it to a vote. Disbelieving that a major terrorist threat was on the horizon, Republicans decided to sacrifice any efforts at counterterrorism and instead criticize the Clinton administration for its failures. In 1996 Congress did pass the Antiterrorism and Effective Death Penalty Act of 1996, but many of the original provisions involving firearms control were eliminated because of the objections of the gun lobby. Two important provisions were retained: chemical markers on high explosives and legal authority to bar terrorists from entering the United States (Alien Terrorist Removal Court).

During his second term in office, Clinton and his administration became more aware of the threat of both domestic and foreign terrorism. His appointment of

George Tenet helped stabilize the CIA, but Clinton still had reservations about the reliability of intelligence coming from the CIA. The presence of Richard Clarke in the White House brought counterterrorism to the forefront of the president's agenda. Bombings of U.S. embassies at Nairobi and Dar-es-Salaam in August 1998 were rude wake-up calls. President Clinton authorized cruise missile attacks on an al-Qaeda training camp and on a factory in Sudan. A large meeting of al-Qaeda leaders was scheduled to be held at the Zawhar Kili training camp complex near Khost, in eastern Afghanistan, on August 20, 1998. Osama bin Laden was supposed to be at this meeting. Seventy-five cruise missiles hit the complex, killing at least twenty and wounding scores of others. This attack proved to be a failure, probably because Pakistani security Inter-Services Intelligence (ISI) warned al-Qaeda about the attack. (At least this is the evidence provided by Steve Coll in his book *Ghost Wars*.) The other cruise missile attack, at the al-Shifa plant in Sudan, was no more successful. A controversy developed because the al-Shifa plant turned out to be a pharmaceutical factory and not a chemical factory producing chemicals for al-Qaeda.

Several times the Clinton administration proposed special operations to be conducted by the military against terrorist targets. Each time senior generals in the Pentagon were reluctant to undertake special operations against terrorism suspects. Yet Richard A. Clarke reports that these senior generals were eager to let the word spread down through the ranks that the politicians in the While House were reluctant to act. They also communicated this to members of Congress and the media.

Hostile criticism about the missile attacks in 1998 from Republicans cooled the Clinton administration's ardor for further efforts to capture or kill bin Laden. Yet both the CIA and FBI reported intelligence to the Clinton administration that al-Qaeda was planning for terrorist activities within the United States. With these warnings still fresh, the Clinton administration slowly closed down any operations against bin Laden.

After the 1998 embassy attacks, the Clinton administration did attempt to disrupt al-Qaeda's financing. It took legal steps to freeze $240 million in al-Qaeda and Taliban assets in American bank accounts. Assets of Afghanistan's national airline, Ariana Afghan, were also frozen. These actions were inconvenient for al-Qaeda and made it shift its assets into commodities—diamonds and blue tanzanite—and the creation or use of Islamic charities to raise funds. Hindering the Clinton administration was the weakness of the international money-laundering laws. These laws were particularly weak in Kuwait, Dubai, United Arab Emirates, Bahrain, and Lebanon. Also, the traditional Islamic banking system, the hawala, heavily used in Afghanistan and Pakistan, was cash based, leaving no written or electronic records. These factors brought limited success to the Clinton administration's efforts to restrict the flow of funds to al-Qaeda.

See Also
African Embassy Bombings; Bin Laden, Osama; Clarke, Richard A.; Qaeda, al-

See Document
Document #31

Suggested Reading
Daniel Benjamin and Steven Simon, *The Age of Sacred Terror* (New York: Random House, 2002); Richard Bernstein, *Out of the Blue: The Story of September 11, 2001, from*

Opinion of Richard Clarke on the Clinton Administration's Efforts on Terrorism in Testimony before the 9/11 Commission

My impression was that fighting terrorism, in general, and fighting al-Qaeda, in particular, were an extraordinarily high priority in the Clinton administration—certainly [there was] no higher priority. There were priorities probably of equal importance such as the Middle East peace process, but I certainly don't know of one that was any higher in the priority of the administration.

Richard A. Clarke, *Against All Enemies: Inside America's War on Terror*, paperback edition (New York: Free Press, 2004), p. 293.

Jihad to Ground Zero (New York: Times Books, 2002); Bill Clinton, *My Life* (New York: Vintage Books, 2005); Steve Coll, *Ghost Wars: The Secret History of the CIA, Afghanistan, and Bin Laden, from the Soviet Invasion to September 10, 2001* (New York: Penguin Books, 2004); Timothy Naftali, *Blind Spot: The Secret History of American Counterterrorism* (New York: Basic Books, 2005); Gerald Posner, *Why America Slept: The Failure to Prevent 9/11* (New York: Ballantine Books, 2003).

Conspiracy Theories

From day after the attacks on September 11, conspiracy theories appeared and began to spread. A disaster of such magnitude, along with some of the mysterious circumstances surrounding it, promoted such theories. The conspiracy theorists started with a hypothesis challenging the official version and began searching for information to support their theories. Any data that did not conform to their preconceived ideas were discounted, particularly if the data came from government sources, the mainstream media, or social scientists. Americans and Europeans have become susceptible to this type of thinking when building conspiracy theories.

A leading conspiracy theorist was the French left-wing activist Thierry Meyssan. His book *L'Effroyable Imposture: 11 Septembre 2001 (The Frightening Fraud: September 11, 2001)* charged that it was a plot by the American government to discredit its enemies and to increase the U.S defense budget This book appeared in 2002 and became an immediate best seller. Among his assertions was that the damage to the Pentagon in Washington, D.C., could not have been caused by a Boeing 757 but was instead a missile strike or a truck bombing made to appear as a plane crash. He also challenged eyewitness testimony. His thesis was that the September 11 attacks were part of a military conspiracy in the United States to impose a military regime. Media in both France and the United States have attacked the book for its bizarre claims. Shortly after the publication of his book, the U.S. Department of Defense declared Meyssan persona non grata. This status meant that Meyssan would be unable to enter the United States for any reason. The U.S. government followed in July 2005 with a document from the U.S. Department of State classifying him as a major source of anti-American propaganda in the world.

Another conspiracy theorist is A. K. Dewdney, a professor emeritus of computer science at the University of Waterloo in Ontario, Canada. His theory, which he calls "Operation Pearl," makes September 11 a U.S. government conspiracy. In his thesis the first three passenger aircraft landed at Harrisburg International Airport, Harrisburg, Pennsylvania, where the passengers disembarked. Three remote-controlled aircraft then were launched against the World Trade Center complex and the Pentagon. Passengers were then packed into United Airlines Flight 93 aircraft, which was then shot down over Shanksville, Pennsylvania. The three empty aircraft were flown over the ocean and disposed of in a watery grave.

Dowdney's thesis lacks credibility for a number of reasons. First, there were too many passengers to cram into one aircraft. Second, two videos and numerous witnesses show both American Airlines Flight 11 and United Airlines Flight 175 crash into the World Trade Center's twin towers. Third, seven witnesses saw a commercial aircraft crash into the Pentagon. Fourth, and most important, it is likely that the U.S. government lacks the capability to carry out such an involved conspiracy without being caught. Richard A. Clarke maintains that conspiracy theorists simultaneously hold two contrary beliefs. The first is that the U.S. government is so incompetent that it can miss explanations the conspiracy theorists can uncover, and second, that the same government can keep a secret of that magnitude.

Conspiracy theories appear at every important event in U.S. history. Marcus LiBrizzi, an English professor at the University of Maine at Machias and an authority on conspiracy theories, however, was shocked at how soon conspiracy theories on 9/11 appeared, because normally it takes a decade or so before conspiracy theories develop enough material to be articulated and to surface.

The leadership of the conspiracy theories on September 11 is a diverse group. The movement's most vocal theorists are David Ray Griffin, a retired professor of postmodern theology; James H. Fetzer, a professor at the University of Minnesota–Duluth; Steven F. Jones, a retired physicist from Brigham Young University; and Jim Marrs, a freelance writer who specializes in conspiracy theories. All of them joined Fetzer's Scholars for 9/11 Truth to coordinate the investigations on the events surrounding 9/11. Soon, however, differences over the interpretation of 9/11 developed between Fetzer and Jones. Jones left the Scholars for 9/11 Truth to form the Scholars for 9/11 Truth and Justice. Even among the leaders of the conspiracist movement, there are wide-ranging views on the nature of the conspiracy. These views range from the impossible to the ridiculous; all, however, blame the U.S. government.

See Also

Fetzer, James H.; Griffin, David Ray; Jones, Steven E.; Marrs, Jim; Meyssan, Thierry; Scholars for 9/11 Truth

Suggested Reading

David Dunbar and Brad Reagan, *Debunking 9/11 Myths: Why Conspiracy Theories Can't Stand Up to the Facts* (New York: Hearst Books, 2006); Jonathan Gurwitz, "Conspiracy Theories Only Flourish in the Darkness," *San Antonio Express-News* (May 24, 2006), p. 7B; John Henley, "US Invented Air Attack on Pentagon, Claims French Book," *Guardian* (April 1, 2002), p. 1.

> **Explanation by Marcus LiBrizzi on Why Conspiracy Theories Proliferate**
>
> "In a world that is increasingly fragmented or even alienating and confusing, I think conspiracy theories give us back that sense of connection that is lost. It's even that old stereotype that everything is connected; I think that's one of the reasons we want to believe in them. [These theories] really tap into one of the most dominant fears in contemporary conspiracy theories . . . new world order. It's kind of like [George] Orwell's *1984*, a nightmarish version of a one-world government, of a real totalitarian government."
>
> Ed Balint, "Catastrophic Events of 9/11 Prove a Magnet for Conspiracy Theories," *Copley News Service* (September 8, 2006), p. 1.

Counterterrorism Center

The Central Intelligence Agency (CIA) decided in 1985 to create a new section to fight against international terrorism. This decision came shortly after intelligence failures in Lebanon led to 241 U.S. Marines' deaths, and the kidnapping and killing of CIA Section Chief William Buckley. President Reagan placed pressure on the then-director of the CIA, William J. Casey, to do something about terrorism. Casey approached Duane R. "Dewey" Clarridge, a respected veteran field officer, to make a recommendation for a way that the CIA could most effectively fight terrorism. Clarridge recommended an interdisciplinary center in the CIA that had an international reach and could utilize all the capabilities of the CIA. Part of its mission was to launch covert action against known terrorists, so the Special Operations Group (SOG) was transferred to the Counterterrorism Center. It was to be a section staffed by 100 persons with representation from the FBI. Casey accepted Clarridge's recommendation and appointed him as its head. Instead of the original plan for a staff of 100, Casey authorized it at a staffing of 250. The Counterterrorism Center became operational in February 1986.

Clarridge's first target as head of the Counterterrorism Center was the Abu Nidal Organization (ANO). In the 1970s and 1980s, the ANO, named after its leader, was the most violent terrorist group in operation and had become the number one terrorist threat. The CIA was able to recruit a source within ANO, and this source provided inside information. Much of this information was published in a State Department publication *The Abu Nidal Handbook*. After this information became public, Abu Nidal became so concerned about penetration of his organization that he ordered the execution of a large number of his followers in Libya. This purge ended the effectiveness of the ANO.

The next target was the Hezbollah (Party of God) in Lebanon. Hezbollah, a Shiite terrorist organization, had killed the 241 Marines in Beirut and had captured a number of Western hostages. Among its victims was William Buckley, the CIA agent in Lebanon, who died from harsh treatment. This campaign against Hezbollah was less successful because it proved impossible to find an agent able to penetrate Hezbollah's leadership. Efforts to launch covert operations were also hampered by a lack of intelligence and the reluctance of the American military to lend support.

Clarridge became frustrated by the lack of support for the Counterterrorism Center. His role in the Iran-Contra scandal also led his superiors in the CIA after Casey's illness to question his judgment. He maintained that Oliver North had misled him in the exchange of hostages from Iran for weapons to be used by the Contras to fight against the Sandinista government in Nicaragua. Clarridge's goal had been to make the center a proactive force against terrorism. Instead, he found that his boss, CIA director William Webster, who had assumed control of the CIA on May 26, 1987, was averse to risk. This lack of support led Clarridge to leave the Counterterrorism Center later in 1987. Later, in June 1988, he was forced to resign from the CIA by Webster.

Clarridge's successor, Fred Turco, picked the next target for the Counterterrorism Center, and it was Peru's Shining Path. Abimael Guzman, a philosophy professor, had founded the Maoist terrorist group in 1970, and it had opened a war against the Peruvian government. The Counterterrorism Center provided the Peruvian police sophisticated electronic surveillance equipment and training that enabled them to capture Guzman in a Lima suburb in September 1992. They found out that Guzman had a special diet and smoked a particular brand of tobacco. After briefing the Peruvian authorities on these facts, Peruvian police identified the stores that handled these items. By searching garbage, it was established where Guzman was staying.

The Counterterrorism Center's activities assumed more importance in 1993. By this time the new head of the Counterterrorism Center was Winston Wiley, who had assumed control in November 1992. Two events mobilized this activity. First was the murder of two CIA employees in Langley by Mir Amal Kasi on January 25, 1993. Believing the CIA responsible for countless Muslim deaths, Kasi opened fire with an AK-47 assault rifle just outside of CIA headquarters, killing the CIA employees. Kasi was from Baluchistan, and he managed to escape back to Pakistan, where he promptly disappeared. A special CIA unit was set up to locate and capture him. Kasi was finally captured on June 15, 1997.

An even bigger task was the investigation of the conspiracy behind the World Trade Center bombing on February 23, 1993. While the domestic investigation was left up to the FBI, the Counterterrorism Center established a subunit to gather intelligence about the bombing. Information was slow to surface, and at first the Counterterrorism Center suspected that it had been a state-sponsored terrorist operation with Iraq, Libya, and Iran as the prime suspects. Slowly the intelligence analysts came to realize that it was an independent operation led by Ramzi Yousef. In a combined CIA/FBI operation Yousef was capture in Islamabad on February 7, 1995.

The Counterterrorism Center continued to select terrorist groups to fight against. First under Geoff O'Connell and then under J. Cofer Black the Counterterrorism Center planned counterterrorist operations. Black's target was Osama bin Laden and al-Qaeda. He was also able to count on an expanded Counterterrorism Center. In 1986, the center had 20 analysts, but by early 2001 it had 340 people, of which more than a dozen were FBI agents. Despite the additions, the staffing of the Counterterrorism Center was too low to handle the volume of information flowing into it. Not surprisingly, considering the staffing, the leaders and the staff of the Counterterrorism Center were caught unaware on September 11, 2001.

American pressure on Sudan led bin Laden to move from Sudan to Afghanistan. Bin Laden, family, and retainers caught an aircraft on May 18, 1996, for the trip. The staff of the Counterterrorism Center thought that this presented a golden opportunity to capture bin Laden in transit. A proposal to do so was given to President Clinton, but it never received presidential approval. Members of the Counterterrorism Center were furious over this lost opportunity.

Throughout the late 1990s the analysts in the Counterterrorism Center were monitoring bin Laden's activities from sources within Afghanistan. The problem was that bin Laden was constantly moving, so that tracking him was almost impossible. Bin Laden was never in one place long enough to either capture or kill him. There was also an ongoing debate in the Clinton administration that was never resolved on whether it was legal to assassinate bin Laden. Attorney General Janet Reno made it plain to the head of the CIA, George Tenet, and then-head of the Counterterrorism Center, Geoff O'Connell, that any attempt to kill bin Laden was illegal. All schemes involved capturing bin Laden first and killing him only in self-defense.

Another problem was the issue of collateral damage in an attack on bin Laden. Isolating bin Laden from civilians was almost impossible. Members of the Counterterrorism Center wanted to proceed with covert action that might lead to collateral damage regardless of the consequences. They considered bin Laden too dangerous to the United States to live.

In the middle of the debate over bin Laden, the destroyer USS *Cole* was attacked in its Aden, Yemen, harbor on October 12, 2000. A small boat filled with explosives blew up alongside the *Cole*, killing nineteen American sailors and wounding scores more. This incident shocked the analysts in the Counterterrorism Center because there had been no intelligence indicating that something like this was going to happen. It took awhile for the analysts to find the evidence connecting this attack with al-Qaeda, but the evidence was found. Counterterrorism Center staffers wanted retaliation, but the American military was reluctant to undertake any operations and so advised the White House. To the leadership of the Counterterrorism Center the only option was to support the Afghan leader General Massoud and his war against the Taliban. But the Clinton administration was reluctant to back Massoud and forbade the Counterterrorism Center from increasing aid. The Clinton administration left office with the problem of bin Laden and al-Qaeda unresolved.

The analysts of the Counterterrorism Center continued to be frustrated by inaction of the Bush administration toward terrorism. Reports indicated increased activity by al-Qaeda, but the problem was that there was no evidence of where or what kind of operation it was going to undertake. A series of warnings came out of the Counterterrorism Center that Tenet took to President Bush and other prominent administration figures. These warnings coincided with similar warnings from the FBI. Some of these warning even made the case that al-Qaeda operatives might carry out an operation in the United States. What weakened these frequent warnings was the lack of specific details. The Bush administration listened to the warnings, noted the lack of specifics, and took no action. President Bush wanted more specific intelligence before he would authorize any action.

Tenet ordered the CIA to round up suspected al-Qaeda members to try to find out information on what al-Qaeda was planning. This tactic had two purposes: to gather intelligence and to delay al-Qaeda missions. Several al-Qaeda plots were uncovered, and a massive amount of intelligence material arrived at the Counterterrorism Center. The problem was that there were not enough translators and analysts to handle this mass of material. Frustration was high among the intelligence analysts because they were fearful that important information was being overlooked. In mid-July, Tenet ordered the Counterterrorism Center analysts to search back in its files and its current information on bin Laden's major plots. He was suspicious that bin Laden might be targeting the United States for a terrorism mission. Tenet took what information the Counterterrorism Center had uncovered and presented the report "Bin Laden Determined to Strike in United States" to President Bush at his Crawford, Texas, ranch on August 6, 2001. In early September the Bush administration began to consider a plan to attack terrorism, especially bin Laden and al-Qaeda, but there was no sense of haste.

After September 11, resources flowed into the Counterterrorism Center. By the summer of 2002, George Tenet had expanded its staff to 1,500. This size staff was able to handle 2,500 classified electronic communications a day, and it could produce 500 terrorist reports a month.

The Counterterrorism Center was also given the responsibility for the interrogations of important al-Qaeda prisoners. A series of secret interrogation centers were established in friendly countries. Top al-Qaeda prisoners were kept at an interrogation center, Bright Lights, the location of which even analysts in the Counterterrorism Center had not been informed of. These interrogations are ongoing, with some of the information making it back to intelligence circles. There have also been reports of CIA interrogators using questionable interrogation techniques, so that the FBI wants nothing to do with these interrogations. Several news reports have confirmed this information, and CIA agents have become increasingly uncomfortable about their legal position over these interrogations. This nervousness about interrogation techniques led to controversy in December 2007, when news surfaced that the secret tapes of CIA interrogations had been destroyed in 2005. This action has been defended by the head of the CIA Michael V. Hayden, but there are congressional efforts to hold hearings on whether this action was illegal.

See Also
Alec Station; Bush Administration; Central Intelligence Agency; Clinton Administration; Tenet, George

See Documents
Document #5; Document #26; Document #42

Suggested Reading
Steve Coll, *Ghost Wars: The Secret History of the CIA, Afghanistan, and Bin Laden, from the Soviet Invasion to September 10, 2001* (New York: Penguin Books, 2004); Ronald Kessler, *The CIA at War: Inside the Secret Campaign against Terror* (New York: St. Martin's Griffin, 2003); Greg Miller, "CIA Destroyed Secret Tapes of Interrogations," *Los Angeles Times* (December 7, 2007), p. A1; John Miller, Michael Stone, and Chris Mitchell, *The Cell: Inside the 9/11 Plot, and Why the FBI and CIA Failed to Stop It* (New York: Hyperion, 2002); Timothy Naftali, *Blind Spot: The Secret History of American Counterterrorism* (New York: Basic Books, 2005); Gerald Posner, *Why America Slept: The Failure to Prevent 9/11* (New York: Ballantine Books, 2003); James Risen, *State of War: The Secret History of the CIA and the Bush Administration* (New York: Free Press, 2006); George Tenet and Bill Harlow, *At the Center of the Storm: My Years at the CIA* (New York: Harper Collins, 2007).

D

Dahl, Jason Matthew (1957–2001)

Jason Dahl was the captain of the crew of United Airlines Flight 93, which was hijacked and crashed on September 11, 2001. He had a training position with United Airlines in its Denver training center, but he took the flight on September 11 to keep his flight certification current. He had picked this flight to enable him to be in Denver in time for his fifth wedding anniversary.

Dahl had an unremarkable childhood. He was born on November 2, 1957, in San Jose, California, the youngest child of a family with three boys and two girls. His father was a railroad switchman who later started a milk-delivery business, and his mother was a housewife. Dahl attended Hillsdale Elementary School. When he was in junior high school, one of his older brothers, Army Specialist 4th Class Kenneth Dahl, died in combat in South Vietnam. Dahl graduated from Andrew Hill High School in San Jose.

From childhood onward, all Dahl wanted to do was fly an airplane. At age thirteen he joined the Civil Air Patrol and won a scholarship for flying lessons. By age sixteen, he was flying solo and always trying to find ways to gain flying time. He attended San Jose State University, from which he graduated in 1980 with a degree in aeronautical engineering. After a tour as a corporate pilot, he obtained a job in 1984 with United Airlines. Years of flying later, Dahl became a flight instructor in the Denver training center. His job was training and testing other pilots. This position meant that he had to arrange flights to retain his flying status. After a failed first marriage and a son, Dahl married Sandy Dahl, a flight attendant with United Airlines. Dahl had started a month-on, month-off program so that he could spend more time with his family.

Dahl assumed command of United Airlines Flight 93 with the expectation that the flight from Newark International Airport to San Francisco International Airport would be routine. His first officer was LeRoy Homer. Everything seemed normal until the hijackers led by Ziad Jarrah invaded the cockpit and seized control of the aircraft at around 9:45 a.m. In the scuffle both Dahl and Homer were injured—how seriously nobody knows. There were both restrained when Jarrah turned the aircraft around and headed toward the Washington, D.C., area. Once the passengers and crew realized from cell phone conversations that the hijackers were on a suicide mission, the passengers revolted and attempted to regain control of the cockpit. There is speculation coming from the black box recording that Dahl and Homer attempted to help, but all of their efforts failed as Jarrah crashed the aircraft into the ground. There were no survivors.

Dahl has been honored as one of the heroes of United Airlines Flight 93. The elementary school he attended was renamed the Captain Jason M. Dahl Elementary School in March 2002. Other tributes to his life from friends and acquaintances have appeared in the succeeding years.

See Also
Beamer, Todd Morgan; Homer, LeRoy Wilton Jr.; Jarrah, Ziad Samir; United Airlines Flight 93

Suggested Reading
Robert Sanchez, "Fallen Eagle, Falling Tears," *Rocky Mountain News* [Denver] (September 7, 2002), p. 6S; Michael Sangiacomo, "Flight 93 Pilot's Family Recalls a Man and a Life," *Plain Dealer* [Cleveland] (September 11, 2002), p. A8; Robert Sanchez, "Pilot's Survivors Battle Pain," *Rocky Mountain News* [Denver] (September 10, 2003), p. 6A.

DCA

Flight attendants have a close-knit community, and the loss of so many flight attendants on September 11 caused American Airlines attendants to form a support group in the Washington, D.C., area. They named this support group the DCA after the codename for Washington National Airport. During the five days when the airline industry was shut down, the DCA set up what the flight attendants called the DCA Gathering Place at a local hotel in Washington, D.C. They rented a room with TV outlets, ordered food, and made sure that the hotel kept away lawyers and the media.

The DCA's first step was to get the word out to flight attendants and pilots of all the airlines who had been stranded to let them know about the DCA Gathering Place. This site became a clearinghouse for stranded flight attendants and pilots needing to contact their families. Members of the DCA also used the place to mourn the loss of close friends. A call went out to counselors and clergy to help provide emotional support. The DCA Gathering Place became a place where attendants could comfort each other and remember their fallen colleagues. Some of the flight attendants brought their children because they did not want to mourn alone. Even some pilots dropped by for help with handling their grief.

American Airlines Flight 77 had taken off from Dulles International Airport, so all of the DCA members knew the pilots and crew. They were particularly upset at the loss of the pilot Charles "Chic" Burlingame, copilot David Charlebois, and the flight attendants Michelle Heidenberger, Renee May, and the married couple, Ken and Jennifer Lewis. The members of the DCA could envision themselves in a similar situation, and they were angry that no training had been provided for suicidal hijackers. All of their training had been to be passive with hijackers until authorities could handle the situation on the ground.

After five days, the airlines started resuming air service, and it appeared that the DCA would terminate activities. On September 15, 2001, DCA flight attendants greeted with flowers the arrival of flights at Dulles American Airlines gates. Afterward, the DCA Gathering Place closed, but one of the members suggested that the DCA continue its activities in other venues.

DCA members decided to continue the DCA by having it donate to charity projects in the names of the flight attendants lost on September 11. The first project was for a Christmas toy drive in the name of Michelle Heidenberger at the St. Ann's Home for Unwed Mothers and Abused Children in Baltimore. Heidenberger had served as a volunteer worker at St. Ann's on her off-duty hours, so this annual drive was a natural. A call went out in December 2001 for teddy bears, and so many arrived that a truck was needed to carry all the bears. The next year, the DCA conducted a similar drive for more toys, a TV, VCR, and DVD player with a video library with more than a thousand titles.

The next DCA project was honoring the memories of Ken and Jennifer Lewis. They had been such a close-knit couple that the flight attendants had named them Kennifer. They had lived in Culpepper, Virginia, so the DCA decided to build a Kennifer Memorial Garden in Culpepper. In September 2002 members of the DCA started to build the memorial with the help of hundreds of volunteers. It took three days to build the garden. There was a formal ceremony to commemorate the garden just before September 11, 2002. It had inscribed on a marble bench the words "KENNIFER: KEN AND JENNIFER LEWIS, SEPTEMBER 11, 2001. AA/77."

Other projects have also been undertaken. A memorial was established at the Walters Museum in Baltimore, in the memory of Renee May. May had done volunteer work there, helping make the building accessible to blind children and soliciting funds to buy books in braille. Members of the DCA are still looking for ways to memorialize other victims on American Airlines Flight 77.

See Also
American Airlines Flight 77; Burlingame, Charles Frank "Chic" III

Suggested Reading
Tom Murphy, *Reclaiming the Sky: 9/11 and the Untold Story of the Men and Women Who Kept America Flying* (New York: AMACOM, 2007).

Department of Design and Construction

The Department of Design and Construction (DDC) of New York City had the overall responsibility for the cleanup of the World Trade Center complex after September 11. Before September 11, the DDC was an obscure department in New York City government. Mayor Rudolph Giuliani had created the DDC in 1996 to oversee the work of building and repairing the municipal infrastructure. By New York City standards the DDC was a small department, with only 1,300 employees. But it had a $3.7 billion design and construction budget. Despite this budget, it was so obscure in the city's administrative hierarchy that the department was not even mentioned in the city's official emergency-response plan.

What made the DDC unique was that its head, Kenneth Holden, and his chief lieutenant, Michael Burton, took charge of the World Trade Center site immediately after the twin towers collapsed and began directing operations. Without authority and without permission, they began to recruit engineers and schedule heavy equipment at the site. Holden was familiar with the construction companies in the New York City area, and he bypassed ordinary bidding procedures to employ four companies: AMEC, Bovis, Tully, and Turner. He made the decision based on personal and corporate reputations. These companies earned immense profits in the cleanup, but they were also at risk financially because the companies never received adequate insurance for the job. Holden and Burton were so successful in mobilizing resources that Mayor Giuliani assigned the DDC to oversee operations at the World Trade Center complex site.

The first task of the Department of Design and Construction was to survey the site. At the first survey of Ground Zero, Holden and Burton escorted representatives from the construction firms, and Richard Tomasetti from the well-respected engineering firm of Thornton-Tomasetti. After this initial survey, six engineers spent two weeks mapping the debris pile. They divided the pile into four quadrants. One quadrant each was assigned to AMEC, Bovis, Tully, and Turner. Except for Tully each of the construction companies was a multinational corporation in the high-rise construction business, and they had little equipment at their disposal. Tully was a family-owned New York paving contractor with little experience in building construction, but it had all the necessary trucks and heavy equipment. All of the companies had experience dealing with the DDC. Within a few weeks there were 3,000 construction workers at the World Trade Center site.

Burton also hired a New Jersey outfit, Weeks Marine, to supply barges to haul the debris from the World Trade Center complex. Until this decision, the trucks hauling the debris were overwhelming the city's transportation system. Marty Corcoran, a marine-construction engineer, persuaded Burton to award the job to Weeks Marine. This decision simplified the debris removal.

Running a complex operation like the cleanup at Ground Zero was a thankless task. Holden's job was to find resources for the cleanup, defend the DDC from political attacks, and allow Burton to do his job. Burton had the responsibility of overseeing the practical details of the cleanup. Together they were an effective team, but they were not without their critics. Both Holden and Burton were hard drivers, and their goal was to clear the debris as soon as possible. There was also the task of

---

Explanation Why the Department of Design and Construction Became So Important after September 11

The agency charged with the managing the physical work was an unlikely one. It was the Department of Design and Construction (DDC), an obscure bureaucracy 1,300 strong whose normal responsibility was to oversee municipal construction contracts—for sidewalk and street repairs, jails, and the like—and whose offices were not even in Manhattan but in Queens. The DDC was given the lead for the simple reason that its two top officials, a man named Kenneth Holden and his lieutenant, Michael Burton, had emerged from the chaos of September 11 as the most effective of the responders. Now they found themselves running a billion-dollar operation with the focus of the nation upon them.

William Langewiesche, *American Ground: Unbuilding the World Trade Center* (New York: North Point Press, 2002), p. 9.

Different Ways the Construction Companies Handled the Cleanup

"Four of the world's largest construction companies were onsite doing the debris clean-up. But if you went from corner to corner to corner, they were all doing it differently. Who was the most efficient and who was the best? That's where the debris people came in and said, 'Hey, if you move this to that site, then you won't have to handle it three times' We worked with those kinds of things."

Comment of Major Kally Eastman, U.S. Army Corps of Engineers, cited in Susan Hagen and Mary Carouba, *Women at Ground Zero: Stories of Courage and Compassion* (New York: Alpha Books, 2002), p. 240.

meeting with all the representatives of interested parties and coordinating activities. To expedite decision making there were twice-a-day meetings in which each interested party had to appear, because decisions were made and orders given out verbally.

The firefighters were unhappy about the fast pace of the debris removal. They blamed Holden, Burton, and the DDC in general for disrespect for the dead. Holden soon became known as the "Trade Center Czar." This resentment led in part to the riot by firefighters on November 2, 2001. In a meeting on November 12, 2001, families of lost firefighters attacked Burton for the rapid pace of debris removal.

Unhappiness over the pace of debris removal continued until the end of the cleanup in May 2002. Some of the responsibility for the cleanup shifted to private companies beginning in December 2001, but the DDC continued to play a major role in decision making. After May 2002, Holden was reappointed to the DDC, but Burton left for another position. Their personal relationship had never been a happy one, and the tensions of the months after September 11 only intensified the strain of their working together.

See Also
Cleanup Operations at Ground Zero; Firefighters at Ground Zero; Giuliani, Rudolph William Louis "Rudy" III

Suggested Reading
Diane Cardwell, "Workers and Residents Are Safe, Officials Say," *New York Times* (November 2, 2001), p. B10; Greg Gittrich, "Last Hard Days at WTC: Crews Ponder Toll As They Search Few Remaining Piles," *Daily News* [New York] (May 10, 2002), p. 8; James Glanz, "Ground-Penetrating Radar to Aid in Cleanup," *New York Times* (December 5, 2001), p. B8; James Glanz and Kenneth Chang, "Engineers Seek to Test Steel Before It Is Melted for Reuse," *New York Times* (September 29, 2001), p. B9; James Glanz and Eric Lipton, "City Had Been Warned of Fuel Tank at 7 World Trade Center," *New York Times* (December 20, 2001), p. B1; William Langewiesche, *American Ground: Unbuilding the World Trade Center* (New York: North Point Press, 2002); Dennis Overbye, "Experts' Eyes Focus on 'the Bathtub' as Debris Is Cleared," *New York Times* (December 4, 2001), p. F3.

Disaster Mortuary Operation Response Team

The most difficult problem facing the authorities after the recovery of remains of victims of the September 11 attacks was identifying the victims. It was a horrendous business at all three sites—World Trade Center complex, the Pentagon, and the United Airlines Flight 93 crash site. Into this void stepped the Disaster Mortuary Operation Response Team (DMORT) movement. Teams from DMORT were to assist local authorities in the handling and identification of bodies or body parts. In New York City, the Office of the Chief Medical Examiner (OCME) was in charge overall.

In the early 1980s the National Funeral Directors Association saw the need for a rapid deployment of mortuary operations in the event of large-scale disasters. To correspond to this need the association formed the Disaster Mortuary Operation Response Team concept. It was a multidisciplinary, nonprofit organization of forensic practitioners capable of responding in the event of a massive loss of life due to a disaster. In 1996 Congress passed the Family Assistance Act, which augmented the mission of the DMORT. On the eve of September 11, 2001, DMORT had two specialized Disaster Portable Morgue Units (DPMUs) stationed at the Federal Emergency Management Agency (FEMA) Logistic Centers in Rockwell, Maryland, and in San Jose, California. These DMORT teams had all the specialists necessary to handle a disaster with huge loss of life: medical examiners, forensic pathologists, forensic anthropologists, fingerprint specialists, forensic orthodontists, DNA specialists, mental health specialists, and an administrative staff to coordinate their activities.

DMORT teams operated at all of the September 11, 2001, sites. This meant that the two teams of specialists had to be subdivided into three parts. Reduction in the number of specialists at any one site led the DMORT teams to draw on local medical volunteers. There was no lack of competent medical personnel ready to volunteer their services.

Because of the nature of the crashes and collapsing buildings, most of the identification of victims has come from recovered body parts. Morgue workers systematically processed each body part individually. It was then catalogued and assigned a number, photographed, x-rayed, and examined further for some kind of identifying characteristic. For those that could not be identified from dental records or some distinguishing characteristic other than DNA, analysis was necessary. This process meant taking DNA samples from family members. DNA analysis allowed an amazing number of victims to be identified, especially at the United Airlines Flight 93 crash site near Shanksville, Pennsylvania. Ultimately, everyone on that plane was identified from body parts at this site. It was much more difficult at the other sites. It was especially difficult at the World Trade Center because the high-temperature fire and changes of temperature caused the DNA to deteriorate, making identification sometimes impossible.

> **DMORT in Action after September 11**
>
> To begin with, even within those short tours, it was possible to make personal friendships with the DMORT teams, similar to the quick relationships forged on vacations or other special occasions. . . . One DMORT member, a woman from Sioux City, Iowa, became so good at reviewing the data input that we named one of the computer screens after her. Others returned more than once, and a few became semipermanent. For them, it was long shifts with no days off. One semipermanent DMORT member observed that life in the conference room consisted of long periods of boredom punctuated by short bursts of panic.
>
> Adrian Jones, "The Days of the Remains," in Yael Danieli and Robert L. Dingman (eds.), *On the Ground after September 11: Mental Health Responses and Practical Knowledge Gained* (New York: Haworth Maltreatment and Trauma Press, 2005), p. 328.

The huge number of deaths at the World Trade Center and the nature of the deaths made it impossible to identify all of the victims. There were more complete bodies found there, but others were so affected by the combination of high-temperature fires and the weight of the collapsing buildings that they simply disappeared. Even with the help of non-DMORT forensic help in New York City, the task verged on the impossible. Because of the heavy demands on the DNA-processing centers around the country, some of the identification took longer than usual and upset some of the families of the victims, but there was no way to rush the process. Once an identification was made, the families were contacted and given various options on what to do with the remains. Some families wanted to wait and see if more remains could be identified, but other families wanted closure and accepted the identified remains for burial services. Remains that nobody claimed were disposed of in a dignified way.

One of the problems with the slow identification process was that it caused difficulty for families needing to file legal papers for life insurance and other important legal documents without death certificates. This fact was more of a problem in Pennsylvania than in New York City, because officials there issued an affidavit that expedited death certificates. Two enterprising men from Pennsylvania offered a solution by calling for an Action of Declaratory Judgment that the court accepted after receiving corroborating evidence that there were no survivors on United Airlines Flight 93. It took only a month after September 11, 2001, for the death certificates to be issued.

See Also
Casualties of September 11; Pentagon Attack; United Airlines Flight 93; World Trade Center, September 11

Suggested Reading
Lawrence Hannah, "Sifting through Ground Zero," *Dominion Post* [Wellington, N.Z.] (September 14, 2002), p. 14; Adrian Jones, "The Days of the Remains," in Yael Danieli and Robert L. Dingman (eds.), *On the Ground after September 11: Mental Health Responses and Practical Knowledge Gained* (New York: Haworth Maltreatment and Trauma Press, 2005); Glenn J. Kashurba, *Quiet Courage: The Definitive Account of Flight 93 and Its Aftermath* (Somerset, PA: SAJ Publishing, 2006).

Dog Rescue and Recovery Teams
Dogs were the unsung heroes of the rescue and recovery at the World Trade Center complex site after September 11. More than 300 dogs worked at the World Trade Center site, of which between 50 and 60 were police dogs. All different types of dogs performed the invaluable service of locating survivors and then locating bodies and body parts. The dogs were divided into two types: search and rescue dogs and cadaver-sniffing dogs. The two types were trained differently. Search and rescue dogs reacted negatively to finding bodies or body parts. To the cadaver-sniffing dogs, it was their job to find remains. In the early days a search and rescue dog and a cadaver-sniffing dog would work as a team. Later, when it became apparent that there were no survivors, the cadaver-sniffing dogs took over.

Regardless of the type of dog, the dogs and their handlers climbed up and down over the debris. Some of the dogs had to wear booties to protect their paws from sharp objects and the heat coming from the debris pile. This duty was exhausting, and the dogs often took naps in stretchers, in beds of trucks, or on a pile of firefighting equipment. There was even a hospital trailer to treat the dogs for injuries. Cleanliness was important, and a bath improved the morale of the dog.

The cadaver-sniffing dogs were experts at finding bodies or body parts. A handler and the dog would traverse back and forth over the debris until the dog would stop and sniff. The dog would start pawing the ground. If a cadaver-sniffing dog got excited, digging and barking, there was a good chance a body or body part was nearby. The handler would then notify the firefighters, who would begin digging until the body or body part could be found. Since the dogs could detect any decomposing flesh, one time a dog smelled a side of beef from one of the restaurants in the World Trade Center. Sometimes, to keep up the morale of the dogs, a police officer would hide in the rubble so the dogs would hit upon a live person.

This action helped both search and rescue and cadaver-sniffing dogs from becoming too depressed.

Some of the dogs became celebrities. One such dog was a golden retriever named Bear. His fame came from finding the most bodies in the rubble, including that of Fire Chief Peter Ganci. He was featured in the *Guinness Book of World Records* as "the most celebrated dog in the world." He worked with his human partner, Scott Shields, who worked for a private safety firm. Not long after working at the World Trade Center site, Bear started having health problems. He developed cancer, arthritis, and other ailments associated with his work at the site. His veterinarian fees were $3,000. Bear was twelve years old when he died on September 23, 2002.

> **Description of One Dog Team at Ground Zero**
>
> Marley [black female Labrador retriever] and Bogush [Tampa Fire and Rescue Lieutenant Mark Bogush] were part of a team of eight people and four dogs from Tampa who arrived at ground zero after a long bus ride. . . . The handlers and their dogs worked 12-hour shifts, searching the rubble. Marley and Bogush rappelled down deep into the destruction, Marley riding piggyback on her handler. "The heat and dust was horribly thick," Bogush says. "It was very hard to see outside." Bogush would tend to Marley's needs by giving her plenty of water and flushing debris out of her nose and eyes.
>
> Mimi Rich, "Dogged Hero," *St. Petersburg Times* [Florida] (November 19, 2001), p. 3D.

Besides assisting in finding remains, dogs also provided another service. Fourteen certified teams of trauma-response dogs had come from around the

Scott Shields (right) gives his rescue dog Bear water from a bottle after exiting the World Trade Center disaster site in this September 13, 2001, photo. Bear died in 2002 from injuries incurred during recovery work from the crash site. (AP IMAGES/Beth A. Keiser, FILE.)

country to serve at Ground Zero. Some donor had provided airline tickets for these teams to come from as far away as Oregon. These affectionate dogs gave assistance to distraught workers who needed reassurance.

See Also
Cleanup Operations at Ground Zero; Ganci, Peter J. "Pete"

See Document
Document #17

Suggested Reading
David W. Ausmus, *In the Midst of Chaos: My 30 Days at Ground Zero* (Victoria, BC [Canada]: Trafford, 2004); Nicole Bode, "Human Pals Mourn WTC Hero Pooch," *Daily News* [New York] (October 28, 2002), p. 18; Mitchell Fink and Lois Mathias, *Never Forget: An Oral History of September 11, 2001* (New York: HarperCollins, 2002); Sarah Huntley, "Dog Handler Recounts Search at Ground Zero," *Rocky Mountain News* [Denver] (September 23, 2002), p. 6A.

Downey, Ray Matthew (1937–2001)

Ray Downey was the chief in charge of the Special Operations Command (SOC) in the Fire Department of New York (FDNY); he died at the World Trade Center complex on September 11, 2001. The Special Operations Command was an elite unit that included the Hazardous Materials (haz-mat) Unit, structural-collapse experts, a fire rescue unit, and two squads of elite firefighters. It had its headquarters on Roosevelt Island, and the SOC had its own budget. Downey and his command were natural candidates to be called to the World Trade Center complex on September 11.

Downey spent his entire career in firefighting. He was born on September 19, 1937. Most of his life Downey lived in Deer Park, Long Island. He was an enthusiastic hockey fan, and his favorite team was the New York Rangers. Downey joined the FDNY in 1962. His two older brothers had already joined, so he knew what to expect. Downey worked in several different fire houses in and around Times Square in Manhattan, and in Rescue Company 2 in Brooklyn. In 1972 Downey became a charter member of FDNY's hockey team, and he played on a hockey team until his death. By 1977 Downey had been promoted to captain, and he worked at the training school to create the first special operations squad—Squad 1. His next assignment was to command his former firehouse Rescue Company 2. After a few years there, he was assigned to the Special Operations Command. He became the resident expert in the FDNY on building collapses, and how to conduct rescues from collapsed buildings and those about to collapse. He was also the FDNY's most decorated member, with twenty-one citations for valor.

By the early 1990s Downey had a national reputation in working with building collapses. He was placed in charge of directing recovery work at the 1993 World Trade Center complex bombing. Then he was assigned to lead the FDNY's emergency rescue team that went to Oklahoma City in 1995 to assist with search and rescue efforts. He had long predicted that there would be another terrorist attack, and in May 2001 he had made a statement that "it's not a question of if, but when the next one comes." In late July 2001, the mayor and Downey's colleagues held an appreciation dinner at Gracie Mansion for his many accomplishments while a member of the FDNY. Downey had planned to retire from the department in 2002.

Downey rushed to the site of the World Trade Center complex on September 11, 2001, to help. His driver dropped him off at the command center near the North Tower shortly before the collapse of the South Tower. Using his expertise on collapsed buildings, Downey remarked that he was afraid that the towers might collapse. Soon afterward the South Tower collapsed. Responding to calls for help when the North Tower fell, Downey dove into the rubble and lost his life. It took over eight months to find his body. After a funeral on May 20, 2002, in Deer Park, Long Island, he was buried in a family plot in St. Charles Cemetery.

> **Personality and Reputation of Chief Raymond M. Downey**
>
> Raymond M. Downey was a tough, taciturn man in his late fifties, with piercing eyes, a shock of snow-white hair, and a poker face matched by a dry sense of humor—so dry that you might not know at first when he was joking. Ray was somewhat of an anomaly in our department, a man who had built an outside reputation because of his expertise in special operations such a building collapse. He had overseen the rescue operation after the World Trade Center bombing in 1993 and had headed the federal Urban Search and Rescue team that led the recovery following the Oklahoma City bombing in 1995. His extensive outside network and reputation gave him an unparalleled Rolodex when it came to tapping resources. It also won him the nickname "The Master of Disaster."
>
> Thomas Von Essen, *Strong of Heart: Life and Death in the Fire Department of New York* (New York: ReganBooks, 2002), pp. 172–173.

See Also

Casualties of September 11; World Trade Center Bombing (1993); World Trade Center, September 11

Suggested Reading

Michael Daly, "Magnificent Fire Chief's Last Call to Duty, *Daily News* [New York] (September 13, 2001), p. 20; Steve Dunleavy, "There Are a Lot of Legends about Ray—They're All True," *New York Post* (May 21, 2002), p. 20; Jose Martinez, "Finest of Bravest Is Laid to Rest," *Daily News* [New York] (May 21, 2002), p. 8; Michele McPhee and Maki Becker, "9/11 Hero's Remains Are with Kin Now," *Daily News* [New York] (May 16, 2002), p. 9; Elizabeth Moore, "Raymond Matthew Downey: A Legend's Family Keeps Hope for Him Alive," *Newsday* [New York] (September 13, 2001), p. 19; Thomas Von Essen with Matt Murray, *Strong of Heart: Life and Death in the Fire Department of New York* (New York: ReganBooks, 2002).

E

Economic Impact of September 11

The financial impact of September 11 was devastating to New York City and to the commercial airline industry. It was this economic damage as much as the physical damage that had appealed to Osama bin Laden. He wanted to attack the United States at its source of strength and cause it economic distress. Bin Laden was partially successful, as property losses, particularly in New York City, were high. Southern Manhattan was the center of the New York City government and international finance, and both were paralyzed. Office buildings were empty, and the subways stopped running. The tens of thousands of people who lived below Canal Street were prevented from going there. All schools and bridges were closed. But where the economic impact was greatest and most long lasting was with the airline industry.

It took the American airline industry nearly five years to recover from September 11. Both American and United airlines lost two aircraft to the hijackers, but insurance covered most of those losses. What hurt the airlines was the loss of customers, many of whom were afraid to fly. Airports had been shut down around the country. Even ten days after September 11 the New York City airports were running 80 percent of their flights but with only 35 percent of passenger seats filled. Lost revenue from the three New York Airports was around $250 million a day.

Compounding the problem was the rocketing cost of oil and the higher aviation premiums from insurers. In the period from September 11, 2001, to September 2004, the airline industry lost $23 billion. In October 2001 airline passenger traffic dropped 23.2 percent in comparison to October 2000. An infusion of $1.5 million of federal aid helped the airline industry, but a series of bankruptcies occurred in the next few years. Only gradually have the airlines begun to creep back to financial health.

New York City had a massive loss of jobs and buildings. Job loss has been estimated at 143,000 a month, with lost wages of $2.8 billion. Nearly 70 percent of the jobs lost and 86 percent of the wages lost were to persons with well paying positions in finance, insurance, and banking. Building loss has been assessed at $34 billion, with only about half of the building loss insured at value. It has been estimated that the city lost $60 billion in revenue, with $82 million coming from lost parking ticket revenue alone.

The least long-lasting economic impact was with the stock market. On September 11, 2001, the hijacked aircraft crashed into the World Trade Center complex before the opening of the stock market. Damage to communications, evacuation orders, and rescue efforts led to the closing of the market for the next four days. When the stock market reopened on Monday, September 17, there was an immediate sell-off. On September 10, the Standard & Poor's 500 Index had closed at 1,092.54, and when trading closed on September 17 the index was at 891.10. By September 24, however, the stock market was climbing again. On October 11, the index closed at 1,097.43.

The American economy rebounded from the September 11 attacks within months. One reason that these attacks did not have a more lasting impact was that they were concentrated by geography and industry. Whereas New York City and to a lesser extent Washington, D.C., suffered economic dislocation from unemployment and property damage, the rest of the country was left relatively untouched.

See Also
World Trade Center, September 11

Suggested Reading
Katherine Griffiths, "US Airline Industry in Tailspin to Disaster," *Independent* [London] (September 10, 2004), p. 46; Mark Kawar, "9/11 Shock Didn't Bring Bears to Stock Market," *Omaha World Herald* (September 17, 2002), p. 1D; Lydia Polgreen, "Study Confirms 9/11 Impact on New York City Economy," *New York Times* (June 30, 2004), p. B6; Sam Zuckerman, "9/11 Before & After: It's the Rebound, Stupid," *San Francisco Chronicle* (December 30, 2001), p. D7.

F

Fadl, Jamal al- (1963–)

American intelligence received its first full disclosure about the capabilities of al-Qaeda from a series of interviews with Jamal al-Fadl beginning in 1996. He had been a low-level member of al-Qaeda before he defected to the Americans. Al-Fadl asserted that he had important information to pass to American intelligence in a series of interviews with American intelligence officials in Eritrea. These officials decided that al-Fadl would be a reliable and valuable source of intelligence and sent him to the United States. His interrogation over the next five years produced a gold mine of information about al-Qaeda and its operations up to 1996.

Al-Fadl was a Sudanese from a relatively affluent family. He was born in 1963 in Rufaa City, Sudan, near Khartoum. After graduation from high school, he went to Saudi Arabia, where he lived on the fringes of society. His roommate was apprehended for possession of marijuana, after which al-Fadl looked to move to another country. He immigrated to the United States in 1986. In his new country, al-Fadl held two jobs: working in a grocery store in Brooklyn, New York, and raising funds for the al-Kifah Refugee Services Office, where his boss was Mustafa Shalabi. Another, unofficial part of his job was to recruit fighters for the Afghan side in the war against the Soviets in Afghanistan.

In time, it was al-Fadl's turn to go to Afghanistan to fight the Soviets. He traveled to Afghanistan, where he attended an al-Qaeda training camp at Khalid ibn Walid. His forty-five days there were filled with weapons training and religious indoctrination. Next, al-Fadl was sent to other training camps for further training. It was about this time that al-Fadl met Osama bin Laden. After completing his training, he joined a combat unit in Afghanistan.

Most of al-Fadl's later training was aimed at turning him into an administrator. As the war in Afghanistan drew to an end with the withdrawal of the Soviet forces, his responsibilities had increasingly transformed his job into an administrative one. Al-Fadl was present at the meeting, in the fall of 1989, where the establishment of al-Qaeda was announced by Abu Ubaidah al-Banshiri, head of the military committee of the Shura (Consulting) Council. Al-Fadl was the third signatory of the document on which the participants pledged their allegiance to al-Qaeda.

Al-Fadl carried out a variety of tasks for al-Qaeda. Besides performing routine courier work, al-Fadl was also appointed as the point man for Osama bin Laden's move from Afghanistan to Sudan. Because al-Fadl was a Sudanese citizen, it was easy for him to buy property for al-Qaeda in his native country. Another one of his crucial missions was to inquire about the availability of chemical weapons in the international underground market. Finally, he was given the task of finding out the availability of weapons-grade uranium. Both of these missions ended in failure.

By the early 1990s al-Fadl was becoming increasingly discontent with his role in al-Qaeda. He believed that others were being rewarded more for their work than he was. He made his feelings known to bin Laden; however, his complaints fell on deaf ears, with bin Laden simply telling him to get back to work. Al-Fadl's salary as an officer in al-Qaeda was $700 a month with health benefits. Others in the organization with similar responsibilities made much more. In retaliation, al-Fadl began to skim funds off the top of the deals he made on behalf of the organization. He was able to accumulate $250,000 before his peers in al-Qaeda caught on to his scheme in 1995. Al-Fadl promised restitution, but he then went into hiding. Uncertain of his fate if he stayed in al-Qaeda, al-Fadl took the first opportunity to turn himself over to American intelligence officers in Eritrea.

Al-Fadl was too low ranking a member to have useful information about possible future terrorist plots, but his information regarding the inner workings of al-Qaeda has been invaluable. Al-Qaeda's terrorist campaign started in 1995, and al-Fadl was already on the outs with the organization by that time. What he did have knowledge about was how al-Qaeda was organized, its leadership structure, and its philosophy. The 9/11 plot had not yet been contemplated by al-Qaeda, but al-Fadl's testimony showed that al-Qaeda was capable of almost anything.

Al-Fadl has remained under the protection of the U.S. government. He pleaded guilty to multiple counts of conspiracy against the United States, charges that carried a maximum prison sentence of fifteen years. Ultimately, the FBI kept him under house arrest for nearly two years before moving him and his family into the Witness Protection Program. Al-Fadl testified against Wadih el Hage with respect to Hage's role in the bombings of the U.S. embassies in Nairobi, Kenya, and Dar es Salaam, Tanzania. Since September 11, al-Fadl has been in constant demand by intelligence organizations for his extensive knowledge of the operations of al-Qaeda.

See Also
Bin Laden, Osama; Hage, Wadih el-; Qaeda, al-

Suggested Reading
John Miller, Michael Stone, and Chris Mitchell, *The Cell: Inside the 9/11 Plot and Why the FBI and CIA Failed to Stop It* (New York: Hyperion, 2002); Timothy Naftali, *Blind Spot: The Secret History of American Counterterrorism* (New York: Basic Books, 2005).

Fahrenheit 9/11

Fahrenheit 9/11 is an award-winning documentary by the filmmaker Michael Moore. It is highly controversial because of its pronounced bias against President Bush and his policies. The documentary opened in movie theaters across the United States on June 25, 2004, and it received mixed reviews, which often reflected the political persuasion and beliefs of the reviewers. Moore had a reputation for making documentaries that evinced a liberal bias, and this documentary fits into that category as well.

The film highlights President George W. Bush's conduct before and after the events of September 11. Moore is particularly harsh toward President Bush's passivity and apparent lack of action against the threat of terrorism before September 11. In his documentary, Moore reported that Bush spent 42 percent of his time on vacation in the period leading up to September 11. Moore also spotlighted the close personal and business relationship between President Bush (and his family) and the Saudi regime. This relationship led to the evacuation of the bin Laden family from the United States just after September 11 in such haste there was no time for debriefing by law enforcement and intelligence officials. Moore was also highly critical of the rationale for the invasion of Iraq. Finally, Moore criticized the national media for cheering on the Bush administration's war against terror and the invasion of Iraq.

Even before its appearance in movie theaters, the documentary was so controversial that it had trouble finding a distributor. Harvey Weinstein, the CEO of Miramax Films, had provided most of the $6 million financial support for the documentary. Miramax is a subsidiary of Walt Disney Company, and Michael Eisner, then the CEO of Walt Disney Company, refused to allow Miramax to distribute the film. This decision was made by Eisner despite the fact that he had not yet seen the documentary. Moore claimed that Eisner had been concerned about retaliation from Florida Governor Jeb Bush, the brother of George W. Bush, concerning Disney's real estate holdings and other interests in Florida. In the trade journals it was already common knowledge that *Fahrenheit 9/11* was going to be a hot property and that it would draw interest from a number of distributors. Weinstein discussed the issue with Eisner, but he lost the argument and the documentary was ultimately not distributed by Miramax. Moore then turned to a second distributor, Lions Gate Entertainment Corporation, which was a Canadian distributor based in Vancouver, British Columbia. To handle such a large booking Lions Gate had to conclude a secondary partnership with IFC Films and Fellowship Adventure Group.

The documentary has been fabulously successful financially. During its opening weekend (July 25–27, 2004), it generated box office revenues of $23.9 million in the United States and Canada despite opening in only about 40 percent of the theaters normally available for top-flight movies. In less than a year the documentary had grossed over $120 million in the United States and over $220 million worldwide. Because of its anti-Bush theme and opposition to the Iraq War, the documentary was an international bestseller. Moore decided to release the documentary in a DVD format, which was made available in stores on October 5, 2004. Around 2 million copies of the DVD were sold on the first day.

Besides producing controversy, the documentary has also received some critical acclaim. In April 2004 the documentary was entered to compete for the prestigious *Palme d'Or* (Golden Palm) Award at the 57th Cannes Film Festival. It was received with great fanfare at its first showing. The nine-person panel for the award had four Americans and only one Frenchman on it. They voted for *Fahrenheit 9/11* as the winner of the 2004 *Palme d'Or* award.

Supporters of President Bush and the conservative movement tried in various ways to block the release of the documentary. They were worried that the documentary might have a negative effect on the 2004 reelection campaign of President Bush. Organizations such as Patriotic Americans Boycotting Anti-American Hollywood (PABAAH) launched an anti-Moore campaign. Subsequently, some Bush supporters held an anti-Moore film festival, called the American Film Renaissance, in Texas, showing films that attacked Moore and his views regarding the Bush administration. The key feature was Michael Wilson's film *Michael Moore Hates America*. To counter the charges from conservatives that he distorted facts in his documentary, Moore hired a staff of researchers and two lawyers to check the facts and claims in *Fahrenheit 9/11*. There appeared to have been a backlash against this anti-Moore campaign and the documentary continued to be shown in theaters, attracting more viewers and making money.

> **Michael Moore's Reaction to the Decision by Disney**
>
> Disney joining forces with the right-wing kooks who have come together to attempt to censor *Fahrenheit 9/11* must mean that Dumbo is now in charge of the company's strategic decisions. First, Disney tried to stop the movie from being released, and now it is aligning itself with the very people who are trying to intimidate the movie theaters from showing the movie. Even Daffy Duck would tell you this makes no sense. This latest development only further disproves what Michael Eisner had claimed about "politics" not being behind Disney's decision not to distribute *Fahrenheit 9/11*.
>
> Quoted in Gabriel Snyder, "'Fahrenheit' Foes Put 'Heart' into Disney Doc," *Daily Variety* (June 29, 2004), p. 1.

See Also

Bush, George W.; Bush Administration

Suggested Reading

William Booth, "'Fahrenheit 9/11' Too Hot for Disney?" *Washington Post* (May 6, 2004), p. C1; David Denby, "Michael Moore's Viciously Funny Attack on the Bush Administration," *New Yorker* (June 28, 2004), p. 108; Lawrence Donegan, and Paul Harris, "American Right Vows to Settle Score as Bush's Nemesis Turns Up the Heat," *Observer* [London] (June 27, 2004), p. 18; Patrick Goldstein, "Eisner Fumbles PR Stunt—and Show Biz Politics," *Gazette* [Montreal] (May 14, 2004), p. D1; Gavin Smith, "Michael Moore Gives Much More," *New Statesman* (July 19, 2004), p. 1; A. O. Scott, "Moore's 'Fahrenheit 9/11' Wins Top Honors at Cannes," *New York Times* (May 23, 2004), p. 6; Wendy Stueck, "Lions Gate hits Jackpot with Fahrenheit 9/11 Distribution," *Globe and Mail* [Canada] (June 29, 2004), p. B1.

Families of Victims of September 11

Soon after September 11, 2001, the families of the victims began to organize into support groups. At first the families underwent a period of mourning. Many of the families did not even have the opportunity to give their loved ones a proper burial and achieve closure. Next, the families had to deal with the real-world repercussions of their loss in the form of financial liabilities and uncertainty. Government programs were available, but dealing with government bureaucracy was confusing and troubling for many of the survivors. Some family members were unable to cope without help. Various organizations and support groups were formed to help the families cope with their losses and to teach them how to handle their new responsibilities. Later, these organizations set up a formidable lobbying group to compel Congress and the Bush administration to examine how the events of September 11 could have happened and how they could have been prevented.

Difficulty of Families Coping with Loss of Loved Ones

I think people don't realize that there's never going to be closure for us. That finding a piece of my husband—I'm the luckiest of the unlucky. But yet I still can't have closure from that because it's not his whole being, and it still brings back the reality of how he died and how devastating it was, and the brutality of it. And I think people don't realize that they're still identifying remains, we're still getting calls. That brings us right back to him dying and his death. As long as that's going on, I always have that fear when somebody calls and I don't know who it is. Is it a telemarketer or is it someone telling me they found more of Patrick? I think it makes it harder when they keep replaying all the tapes. When most people die, you don't get a tape of it that's replayed on national TV. And we have to live with that and we don't have control over that. Most people, fortunately, don't have a tape of their loved one dying.

Interview with Mary Danahy in Julie Scelfo et al., "After 9-11: A Year of Change," *Newsweek* (September 9, 2002), p. 40.

The largest and one of the most active groups in the Families of Victims of 9/11 movement is known as the Voices of September 11. It is a nonprofit, nonpartisan organization founded by its current President Mary Fetchet in October 2001. Fetchet, a clinical social worker from New Canaan, Connecticut, lost her twenty-four-year old son in the collapse of the South Tower of the World Trade Center complex on September 11. Headquarters for the Voices of September 11 is in New Canaan. Fetchet and Beverly Eckert, an insurance specialist, started out by setting up an Internet clearinghouse for disseminating information about all aspects of September 11 for the families of the victims. The goal of the Voices of September 11 group has been to serve as an advocate for the 9/11 families. As one of the largest of the support groups for the 9/11 families, with around 5,500 members, it has proven to be a potent lobbying force. Fetchet and her colleagues in other groups fought hard for the creation of the 9/11 Commission. Fetchet has testified before several committees of Congress on the need to investigate what happened on September 11 and to understand why it happened.

Another leading 9/11 family group is the Families of September 11 (FOS11), a nonprofit organization founded in October 2001 by Donald W. Goodrich and Carie Lemarck. Both founders lost relatives on September 11. Families of September 11 attempts to be highly inclusive in its membership by admitting to membership families of the victims of September 11, survivors, and anyone who will support its mission. The primary goals of FOS11 are to support the families of the victims of September 11 by providing information on topics relevant to their situation and to engage in lobbying efforts on issues relating to the domestic and international efforts to combat terrorism. Representatives from FOS11 were active in lobbying for the creation of the 9/11 Commission, and they have campaigned for the Congressional implementation of the 9/11 Commission's recommendations.

The World Trade Center United Family Group, or WTC United, is another important member of the families of 9/11 movement. This nonprofit organization was established shortly after September 11. Its goal was to ensure that the memories and the legacies of the victims of 9/11 are protected. Members are also active in lobbying the U.S. Congress on issues important to them. All members of the board, except one, lost family members on September 11. The current board chair is Patricia Riley, whose sister, Lorraine Lee, died on September 11. This group has been active in working for the 9/11 Memorial to be built on the former World Trade Center complex site.

Mayor Michael R. Bloomberg appointed Christy Feret as New York City's liaison with various organizations representing the interests of the relatives of the victims of September 11. Her husband had been the executive director of the Port Authority of New York and New Jersey, and he died on September 11. It has been a stormy tenure in office for Feret because the families have been critical of many of the decisions made by the mayor's office. A major source of contention has been the proposed memorial to the victims of September 11 that is to be constructed on the World Trade Center complex site. The 9/11 families wanted the memorial to be built first, but the decision to

Family members of 9/11 victims testify on proposed intelligence reforms during a hearing by the Senate Government Affairs Committee on Capitol Hill in Washington, Tuesday, August 17, 2004. From left to right are Mary Fetchet, who lost her son Brad in the World Trade Center attack; Stephen Push of Washington, who heads Families of September 11 and whose wife died on American Airlines Fight 77; and Kristen Breitweiser, whose husband died in the World Trade Center attack. (AP IMAGES/Scott Applewhite.)

build the Freedom Tower first was made by Governor Pataki for financial and political reasons. Although the major decision had been made by Governor Pataki, the details of the decision became a source of contention between the mayor's office and representatives of the families. Other issues have also caused friction.

Where the families of 9/11 movement made the biggest impact was in the creation of the 9/11 Commission and the passage by Congress of most of that commission's recommendations. For almost two years representatives from the various groups formed by 9/11 families lobbied the halls of Congress and the White House for the establishment of such a commission. The Bush administration tried to stonewall the request, but eventually President Bush gave in and agreed to cooperate. President Bush's selection of Henry Kissinger to be the cochair of the commission was unsatisfactory to the families because of his business dealings with prominent Saudi families, including the Bin Laden family. The newly formed Family Steering Committee made it a condition of its support for the commission that members of the committee disclose their business ties, and Kissinger consequently resigned from the commission. Throughout the remainder of the activities of the 9/11 Commission, there was constant agitation by the Family Steering Committee and its subgroup, the Jersey Girls. Their biggest concern was that nobody was being held accountable for what had happened on September 11. Regardless, the Family Steering Committee and the other groups lobbied Congress for passage of the necessary legislation to implement the 9/11 Committee's recommendations.

See Also
Family Steering Committee; Jersey Girls; National Commission on Terrorist Attacks upon the United States

See Document
Document #32

Suggested Reading
Bob Braun, "Kean Feels the Wrath of Irate 9/11 Families," *Star-Ledger* (February 12, 2004), p. 1; Gail Russell Chaddock, "A Key Force behind the 9/11 Commission," *Christian Science Monitor* (March 25, 2004), p. 3; Thomas H. Kean, Lee H. Hamilton, and Benjamin Rhodes, *Without Precedent: The Inside Story of the 9/11 Commission* (New York: Knopf, 2006); Jerry Zremski, "Families of 9/11 Victims Urge Action on Report," *Buffalo News* (August 16, 2004), p. A1.

Family Assistance Center

One of the many tragic events in the aftermath of September 11 was the fact that families had to deal with federal and state agencies in order to receive financial assistance. In a single blow, families had lost their financial providers and bills kept coming in with relentless regularity. To handle this problem, the Federal Emergency Management Agency, with the cooperation of Mayor Giuliani's administration, set up the Family Assistance Center (FAC) on Pier 94 in the weeks following September 11. A large number of booths were set up by ten federal, state, and private agencies, covering an area the size of several football fields. These booths housed agencies ranging from the Red Cross to the Social Security Administration, and there was also a food service area. There were also interpreters available for almost every language imaginable. A second site was set up later at the former location of the New York State Department of Motor Vehicles. In the period from September 11 until the end of November 2001, more than 26,000 people sought help at one of the two Family Assistance Centers.

The goal of this gigantic financial flea market was to inform bereaved relatives on what financial support they were entitled to and how to obtain it. Many of the original users of the Family Assistance Centers came there seeking information on victims and their loved ones. As it became apparent that there would be no more survivors, people started coming for financial assistance. Red tape was cut to the minimum. One of the most valuable services was provided by the FBI as it offered assistance for defraying travel costs in bringing relatives to New York City to attend funerals.

Although the Family Assistance Center had been established in the weeks following September 11, help was initially slow in coming. Early in the process, the families had to cope with their problems on their own. Representatives from the various agencies were eager to help, and they attempted to make the process as easy as possible. Beginning in late September, Mayor Giuliani arranged to have nearly 500 lawyers appear at the Family Assistance Centers to help explain the legal details of the financial help process to the families. They explained the need for documentation of relationships. Under New York State law, a death certificate cannot be issued without a body unless either three years have passed since the death or a court hearing is held. What the lawyers helped to do was to shorten the legal process by attesting to affidavits on the deceased and having them notarized on the spot. This meant that papers could then be forwarded to a judge immediately for a court hearing. After an affidavit was approved by a judge, the judge then ordered the medical examiner to issue a death certificate.

It was not until early October that the first death certificates began to be issued. These death certificates allowed the widows, widowers, and other family members to begin to claim benefits at various agencies. It was a material and mechanical process because people were awarded benefits based on the nature of their relationship with the person who had died at the World Trade Center complex. Even significant others who could prove cohabitation received compensation. The main problem, of course, was the difficulties associated with attracting people to the FAC in the first place. Certain families were so grief stricken that they were unable to function with respect to processes associated with the demise of their loved ones. They were reluctant to show up even if the compensation they would receive was urgently necessary for paying rent and bills.

Firefighter families received special attention from the Fire Department of New York (FDNY). Although firefighters who had died on September 11 were initially kept on the Fire Department's payroll, this was only a temporary solution, and it was not going to last forever. Officers from the FDNY were assigned to the Family Assistance Center to assist the firefighters' families. They guided the families through the process, sometimes with widows having difficulty coping with their loss.

Immediate Reaction of Families to the Family Assistance Center

In the beginning, it was just a total sense of numbness with the families. Those first couple of weeks people were really just hanging on to the possibility that their loved ones were still going to be found, and so we would refer to the victims as a missing person, and we were always very careful about how we worded everything with the clients, never wanting to assume that this person was not coming home again. . . . It was also tough wanting to be able to make the process as easy for them as we possibly could, yet having guidelines and rules we have to follow. Dealing with their frustration of: "Why do you need my marriage certificate and if I don't have this do I have to come back tomorrow? I've been here all day waiting." People would say, "This has become my full-time job. This is all I do now: give my DNA sample and come here to file missing-persons reports."

Interview of Christy Gibney Carey, the director of the Family Assistance Center, in Julie Scelfo et al., "After 9-11: A Year of Change," *Newsweek* (September 9, 2002), p. 40.

See Also
Firefighters at Ground Zero

Suggested Reading
Nina Bernstein, "The Family Center; On Pier 94, a Welfare State That Works, and a Possible Model for the Future," *New York Times* (September 26, 2001), p. B9; John W. Bloom, "The Family Assistance Center at Pier 94," in Yael Danieli and Robert L. Dingman, eds., *On the Ground After September 11: Mental Health Responses and Practical Knowledge Gained* (New York: Haworth Maltreatment and Trauma Press, 2005); Alan J. Borsuk, "Air Centers Overflow with Attack Victims," *Milwaukee Journal Sentinel* (November 26, 2001), p. 1A; Shaila K. Dewan, "Death Certificates; A Grim Formality Is Made Easier for Families," *New York Times* (September 27, 2001), p. B10; Kevin Fagan, "Grim Reality Setting In for Survivors," *San Francisco Chronicle* (September 19, 2001), p. A3; John McCole, *The Second Tower's Down* (London: Robson Books, 2002); David Usborne, "The Bereaved—This Was the Day Relatives Finally Accepted Their Loved Ones Were Not Coming Home," *Independent* [London] (September 27, 2001), p. 3.

Family Steering Committee
The Family Steering Committee was an ad hoc group of twelve representatives from the families of 9/11 movement that had considerable influence on the founding and the operations of the 9/11 Commission. Eleven of the twelve members were women: Carol Ashley, Kristen Breitweiser, Patty Casazza, Beverly Eckert, Mary Fetchet, Monica Gabrielle, Mindy Keinberg, Carie Lemack, Sally Regenhard, Lorie Van Auken, and Robin Weiner. They had all lost relatives during the terrorist attacks on September 11, 2001. The only male member of the committee was Bill Harvey, whose wife, Sarah Manley, had been killed at the World Trade Center only a month after they were married.

A subgroup of the Family Steering Committee was the Jersey Girls. This small group of four women from New Jersey (Karen Breitweiser, Patty Casazza, Lorie Van Auken, and Mindy Keinberg) had all lost their husbands at the World Trade Center complex. Three of their husbands had been coworkers at Cantor Fitzgerald, a financial services firm on Wall Street. They had formed their group to lobby Congress and the White House to look more closely into what had happened on September 11. They insisted that there needed to be an inquiry into what had happened on September 11 and what had gone wrong. Members of this group worked the halls of Congress, and their vocal demands in the national media that the Bush administration cooperate finally led to the creation of the 9/11 Commission.

Once it became apparent that there was going to be a 9/11 Commission, the Jersey Girls and representatives of other family groups formed the Family Steering Committee. This ad hoc group took on the responsibility of chief watchdog and critic of the 9/11 Commission. Members had a number of complaints about the composition of the staff of the Commission, and they made their position well-known through the media. Members were particularly unhappy about the close Republican ties of the executive staff director, Philip Zelikow. They also placed considerable pressure on government agencies and the White House to produce the necessary governmental documents for the 9/11 Commission to carry out its investigation. When it became apparent that the White House was purposefully delaying the release of certain documents, the Family Steering Committee first placed pressure on Thomas Kean, the co-chair of the 9/11 Commission, to do something about it, and then the members lobbied for an extension of time for the 9/11 Com-

Patty Casazza (right), whose husband was killed in the 9/11 attacks, flashes a thumbs-up in support of the Intelligence Reform Bill as legislators line up to get cleared for a White House party, December 6, 2004. Others in the picture are Mary Fetchet (second from right) and, from right to left, Carol Ashley, Cane Le Wack, Bill Harvey, and Charles Wolf, all relatives of 9/11 victims. (AP IMAGES/Manuel Balce Ceneta.)

mittee. What disappointed the Family Steering Committee the most about the 9/11 Commission's report was the lack of accountability in its conclusions. The final report pointed out deficiencies, but no one was held accountable for bad decisions or the failure of key officials to do their jobs prior to September 11.

After the *9/11 Report* was issued, the members of the Family Steering Committee began lobbying Congress to pass the recommendations of the 9/11 Commission into law. They used their moral authority to confront members of Congress who were reluctant to act. One of their tactics was to keep a "watchdog list," comprising members of Congress who opposed the Commission's recommendations. When Republicans in Congress wanted to add extraneous antiterrorism language to a bill implementing the 9/11 Commission's recommendations, the Family Steering Committee opposed these additions. After the final passage of a streamlined bill that included most of the recommendations of the 9/11 Commission, the Family Steering Committee disbanded. Its mission had been accomplished, but this did not mean that the former members retired from the fray. They returned to their respective organizations to continue their activism on behalf of the families of the victims of 9/11 at a different organizational level.

See Also
Bush Administration; Jersey Girls; Kean, Thomas Howard; National Commission on Terrorist Attacks upon the United States

See Document
Document #32

Suggested Reading
Bob Braun, "Kean Feels the Wrath of Irate 9/11 Families," *Star-Ledger* (February 12, 2004), p. 1; Kristen Breitweiser, *Wake-Up Call: The Political Education of a 9/11 Widow* (New York: Warner Books, 2006); Gail Russell Chaddock, "A Key Force behind the 9/11 Commission," *Christian Science Monitor* (March 25, 2004), p. 3; Dan Eggen, "9/11 Panel May Seek Extension," *Washington Post* (November 27, 2003), p. A2; Edward Epstein, "Sept. 11 Families Want Intelligence Reforms, But Not GOP Plan," *San Francisco Chronicle* (September 29, 2004), p. A7; Jerry Zremski, "Families of 9/11 Victims Urge Action on Report," *Buffalo News* (August 16, 2004), p. A1.

Federal Aviation Administration (FAA)

The Federal Aviation Administration (FAA) has the authority and the responsibility to regulate and monitor all U.S. civil aviation. All functions of the Civil Aeronautics Administration (CAA) and the Civil Aviation Board (CAB) had been transferred to the FAA by the Federal Aviation Act of 1958. The FAA has a mandate to both regulate and promote civil aviation in a manner to best foster its development and safety. The FAA's dual responsibility—both to promote development and to provide safety—consists of two competing functions that were never reconciled. The FAA did not receive any Congressional guidelines on how to reconcile these competing functions, so market forces came to dominate the process. In time, the commercial airline industry was regulating the FAA. Even when Congress passed the 1996 Reauthorization Act under Title IV and tried to eliminate the word "promotion" from the description of the FAA's mandate by designating "assigning, maintaining, and enhancing safety and security as the highest priorities in air commerce," this Congressional mandate was implemented in only a cursory fashion. Before September 11, 2001, the FAA had other concerns that its leadership considered more pressing than international terrorism: safety, consumer service, capacity, and economic issues. Its mission was made doubly difficult by the fact that it lacked both the funding and personnel to enforce its regulations.

Cozy Relationship between the FAA and the Airline Industry

The broader outcome resulting from the minimalization of the FAA as a regulatory body was a disoriented, fragmented, and highly inefficient agency. A culture of compromise festered within the organization for years and came to permeate every level of it. Although isolated pockets of dedicated employees existed throughout the FAA, the majority of the leadership throughout the agency's history had been devoted to making things as easy as possible for the airlines. Even on the rare occasion when the FAA pushed back, the airlines were almost always able to leverage their influence both inside and outside of the agency to get what they wanted. As a result, FAA security policy was treated more as a political issue than a mandated responsibility.

Andrew R. Thomas, *Aviation Insecurity: The New Challenges of Air Travel* (Amherst, NY: Prometheus Books, 2003), pp. 55–56.

The FAA also had to face a powerful aviation lobby that wanted as few restrictions on their operations as possible. By 2000, the airline industry was spending $46,020,819 annually on lobbyists. The airline industry also gave large amounts of money to politicians running for Congress, mostly to Republicans. This lobby was particularly powerful on issues relating to regulation that might cost the airline industry money. In the 1960s the FAA had tried to introduce armed federal marshals on flights, but the pilots and the airlines feared the possibility of a shootout more than they feared the prospects of a hijacking. It took a series of aircraft hijackings in the late 1960s and early 1970s to persuade the federal government and the airline industry to set up a screening system for passengers and luggage, which went into effect on January 5, 1973. The FAA was less successful in getting airlines to install bulletproof cockpit doors. Moreover, there were numerous unclassified reports from various government agencies outlining the vulnerabilities of the American domestic commercial aviation system. The findings of these reports had been publicized in the mass media, and the problems they underlined were well-known within the aviation industry.

The commercial airlines tended to ignore warnings from American authorities. American intelligence warned the FAA and the airlines—Trans World Airlines, Pan American Airlines, and Delta—of the danger of a terrorist attack on aircrafts flying from Germany to the United States. Nothing was done by the airlines to institute special screening procedures for those flights. The result was the explosion of a luggage bomb that caused the downing of Pan Am Flight 103 over Lockerbie, Scotland, killing 259 crew and passengers and 11 people on the ground. After an exhaustive investigation, it was concluded that agents from Libya had planted the bomb.

By this time, there was a screening process at each airport in the United States, but it was so ineffective as to be considered almost a joke. Several times there had been tests of the security system and the system had failed miserably each time. But any efforts to upgrade the system were fought bitterly by the airline industry, because delays in the processing of passengers and luggage cost them money.

The FAA had a counterintelligence unit, but it had difficulty obtaining information from other government agencies. Its forty-person unit operated twenty-four hours per day collecting information to the extent that the FBI, CIA, and the State Department shared their intelligence with it. These agencies gave out only general information. The FAA had a no-fly list, but none of the September 11 hijackers were on it. In fact, the list had less than twenty names on it. The CIA had a list of suspected terrorists, but it was not shared with the FAA because the list was classified. Although the State Department had a watch list with 61,000 names on it, neither the FAA nor the airlines had access to the list. What is more significant is that the FAA did not want or ask for access to the watch list because the airlines would have been unwilling to check it because of cost and time constraints.

The FAA was completely unaware of any hijacking plots, but civil aviation security officials knew about Osama bin Laden and al-Qaeda's interest in plots aimed at civil aviation. They had intelligence dating from the 1990s that al-Qaeda affiliates were interested in hijackings and the possible use of aircraft as a weapon. Moreover, FAA intelligence analysts were aware of the increased intelligence activity forecasting possible terrorist acts in the summer of 2001. The FAA issued a series of alerts to air carriers about possible terrorist activity directed toward civil aviation operations. However, most of the FAA's concern was related to explosives being smuggled into aircraft. This had also been the main area of focus for the Commission on Aviation Safety and Security, also known as the Gore Commission, which President Clinton had authorized in 1996. That commission had been reluctant, however, to assume the role and duties of screening airport passengers and luggage because it would have meant hiring 50,000 new federal employees at a cost of several billion dollars at a time when the Clinton administration and Congress were busy cutting the number of federal employees and the federal budget.

Federal Aviation Administration starts its check on airline passengers with a process known as prescreening. Passenger prescreening begins with the ticketing process and concludes with the passenger check-in at the airport ticket counter. Prescreening occurs when passenger names are checked against the FAA's list of individuals known to pose a threat to commercial aviation. On September 11, 2001, there were only twelve names on the list, and none of the names of the 9/11 hijackers were on it. This meant that none of the 9/11 hijackers were subjected to extra security measures at the airport. The hijackers did have to go through the Computer-Assisted Passenger Prescreening Program (CAPPS) for examination of luggage for explosives. They all passed the CAPPS inspection because explosives were not part of their plot.

The checkpoint screening system failed miserably on September 11, 2001. Numerous studies had noted various weaknesses in the checkpoint screening system. The FAA had attempted since 1996 to set certification requirements for screening contractors, but these requirements had not been implemented by September 11, 2001. Counteracting these security efforts were FAA's instructions to checkpoint supervisors "to use common sense about what items should not be allowed on an aircraft." This loose definition of what was allowed created confusion among the screeners. Among the items that the nineteen hijackers carried through the checkpoint system were chemical sprays, utility knives, and box cutters. Even though utility knives were permissible under FAA regulations, box cutters and chemical sprays were not. Several of the hijackers set off alarms at security checkpoints; however, all of them were allowed to board their planes.

Two of the hijacked airliners had departed from Logan International Airport. Logan International Airport had long been known as one of the least secure airports in the United

---

Lack of Attention to FAA's Intelligence Unit by FAA Senior Management

Moreover, the FAA's intelligence unit did not receive much attention from the agency's leadership. Neither Administrator Jane Garvey nor her deputy routinely reviewed daily intelligence, and what they did see was screened for them. She was unaware of a great amount of hijacking threat information from her own intelligence unit, which, in turn, was not deeply involved in the agency's policymaking process. Historically, decisive security action took place only after a disaster had occurred or a specific plot had been discovered.

The 9/11 Commission Report: Final Report of the National Commission on Terrorist Attacks Upon the United States (New York: Norton, 2005), p. 83.

States. As the eighteenth busiest airport in the country, it had the fifth-highest number of security breaches from 1991 to 2000. The Massachusetts Port Authority (Massport) ran the airport and it had more security violations than any other airport authority in the United States. All of this was well-known before September 11, but nothing was done to rectify the situation. Even an April 2001 memorandum from Massport's Director of Security, Joe Lawless, on the need for Logan International Airport to address its known security vulnerabilities was ignored. Lawless had been a career law enforcement officer, who had worked as a state trooper and then provided security for former Massachusetts Governor William F. Weld. He had tried to institute mandatory criminal background checks on airline employees and subcontractors after discovering that the airline checks had failed to detect the criminal records of some employees. His reward for trying to improve security was to become a designated scapegoat for what happened at Logan International Airport on September 11, and he was subsequently demoted to a lower-level job.

Once the 9/11 terrorists had passed through the screening process and boarded, there were no impediments to a successful hijacking. Because these flights were domestic, federal marshals were not flying on them. Airlines had fought against having air marshals on domestic flights because of the expense and lost revenue of giving up a first-class seat. Cockpit doors had not been hardened; thus the hijackers would have had little difficulty breaking down the door of the cockpit. Although the cockpit doors were locked during the flight, the door was designed to withstand only 150 pounds of pressure.

Besides breaking down the cockpit door, there were two other ways for the hijackers to gain access to the cockpit. All flight attendants were required to carry keys to the cockpit at all times during the flight in case of an emergency. All it would take for a hijacker to gain control of a key was to assault the flight attendant and take the key away from him or her. The other way to gain access to the cockpit was to create such a disturbance that would ensure that the pilot or copilot would open the cockpit door, as required by regulations. Then the hijacker could overpower the pilot and walk into the cockpit without resistance.

The policy of the airlines at the time of the terrorist attacks was for flight crews not to fight against hijackers and to dissuade passengers from interfering. This policy was known as the "Common Strategy," and its premise was to placate the hijackers and get the plane on the ground where law enforcement teams could storm the aircraft. The safety of the aircraft and its passengers was paramount. What this policy failed to take into account was a suicide mission.

The FAA also had a mandate to notify NORAD (North American Aerospace Defense Command) in the event of a hijacking of an aircraft. In the event of a hijacking, a chain of command, which had been established expressly for this purpose, would have to be followed. Commercial pilots were to notify air traffic controllers by radio or a code 7500 transponder message. FAA controllers were then required to report the hijacking up a complicated and time-consuming multilayered chain of command, beginning with the Pentagon's National Military Command Center (NMCC). Then the NMCC was to request approval of military assistance to the aircraft involved in the hijacking from the Secretary of Defense. Only after receiving the necessary approval from the Secretary of Defense would NORAD issue orders for jets to scramble toward the hijacked aircraft. A flight of jets had orders to locate the aircraft and monitor it from a distance of five miles. This standard operating procedure (SOP) had no provision for encountering a hijacked airplane on a suicide mission. It would take a presidential order for the military jets to fire and shoot down an American commercial aircraft.

The FAA's response after the hijackings on September 11 was confused, and there was little reliance on the SOP upon contact with NORAD. The response on the ground was incredulous, confused, and unhurried. Nobody knew what to do. Never having experienced such a situation, the system failed to do anything useful.

As news of the hijackings of the four airlines spread, there were fears and rumors that other aircraft had been hijacked. One such erroneous report was disseminated by the Boston office of the FAA, which reported that a fifth aircraft had gone missing. This missing aircraft, according to the report, was Delta Flight 89. But Delta Flight 89 had not been hijacked and landed safely in Cleveland, Ohio, at about 9:47 a.m. This misinformation only added to the confusion of an already chaotic situation. Ultimately, 3,949 commercial aircraft landed at the closest available airport on orders from the FAA.

There were other irregularities in the immediate aftermath of the attacks. When the Herndon office of the FAA received a request at 9:07 a.m. on September 11 from the Boston Center to warn all pilots about possible cockpit invasions, the Herndon FAA did not send out the warning. Questioned about this by the 9/11 Commission, FAA personnel stated that it was not the FAA's responsibility to relay such a message.

The FAA ended up losing control of aviation security to the new Transportation Security Administration (TSA), but the airline industry's lobbyists made sure that the airline industry survived intact. These lobbyists were so successful that Congress passed and President George W. Bush signed the Air Transportation Safety and System Stabilization Act, which gave the airline industry $5 billion in grants and $10 billion in secured loans. Title IV of the Act offered 9/11 victims compensation of $1.6 million each in taxpayer money if they signed a waiver forgoing their right to sue the airlines for additional compensation. Title V of the law required the federal government to take over the responsibility and the cost of aviation security. After taking the money, airlines began to downsize, laying off about 20 percent of their staff in the next few years. The airlines also began cutting service to dozens of cities around the United States.

See Also
American Airlines Flight 11; American Airlines Flight 77; United Airlines Flight 93; United Airlines Flight 175

See Documents
Document #9; Document #10; Document #12; Document #35; Document #36

Suggested Reading
Tom Murphy, *Reclaiming the Sky: 9/11 and the Untold Story of the Men and Women Who Kept America Flying* (New York: AMACOM, 2007); Sean P. Murphy, "Logan Security Head Issued Warning: April Memo Noted Terrorist Activity," *Boston Globe* (April 7, 2002), p. 1; Sean P. Murphy, "In Letter before Attacks, FAA Urged Easing Background Checks, *Boston Globe* (December 12, 2001), p. B4; Timothy Naftali, *Blind Spot: The Secret History of American Counterterrorism* (New York: Basic Books, 2005); Andrew R. Thomas, *Aviation Insecurity:*

The New Challenges of Air Travel (Amherst, NY: Prometheus Books, 2003); Susan B. Trento and Joseph J. Trento, *Unsafe at Any Altitude: Failed Terrorism Investigations, Scapegoating 9/11, and the Shocking Truth about Aviation Security Today* (Hanover, NH: Steerforth Press, 2006).

Federal Bureau of Investigation (FBI)

The record of the Federal Bureau of Investigation (FBI) prior to September 11, 2001, has been controversial. Numerous times there were solid leads that might have led FBI agents to the Islamist extremists planning the attack, but the FBI failed to take advantage of those leads. Part of the difficulty was that the FBI had an "arrest and convict" mentality before 9/11. Its unofficial golden rule was that, whenever there was a possibility that intelligence gathering would conflict with the making of legal cases, intelligence gathering lost out.

Since the mid-1990s, the FBI has had expanded powers to investigate potential and actual terrorists. A 1995 presidential directive gave the FBI the lead authority in both investigating and preventing acts of terrorism wherever in the world American lives or American interests were threatened. Much like the CIA, the FBI was reluctant to share its intelligence information with other law enforcement agencies. The FBI used Rule 6E of the Federal Rules of Criminal Procedure, which states that information arising from grand jury testimony is secret, as an excuse never to give out investigative information. Another barrier to the free flow of information was the Foreign Intelligence Surveillance Act (FISA) court created in 1979, which served as the arbiter of information that could be shared between government agencies. Like the CIA and the NSA, the FBI avoided the FISA court by simply not asking for permission to share.

The FBI created two units at its headquarters to handle and respond to the growing threat of terrorism in the United States and abroad. One was the Radical Fundamentalist Unit (RFU). The mission of this unit was to research radical fundamentalist activities at mosques and gather intelligence for possible court cases if there was evidence of law breaking. The other was the Usama bin Ladin Unit (UBLU). This unit was more localized, and its mission was to follow the activities of al-Qaeda members in the United States. Both units had a mandate to monitor the activities of possible agents and to prepare court cases against those agents in cases where laws were broken. There was significant overlap between the two units because of the nature of their assignments. Coordination between the two units was always a problem, even though both units resided at FBI headquarters. Another difficulty was that assignment to either unit was not considered a good career move within the FBI, so qualified agents left as soon as possible. Consequently, there was a lack of experienced intelligence gatherers in both units.

The FBI had internal communication problems as well. It had finally developed its own computer system in the mid-1990s, but the system had never worked properly or adequately. At the time of the attacks of September 11, it was a system on which nothing more than the simplest searches could be performed. The system also did not provide access to the Internet. Old-time FBI agents refused to use it. It was a system that had been modeled after the FBI's court-case system, and it was never designed to improve communications between regional field offices and FBI headquarters. People who have used the FBI computer system said

FBI's Risk Avoidance Philosophy

The FBI did not turn itself into a risk-aversive Bureau because it wanted to be that way. It did not turn into an FBI that paraded its political correctness as an all-purpose excuse for not doing its job because that was the kind of Bureau it wanted to be. You can't protect a country that doesn't want to be protected. And for at least a quarter century, we sent every signal to the FBI that we did not want to be protected, and we punished the FBI whenever it tried to protect us.

Richard Gid Powers, *Broken: The Troubled Past and Uncertain Future of the FBI* (New York: Free Press, 2004), pp. 427–428.

to John Schwartz that the "bureau has often intentionally disregarded industry standards, in part because of fears that such systems might be more vulnerable to hackers."

Before September 11, 2001, the FBI had already begun to consider implementing a new computer system. It has ultimately adopted a computer system with the name of "Trilogy," but the system has never become operational, despite $626 million in expenditures. Since 2005 the Virtual Case File System has been in a state of constant upgrades and rebuilding, and it appears that the system will not be ready for use until 2009 and will entail a huge cost overrun.

The FBI's internal system for handling communications created additional obstacles in carrying out its mission. It had a system of assigning communications and memos (called "leads") to individuals at FBI headquarters for further investigation. The problem was that the lead system had been overwhelmed. In mid-2002 the Joint Committee on Intelligence of the U.S. Congress found that the FBI's Counterterrorism Division had 68,000 outstanding unassigned leads dating back to 1995. The Phoenix Memo was a victim of this system.

But of all the reasons why the FBI failed to uncover the September 11 conspiracy, the most compelling one is that the FBI underestimated the terrorist threat. Efforts to assess the counterterrorism efforts of the FBI were met with defensiveness rather than cooperation. When Richard Clarke, the National Security Council's counterterrorism expert, quizzed FBI agents in late 1999 about their counterterrorism activities, he received assurances that the FBI had things under control, even though this was not the case. Dale Watson, the FBI's antiterrorism unit chief, tried to get FBI field offices to concentrate on counterterrorism, but he ended up concluding that too few FBI agents were working on terrorism cases or even knew what to do with regard to terrorism. His efforts proved futile, as shown by the fact that there were fewer FBI agents assigned to counterterrorism activities on September 10, 2001, than there had been in 1998.

Since September 11, the FBI has been busy reforming its practices to avoid the intelligence

FBI's Role in Allowing September 11 Attacks

It [September 11] happened because of the Bureau's ongoing belief that the threat was the work of disorganized zealots who lacked the competence to deliver weapons of mass destruction. It happened because of the Justice Department's treatment of that threat as a series of legal cases to be prosecuted rather than a worldwide conspiracy to be fought from a global intelligence perspective. It happened because a tradition of interagency biases and "need to know" secrecy prevented the vital sharing of intelligence.

Peter Lance, *1000 years for Revenge: International Terrorism and the FBI—The Untold Story* (New York: ReganBooks, 2003), p. 432.

lapses that occurred in the days, months, and years leading up to the terrorist attacks. Intelligence gathering is now a top priority for the Bureau. In fact, the FBI is now being criticized for concentrating its efforts and resources so much on gathering intelligence to prevent terrorist activities that it is neglecting its traditional job of crime fighting.

See Also
Foreign Surveillance Intelligence Act of 1978; Phoenix Memo; Tenet, George

See Documents
Document #28; Document #29; Document #30; Document #33; Document #40

Suggested Reading
Louis J. Freeh and Howard Means, *My FBI: Bringing Down the Mafia, Investigating Bill Clinton, and Fighting the War on Terror* (New York: St. Martin's Press, 2005); Bob Graham, *Intelligence Matters: The CIA, the FBI, Saudi Arabia, and the Failure of America's War on Terror* (New York: Random House, 2004); Joint Inquiry into Intelligence Community Activities before and after the Terrorist Attacks of September 11, 2001, *Hearings Before the Select Committee on Intelligence U.S. Senate and the Permanent Select Committee on Intelligence House of Representatives* (Washington, D.C.: U.S. Government Printing Office, 2004), 2 vols.; Peter Lange, *1000 Years for Revenge: International Terrorism and the FBI—the Untold Story* (New York: ReganBooks, 2003); John Miller, Michael Stone, and Christ Mitchell, *The Cell: Inside the 9/11 Plot, and Why the FBI and CIA Failed to Stop It* (New York: Hyperion, 2002); Gerald Posner, *Why America Slept: The Failure to Prevent 9/11* (New York: Ballantine Books, 2003); John Schwartz, "[FBI] Computer System That Makes Data Secure, but Hard to Find," *New York Times* (June 8, 2002), p. A10.

Freeh

Watson

Mueller

Bald

File photos showing former FBI Director Louis Freeh, FBI Terrorism Chief Dale Watson, FBI Director Robert Mueller, and FBI Executive Assistant Director Gary Bald. (AP IMAGES.)

Federal Emergency Management Agency (FEMA)
The Federal Emergency Management Agency (FEMA) has had a mixed record in dealing with the aftermath of September 11. The legislative mandate for FEMA was to provide direct assistance to those who had been impacted by a natural or man-made disaster. In September 2001 it was a large agency, with 2,600 employees and nearly 4,000 standby reservists. On September 11 Joe M. Allbaugh was the director of FEMA. Allbaugh was a Texan with close ties to President George W. Bush.

Where FEMA excelled was in its prompt response to the disaster. Emergency services personnel from eighteen states responded almost immediately to the sites of the attacks. FEMA sent twenty-eight urban search-and-rescue task forces to the sites of the disasters. Each task force had sixty-two members. The urban search-and-rescue task forces sent to the World Trade Center complex site to locate survivors worked twenty-four-hour days, with the personnel working two twelve-hour shifts. Conditions were horrible, and the dust from the debris made the task extremely difficult for the searchers. They employed portable cameras to spot survivors, sniffer dogs to smell for survivors, and sensitive life-detector sensors to look for signs of life. Despite these heroic efforts, few survivors were found because of the horrendous impact of the collapse of the twin towers. As it became apparent that there would be no more survivors, FEMA started pulling out its search-and-rescue teams. The last to leave was an Oakland, California, unit, which left on October 6, 2001. A spokesperson for FEMA stated that the site had been turned over to the New York City Fire Department and the Army Corps of Engineers.

FEMA also sent in Critical Incident Stress Management (CISM) teams to help the workers at the site of the attacks. These teams had psychologists, psychiatrists, social workers, and professional counselors whose mission was the prevention and mitigation of disabling stress among the personnel working at the World Trade Center site. There were nearly as many members of these CISM teams as there were workers at the site. This caused some difficulty because members of these teams were so eager to help that they became intrusive. They soon earned the nickname "therapy dogs" from workers at the site. Members of these teams undoubtedly helped some of those working at the site, but others resented their constant interference with the urgent job at hand.

The Federal Emergency Management Agency's biggest failure was in its handling of the September 11 disaster relief funds. September 11 had caused the loss of 75,000 jobs and $4.5 billion in lost income. Despite promises of quick financial relief for those who had lost their jobs, FEMA's administrators changed the rules in the aftermath of September 11, making it more difficult for people to qualify for financial relief. Thousands of people were denied housing aid after FEMA decided to limit benefits to those who could prove that their lost income was a "direct result" of the attacks rather than merely the "result" of the attacks, which had been the previous standard. This seemingly minor change in language led to FEMA's rejection of the claims of 70 percent of the people applying for relief under the mortgage and rental program after losing their jobs. Between September 11, 2001, and April 2002, less than $65 million was paid out by FEMA to help families in the disaster area pay their bills, avoid eviction, and buy food.

Decisions on accepting or rejecting claims were made by FEMA agency evaluators (two-thirds of whom were temporary workers) at processing centers in Texas, Maryland, and Virginia. These evaluators had little or no knowledge of New York City or its culture, institutions, or geography. Moreover, the application form had not been changed to make it possible for evaluators to determine whether job losses were directly related to the disaster, and all the forms were printed exclusively in English. It was only on November 14, 2001, that the application form was revised and issued in six languages, but even the new forms did not explain how FEMA defined "direct result."

Furthermore, some odd decisions were made by the FEMA evaluators. One applicant provided the name of the restaurant where he had worked in the World Trade Center and his supervisor's telephone number, as required by the application. His application was denied because the evaluator was unable to make contact by telephone with the restaurant, which had of course been destroyed on September 11.

As bad as the situation was in New York City, it was even worse in Virginia. Thousands of workers had been thrown out of work by the closing of Reagan National Airport in Washington, D.C., in September, but the evaluators were slow to recognize this fact. Only a handful of applications from those workers had been approved by April 2002.

Criticisms of FEMA reached the halls of Congress. Under pressure from politicians, FEMA reevaluated its program in late June 2002 and eased its eligibility criteria. But the bad feelings were hard to overcome.

The immediate result of the change in direction was that FEMA approved more applications. Between September 2001 and June 2002, FEMA sent $20.6 million to 3,585 households. After June 2002, FEMA dispersed $25.3 million to 3,053 households in less than two months. This relaxation of eligibility rules helped the financial situation for people in New York and Virginia, but there was still widespread distrust of FEMA.

> **Commentary on the Distrust of FEMA**
>
> Thousands of people have lost trust in the agency because of the prior rejections and false promises the first time around. It's going to take more effort and stronger outreach from FEMA to convince those who are now so frustrated with the process that they haven't even considered applying for assistance under the new guidelines.
>
> Comments by New York Democratic Representative Carolyn B. Maloney, quoted in David W. Chen, "More Get 9/11 Aid, but Distrust of U.S. Effort Lingers," *New York Times* (August 27, 2002), p. B1.

See Also
World Trade Center, September 11

See Documents
Document #21

Suggested Reading
David W. Chen, "More Get 9/11 Aid, but Distrust of U.S. Effort Lingers," *New York Times* (August 27, 2002), p. B1; Diana B. Henriques and David Barstow, "Change in Rules Barred Many from September 11 Disaster Relief," *New York Times* (April 26, 2002), p. A1; William Keegan Jr., *Closure: The Untold Story of the Ground Zero Recovery Mission* (New York: Touchstone Books, 2006); Kirsten B. Mitchell, "Government Trying to Decide FEMA's Fate," *Tampa Tribune* (August 7, 2002), p. 1.

Feehan, William M. "Bill" (1929–2001)
Bill Feehan, the Deputy Fire Commissioner of the Fire Department of New York (FDNY), was killed at the World Trade Center complex on September 11, 2001. He was well past retirement age, but Feehan had been retained by the FDNY

because of his contributions to the FDNY and because of the affection of his fellow firefighters. During his forty-two years in the FDNY, he had held every position in the fire department, from firefighter to acting commissioner.

Feehan was slow coming to the Fire Department of New York. He was born on September 29, 1929, on Long Island, and he grew up in Jackson Heights, Queens, New York. After graduating from the local high school, he attended and graduated from St. John's University in 1952. Feehan then served a tour of duty in the U.S. Army in the Korean War. Returning to civilian life, Feehan married in 1956, and he worked as a substitute teacher for ten years. He was a lifelong resident of Queens.

Deciding that his first love was firefighting, Feehan joined the Fire Department of New York on October 10, 1959. Once Feehan joined the FDNY, his advancement was rapid. After serving his probationary period, he held the rank of firefighter until 1963. Feehan became a lieutenant in 1964. He rose in the ranks until Mayor Dinkins appointed him Acting Fire Commissioner in 1993–1994. On the eve of September 11, he was serving as the Deputy Fire Commissioner.

Feehan's life began to revolve completely around the FDNY after his wife died in 1995. He was so preoccupied with fire department work that he neglected other aspects of his personal life. He was completely oblivious to the fact that he qualified for Social Security. His commitment to the fire department made him an indispensable asset to Thomas Von Essen, Commissioner of the Fire Department of New York.

On September 11, 2001, Feehan headed to the World Trade Center complex as soon as he heard about an emergency there. As Deputy Fire Commissioner, Feehan had no command responsibility, but he knew all the fire station chiefs and they respected him. He found his old friend, Chief Pete Ganci, at the World Trade Center site. Ganci was the head of all the uniformed firefighters in the FDNY, and he had command responsibility. Feehan accompanied Ganci when the command center was moved outside of the lobby of the North Tower. Soon afterward the South Tower collapsed. When the North Tower collapsed later, it caught both Feehan and Ganci, who were helping to evacuate the building and rescue the survivors. They died together and were buried under four feet of rubble. Their bodies were found by a dog rescue team less than a day later. Feehan's funeral was held in St. Mel's Church in Flushing, Queens, on September 15, 2001.

See Also
Firefighters at Ground Zero; Ganci, Peter J. "Pete"; Von Essen, Thomas; World Trade Center, September 11

Suggested Reading
Michele McPhee and Steve McFarland, "He Was 'Heart & Soul' of Dept. Everyone Knew Feehan," *Daily News* (September 16, 2001), p. 20; Ronnie Rabin, "William M. Feehan: Feehan Was Fighting Fires Right Up to the End," *Newsday* (September 13, 2001), p. 25; Thomas Von Essen with Matt Murray, *Strong of Heart: Life and Death in the Fire Department of New York* (New York: ReganBooks, 2002).

Fetzer, James H. (1940–)
James H. Fetzer is one of the leading conspiracy theorists in the United States and head of the Scholars for 9/11 Truth. His academic training was in philosophy, but he has long had a fascination with government conspiracies, going

back to the assassination of John Fitzgerald Kennedy. This belief in government conspiracies has made him direct his attention to the attacks of September 11, 2001.

Fetzer had a vagabond academic career before landing at the University of Minnesota at Duluth. He was born on December 6, 1940, in Pasadena, California. After attending South Pasadena High School, Fetzer matriculated at Princeton University, where he received a BA in philosophy. He graduated magna cum laude in 1962. Fetzer then entered the U.S. Marine Corps as a 2nd Lieutenant, serving in an artillery unit. In 1966, shortly after reaching the rank of captain, Fetzer resigned his commission to attend graduate school at Indiana University. Four years later, in 1970, Fetzer received a PhD in the history and philosophy of science. His first academic appointment was at the University of Kentucky. Leaving the University of Kentucky without tenure in 1977, he taught at a variety of universities—University of Virginia, University of Cincinnati, University of North Carolina at Chapel Hill, and the University of South Florida—before finding an academic home at the University of Minnesota at Duluth in 1987. After obtaining tenure and then becoming a Distinguished McKnight Professor at the university, he stayed there until his retirement in 2006.

Fetzer's area of academic specialty was in the philosophy of science and the theoretical foundations of computer science. His academic research in these fields was productive and he published twenty books as well as numerous articles and reviews. Fetzer also started the international journal, *Minds and Machines*, which he edited for eleven years. He also founded the academic journal *Studies in Cognitive Systems*.

Outside of his academic career Fetzer adopted a conspiracy theorist's view of history. His first venture into conspiracy theories was his investigation into the alleged conspiracy behind the assassination of John Fitzgerald Kennedy in Dallas, Texas, on November 22, 1963. Fetzer came to the conclusion that the U.S. government had planned and executed the assassination of Kennedy. According to his view, Lee Harvey Oswald was a mere pawn in the conspiracy. Fetzer has spent years proclaiming his thesis at conferences and on talk shows.

Because of his inclination toward government conspiracies, it was easy for Fetzer to embrace the idea that a U.S. government conspiracy had led to the September 11 attacks. In his view motivation for the involvement of the U.S. government in the September 11 conspiracy was political and economic gain. The purported political gain was the needed justification for the invasion of Iraq and the economic gain was reaped by certain friends of the members of the Bush administration. Fetzer has rejected the idea that the hijacked airliners brought down the twin towers, and he has insisted instead that controlled demolitions were used. According to Fetzer, demolitions were also used to bring down Seven World Trade Center. In recent remarks Fetzer has left open the possibility that there may be other valid theories about what caused those buildings to collapse, including the possibility of the use of high-tech weapons.

To spread his conspiracy theories Fetzer founded a group called "Scholars for 9/11 Truth." His cofounder was Steven E. Jones, a former physicist from Brigham Young University. They were able to lead their group together for a year before Jones broke away to form a rival group: Scholars for 9/11 Truth and Justice. Their main source of contention was that Jones wanted to keep speculation grounded on scientific possibilities, while Fetzer was prone to more extreme speculations.

Fetzer's motivations and actions have attracted critics. His rabid hatred of the Bush administration and his calls for a military coup to overthrow it have hurt his credibility. Moreover, his constant shifts on the subject of how the U.S. government could have pulled off the 9/11 conspiracy cause critics to question his knowledge of the affair. Despite these attacks on his credibility, Fetzer remains one of the leading proponents of the view that a U.S. government conspiracy led to the attacks on September 11, 2001.

See Also
Conspiracy Theories; Jones, Steven E.; Scholars for 9/11 Truth

Suggested Reading
Andrew Cline, "A Conspiracy against Us All," *National Review* (September 11, 2006), p. 1; John Gravois, "Professors of Paranoia? Academics Give a Scholarly Stamp to 9/11 Conspiracy Theories," *The Chronicle of Higher Education* 52.42 (June 23, 2006), p. A10; John Gravois, "A Theory That Just Won't Die," *National Post* [Canada] (July 28, 2006), p. A14; Doug Todd, "The 9/11 Truth of Dr. James Fetzer; Boon or Boondoggle: A Review," *Free Press* [Columbus, OH] (February 22, 2007), p. 1.

Fire House 40/35

Firefighters from Fire House 40/35 in mid-Manhattan responded to the September 11 attacks, and in the process of handling evacuations and firefighting, twelve of the thirteen of those responding died. All of the firefighters died in the collapse of the South Tower of the World Trade Center complex. Like many firefighters in New York City, most of the men of the 40/35 came from firefighting families. They had a strong commitment to their jobs and to their unit.

Fire House 40/35 was considered to be one of the better firefighting units in New York City. The strength of the unit was fifty men working in shifts—eleven at any given time. There were eight officers in 40/35—two captains and six lieutenants. This house contained both an engine (Engine 40) unit and a ladder (Ladder 35) unit for both rescue and firefighting operations. There was a lively rivalry between the two units as to whose role was more important.

September 11 started out peacefully enough at Fire House 40/35, but after the news of the aircraft crashes into the North and South Towers of the World Trade Center complex, everything changed in an instant. Captain Frank Callahan was the shift commander at the time of the attack. A veteran of almost twenty-eight years in the fire department, he was an old-school firefighter, and he held the men under his command to the highest standards of performance. Callahan had assumed command of Ladder 35 in July 1998. After hearing about the second crash into the South Tower, Fire House 40/35 mobilized and headed for the scene of the emergency at 9:08 a.m. They arrived there and immediately began evacuating personnel and fighting the fire in the South Tower, when it suddenly collapsed on top of them. Of the thirteen firefighters on the scene, only Kevin Shea survived, but he was badly injured. Shea had been blown out of danger, suffering a concussion, a broken neck, and other serious injuries. He was found by Todd Maisel, a photographer for the *New York Daily News*.

The bodies of eleven of the twelve members of Fire House 40/35 were gradually recovered. The first to be found was the body of Bruce Gary. His body was

Firefighters and emergency personnel remove debris from the site of the World Trade Center towers on September 13, 2001. (AP IMAGES/Stephen Chernin.)

found under four stories of rubble some three weeks after September 11. Beside him was a medical bag that he must have been carrying and the bodies of several firemen and civilians. On January 1, 2002, Michael D'Auria's body was located. In early February 2002, two other bodies—belonging to Mike Boyle and David Arce—were found. They had been lifelong friends. Then, on March 21, 2002, searchers found the bodies of Lieutenant John Gintly, Michael Lynch, and Vince Morello. Ultimately, the only body not recovered was that of Steve Mercado.

The loss of so many men from a single firehouse was devastating. Even before most of the bodies had been found, the families had held ceremonies honoring the deceased. Because the families of the firefighters were so close, there was a strong support system. Nevertheless, some of the wives had severe adjustment problems. The families achieved closure, but the loss of their husbands left the wives raising their families as single parents.

See Also
Firefighters at Ground Zero

Suggested Reading
Charles Brice, "Inside Story of New York's Heroes," *Advertiser* [New York] (September 7, 2002), p. W11; David Halberstam, *Firehouse* (New York: Hyperion, 2002).

Firefighters at Ground Zero
Firefighters from the New York City Fire Department (NYFD) immediately responded to the first airliner crashing into the North Tower of the World Trade

Center. American Airlines Flight 11 crashed into the tower at 8:46:40 a.m. The NYFD units were in the middle of a shift change. This meant that the maximum number of firefighters (those whose shifts had just ended and those whose shifts were just starting) were able to respond to the emergency. Engine Company 10 and Ladder Company 10 were the first to respond because their firehouse was located across Liberty Street from the World Trade Center. Other fire stations also reacted quickly. Within thirty minutes more than 100 fire trucks had appeared at the World Trade Center complex. Firefighters were on duty fighting the fire and handling survivors when United Airlines Flight 175 hit the South Tower of the World Trade Center at 9:03:11 a.m. Firefighters continued fighting the fire and trying to save survivors until both towers collapsed. One of the problems the fire-fighters had to overcome was climbing up between sixty and eighty floors while hauling the self-contained breathing apparatus (SCBA), with the pants, jacket, and helmet weighing an additional 70 pounds.

The NYFD is huge. In the five boroughs of New York City there were 2,629 fire officers, 8,599 firefighters, 3,000 emergency technicians and paramedics, and 2,000 civilians. They were organized into 203 engine companies, 143 ladder companies, 5 rescue companies, 7 investigative squads, 3 marine companies, and a hazardous materials (hazmat) company. These units were stationed in 225 firehouses scattered throughout the five boroughs. This demonstrates the extent of the manpower that responded to the crisis on September 11. Some reports have estimated that somewhere around 10,000 firefighters made it to the World Trade Center on September 11.

Two factors hindered the efforts of firefighters to be more effective. One was the failure of the communication systems. Radios did not work, and other communication systems were overwhelmed by the traffic. Almost as serious was the lack of coordination between the firefighters and the police. Distrust between the two agencies had a lengthy history, as firefighters believed that the police department was favored over the fire department by New York politicians. These feelings of hostility were reciprocated by the police, even though both departments had traditionally recruited from the same segments of the population—Irish and Italians.

An example of the way this discord influenced operations on September 11 was the helicopter rescue issue. In the 1993 World Trade Center bombing, police helicopters rescued people from the rooftop by helicopter. Afterward the Fire Department's Chiefs Association claimed that this was grandstanding and complained to the mayor. After some infighting, the Fire Department and the Police Department came to a compromise. Police helicopters would thereafter attempt rooftop rescues only when requested by a fire chief.

At the same time the roof exits on both towers at the World Trade Center had been securely locked by the Port Authority, ostensibly to prevent vandals, daredevils, and suicides from gaining access to the rooftop. New York City building code regulations did call for access to rooftops in emergencies, but the World Trade Center complex was exempt from the code. The New York City Fire Department had agreed with this decision.

On September 11 the rooftop doors remained shut, dooming those unable to climb down the staircases. The rooftop doors could be opened by using the computers on the twenty-second floor, but this system failed because of the explosion and fire. Moreover, the firefighters were unable to communicate with the police helicopters because of the collapse of the communication systems. Police helicopters flew over the twin towers, but there was no authorization to rescue people from the rooftops even if they had been able to make it to the rooftops of either tower.

The firefighters never had a chance to put out the fire because it was a high-rise fire. A high-rise fire is one that can only be extinguished from inside the building because no ladder truck and no stream of water can reach that high, making it the most dangerous type of fire to fight. In many cases, the only hope is that the building remains standing and the fire burns itself out.

A characteristic of the twin towers was that there were large areas of 20,000 to 30,000 square feet on each floor. This fact made firefighting almost impossible, but the firefighters tried their best anyway. Half of the firefighters tried to fight the fire and the other half were busy evacuating people from the burning buildings. The fire chiefs had become concerned about the possibility of the towers collapsing, but too many people were in distress to pull the firefighters out. Consequently, losses among the firefighters when the towers collapsed were horrific. The final tally of firefighters killed on September 11 was 343. Among the dead were the first deputy fire commissioner, the chief of the department, 23 station chiefs, 21 captains, 46 lieutenants, 249 firefighters, 1 fire marshal, 2 paramedics, and 1 chaplain. Others were injured, and some of the surviving firefighters have had serious health problems since. New York firefighters have always had a reputation for bravery, and September 11 was no exception. It was part of a long history of fighting dangerous and deadly fires.

After it became apparent that there would be no more

Difficulties in Fighting High-Rise Fires

The best-kept secret in America's fire service is that firefighters cannot extinguish a fire in a 20–30,000 square-foot open floor area in a high-rise building. A fire company advancing a 2½-inch hose line with a 1¼-inch nozzle discharges only 300 gallons per minute and can extinguish only about 2,500 square feet of fire. The reach of the streams is only 50 feet . . . . A fully involved, free burning 20,000 square-foot floor area cannot be extinguished by a couple of firefighters spraying a hose stream from a stairway.

Comments of Vincent Dunne, a retired Deputy Chief in the FDNY in Richard Bernstein, *Out of the Blue: The Story of September 11, 2001, From Jihad to Ground Zero* (New York: Times Books, 2002), p. 210.

Code of the Firefighters

The fireman's calling is to save people, whoever and however they can, and the chief's duty is to save people while losing none of his own. Firemen run into burning buildings and up smoky staircases with air tanks and masks and fifty pounds of hose over their shoulders because that's the honor and the glory. There is a code. You do everything you can to save people. You never leave another firefighter alone in the burning building. If you're not willing to take the chances firefighters have to take, you should have gone into another profession. A newcomer has to fit in and prove himself, or he will find the rest of the company or squad putting him in for a transfer—to some company or squad where there aren't very many fires.

Philosophy of Peter J. Ganci, FDNY's highest ranking uniformed officer and victim of 9/11, as reported in Richard Bernstein, *Out of the Blue: The Story of September 11, 2001, from Jihad to Ground Zero* (New York: Times Books, 2002), pp. 151–152.

survivors, the firefighters began searching for bodies and body parts. Even the recovery of a small part of a body meant that DNA analysis would allow the deceased to be identified. The firefighters had a code that they did not leave comrades behind. They worked diligently to recover whatever body parts could be found, but particular emphasis was put on finding the remains of firefighters. When the mayor's office announced that the number of firefighters, police, and Port Authority personnel at the site would be reduced in early November 2001, the firefighters protested to the point of almost rioting at the World Trade Center site. They felt that moving the debris had become more important to the city government than finding the remains of the victims. Bad feelings developed between the firefighters and Mayor Rudy Giuliani. Only after a direct appeal by firefighters who had lost relatives in the attacks did the mayor back down and allow more firefighters to search for body remains.

> **Frustration of a Firefighter at Ground Zero**
>
> What we were trained to do and what we were able to do that day were two completely different things. The total sense of uselessness I felt all day, knowing that all those people were in those buildings and we couldn't get to them, that we couldn't help them, was unbelievable. And there are still so many people missing. One of the drill instructors I know lost his brother. Every spare moment he has, he goes down there and he digs. Maybe he'll never find his brother, but he's got to do something. It's a total feeling of uselessness, but at least he can say he tried.
>
> Comments of Maureen McArdle-Schulman, quoted in Susan Hagen and Mary Carouba, *Women at Ground Zero: Stories of Courage and Compassion* (New York: Alpha Books, 2002), p. 39.

The efforts and sacrifices of the New York City firefighters have been recognized. On June 10, 2006, a bronze memorial was dedicated to the memory of the dead firefighters with names listed on the memorial according to rank. It begins with First Deputy Commissioner William F. Feehan and ends with Paramedic Ricardo J. Quinn.

The toll on the New York City firefighters was extreme. Besides the heavy loss of experienced personnel and the loss of ninety-one vehicles, there were still 415 members of the department on medical leave or light duty six months after September 11. Stress-related problems have been particularly severe. To replace the lost firefighters the department lowered entrance requirements for its recruits. One firefighter said, "It is going to take us a couple of generations, at least, to get the Fire Department back to where it was prior to 9/11."

See Also

Bucca, Ronald; Downey, Ray Matthew; Feehan, William M. "Bill"; Fire House 40/35; Ganci, Peter J. "Pete"; Von Essen, Thomas

See Documents

Document #14; Document #25

Suggested Reading

Stefan Aust et al., *Inside 9-11: What Really Happened* (New York: St. Martin's Press, 2001); Al Baker, "The True Toll on Firefighters Is Still Untold," *New York Times* (March 10, 2002), p. 41; Richard Bernstein, *Out of the Blue: The Story of September 11, 2001, from Jihad to Ground Zero* (New York: Times Books, 2002); David W. Dunlap, "A 'Silent Roll Call' of 9/11's Firefighter Heroes," *New York Times* (June 10, 2006), p. 1; Jim Dwyer and Kevin

Firefighters dig through the rubble covering the remains of the South Tower of the World Trade Center in October 2001. (AP IMAGES/Michael Conroy.)

Flynn, *102 Minutes: The Untold Story of the Fight to Survive inside the Twin Towers* (New York: Times Books, 2005); David Halberstam, *Firehouse* (New York: Hyperion, 2002); Peter Lange, *1000 Years for Revenge: International Terrorism and the FBI—the Untold Story* (New York: ReganBooks, 2003); Dennis Smith, *Report from Ground Zero* (New York: Viking, 2002); Thomas Von Essen with Matt Murray, *Strong of Heart: Life and Death in the Fire Department of New York City* (New York: ReganBooks, 2002).

Firefighter Riot on November 2, 2001

The firefighters of the New York Fire Department (NYFD) were possessive of their dead after the September 11 attacks on the World Trade Center complex. After all, the firefighters had just lost 343 members of a close-knit fraternity of brothers. They had made a special ceremony of the recovery of their fallen comrades. In some cases, these efforts caused resentment among members of the New York Police Department (NYPD), Port Authority police, and the 3,000 or so construction workers. Tempers flared on several occasions between firefighters and others.

Work at the World Trade Center site was always chaotic, so Mayor Rudolph Giuliani proposed that the number of firefighters, police, and Port Authority police be reduced to twenty-five representatives each on the grounds of safety. At that time, around 100 firefighters were active in helping locate bodies and body parts. The firefighters, unlike the NYPD police and the Port Authority police, were furious at this announcement. They charged that the Giuliani administration wanted to

accelerate the disposal of debris
at the expense of finding the
remains of the victims. Complaints made their way up the
ladder to the management of
both firefighter unions. Union
leaders decided to organize a
demonstration at Ground Zero
on November 2, 2001. This
demonstration was scheduled
seven weeks and three days after
September 11.

The heads of the Department
of Design and Construction
(DDC) found themselves in
the middle of the controversy.
Kenneth Holden and Michael
Burton, the two top officials at
DDC, agreed that there were
safety issues involved with having so many people at the site,
but they also knew that Giuliani's decision would cause
political trouble. Holden was a veteran civil service administrator and to buck Giuliani would have been a career breaker. Both leaders wanted to clear the debris out
of the World Trade Center site as soon possible, but not at the expense of finding
the remains of the victims.

Union leaders assured the Giuliani administration that the demonstration
would be orderly, but tensions were so high that the situation soon developed into
a confrontation between the firefighters and the police. Around 500 firefighters
joined the demonstration at the beginning, but during the course of the demonstration another 500 showed up. Since there was no love lost between the NYPD
police and the FDNY firefighters, pushing and shoving soon turned into an
attempt by the firefighters to break police lines. The police responded by meeting
force with force. Soon police began arresting the most violent of the demonstrators. Twelve firefighters were arrested, including the two heads of the firefighter
unions. These arrests further infuriated the firefighters.

The Giuliani administration, including Mayor Giuliani and the Fire Commissioner, Thomas Von Essen, knew that they had a serious public relations problem.
Giuliani was furious at the riot. At first, the mayor wanted to arrest some of the
construction workers for supporting the demonstration, but cooler heads soon
prevailed. Then, on the evening of November 12, 2001, the families of the dead
firefighters vented their frustrations at the inability of the search and rescue teams
to find bodies, and they expressed their concern about the rapid pace of the
cleanup at Ground Zero. It was an emotional meeting in which the widows
attacked the leaders of the Department of Design and Construction in a variety of
ways and for a variety of reasons. They accused the Medical Examiner and Burton

New York City firefighter Declan Grant (right) participates in a demonstration conducted by firefighters outside City Hall in New York, November 2, 2001. Firefighters marched from Ground Zero to City Hall to demand that they be allowed to continue searching for victims' remains at the site of the World Trade Center Attack. (AP IMAGES/Tina Fineberg)

of lying. The mayor came away from this meeting relatively unscathed, but he was aware that things had to be calmed down.

Mayor Giuliani decided to compromise. He authorized first fifty and then seventy-five firefighters to remain at the site to help recover human remains. These concessions, including the release of the twelve arrested demonstrators without charges, did little to reconcile the firefighters with the Giuliani administration. Strong feelings remained after the Giuliani administration stepped down on January 1, 2002. Some of the distrust on the part of the firefighters carried over to the new mayor and his administration.

See Also
Department of Design and Construction; Firefighters at Ground Zero; Giuliani, Rudolph William Louis "Rudy" III

Suggested Reading
Maki Becker, "Widows Vent to Mayor in Secret Talks," *Daily News* [New York] (November 13, 2001), p. 5; William Langewiesche, *American Ground: Unbuilding the World Trade Center* (New York: North Point Press, 2002); Frank Lombardi and Michele McPhee, "Bravest vs. Finest in Melee at WTC," *Daily News* [New York] (November 3, 2001), p. 3; Frank Lombardi and Dave Goldiner, "City Adds Bravest at WTC, Hikes Number of Fire-fighters to 75 from 50 after Protests," *Daily News* [New York] (November 17, 2001), p. 17; Jennifer Steinhauer, "Mayor Criticizes Firefighters Over Stand on Staffing at Trade Center Site," *New York Times* (November 9, 2001), p. D5.

Floyd, Nancy (1960–)

Nancy Floyd was the FBI agent whose association with the undercover informant Emad Salem helped reveal and break up the conspiracy by the followers of Abdel Rahman to bomb New York City landmarks. She was a specialist on tracking Russian agents, but her contact and subsequent involvement with Salem transformed her career. Ultimately, this association hurt her FBI career because of her outspokenness about how her superiors had mishandled the Salem affair.

Floyd, who was born in 1960, had wanted to be in government service from an early age. Her father was an officer in the U.S. Air Force who reached the rank of major before suffering a fatal heart attack at age 53. She moved around with her family, living both in Europe and at various air force bases in the United States. Floyd ended up living in Dallas, Texas. She attended the University of Texas at Arlington, where she received a BS in criminal justice. After graduating in 1982, she worked at various other jobs before applying to join the FBI in 1985. Floyd was one of eight women out of sixty trainees in her class at the FBI Academy in Quantico, Virginia.

Most of Floyd's FBI career has been spent at the New York City Field Office. However, her first assignment was as a special agent in the Savannah, Georgia Field Office. After a couple of years, she was transferred the New York City Field Office. Once there, she was assigned to Branch A in the Bureau's Foreign Counterintelligence Division (FCI). The mission of the FCI was the gathering of intelligence on the intelligence unit of the Russian army (*Glavnoe Razvedyvatelnoe Upravlenie*, or GRU). Her mentor was the legendary agent Len Predtechenskis.

Floyd first made contact with Emad Salem while trying to locate Russian agents. Salem was working at a down-and-out hotel when Floyd approached him for information about a Russian agent who had possibly been using the hotel. Salem rounded up the information she had asked for, and then began volunteering other information. It was Salem who alerted her to how dangerous Sheikh Omar Abdel Rahman was to the United States. Salem also showed an eagerness to do undercover work, but he was more comfortable dealing with Floyd than with his two FBI handlers. His only stipulation regarding his services was that he would not wear a wire.

Salem soon began to produce first-class intelligence on the extremists who were centered around the al-Kifah Refugee Center. He learned about possible bomb-making activities when the extremists approached him about working on a bomb, but he was not told where they planned to plant the bomb.

At this critical stage, a change of supervisors led to the termination of Salem's undercover work for the FBI, much to Floyd's disgust. The new supervisor, Carson Dunbar, insisted that Salem wear a wire so that a court case could be pursued against the terrorist targets. Dunbar was also suspicious of Salem, and he questioned Salem's reliability. Dunbar was also critical of Floyd's close personal relationship with Salem. Salem refused to wear a wire and his employment with the FBI was terminated at a key juncture in 1992.

After the World Trade Center bombing in February 1993, the FBI changed its mind and rehired Salem. Salem still only had confidence in Floyd, but he was persuaded to wear a wire. His secret recordings led to the break-up of a plot to bomb key New York City landmarks. His lack of trust in the FBI culminated in his recording his contacts with various FBI agents. On some of these secret recordings, Floyd had made some disparaging remarks about her FBI superiors, which caused these supervisors to report her for disciplinary action.

For the next five and a half years, Floyd's conduct during the Salem affair was investigated. The Office of Professional Responsibility (OPR) began an investigation of Floyd that ruined her career. Any chance of promotion to higher positions in the FBI for Floyd ended during the investigation. Ultimately, the OPR investigation concluded that Floyd was guilty of insubordination against Carson Dunbar. The original penalty was suspension for thirty days, but her appeal reduced the suspension to fourteen days. Floyd remained in the New York office until she decided to request a transfer to a remote field office. During this time, she received a direct order not to have any contact with Salem. She was still in New York City on September 11, 2001.

Suggested Reading
Peter Lange, *1000 Years for Revenge: International Terrorism and the FBI—the Untold Story* (New York: ReganBooks, 2003).

Foreign Intelligence Surveillance Act of 1978

The Foreign Intelligence Surveillance Act of 1978 (FISA) was passed as a result of the abuses of the Federal Bureau of Investigation (FBI) in conducting warrantless surveillance of American citizens in the 1960s and early 1970s. Recommendations came out of the 1975 Church Committee on ways to prevent the warrantless surveillance of U.S. citizens by the FBI. Committee members also wanted to end decades of presidentially approved electronic surveillance for national security purposes without a judicial warrant, and thus prevent irregularities in surveillance activities. This committee also believed that the U.S. judiciary lacked the expertise to rule on matters concerning foreign intelligence surveillance. Provisions of the FISA allowed for a special court to be established that would issue warrants after receiving requests from law-enforcement agencies. This court was given the name of Foreign Intelligence Surveillance Court (FISC). A search warrant or a wire tap could be issued by the FISC if the subject was an agent of a foreign power, which was defined as either a foreign country or an international terrorist group, or if the subject was engaged in international terrorism or activities in preparation for terrorism on behalf of a foreign power. FISC's orders are classified and kept secret. In the history of the FISC, only a few warrants have ever been turned down, because FISA permits search warrants to be issued based on a lower standard than the standard of probable cause used for criminal search warrants.

Despite the reputation of the Foreign Intelligence Surveillance Court for almost never turning down a request from a law-enforcement agency, the FBI had been reluctant to apply for warrants from the court before September 11, 2001. An elaborate and time-consuming procedure had to be followed to apply for a warrant from the FISC. Once the agents at a field office had determined that there was probable cause for a FISA warrant, an electronic communication (EC) with supporting documents would be sent to the FBI headquarters unit overseeing the investigation. That unit would add any supporting documents and send the package to the National Security Law Unit (NSLU). This unit comprises lawyers with expertise in national security law. Lawyers in the NSLU would review the case on its merits. If these lawyers agreed that the case met the threshold of probable cause, then the dossier would be forwarded to the Department of Justice. If not, the case would end at the NSLU. At the Department of Justice, the case would be examined anew by its Office of Intelligence Policy Review (OIPR), where lawyers would once again examine the case for a FISA warrant. Only if the case could pass all of these roadblocks could it be forwarded to the FISA court in the form of a declaration and be signed off by a FISA court judge.

Part of the problem was that the FBI's lawyers interpreted the FISA law in a more restrictive manner than the legislation had intended. This strict interpretation of the law was the case with the FISA request from the Minneapolis Field Office for a warrant concerning Zacarias Moussaoui, the so-called twentieth hijacker on September 11, 2001. FBI agents had requested authority for a warrant several times for Moussaoui, including one from the FISC, but each time their request was turned down by FBI headquarters. Moussaoui had been in Chechnya assisting the Chechen rebels fighting against Russia. The head of the Radical Fundamental Unit (RFU) at FBI headquarters refused to classify the Chechen rebels as part of a so-called recognized foreign power.

The final interpretation of FBI headquarters in the Moussaoui case was that Moussaoui was not associated with a foreign power, nor was the Chechen rebel group a recognized terrorist group. This decision was made despite the warning from French security agents that Moussaoui had been associating with Muslim extremists and even though it was well-known in intelligence circles that the Chechen rebels had extensive contacts with al-Qaeda.

Everything changed after the events of September 11, and the FBI had no trouble obtaining a criminal warrant against Moussaoui in the aftermath of the attacks. An examination of his computer after September 11 revealed his contacts with the Hamburg Cell, which had carried out the 9/11 attacks, and al-Qaeda. The FBI's strict adherence to its interpretation of the FISA has been blamed as part of the "Wall" that hindered the flow of information and thwarted the effectiveness of the FBI's efforts against terrorism.

Since September 11, 2001, the controversy over the Foreign Intelligence Surveillance Court has intensified. The Bush administration made its view known that the onerous requirements of FISA stood in the way of intelligence gathering. In a secret court proceeding before the FISA Appeals Court on September 9, 2002, with only government lawyers present, the Bush administration presented its case that the FISC had hindered the flow of information and had obstructed the president's authority to conduct warrantless searches to obtain foreign intelligence information. The court accepted the government's position and the U.S. Supreme Court refused to hear any appeals. This judgment was the legal grounds for subsequent warrantless searches, which were conducted by the National Security Agency in secret and under presidential authority.

Despite the efforts of the Bush administration to bypass the FISC system, FISA courts still exist and the number of warrant requests coming before them has increased significantly in recent years. The use of FISA and its courts does protect the government from accusations that it violates the Fourth Amendment rights of U.S. persons. Since the disclosure of the warrantless searches, President Bush has instructed the various intelligence organizations that the FISC system be used for all intelligence-gathering activities. The debate over FISA and its courts is ongoing, with many critics believing that both the law and its implementation are hindering the War on Terrorism.

See Also
Federal Bureau of Investigation (FBI); Moussaoui, Zacarias; Wall, The

See Documents
Document #28; Document #30

Suggested Reading
Bob Graham, *Intelligence Matters: The CIA, the FBI, Saudi Arabia, and the Failure of America's War on Terror* (New York: Random House, 2004); James E. Meason, "The Foreign Intelligence Surveillance Act: Time for Reappraisal," *International Lawyer* 24(Winter 1990)1043; Gary Schmitt, "Constitutional Spying: The Solution to the FISA Problem," *Weekly Standard* 11.16 (January 2–January 9, 2006), pp. 1–2; John Yoo, *War by Other Means: An Insider's Account of the War on Terror* (New York: Atlantic Monthly Press, 2006).

Freedom Tower

The replacement for the twin towers destroyed on September 11, 2001, is known as the Freedom Tower. Almost from the beginning, the project to replace the World Trade Center complex and the twin towers has been mired in controversy and politics. Part of the reason for the conflict has been the involvement of so many players in the rebuilding project. The Lower Manhattan Development Corporation has the overall responsibility for guiding the entire project, but the Port Authority of New York and New Jersey, the Metropolitan Transportation Authority, the New York Police Department (NYPD), the developer Larry Silverstein, and politicians such as Governor George Pataki and New York City Mayor Michael Bloomberg, have all played active roles in the process. Add to this the lobbying from the Families of 9/11 Movement, and it can easily be seen that any type of decision making would be difficult and time-consuming. Moreover, there have been irreconcilable differences between the stakeholders at times, which has further complicated the process.

It took nearly two years after September 11, 2001, for the concept of the Freedom Tower to win approval. A German architect, Daniel Libeskind, was selected in 2003 by the Lower Manhattan Development Corporation to design the building. Libeskind's original plan was to build the memorial to the victims of September 11 first, complete Church Street buildings next, and finally construct the Freedom Tower last. This plan was revised by Governor Pataki, who insisted that the Freedom Tower should be built first. In the meantime, a feud developed between the lead architect, Libeskind, and the developer's choice of architect, David Childs.

The original design was for a futuristic building that would reflect the city's self-confidence and that could withstand any type of terrorist attack. It was designed as a twisting obelisk of steel and glass rising to 1,776 feet. There would be about 2.6 million square feet of office space in the lower 69 stories, but the building would be 102-stories tall overall. The bottom half of the building would contain offices while the top half would be a broadcast tower with restaurants at the top. Part of the top half would have an open space for wind turbines that could fulfill

Architects David Childs (right) and Daniel Libeskind (left) in 2005, posing next to the model of the redesigned Freedom Tower during a news conference in New York. (AP IMAGES/Mary Altaffer.)

20 percent of the building's energy needs. Original site for the building was to be within twenty-five feet from the West Street-Route 9A. The cost of the building had been estimated in the $2 billion range.

The Freedom Tower was in the initial construction phase in the spring of 2005 when the New York Police Department criticized the building's location and insisted that it would present serious security concerns. The NYPD feared that a large truck bomb attack would seriously damage the Freedom Tower. After all, it had happened in the 1993 World Trade Center bombing. After some negotiations, Governor Pataki announced in May 2005 that the building would be moved further from West Street, and that the tower's exterior would be strengthened to withstand a truck bombing. These requirements meant that the Freedom Tower would have to be redesigned almost from scratch. In this new design, there would be a twenty-story fortified wall around the base of the tower. These modifications brought the estimated cost of the Freedom Tower to the $3 billion range.

The twin towers had structural problems that contributed to their collapse, so the Freedom Tower would also have to meet higher structural standards. Elevators and stairwells are to be protected by walls of concrete and steel two feet thick. There will be wider exit stairs, improved emergency systems, and better fireproofing. The ultimate assessment of the building, however, will be conducted by structural engineers, who must give their approval that the proposed design of the building is structurally sound. This creates a further problem in that, as Guy Nordenson, a structural engineer and a professor of architecture at Princeton University, points out, "the computer software that is being used to simulate the blast effects is proprietary and classified by the federal government." This means that the structural engineers only have access to the data produced by the government's software without being able to judge the reliability of the tests.

Once the security and structural problems posed by the design of the Freedom Tower had been resolved, the next obstacle was finding potential tenants for the building. A residue of fear had built up over working at a place where so many had died so recently. Moreover, the building would serve as a prime target for future terrorist activity. To encourage the private sector to move into the building, the governors of New York and New Jersey, and the mayor of New York City committed state and federal agencies to occupy 1 million of the 2.6 million square feet in the Freedom Tower. Despite this decision, there has been widespread resistance to the idea of working in the Freedom Tower by the employees of these governmental agencies. A secondary issue is the escalating cost of construction, which means that leasing space in the Freedom Tower might eventually be too expensive for most businesses and corporations.

Wrangling over terms between the state and local governments and the developer, and the constant changing of agendas by the various players, has slowed down the pace of construction of the Freedom Tower. It was originally envisaged that the tower would be operational sometime in 2009, but it now seems likely that the building will be completely finished sometime in 2011.

See Also
World Trade Center Bombing (1993)

Suggested Reading
Charles V. Bagli, "A Blueprint for Conflict at Ground Zero," *New York Times* (February 19, 2006), p. 33; Glenn Collins and David W. Dunlap, "Seeking Better Security at a Symbol of Resolve," *New York Times* (June 7, 2005), p. B4; Patrick McGeehan, Kate Hammer, and Colin Moynihan, "Employees Say No to Working in Freedom Tower," *New York Times* (September 19, 2006), p. B1; Guy Nordenson, "Freedom from Fear," *New York Times* (February 16, 2007), p. A23; David Usborne, "The Big Freeze at Ground Zero," *Hamilton Spectator* [Ontario, Canada] (June 3, 2005), p. A13.

Freeh, Louis (1950–)

Louis Freeh was the director of the Federal Bureau of Investigation (FBI) during most of the early days of the September 11 plot. He was the fifteenth head of the FBI, and his tenure in office lasted from September 1, 1993, until June 2001. In those eight years, Freeh transformed the FBI and its culture according to his own views and ideas. He had been a field operative earlier in his career and he distrusted FBI headquarters. This distrust led him to institute certain policies and to engage in downsizing that weakened FBI headquarters. This weakening was so severe that headquarters was unable to process information from the field offices that might have had an impact on counteracting and preventing al-Qaeda operations in the United States.

Freeh spent his entire professional life in government service. He was born on January 6, 1950, in Jersey City, New Jersey. His father ran a real estate firm after spending most of World War II as a combat engineer, and his mother worked as a secretary in the same firm. Freeh attended Immaculate Heart of Mary Grammar School, St. Joseph of the Palisades Junior High, and then St. Joseph's High

School. After graduation from high school, Freeh entered Rutgers University where he was a Phi Beta Kappa graduate. He then entered Rutgers Law School, and he graduated with a JD in 1974. During part of this time, Freeh worked in the office of Republican Senator Clifford P. Chase. Later, Freeh obtained an LLM degree from New York University Law School in 1984. In the meantime, Freeh joined the FBI in the summer of 1975 and graduated from the FBI Academy in Quantico, Virginia, in August of the same year. His first assignment was with the New York City Field Office and he was later transferred to the FBI headquarters in Washington, D.C. He became bored with the office work at FBI headquarters.

In 1981 Freeh made a career change by leaving the FBI for a legal position in government service. He became an assistant U.S. attorney for the Southern District of New York, working as a federal prosecutor in Manhattan. His duties there were handling investigations and conducting trials of Mafia figures. He moved steadily up the legal ladder in this office, becoming Chief of the Organized Crime Unit, Deputy United States Attorney, and Associate United States Attorney. Then, in 1991, President George H. W. Bush appointed Freeh as United States District Court Judge for the Southern District of New York. He remained in this position until President Bill Clinton appointed him FBI director in 1993.

Freeh's tenure as FBI director was characterized by numerous problems, both inherited and new. Two investigations were ongoing—the Ruby Ridge incident in Idaho and the Branch Davidian standoff in Waco, Texas—when Freeh assumed office in 1993. He took a neutral position on both of these investigations by maintaining his distance from blame that accumulated in both incidents. Critics in Congress and in right-wing circles accused the federal government of misconduct in using force to capture the Weaver family, and in the siege of the Branch Davidians, when David Koresh refused to surrender to federal agents, leading to heavy casualties. Several high-profile cases did take place during Freeh's stay as director: the Centennial Olympic Park bombing, the negotiations with the Montana Freemen, the capture of the Unabomber, the Robert Hanssen spy case, and the Wen Ho Lee investigation. Freeh also had to deal with the fallout from the Clinton sex and perjury scandals.

Freeh valued his independence, and, early in his tenure as FBI director, he alienated President Bill Clinton by rejecting Clinton's attempts to forge a closer working relationship with him. His official reason for rejecting any alignment with the president was the possibility of legal action against him, but Freeh also wanted complete independence in carrying out his duties. This attitude soon resulted in a souring of relations with President Clinton. Freeh did retain good working relations with the Democrats who controlled Congress. This friendliness with Democrats ended in 1994, however, when the Republicans assumed control of Congress. Freeh soon began to cultivate the Republican leaders. Whether this was a calculated policy or not, Freeh's former good relationships with Democrats ended abruptly. From the time the Republicans gained control of Congress until he resigned, his position was impregnable because of his support from Republicans in Congress.

Toward the end of the Clinton administration, Clinton and Freeh had developed, according to Clinton, "an openly adversarial relationship." Freeh believed that the Clinton administration had prevented the FBI from receiving cooperation from Saudi officials over the Khobar bombing that had taken place on June 25, 1996. Prince Bandar, the Saudi Ambassador to the United States, told Freeh this. He added that the Clinton administration had impeded the FBI's efforts to receive Saudi cooperation because it did not want to risk worsening relations with Iran. In fact, it was Saudi Arabia that wanted to avoid trouble with Iran, and thus limited its cooperation on the Khobar investigation. In actuality, the Clinton administration considered military options against Iran, but Freeh was never informed of them.

Clinton came to distrust Freeh so much that he no longer invited Freeh to top-level national security briefings. This isolation led to some embarrassing incidents such as when President Clinton authorized cruise missiles to be shot at al-Qaeda camps in Afghanistan without notifying Freeh in advance. Freeh's relationship with Janet Reno, the U.S. Attorney General, was also strained. Freeh had enough support among Republicans in Congress and in the media that it was politically impossible for President Clinton to fire him.

Freeh's biggest impact on the FBI was the type of culture he left behind. He had been a field agent earlier in his career and his experiences had led to a deep distrust of FBI headquarters. His tour of duty at FBI headquarters only reinforced this distrust. As soon as Freeh became director, he reduced staff at headquarters. Nearly fifty top-level posts were eliminated and some 600 supervisory agents were reassigned to the field in this purge. This purge led to a large number of senior agents leaving the FBI. Freeh admitted in 2001 that 41 percent of FBI special agents had less than six years of experience. He was also more comfortable with agents in the field than at FBI headquarters.

Freeh was also distrustful of technology. He refused to use a computer in his office. Consequently, the FBI was a paper-based organization to such an extent that it was constantly flooded with paperwork and its analysts at headquarters were unable to keep up with the flow of documents. The FBI's computer system, known as the Automated Case Support system, has been described by Ronald Kessler as "so flawed that memos sent to agents never arrived, and there was no way for the sender to know if a memo had been received." It took twelve commands to store a document on the FBI's computer system. Moreover, the case organization system meant that the computer was unable to send relevant information from one case file to another. Freeh maintained in his memoirs that it was Congress's fault for not appropriating sufficient funds for installing a new computer system.

When Freeh left his position as director of the FBI, it was an organization that operated well in the field offices but exhibited a lack of coordination at headquarters. What has been termed a risk avoidance culture has also caused some controversy, as every decision during Freeh's tenure went through the legal staff first, and the most conservative interpretation of the law was usually upheld by the lawyers. This was partially the reason why Zacarias Moussaoui's laptop was not examined until after September 11. Freeh's relationship with the FBI's top counterterrorism expert, John O'Neill, was strained because of this policy. Freeh's replacement as the director of the FBI was Robert Mueller.

Freeh has returned to the legal profession. In September 2001, he became the senior vice chairman for MBNA America, a large credit card company. Several companies have also appointed him to their board of directors. Freeh wrote an editorial in the November 17, 2005, edition of the *Wall Street Journal* that was critical of the 9/11 Commission. He also authored, with Howard Means, a 1995 book about his career in the FBI: *My FBI: Bringing Down the Mafia, Investigating Bill Clinton, and Fighting the War on Terror*. Most of his criticisms in the book are directed against former President Bill Clinton and his former counterterrorism advisor, Richard A. Clarke.

See Also
Clarke, Richard A.; Clinton Administration; Federal Bureau of Investigation; O'Neill, John

See Document
Document #33

Suggested Reading
Daniel Benjamin and Steven Simon, *The Age of Sacred Terror* (New York: Random House, 2002); Richard A. Clarke, *Against All Enemies: Inside America's War on Terror* (New York: Free Press, 2004); Louis J. Freeh and Howard Means, *My FBI: Bringing Down the Mafia, Investigating Bill Clinton, and Fighting the War on Terrorism* (New York: St. Martin's Press, 2005); Ronald Kessler, *The CIA at War: Inside the Secret Campaign Against Terror* (New York: St. Martin's Griffin, 2003); Peter Lange, *1000 Years for Revenge: International Terrorism and the FBI—the Untold Story* (New York: ReganBooks, 2003); Murray Weiss, *The Man Who Warned America: The Life and Death of John O'Neill, the FBI's Embattled Counterterror Warrior* (New York: ReganBooks, 2003); Richard Gid Powers, *Broken: The Troubled Past and Uncertain Future of the FBI* (New York: Free Press, 2004).

Fresh Kills Landfill

The debris from the World Trade Center complex site was transported to the Fresh Kills Landfill on Staten Island, New York. This island had been used as a landfill for New York City for half a century before it was closed down in March 2001. It was a landfill covering 2,200 acres, and in places it reached 200 feet above the surrounding water. Plans had been made to turn the landfill into a park. Because it had been one of the largest open spaces in the New York City area, the landfill was a natural depository for the debris from the World Trade Center complex site.

Almost from day one, debris came from the World Trade Center site to the Fresh Kills Landfill. At first the debris came by truck, but within days it began to come by barge. Once a debris load arrived at the Fresh Kills Landfill, it underwent a

---

Nature of the Procedures at the Fresh Kills Landfill

Those procedures remained remarkably stable over the course of the operation, because though the conditions at the Trade Center site frequently changed (resulting in production spikes), once the heavy steel had been redirected to New Jersey, the nature of the output destined for Fresh Kills remained largely the same: bargeloads of rubble consisting of broken and crushed concrete, asbestos, asphalt millings, rebar, and other forms of light steel—all stirred through with a homogenized mixture of details from 50,000 working lives, nearly 3,000 of which had just ended violently. Fresh Kills's job was to separate the human mixture from the rest—to dehomogenize the debris.

William Langewiesche, *American Ground: Unbuilding the World Trade Center* (New York: North Point Press, 2002), p. 194.

detailed inspection for body parts and any type of evidence that could be used to understand the nature of the attack. The method used for sorting the materials was complex. First, large items—those larger than six inches—were isolated from the rest of the materials. The remaining materials were then placed in one of four large sorters. These sorters separated the materials into three sizes: less than a quarter of an inch, more than a quarter inch to three inches, and from three to six inches. Because almost all of the material below the size of a quarter of an inch consisted of asphalt milling and dirt, the inspectors only gave them a brief inspection. The two other piles were closely inspected along an assembly line of inspectors. Inspectors were on ninety-minute rotations to keep them alert. Soon after this final inspection, the debris was buried in the landfill.

The only item from the debris not buried was the structural steel. Retaining structural steel would have caused burial problems at the Fresh Kills Landfill. The solution was to sell and send the structural steel to scrap yards in New Jersey. This sale of the structural steel helped defray some of the expense of the World Trade Center complex cleanup.

The process of handling debris at the Fresh Kills Landfill continued beyond the end of the work at the World Trade Center complex in May 2002. Materials ceased arriving, but there was a backlog of work still to be done. The closing ceremony at the World Trade Center complex was held on May 30, 2002. Once the

New York police officers in biohazard suits painstakingly sift through the wreckage of the World Trade Center as it is dumped at the Fresh Kills Landfill on Staten Island in New York, in October 2001. (AP IMAGES/Beth A. Keiser.)

work was completed at the landfill several months later, it was closed again. Plans are still active to make it into a park, but for now it serves as a memorial for the victims of September 11.

See Also
Cleanup Operations at Ground Zero

Suggested Reading
William Langewiesche, *American Ground: Unbuilding the World Trade Center* (New York: North Point Press, 2002).

G

Ganci, Peter J. "Pete" (1946–2001)

Peter Ganci was one of the highest-ranking Fire Department of New York (FDNY) officers to die at the World Trade Center on September 11. He started out in the ranks and worked himself up through the ranks to Chief of the Fire Department of New York. Eleven thousand uniformed officers and firefighters reported to him. Ganci was also one of the most highly decorated firefighters in the history of the FDNY. Members of the fire department loved him because he always considered himself one of them.

Ganci spent his entire life as a firefighter. He was born on October 27, 1946, and raised in North Massapequa, New York. His mother died young, and he was raised by his father. He attended St. Killian's School and Farmingdale High School. He joined the Farmingdale Volunteer Fire Department when he was eighteen, and he never left it, even after employment as a firefighter with the New York City Fire Department. At twenty, he entered the U.S. Army, serving with the 82nd Airborne at Fort Bragg, North Carolina. After serving in the military for two years, Ganci returned to civilian life in 1968 and became a firefighter with Engine Company 92 in the Bronx. After marriage and three children, he opened a bar and restaurant in North Massaquequa, Potter's Pub, to supplement his income. Ganci rose rapidly in the FDNY. He made lieutenant in 1977, captain in 1983, and Chief of the FDNY in 1987. He had a reputation as "a tough, hard-ass firefighter who was fearless." Ganci received numerous citations for bravery in his thirty-three years in the FDNY. As a lieutenant he was cited for saving the lives of three children. His office was at headquarters in Brooklyn.

Ganci responded to the crisis at the World Trade Center like the rest of the New York City Fire Department. He was in his office in Brooklyn when the first plane hit the north tower of the World Trade Center complex. He and his commanders immediately traveled to the World Trade Center complex and established a command center. While there, the fire commissioner, Thomas Von Essen, and the deputy fire commissioner, Bill Feehan, joined him for consultation. Von Essen left to report on the state of affairs to Mayor Giuliani, but Feehan stayed with his old friend Ganci. After the second plane crashed into the south tower, Ganci ordered three command centers to be set up—one in the each tower's lobby and one on the adjacent West Street. Shortly after he received a warning about the danger of collapse of the towers, the south tower collapsed. Then the north tower collapsed twenty-nine minutes after the south tower, burying Ganci and Feehan under four feet of rubble. The search-and-rescue dog, Bear, discovered both Ganci and Feehan's bodies only hours after the collapse of the towers. Ganci was buried with full honors befitting one of the most loved figures in the FDNY.

Reputation of Ganci among Firefighters

To them [fraternity of firefighters] Ganci was the complete fireman; his bravery was laced with an almost reckless competitiveness, the desire that all fireman have to be able to say later, "I opened the door first" or "I got to the fire first." Or, to put this another way, he was known for his instinct to be in front in a fire, to embody the New York Fire Department's sobriquet—the bravest.

Richard Bernstein, *Out of the Blue: The Story of September 11, 2001, From Jihad to Ground Zero* (New York: Times Books, 2002), p. 150.

See Also

Firefighters at Ground Zero; Feehan, William M. "Bill"; Von Essen, Thomas

Suggested Reading

Richard Bernstein, *Out of the Blue: The Story of September 11, 2001, from Jihad to Ground Zero* (New York: Times Books, 2002); Thomas Von Essen with Matt Murray, *Strong of Heart: Life and Death in the Fire Department of New York City* (New York: ReganBooks, 2002).

Giuliani, Rudolph William Louis "Rudy" III (1944–)

Mayor Rudolph Giuliani achieved worldwide fame for his role in the aftermath of the September 11 attack. He was born on May 28, 1944, in Brooklyn, New York. His family was working class. Giuliani attended and, in 1961, graduated from Bishop Loughlin Memorial High School in Brooklyn. His collegiate years were spent at Manhattan College in the Bronx where he graduated in 1965. Next, Giuliani obtained a law degree from New York University Law School in 1968. His first job was clerking for Judge Lloyd MacMahon, U.S. District Judge for the Southern District of New York.

The bulk of Giuliani's career has been spent in government service. His first position was with the Office of the U.S. Attorney in 1970. After a stint as the chief of the narcotics unit and Executive U.S. Attorney, he left for Washington, D.C., in 1975 to become the associate deputy attorney general and chief of staff to the deputy attorney general. Giuliani briefly left government service in 1977 to practice law at the Patterson, Belknap, Webb and Tyler law firm. Then, in 1981 the Reagan administration recruited Giuliani to the office of associate attorney general. Giuliani then was appointed the U.S. Attorney for the Southern District of New York where he earned a reputation for tackling high-profile cases—including those of Wall Street icons Ivan Boesky and Michael Milken.

Giuliani's law-and-order reputation led to his running for the post of New York City mayor. His first attempt as the Republican candidate was unsuccessful; he lost to David Dinkins in 1989 in a close race. His second attempt in 1993 led to his election as mayor after a campaign featuring attacks on crime and rising taxes. Giuliani won reelection in 1997 by a large margin. His law-and-order campaign led to a reduction in crime in New York City. New York City's limit on mayoral terms meant that Giuliani could not run for a third term as mayor, but he was still mayor in September 2001.

Giuliani's career received a boost because of his role in the management of New York City in the aftermath of the September 11, 2001, attacks on the World Trade Center. His response immediately after the assault on the twin towers was to coordinate the response of various city departments, and he made quick contact with state and federal authorities. Giuliani made contact with President George W. Bush and received assurances of federal aid. In the next new few weeks Giuliani held meetings several times a day to coordinate aid and relief. He also worked closely with the fire commissioner, Thomas Von Essen, and the police commissioner, Bernard Kerik, on the activities at the World Trade Center site. Von Essen described the mayor's style as barking, pleading, commiserating, and questioning. At every meeting Giuliani demanded measurable progress on the situation from his subordinates. He was also present and often talked at ceremonies honoring the dead. Giuliani did run into some difficulty trying to reduce the number of firefighters at the World Trade Center site, and he had to back down in a confrontation that took place in early November 2001. This conflict with the firefighters made him furious, but he realized that he had a growing public relations problem unless he compromised.

Because the scheduled date of the mayoral primary was September 11, this primary had to be rescheduled. Few people could make it to the polls on September 11 because the city had been closed down. Giuliani first sought an emergency override of the term-limit law, but this attempt ran into political oppositions, as did his effort to have his term of office extended four months. He left the mayoral office on December 31, 2001.

> **Mayor Giuliani's Role after September 11**
>
> Through it all, the mayor [Giuliani] barked, pleaded, commiserated, prodded, and questioned, just as he always had. At every meeting he wanted to see measurable progress on what you had been working on earlier; he demanded the latest facts and figures from the site; and he piled on the tasks. If you couldn't deliver, he made it clear, you had to get out of the way.
>
> Thomas Von Essen with Matt Murray, *Strong of Heart: Life and Death in the Fire Department of New York* (New York: Regan-Books, 2002), p. 201.

Giuliani left public life with a national reputation. *Time* magazine named Giuliani its Person of the Year for 2001. Shortly after leaving office, Giuliani founded a security consulting business, and he purchased the accounting firm Ernst & Young's investment banking unit, which he named Giuliani Capital Advisors LLC. He also traveled around the country making speeches. He campaigned vigorously for the reelection of President George W. Bush. Bush responded by inviting Giuliani to replace Tom Ridge as Secretary of Homeland Security, but Giuliani turned down the offer. Then in March 2005, Giuliani joined the firm of Bracewell & Patterson LLP, which was promptly renamed Bracewell & Giuliani LLP. Giuliani has maintained his political contacts in the Republican Party, and he has constantly been advanced as a candidate for national office. In the meantime, he was appointed to Congress's Iraq Study Group (ISG). This group had the mission to assess the military situation in Iraq under the sponsorship of the U.S. Institute of Peace.

Giuliani's role has a hero of September 11 has been challenged in recent years. Much of the criticism has come from family members of the victims of September 11. The most vocal have been the families of firefighters. They have criticized Giuliani for

New York Mayor Rudolph Giuliani (center), Fire Commissioner Thomas Von Essen (left), and Chief of the New York Fire Department Peter Ganci (right), cut the ribbon on a new firehouse for Engine Company 75, Ladder 33 and Battalion 19, in the Bronx, on August 16, 2000. Looking on from the background are Captain Thomas Kelly (left) and Captain John Stark (right). (AP IMAGES/Ed Bailey.)

separating the police and firefighter command posts on the morning of September 11 and for not holding emergency drills to check on communication equipment prior to the attacks. Another criticism has been the ineffectiveness of the Office of Emergency Management because of its locations in the World Trade Center complex.

Rudy Giuliani has continued to pursue a political career. In 2007 he announced his intention to seek the 2008 Republican presidential nomination. He ran a lackluster campaign trying to capitalize on his 9/11 reputation. Because of his previous positions on gun control and abortion, he had trouble convincing social conservatives in the Republican Party to support him. After low vote totals in the primaries, Giuliani dropped out of the presidential race on January 31, 2008.

See Also
Kerik, Bernard Bailey; Office of Emergency Management (OEM); World Trade Center, September 11; Von Essen, Thomas

Suggested Reading
Wayne Barrett and Dan Collins, "The Real Rudy: The Image of Rudy Giuliani as the Hero of September 11 Has Never Been Seriously Challenged. That Changes Now," *American Prospect* 17 (September 1, 2006); Jack Newfield, *The Full Rudy: The Man, the Myth, the*

Mania (New York: Thunder's Mouth Press, 2003); Robert Polner, *America's Mayor: The Hidden History of Rudy Giuliani's New York* (New York: Soft Skull Press, 2005); Fred Siegel, *The Prince of the City, Giuliani, New York, and the Genius of American Life* (New York: Encounter Books, 2005); Thomas Von Essen with Matt Murray, *Strong of Heart: Life and Death in the Fire Department of New York* (New York: ReganBooks, 2002).

Giuliani Time (Documentary)

Giuliani Time is a documentary that debates the career of former New York City mayor Rudolph "Rudy" Giuliani. Kevin Keating is an award-winning director of documentaries *When We Were Kings* and *Harlan County, U.S.A.* He began work on the documentary *Giuliani Time* in 1998 during Mayor Giuliani's second term. Keating is no admirer of Giuliani although he allows some of Giuliani's allies to speak of his accomplishments. The main voices in the documentary are critical of Giuliani, particularly Wayne Barrett, a *Village Voice* journalist and the author of an unauthorized critical biography of Giuliani. Little is said of Giuliani's role in the September 11, 2001, attack. The film shows that "his decisiveness, forensic intelligence and wit could be impressive," but it also reveals his "high-handedness, arrogance and meanness." This documentary had little impact on Giuliani's presidential campaign; it was considered too partisan. Even Democratic activists showed little interest in using this documentary against Giuliani.

See Also
Giuliani, Rudolph William Louis "Rudy" III

Suggested Reading
Robin Finn, "Giuliani, through a Lens, Darkly," *New York Times* (May 12, 2006), p. B2; Michael Powell, "'Giuliani Time' Recalls Ex-Mayor's Less Heroic Deeds," *Washington Post* (May 26, 2006), p. C5; A. O. Scott, "Confronting the Legacy of Giuliani: Crime, Race and Urban Politics," *New York Times* (May 12, 2006), p. PT1.

Glick, Jeremy (1970–2001)

Jeremy Glick was one of the passengers on United Airlines Flight 93 who attempted to regain control of the aircraft from al-Qaeda hijackers on September 11, 2001. Glick was a former national collegiate judo champion, and he used his physical abilities to attack the hijackers. The fact that the aircraft crashed does not lessen the courage of Glick's and his fellow passengers' attempt to gain control.

Glick was always athletic and public service–minded. He was born on September 3, 1970, into a Jewish family of six. Glick and his brothers and sisters grew up in Saddle River, New Jersey. He attended Saddle River Day School, graduating in 1988. Always interested in athletics, Glick started training in judo at age seven. In high school, he was also a member of the wrestling team. After high school, Glick studied English at Rochester University. He took time off in 1991 to spend ten months in Israel performing community service and studying Hebrew. During his senior year, Glick participated in the national collegiate judo championship in San Francisco as an independent. He arrived there without a coach or any backing, but his grade school coach was there with another team. This coach helped him, and Glick won the national title in his weight class. He was also elected president of the Alpha Delta Phi fraternity. Glick graduated from Rochester University in 1993. Next, he traveled to Japan where he taught English.

Glick had another reason to compete in the national collegiate judo championship. He was interested in courting a girl from his high school, Lyzbeth Makely, who lived in San Francisco. Their courtship culminated in marriage in 1996. By this time Glick had found a position as a sales rep with Giga Information Group. Then in 2000, he changed jobs and found a position with Vividence, an Internet service provider of products about the behavior, thoughts, and attitudes of Web customers. Although his job meant some traveling, the birth of a daughter, Emerson Glick, made him reluctant to travel from his lakeside home in Hewitt, New Jersey. His daughter was only twelve weeks old when Glick left for a business trip in September 2001.

Like several others on United Airlines Flight 93, Glick was not supposed to have been on that plane. He had planned to leave on September 10, 2001, but because of a fire at the Newark International airport, his flight was rerouted to Kennedy International Airport. Glick decided to take a flight the next morning. On September 11, Glick boarded the plane at Newark International Airport for a business trip to San Francisco. After a forty-five-minute delay, the aircraft lifted off. At approximately 9:28 a.m., the hijackers seized control of the aircraft. Soon afterward, Glick was one of those who used the GTE Airfone to call loved ones. His conversation with his wife confirmed what others were saying: that the hijackers were on a suicide mission. In a twenty-minute conversation, he told his wife of the plans to regain control of the aircraft. The passengers had voted to attack the hijacker. He joked that he still had the butter knife from breakfast. Glick also told his wife to take care of their newborn daughter, and to have a good life. He left the phone on and joined the attackers. Todd Beamer, Mark Bingham, Thomas Burnett, and the others came close to regaining control of the airliner, but the pilot of the hijack team, Ziad Jarrah, put the airliner into a dive and crashed the aircraft near Shanksville, Pennsylvania.

> **Glick's Comments to His Wife on September 11**
>
> "I need you to be happy in the rest of your life," Jeremy told Lyz. "I'll support any decisions that you make." He told her to love their baby and to tell Emerson how much he loved her.
>
> Jere Longman, *Among the Heroes: United Flight 93 & the Passengers & Crew Who Fought Back* (New York: Perennial, 2003), p. 146.

Since September 11, 2001, Glick and his companions have become heroes. They prevented the terrorists from carrying out their mission to crash the airliner into the U.S. Capitol or possibly even the White House. A memorial service was held at the upstate ski resort of Wyndam, New York, where Glick often ski boarded in his youth. This status of hero was small consolation to the widows and children left behind. Glick's wife kept a journal by writing letters to her husband and her daughter. This exercise led to a book *Your Father's Voice* published in 2004. Glick has been honored by the Rochester University, which has endowed a scholarship in his name to support his commitment to the value of a fraternity experience and its rewards.

See Also
Beamer, Todd Morgan; Bingham, Mark Kendall; Burnett, Thomas Edward; Jarrah, Ziad Samir; United Airlines Flight 93

See Document
Document #16

Suggested Reading
Lisa Beamer and Ken Abraham, *Ordinary People, Extraordinary Courage* (Wheaton, IL: Tyndale House Publishers, 2002); Cindi Lash, "An Eloquent Journal of 'Your Father's Voice'," *Pittsburgh Post-Gazette* (November 29, 2004), p. A1; Cindi Lash, "Liz Glick: Widow of Flight 93 Passenger Jeremy Glick," *Pittsburgh Post-Gazette* (September 11, 2002), p. B4; Jere Longman, *Among the Heroes: United Flight 93 and the Passengers and Crew Who Fought Back* (New York: HarperCollins, 2002); Tom Zucco, "Heroes Come from All Walks of Life," *St. Petersburg Times* [Florida] (September 18, 2001), p. 1D.

Goss, Porter J. (1938–)

As a Republican congressman active in intelligence affairs and later head of the CIA, Porter Goss has been concerned about the effectiveness of American intelligence gathering before and after September 11, 2001. Early in his career, until ill health led to his retirement, he was a CIA operative. Goss then turned to politics, becoming a congressman from the 14th congressional district of Florida. Again in the House of Representatives Goss specialized in intelligence, serving as the chairman of the House Intelligence Committee.

Goss had a privileged upbringing. He was born on November 26, 1938, in Waterbury, Connecticut. His early education was at the exclusive Fessenden School in West Newton, Massachusetts, and the equally elite Hotchkiss High School in Lakeville, Connecticut. Goss graduated from that high school in 1956. Next, he attended Yale University where his Bachelor of Arts degree was in ancient Greek. Goss belonged to several prominent societies at Yale. Some of his classmates were William H. T. Bush, the uncle of President George W. Bush, and John Negroponte, career diplomat and Director of National Intelligence from 2005 to 2006.

Most of Goss's early career was with the CIA. It was while he was still at Yale University that the CIA recruited him. His career in the CIA was with the Directorate of Operations (DO). This directorate carries out the clandestine operations of the CIA. Goss worked as a CIA agent in the DO from 1960 until 1971. Most of his activities in the CIA are still classified, but it is known that his area of operation included Latin America and the Caribbean and later Europe. He participated in the events surrounding the Cuban Missile Crisis in 1962. In 1970, while he was in London, health problems led him to resign from the CIA.

Goss began his political career in 1975. He served as mayor of Sanibel City, Florida, in 1975–1977 and again in 1981–1982. In 1988 he ran for the House seat in Florida's 13th congressional district. Goss defeated a former holder of that congressional seat and retained it until 1993. In 1993 he became the congressional representative from Florida's 14th congressional district, and he held this seat until May 5, 2006, when he resigned it to head the CIA. In his sixteen years in Congress, Goss served on specialized committees that had oversight on intelligence. Although Goss had always been supportive of the CIA, he endorsed legislation in 1995 that would have cut intelligence personnel by 20 percent over a five-year period as a budget-cutting measure. Goss served as chair of the House Permanent Committee on Intelligence from 1997 to 2005, and he helped establish and served on the Homeland Security Committee. Throughout his political career, Goss defended the CIA and supported budget increases for it. He also was a strong supporter of George Tenet, the director of the CIA.

The September 11 attacks brought Goss to the political forefront. Goss was having a breakfast meeting with Senator Bob Graham (D-FL) and the chief of Pakistani intelligence, Lieutenant General Mehmoud Ahmed, when news surfaced of the attacks on September 11. They had been discussing what was going on in Afghanistan and the capabilities of al-Qaeda. Goss's immediate response was to find out how this could have happened. In particular, why had the intelligence community not been able to detect the plotters? Goss found that his good friend Senator Graham had the same questions. Together, in their respective houses of Congress, they began to call for a bipartisan investigation into the events surrounding September 11. Both in the Senate and in the House of Representatives there was reluctance to proceed. Opposition was even stronger in the Bush administration against such an investigation. Everyone was afraid of a "gotcha" investigation that would lay blame on them. This fear on both the Republican and the Democratic sides slowed down the setting up of a Senate-House Joint Inquiry on Intelligence, and the length of time provided to produce a report was unrealistically short. Despite the short time span—and reluctance and sometimes nonexistent cooperation from the CIA, the FBI, and the White House—a valuable report was finally issued with sections of it censored.

Goss opposed the creation and many of the recommendations of the 9/11 Commission. Like many of his fellow Republicans, he was fearful that the commission would be a witch hunt against the Bush administration. Even after it was apparent that the 9/11 Commission was bipartisan, Goss opposed its recommendations on intelligence matters. His biggest concern was the recommendation for a national intelligence director whose job would be to oversee all intelligence agencies.

Goss's Opposition to the 9/11 Commission

Breitweiser said that when the victims' families met with Goss to advocate an independent commission to investigate the attacks, he was not supportive. Four steering committee members said that when they made the rounds on Capitol Hill, Goss's staff turned them away, saying that he wasn't there. Mindy Kleinberg, whose husband, Alan, worked on the 104th floor of the World Trade Center, recalled pushing into Goss's office, only to find the congressman hiding: "They said he wasn't there—he was right behind the door."

Laura Blumenfeld, "Goss Hailed as Old Pro, Assailed as Partisan," *Washington Post* (September 13, 2004), p. A1.

As a conservative Republican, Goss has defended the Bush administration in its war on terrorism. He also has been a severe critic of what he calls the failures of the Clinton administration. His loyalty to the Bush administration was noted. When George Tenet resigned as director of the CIA on June 3, 2004, Goss was a natural candidate. President George W. Bush rewarded Goss for his loyalty by nominating him to become director of the CIA. Despite opposition from some Democratic senators, Goss won conformation from the Senate by a vote of 77–17 on September 22, 2004. During his conformation hearings, Goss promised that he would bring change and reform to the CIA.

Goss's tenure as head of the CIA was a mixed record. He arrived at CIA headquarters on September 24, 2004, with a mandate for change, but the top leadership of the CIA showed reluctance to accept him. These leaders were already distressed by how the CIA had been made a scapegoat for past mistakes by both the Clinton and Bush administrations. Several of Goss's top subordinates, particularly his chief advisor Patrick Murray, clashed with senior CIA management, leading three of the top officials—John McLaughlin, Steve Kappes, and Michael Sulick—to resign from the CIA. An attempt by Goss to make the CIA more loyal to the Bush administration also produced criticism. His memo to CIA staff that it was their job "to support the administration and its policies" was the cause of the resentment. Finally, it was Goss's promotion of his friend Kyle Dustin "Dusty" Foggo to a high CIA position from the ranks and his links to former congressman Randy "Duke" Cunningham, who was convicted of accepting bribes, that lowered morale in the CIA.

Eventually, Goss lost out in a power struggle with his nominal boss, John Negroponte. One of the reforms called for in the final report of the 9/11 Commission was coordination of intelligence efforts. This need led to the creation of the position of Director of National Intelligence (DNI) and the appointment of Negroponte, a career diplomat, to that post. Goss and Negroponte had disagreements about how to reform intelligence gathering. Goss was reluctant to transfer personnel and resources from the CIA to the National Counterterrorism Center (NCTC) and the National Counter Proliferation Center (NCPC). These disagreements led to Goss's surprising resignation as Director of the CIA on May 5, 2006, after only nineteen months tenure. His replacement was Negroponte's principal deputy director for national intelligence, four-star Air Force General Michael Hayden.

Representative Porter Goss (left, R-FL) and Senator Bob Graham (right, D–FL), chairmen for the House and Senate Intelligence Committee's Joint Inquiry into intelligence failures leading up to the September 11 attacks, at their hearing on Capitol Hill, September 24, 2002, in Washington. (AP IMAGES/Ken Lambert.)

See Also

Bush Administration; Clinton Administration; Central Intelligence Agency

Suggested Reading

Bob Graham, *Intelligence Matters: The CIA, the FBI, Saudi Arabia, and the Failure of America's War on Terror* (New York: Random House, 2004); James Risen, "Rifts Plentiful as 9/11 Inquiry Begins Today," *New York Times* (June 4, 2002), p. A1.

Graham, Daniel Robert "Bob" (1936–)

Bob Graham, a former governor of the state of Florida and longtime U.S. Senator from Florida, was active in the investigation of intelligence failures of American agencies before the September 11 attacks. He is a lifelong Democrat who has never lost an election in his home state. In the U.S. Senate, Graham specialized in the committee dealing with the intelligence community.

Graham was a successful politician from the beginning. He was born on November 9, 1936, in Coral Gables, Florida. His father was a Florida state senator, mining engineer, and dairy cattleman, and his mother was a schoolteacher. He was the youngest of four children. Graham had family contacts with the *Washington Post* because his brother, Philip Graham, was the husband of Katharine Graham. His political career began in high school at Miami Senior High School when he was elected the student body president. After graduating from high school in 1955, Graham attended the University of Florida. There he was a member of a fraternity and received several student awards. Graduating in 1955, Graham next sought a law degree at Harvard Law School, receiving an LLB in 1962. His family owned Graham Dairy in Miami Lakes, Florida, but the family decided to redevelop the land into a residential and commercial community. Graham participated in this redevelopment and holds a substantial share in the Graham Companies.

Graham decided in the early 1960s to pursue a political career. He ran for the Florida House of Representatives in 1966 and won. Reelected to the Florida House of Representatives in 1968, he opted to run for the Florida State Senate in 1970. Graham was voted into the Florida State Senate in 1970 and again in 1974. Successful in all of his elections, Graham ran for governor of Florida in 1978, winning again. He remained governor of Florida from 1979 to 1987. After two tours as governor, Graham turned to the U.S. Senate. Graham was elected to the U.S. Senate in 1986 and remained there until 2005. Graham toyed with running for President of the United States in the 2004 election, but after announcing his candidacy, he found it difficult to raise funds and withdrew on October 7, 2003. It did not help that he had to undergo heart surgery and received an artificial replacement heart valve in early 2003. Also, his habit of keeping a notebook of his activities made politicians nervous.

Graham was a successful senator, but it was as co-chair of the Senate Select Committee on Intelligence and the House Permanent Select Committee on Intelligence Joint Inquiry into the Terrorist Attacks of September 11 (Joint Committee on Intelligence) that he made a contribution to the understanding of the intelligence failures leading to the September 11 attacks. On September 11, 2001, Graham was having a breakfast meeting with Congressman Porter Goss (R-FL) and the chief of Pakistani intelligence, Lieutenant General Mehmood Ahmed, when news surfaced of the attacks. They had been talking about what was happening in Afghanistan and the capabilities of al-Qaeda.

From this time onward, Graham wanted to know why September 11 happened. Republicans in both Congress and the White House, however, were reluctant to have an investigation for political reasons. They were afraid of an out-of-control investigation that might tarnish the reputation of the Bush administration. Even the Democrats in Congress were somewhat leery because there might be attacks on the Clinton administration. Both Graham and Goss pursued their goal of a bipartisan investigation that would bring about reform in the intelligence community.

Graham worked closely with his co-chair and longtime friend Porter Goss to ferret out weaknesses in intelligence gathering and errors in judgment by intelligence administrators. It was in this committee that the Phoenix Memo, the Moussaoui debacle, the Rowley letter, and the failure of the intelligence agencies to cooperate were pointed out. Despite difficulties in obtaining materials from the CIA, the FBI, and the White House, the final report from the committee was devastating. It pointed out gross failures within the intelligence community that needed to be corrected and fast. Graham chronicled his tenure on the committee in his book *Intelligence Matters: The CIA, the FBI, Saudi Arabia, and the Failure of America's War on Terror* (2004). On his retirement from the U.S. Senate Graham listed his greatest accomplishment in office as "intelligence reform and the new programs to create another generation of intelligence officer." Graham was particularly pleased with the creation of the post of National Intelligence Chief.

Since his retirement, Graham has been active. He taught a one-year term as an Institute of Politics Fellow at Harvard University's John F. Kennedy School of Government. Another of his goals has been the establishment of the Bob Graham Center for Public Service at the University of Florida. He has also been traveling extensively with his wife, Adele.

See Also

Federal Bureau of Investigation; Phoenix Memo; Senate Select Committee on Intelligence and the House Permanent Select Committee on Intelligence Joint Inquiry into the Terrorist Attacks of September 11

Suggested Reading

Bill Adair, "Dress in Gray Suit, Discuss CIA, Mingle," *St. Petersburg Times* [Florida] (February 23, 2003), p. 1F; Bill Adair, "Work That Gave Graham Expertise Muzzles Him," *St. Petersburg Times* (April 28, 2003), p.1A; Bob Graham, *Intelligence Matters: The CIA, the FBI, Saudi Arabia, and the Failure of America's War on Terror* (New York: Random House, 2004); Kathy Kiely, "Intelligence Chairmen Draw Praise for Integrity," *USA Today* (June 5, 2002), p. 8A; New York Times Staff, "Senator Bob Graham, 'Victory in the War on Terrorism Will Not Be Won on the Defensive'," *New York Times* (September 10, 2002), p. A19; Brad Smith, "Citizen Graham," *Tampa Tribune* (December 19, 2004), p. 1.

Criticism That the Final Report Was Not Critical Enough

Senator Bob Graham of Florida, the Democrat who is co-chairman of the joint inquiry, did not publicly respond today, but his aides said that he disagreed with Mr. Shelby's assertions that the final report was not critical enough of officials in the intelligence. The Graham aides pointed out that the report has what they described as strong accountability provisions. They said the report calls for the joint panel to submit its findings to the inspectors general of the relevant agencies to point out either unsatisfactory or exemplary performances by individuals. The inspectors general will then be asked to recommend to their agencies and to Congress specific actions to be taken.

James Risen, "Dissent on Assigning Blame as 9/11 Panel Adopts Report," *New York Times* (December 11, 2002), p. A1.

Griffin, David Ray (1939–)
Dr. David Ray Griffin is a retired professor of philosophy of religion and theology at Claremont University and a leading proponent of the September 11 conspiracy theory that the U.S. government was responsible for the attacks. He has had a long and distinguished academic career and is a leading proponent of postmodern theology. Griffin also views the U.S. government as a direct conspirator in the attacks on the World Trade Center complex and the Pentagon.

Griffin had a distinguished academic career. He was born in 1939 and grew up in a small town in Oregon. Active in the Disciples of Christ Church, he decided to become a minister. He attended Northwest Christian College beginning in 1958 but soon became disenchanted with the conservative-fundamentalist theology taught there. Despite this alienation, Griffin remained at the college and obtained a BA in 1962. Abandoning his plans for the ministry, he entered the University of Oregon to obtain a master's degree in counseling. While at the university, he heard the distinguished theologian and philosopher Paul Tillich in a lecture series. These lectures convinced Griffin to change his academic focus to philosophical theology. He began this course of study at the School of Theology at Claremont University in 1963. Griffin took the 1965–1966 academic year off to study theology at the Johannes Gutenberg University in Mainz, Germany. Returning to Clermont University, Griffin received his PhD in 1970. His first academic job was as assistant professor of theology at the University of Dayton, beginning in 1968. He remained at the University of Dayton teaching theology and Eastern religions until 1973. Accepting a teaching position at Claremont University in 1973, Griffin spent the remainder of his academic career there until his retirement in 2004. In the intervening years, he taught at Cambridge University and the University of California–Berkeley. Then, in 1983, he started the Center for a Postmodern World in Santa Barbara, California. He also became the editor of the SUNY Series in Constructive Postmodern Philosophy in the years between 1987 and 2004. During the course of his academic career, he wrote 24 books and 180 articles.

Since retirement, Griffin has turned his attention from theology to conspiracy politics. According to his own version, Griffin was initially skeptical about the various conspiracy theories surrounding the events of September 11, 2001. Gradually, however, he became convinced that the U.S. government had played a hand in the September 11 attacks. His first book on the topic, *The New Pearl Harbor: Disturbing Questions about the Bush Administration and 9-11,* appeared in 2004. In it Griffin charged that there was evidence that members of the U.S. government had participated in a conspiracy that led to attacks on September 11. Griffin followed this book with another critical of the *9/11 Commission Report.* This book, titled *The 9/11 Commission Report: Omissions and Distortions,* continued the advancement of his thesis that the U.S. government had been involved in the attacks on September 11. His latest book, *Christian Faith and the Truth behind 9/11: A Call to Reflection and Action,* tied his views on the 9/11 plot with how it impacts Christians. Griffin was a charter member of the Scholars for 9/11 Truth, and he has been active in its affairs.

Griffin's views have not gone unchallenged. Critics have pointed out that most of the claims in his books can be explained by chaos surrounding that fateful day when everyone was caught unprepared. Others have stated that Griffin is merely another in a long line of conspiracy theorists who appear after a national emergency. At least one of Griffin's critics, former CIA agent Robert Baer, has maintained that the Bush administration's climate of secrecy and defensiveness has created the atmosphere for conspiracy theories to promulgate.

See Also
Conspiracy Theories; Scholars for 9/11 Truth

Suggested Reading
Reyhan Harmanci, "David Ray Griffin: Theologian Scoffed at 9/11 Conspiracy Theories, Then Looked Closer," *San Francisco Chronicle* (March 30, 2006), p. H24; Michael Powell, "The Disbelievers: 9/11 Conspiracy Theorists Are Building Their Case against the Government from Ground Zero," *Washington Post* (September 8, 2006), p. C1; Douglas Todd, "Another Conspiracy Theory: A Respected Theologian Has Waded into the Debate, and Readers Are Lapping It Up on Two Continents," *Ottawa Citizen* [Canada] (December 4, 2004), p. A17.

Guantánamo Bay Detainment Camp
The Guantánamo Bay Detainment Camp is situated on the Cuban mainland. Guantánamo Bay is an area of forty-five square miles that has been occupied by the United States since 1903. U.S. President Theodore Roosevelt signed an agreement with the Cuban government leasing the bay for 2,000 gold coins per year on February 16, 1903. The original intent of the base was to serve as a coaling station for the U.S. Navy. A subsequent lease was signed on July 2, 1906, on the same terms. A new lease was negotiated between the Cuban government and Franklin Delano Roosevelt in 1934. Shortly after the Cuban Revolution in 1959, the Castro government demanded that the Guantánamo Bay area be returned to Cuban sovereignty, but the American government refused, citing that both parties had to agree to the modification or abrogation of the agreement. The United States sends a check to the Cuban government for the lease amount every year, but the Cuban government has refused to cash the checks.

In its invasion of Afghanistan, the U.S. military captured a large number of al-Qaeda fighters. What to do with these and other prisoners captured in Afghanistan became a national problem. The Bush administration determined that those captured were enemy combatants, not prisoners of war. This decision came after lawyers from the White House, the Pentagon, and the Justice Department had issued a series of secret memorandums that maintained the prisoners had no rights under federal law or the Geneva Conventions. In this ruling enemy combatants were not covered by the Geneva Conventions for treatment as prisoners of war, and they could be held indefinitely without charges. A number of conservative lawyers in the Justice Department's Office of Legal Counsel (OLC) provided the legal opinions for this decision. The Bush administration issued this decision on January 22, 2002. Finally, after considering several sites to hold these prisoners, the U.S. military decided to build a prison at Guantánamo Bay, Cuba: the Guantánamo Bay Detention Camp. Camp X-Ray was the first facility, and the first 110 prisoners arrived there on January 11, 2002. These prisoners were held in wire cages. Later, Camp Delta was constructed, but neither camp was up to standards for prison inmates in the United States. At their peak, the camps held 680 prisoners.

The Bush administration picked Guantánamo Bay area for a specific reason. If the prisoners were held on U.S. soil, then the prisoners might claim access to legal representation and American courts. Guantánamo Bay had a unique legal situation because the land is leased from Cuba and not technically on American soil. Because the United States has no diplomatic relationship with Cuba, the prisoners can have no access to the Cuban legal system. The prisoners reside in legal limbo with few if any legal rights.

The camp is run by the military. At the beginning, command responsibility for the base was divided between Major General Michael Dunlavey, an army reservist, and Brigadier General Rick Baccus, of the Rhode Island National Guard. Dunlavey maintained a hard-line attitude toward the detainees, but Baccus was more concerned about their possible mistreatment. They quarreled over interrogation techniques and other issues. This situation changed when Army Major General Geoffrey Miller replaced them and assumed command at Guantánamo in November 2003. Miller had no experience running a prison camp, and he was soon criticized for allowing harsh interrogation techniques. Later, Miller was transferred to Iraq where he took over responsibility for military prisons there.

After Camp Delta was built, the detainees lived in better but restrictive conditions. At Camp X-Ray, the original camp, the detainees lived behind razor wire in cells open to the elements and with buckets in place of toilets. At Camp Delta the detainees were held in trailer-like structures made from old shipping containers that had been cut in half lengthwise with the two pieces stuck together end to end. Cells were small, six feet eight inches by eight feet, with metal beds fixed to the steel mesh walls. Toilets were squatting-style flush on the floor, and sinks were low to the ground so that detainees could wash their feet before Muslim prayer. There was no air-conditioning for the detainees, only a ventilation system that was supposed to be turned on at 85 degrees but rarely was. Later, a medium-security facility opened up, and it gave much greater freedom and better living conditions to the detainees.

The Bush administration gave the CIA responsibility for interrogations. Because these enemy combatants had no legal standing in American courts, they were treated as merely sources of intelligence. President Bush had determined this stance after deciding that al-Qaeda was a national security issue, not a law enforcement issue. Consequently, the FBI was completely left out of the loop. But this did not mean that the FBI gave up. For various reasons, FBI personnel did interrogate the detainees on occasion.

To encourage cooperation, levels of treatment for detainees are determined by the degree of the detainee's cooperation. Level one was for cooperating prisoners, and they received special privileges. Level two included more moderately cooperative detainees, and they received a few privileges like a drinking cup and access to the library. Level three was for the detainees who absolutely refused to cooperate. They were given only the basics—a blanket, a prayer mat and cap, a Koran, and a toothbrush.

The CIA determined that the most important al-Qaeda prisoners should not be held at the Guantánamo Bay Detention Camp. There were simply too many American officials from too many agencies trying to interrogate the prisoners. Moreover, it was too public. CIA leaders wanted a secret location where there would be no interference in the interrogations. Several secret interrogation sites were set up in friendly countries where the CIA could do what they wanted without interference.

Soon after the prisoners had been transferred to the Guantánamo Bay Detention Camp, reports began to surface about mistreatment of the detainees. A CIA analyst visited the camp in the late spring of 2002, and he was aghast at the treatment of the prisoners. Because he spoke Arabic, he was able to talk to the detainees. In his report this analyst claimed that half of the detainees did not belong there. This report traveled around the Bush administration, but nothing was done about it. The American public was still upset over September 11, and public reports about mistreatment of those held at Guantánamo Bay garnered little sympathy.

The Bush administration decided in the summer of 2006 to transfer the top captured al-Qaeda leaders to the Guantánamo Bay Detention Camp. In September 2006, the transfer of these fourteen detainees was complete. Then, beginning in March 2007, court proceedings were started to determine their status. In the most important case, that of Khalid Sheikh Mohammed, the accused made a total confession of all his activities both in and outside al-Qaeda. Among these were the planning for the September 11 attacks and the execution of Daniel Pearl. His justification was that he was at war against the United States. Proceedings against the other detainees continued in the spring of 2007.

See Also
Bush Administration

See Documents
Document #24; Document #42

Suggested Reading
Edward Epstein, "Guantanamo Is a Miniature America," *San Francisco Chronicle* (January 20, 2002), p. A6; Jonathan M. Hansen, "Making the Law in Cuba," *New York Times* (April 20, 2004), p. A19; Seymour M. Hersh, *Chain of Command: The Road from 9/11 to Abu Ghraib* (New York: HarperCollins, 2004); Erik Saar and Viveca Novak, *Inside the Wire: A Military Intelligence Soldier's Eyewitness Account of Life at Guantanamo* (New York: Penguin Press, 2005); John Yoo, *War by Other Means: An Insider's Account of the War on Terror* (New York: Atlantic Monthly Press, 2006).

H

Hage, Wadih el- (1960–)

Wadih el-Hage is a mysterious al-Qaeda operative, who besides serving as Osama bin Laden's secretary in Sudan, was a key participant in the African Embassy bombings in 1998. At the time of these activities, el-Hage was an American citizen married to an American convert to Islam. Although el-Hage was never one of the leaders of al-Qaeda, he was a valuable asset used on various occasions for odd jobs.

El-Hage has an unconventional background. He was born in 1960 in Lebanon into a Lebanese Catholic family. His birth was difficult, and he was born with a withered right arm. He had a solid education in Lebanese schools. His conversion to Islam took place in Lebanon sometime in the late 1970s. El-Hage was already a Muslim by the time he immigrated to the United States in 1978. That same year he enrolled at the University of Louisiana at Lafayette to study urban planning. It took him eight years to complete his degree. During his schooling, el-Hage became attracted to military Islamist theology. After his conversion to militancy, he traveled to Pakistan to help in the Afghan-Soviet War, but his disability prevented him from participating in the fighting. Instead, he worked for the Saudi charity Muslim World League.

El-Hage returned to the United States in 1985 in time to be married. He married April Ray, a recent convert to Islam. They were eventually to have seven children. Despite his degree in urban planning, el-Hage had to take a series of menial jobs to support his family. He decided to move his family to Quetta, Pakistan. El-Hage stayed there for only about a year and a half. Between 1987 and 1990, he made frequent trips to Brooklyn's al-Kifah Refugee Center. El-Hage ran the al-Kifah Refugee after the death of Mustafa Shalabi. There he met several of the Muslim extremists who later participated in the 1993 World Trade Center bombing. His name came up in the trial of the 1993 bombers, but at the time of the bombing, el-Hage had been in Sudan working as bin Laden's secretary. This position lasted until bin Laden returned to Afghanistan.

Between 1996 and 1997, el-Hage held two jobs. He worked at Lone Star Tires as a manager in Arlington, Texas. His other job was allegedly doing charity work in Nairobi, Kenya. In reality, el-Hage was building an al-Qaeda cell network in Nairobi to plan and implement the bombing of the American embassy in downtown Nairobi. While in Nairobi, he roomed with the operational commander of the mission Haroun Fazil.

After the bombing, el-Hage was arrested by Kenyan authorities. American authorities used rendition to take him back to the United States. He was placed on trial in a Manhattan federal court where he was charged with perjury for his untrue statements about his relationship with bin Laden and for his participation in an al-Qaeda conspiracy to kill Americans. Because he was never charged with complicity in the American embassy bombing in Nairobi, the maximum penalty prosecutors could request was life imprisonment without parole. A federal jury convicted el-Hage of perjury, and he received the penalty of life imprisonment without parole. El-Hage is now serving this sentence in a maximum-security federal prison.

El-Hage was not a participant in the September 11 plot, but his career shows how militant Islamists placed their cause above all else. El-Hage had a large family and with some effort could have found a decent job to support his family. Instead, he joined al-Qaeda and worked against his adopted country. His lawyer appealed his case, but in November 2005 a federal judge in Manhattan refused to overturn the 2001 conviction of el-Hage.

See Also
African Embassy Bombings; Bin Laden, Osama; Kifah Refugee Center, al-; Rendition; World Trade Center Bombing (1993)

Suggested Reading
Peter L. Bergen, *Holy War Inc.: Inside the Secret World of Osama bin Laden* (New York: Free Press, 2001); Simon Houpt, "Embassy Bombers Sentenced to Life," *Globe and Mail* [Canada] (October 19, 2001), p. A5; Elizabeth Neuffer, "Four Guilty in Embassy Bombings," *Boston Globe* (May 30, 2001), p. A1; Robert Tait, "Bin Laden Men Jailed for Embassy Bombs," *Scotsman* [Glasgow] (October 19, 2001), p. 9; Benjamin Weiser, "Going on Trial," *New York Times* (February 4, 2001), p. 27; Benjamin Weiser, "Jury Rejects Death Penalty for Terrorist," *New York Times* (July 11, 2001), p. B1; Benjamin Weiser, "Judge Upholds Conviction in Terror Case," *New York Times* (November 3, 2005), p. B1.

Hamburg Cell

A group of radical Islamists formed a terrorist cell affiliated with al-Qaeda in Hamburg, Germany. This cell began when Mohamed Atta, Ramzi bin al-Shibh, and Marwan al-Shehhi began rooming together on November 1, 1998, in an apartment on 54 Marienstrasse in Hamburg. They were members of a study group at the al-Quds Mosque run by Mohammad Belfas, a middle-aged postal employee in Hamburg originally from Indonesia. Both in the study group and at the apartment they began talking about ways to advance the Islamist cause. Soon the original three attracted others of a like mind. The nine members of this cell were Mohamed Atta, Said Bahaji, Mohammad Belfas, Ramzi bin al-Shibh, Zakariya Essabor, Marwan al-Shehhi, Ziad Jarrah, Mounir el Motassadez, and Abdelghani Mzoudi. At first Belfas was the leader of the group, but he was soon replaced by Atta and left the cell. Atta then became the formal leader of the Hamburg Cell, but bin al-Shibh was its most influential member because he was better liked in the Muslim community than the dour Atta.

At first the members of the Hamburg Cell wanted to join the Chechen rebels in Chechnya in fighting against the Russians. Before this move could take place, the leaders of the cell met with Mohamedou Ould Slahi, an al-Qaeda operative in Duisburg, Germany, who advised that they undertake military and terrorist training in Afghanistan first. Atta, bin al-Shibh, Jarrah, and al-Shehhi traveled to Kandahar, Afghanistan, where they underwent extensive training in terrorist methods. They also met with Osama bin Laden, at which time Atta, Jarrah, and Shehhi were recruited for a special martyrdom mission to the United States.

Bin al-Shibh was to have been a part of this mission, but he was never able to obtain a visa to travel to the United States. Instead, bin al-Shibh stayed in Hamburg, serving as the contact person between the Hamburg Cell and al-Qaeda. He also served as the banker for the September 11 plot.

The most dedicated members of the Hamburg Cell participated in the September 11, 2001, plot. Other members of the group, however, provided moral and technical support. Mamoun Darkanza was the money man for the Hamburg Cell. What made those in the Hamburg Cell so important was that they were fluent in English, well-educated, and accustomed to the Western lifestyle, so they could fit in any of the Western countries. They also had the capability to learn how to pilot a large aircraft with some training.

Bin al-Shibh shut down the Hamburg Cell as soon as he learned the date of the attacks. He made certain that anyone connected with the Hamburg Cell was forewarned so that they could protect themselves. Bin al-Shibh destroyed as much material as possible before leaving for Pakistan. Only later did German and American authorities learn of the full extent of the operations of the Hamburg Cell.

German authorities had been aware of the existence of the Hamburg Cell, but German law prevented action against the cell's members unless a German law was violated. This restriction did not prevent a veteran CIA officer attached to the American consulate in Hamburg, Thomas Volz, from attempting to persuade the German authorities to take action against the Islamist extremists in the Hamburg Cell. Volz had become suspicious of several members of the Hamburg Cell and their connections with other Muslim terrorists. He hounded the German authorities to do something until his actions alienated them to the point that they almost had him deported from Germany.

After the September 11 attacks, German authorities began a serious investigation of the Hamburg Cell and its surviving members. By this time there was little to examine or do except to arrest whoever had been affiliated with it. German authorities learned the extent to which al-Qaeda had been able to establish contacts in Germany and elsewhere in Europe.

See Also

Atta, Mohamed el-Amir Awad el-Sayed; Bin al-Shibh, Ramzi; Quds Mosque, al-; World Trade Center, September 11

Suggested Reading

Richard Bernstein, *Out of the Blue: The Story of September 11, 2001, from Jihad to Ground Zero* (New York: Times Books, 2002); Terry McDermott, *Perfect Soldiers: The 9/11 Hijackers: Who They Were, Why They Did It* (New York: HarperCollins, 2005); Gerald Posner, *Why America Slept: The Failure to Prevent 9/11* (New York: Ballantine Books, 2003); Marc Sageman, *Understanding Terror Networks* (Philadelphia: University of Pennsylvania Press, 2004).

Hamburg Cell (TV Movie)

On August 23, 2004, a fictionalized study of the September 11 skyjackers premiered at the Edinburgh International Film Festival. It was a project co-produced by Channel 4 in the United Kingdom and CBS in Canada. Antonia Bird, a British movie director with a reputation for controversially themed movies, made this semi-documentary based on a film script by Ronan Bennett. Bennett is famous as a prominent Irish Republican sympathizer.

The director tried to make the story line as realistic as possible. Two actors with Arab backgrounds played Mohammed Atta (Maral Kamel) and Ziad Jarrah (Karim Saleh). The central figure in the movie is the character Jarrah. It shows him in the process of changing from a moderate Muslim into a terrorist. Most of the action in the movie dealt with the background and planning of the September 11 operation. Using computer-generated imagery, the enactment of the events of September 11 was enhanced. This movie appeared in Great Britain and Germany, but not in the United States. Some of the British families of September 11 victims were disturbed by the showing of the movie, and they expressed their unhappiness openly.

See Also

Atta, Mohamed el-Amir Awad el-Sayed; Hamburg Cell; Jarrah, Ziad Samir; World Trade Center, September 11.

Suggested Reading

Malcolm Fitzwilliams and Anthony Barnes, "Parents of British Victim Attack Cruel and Insensitive TV Drama about 9/11 Hijackers," *Independent on Sunday* [London] (August 29, 2004), p. 6; S. F. Said, "The Ordinary Terrorists: Controversial Director Antonia Bird's Latest Film Is Her Most Ambitious Yet," *Daily Telegraph* [London] (August 31, 2004), p. 19.

Hamdani, Mohammad Salman (1977–2001)

Mohammad Hamdani was an American Muslim in medical technician training with the New York City Police Department who died helping people evacuate the buildings at the World Trade Center complex on September 11, 2001. His unexplained disappearance led the Joint Terrorist Task Force to suspect him of terrorism. Only after his body was found at the World Trade Center site was he exonerated.

Hamdani came to the United States at an early age. He was born on December 28, 1977, in Pakistan. His family moved to the United States when he was only one year old. He was the eldest son. His father runs a candy store in Brooklyn, and his mother is a literacy teacher in a middle school. Hamdani grew up and was educated in New York City. His childhood was typically American; he loved baseball and the Star Wars movies. He graduated from Queens College with a degree in biochemistry. His goal was to become a medical doctor, but in the meantime he worked as a laboratory research assistant at the Howard Hughes Medical Institute at Rockefeller University. Hamdani had applied and been accepted to the medical technician program of the NYPD and had begun its training program.

On September 11 Hamdani responded to the emergency at the World Trade Center complex. Hamdani was evidently heading to his job on the elevated train from his home in Queens when he witnessed the first aircraft crash into the North Tower. He headed to the World Trade Center complex with his medical bag to help the injured. Unfortunately, he was killed in the collapse of the buildings, but his body was not recovered until months later.

Hamdani's unexplained disappearance led to suspicion that he was somehow involved in the World Trade Center attacks. The Joint Terrorist Task Force began to look for him for questioning. An unofficial poster appeared all over the World Trade Center site with his picture and personal background, noting that the Joint Terrorist Task Force was seeking him. Rumors began to spread, and a newspaper article charged that he was part of the al-Qaeda plot against the World Trade Center. These rumors gained some credibility when an article in the *New York Post* repeated them. This theorizing continued even though unofficial sources in the NYPD believed that Hamdani had died at the World Trade Center complex. His mother refused to believe that he was dead, and she believed that he had been arrested by the government after the September 11 attacks. All of this speculation ended when his remains were found along with his medical bag and an identification card on March 29, 2002.

Unselfish Acts of Hamdani

Yet another confirmed death, the awful doing of terrorists. But the story of 23-year-old Salman, as his family called him, was unlike those of most of the people missing in the attack on the World Trade Center. A mystery surrounded his disappearance. He did not work at the trade center. He had no appointment there. He did not show up at work on Manhattan's Upper East Side. And he never came home. When there are questions there are often rumors, which there were about Mr. Hamdani, scurrilous whisperings that he was either connected to the terrorists or hiding out, scheming to profit from the tragedy. . . . Mr. Hamdani, who wanted to be a doctor, must have seen the destruction from the elevated No. 7 subway line, and instead of going to his job as a research assistant at Rockefeller University, headed south. "He gave his life for humanity," said his mother, Talat Hamdani, a teacher at a middle school in Queens. "He did not know a single soul down there, he did not have to go there. He was a son of New York City." And, as overused as the word is, a hero.

Joyce Purnick, "A Son Lost, A Reputation Redeemed," *New York Times* (March 25, 2002), p. B1.

Both his family and his fellow Muslims at the Islamic Cultural Center of New York were bitter about Hamdani's treatment. Hamdani had become an American citizen, and he had never expressed any sympathy toward Muslim extremism. His family and friends thought he had been unfairly treated. Police Commissioner Edmond Kelly attended Hamdani's funeral and spoke of his courage in trying to help those victims of the World Trade Center attacks.

See Also

Casualties of September 11

Suggested Reading

David W. Ausmus, *In the Midst of Chaos: My 30 Days at Ground Zero* (Victoria, BC [Canada]: Trafford, 2004); Glenda Cooper, "A Muslim Family in N.Y. Fears for a Son Who Loved America," *Washington Post* (September 18, 2001), p. A22; William J. Gorta and Simon Crittle, "Missing—or Hiding?—Mystery of NYPD Cadet from Pakistan," *New York Post* (October 12, 2001), p. 11; Joyce Purnick, "Praying for a Son to Be in Jail," *New York Times* (October 29, 2001), p. F1; Joyce Purnick, "A Son Lost, a Reputation Redeemed," *New York Times* (March 25, 2002), p. B1.

Hamilton, Lee H. (1931–)

Lee H. Hamilton was the co-chair of the 9/11 Commission. He is a former Democratic congressman from Indiana, having served from 1965 to 1999. After leaving Congress, he became the president and director of the Woodrow Wilson

International Center for Scholars. His reputation for bipartisanship and ability to work on commissions made him a natural choice for the 9/11 Commission.

Hamilton started out his career as a lawyer. He was born on April 20, 1931, in Daytona Beach, Florida. His family moved first to Tennessee before settling in Evansville, Indiana. He graduated from Central High School, Evansville, in 1948. His basketball ability in high school continued in college at DePauw University. He graduated from DePauw University in 1952. Hamilton was inducted into the Indiana Basketball Hall of Fame in 1982. His next venture was studying aboard at Goethe University, Frankfurt on the Main, West Germany, in the academic year 1952–1953. Upon returning the United States, Hamilton entered law school at Indiana University. After graduating with a JD in 1956, he practiced law in Chicago and Columbus, Indiana. He decided in 1964 to run for public office in the 9th Congressional District of Indiana. Winning election in 1965, he represented that district until 1999.

In his thirty-four years in the House of Representatives, Hamilton garnered expertise on foreign policy and intelligence issues. He served as member and chair of the House Committee on Foreign Affairs and as the chair of the House Permanent Select Committee on Intelligence among other positions. He was also chair of the House Committee to Investigate Covert Arms Transactions with Iran. Over the years Hamilton established his credentials as the leading congressional expert on foreign affairs. It was this expertise and his ability to work both with Republicans and Democrats that made his appointment to the 9/11 Commission possible.

Hamilton played a positive role as co-chair of the 9/11 Commission. Thomas Kean appointed him co-chair of the commission in the spirit of bipartisanship. They worked closely together and displayed a common front before the media. His foreign-policy and intelligence-gathering expertise proved useful in the compiling of the final version of the *9/11 Commission Report*. Both Hamilton and Kean, however, chaffed at the roadblocks put up to hinder the commission's access to information. They were particularly unhappy with the FAA and NORAD's failures to produce documents. Their unhappiness has been articulated in their 2006 book *Without Precedent: The Inside Story of the 9/11 Commission*.

Hamilton has been active since the release of the *9/11 Commission Report*, responding to critics. A whole industry of critics of the 9/11 Commission has surfaced, attacking its findings, omissions, and alleged distortions. Hamilton has responded to these critics by pointing out the immensity of the project and the limited amount of time to undertake it. Perhaps the most serious charge was the failure of the 9/11 Commission to handle the Able Danger story.

> **Comment on What the 9/11 Commission Accomplished by Lee Hamilton**
>
> An awful lot that we recommended has been adopted. If you looked at all of our recommendations with regard to intelligence, they basically have been enacted into law and enacted into law in a remarkably quick period of time. And if you look at the other recommendations, you can see progress on almost all of them . . . It is not a record we should be totally discouraged about.
>
> Quoted in David T. Cook, "Thomas Kean and Lee Hamilton," *Christian Science Monitor* (December 6, 2005), p. 25.

News of Able Danger came late in the 9/11 Commission deliberations, and it was simply not considered reliable.

9/11 Commission chairman Thomas Kean (left) and vice chairman Lee Hamilton (right) discuss the commission's final report after its release in Washington, July 22, 2004. The report concluded that a "failure of imagination"—not government neglect—allowed nineteen hijackers to carry out the 9/11 attacks. (AP IMAGES/Dennis Cook.)

See Also
Able Danger; Kean, Thomas Howard; National Commission on Terrorist Attacks upon the United States

See Document
Document #34

Suggested Reading
Thomas H. Kean, Lee H. Hamilton, and Benjamin Rhodes, *Without Precedent: The Inside Story of the 9/11 Commission* (New York: Knopf, 2006); Kathy Kiely, "Intelligence Chairmen Draw Praise for Integrity," *USA Today* (June 5, 2002), p. 8A.

Hanjour, Hani Saleh Husan (1972–2001)

Hani Saleh Hanjour was the leader and probable pilot of the terrorist group that seized the American Airlines Flight 77 and crashed it into the Pentagon on September 11, 2001. He was a last-minute recruit because the September 11 conspirators needed one more pilot. Although Hanjour was a terrible pilot, he had enough skill to guide an airliner into a stationary target.

Hanjour had advantages in life, but he lacked the abilities to capitalize on them. He was born on August 30, 1972, in Ta'if, Saudi Arabia. His father was a successful food-supply businessman in Ta'if. Hanjour was a devout Muslim, and it colored all of his conduct. Because he was an indifferent student, Hanjour was only persuaded to stay in school by his older brother. This older brother, who was living in Tucson, Arizona, encouraged him to come to the United States. Hanjour arrived in the United States on October 3, 1991. He stayed in Tucson, Arizona, where he studied English at the University of Arizona. After completing the English program in three months, Hanjour returned to Ta'if. He spent the next five years working at his family's food-supply business. In 1996 he briefly visited Afghanistan. Following this visit, Hanjour decided to move back to the United States. He stayed for a time with an Arab American family in Hollywood, Florida. Then in April 1996, Hanjour moved in with a family in Oakland, California. This time he attended Holy Names College and attended a course in intensive English. Hanjour decided to become a pilot and fly for Saudi Airlines. Hanjour also enrolled in a class at Sierra Academy of Aeronautics, but he withdrew because of the cost. After leaving Oakland in April 1996, he moved to Phoenix, Arizona. This time he paid for lessons at CRM Flight Cockpit Resource Management in Scottsdale, Arizona, but his academic performance there was disappointing. His instructors found him to be a terrible pilot, and it took him a long time to master the essentials of flying. While in Phoenix, he roomed with Bandar al-Hazmi. In January 1998, Hanjour took flying lessons at Arizona Aviation, and after a three-year struggle, he earned his commercial pilot rating in April 1999. Hanjour was unable to find a job as a pilot. His FAA license expired in 1999 when he failed to take a mandatory medical test.

Frustrated in his job hunting, Hanjour traveled to Afghanistan. He arrived there just as Khalid Sheikh Mohammed's men were looking for another pilot for the September 11 plot. Hanjour was made to order. After his recruitment by al-Qaeda, he returned to the United States. In September 2000, when he moved to San Diego, California, Hanjour met up with Nawaf al-Hazmi. Hanjour returned to Phoenix to continue his pilot training at the Jet Tech Flight School. He was so inept as a flyer and his English was so bad that the instructors contacted the FAA to check on whether his commercial license was valid. The FAA confirmed that his commercial license was indeed valid. Hanjour spent most of his time there on the Boeing 737 simulator. Next, he moved to Paterson, New Jersey, in the early spring of 2001. There he met several times with other members of the September 11 conspiracy. On September 11, 2001, Hanjour was the hijackers' pilot of American Airlines Flight 77. Despite his lack of ability, he managed to fly that aircraft into the Pentagon.

See Also
American Airlines Flight 77; Mohammed, Khalid Sheikh; Pentagon Attack; Pilot Training for September 11

Suggested Reading
Bob Graham, *Intelligence Matters: The CIA, the FBI, Saudi Arabia, and the Failure of America's War on Terror* (New York: Random House, 2004); Terry McDermott, *Perfect Soldiers: The Hijackers: Who They Were, Why They Did It* (New York: HarperCollins, 2005).

Hazmi, Nawaf bin Muhammad Salim al- (1976–2001)
Nawaf al-Hazmi was one of the hijackers of American Airlines Flight 77, which crashed into the Pentagon on September 11, 2001. He was intended to be one of the team pilots, but he lacked the skills to fulfill that role. Instead, al-Hazmi worked behind the scenes to provide logistical support to all the teams.

Al-Hazmi became an Islamist militant at an early age. He was born on August 9, 1976, in Mecca, Saudi Arabia. His father was a grocer. An older brother was a police chief in Jizan, Saudi Arabia. As a teenager, al-Hazmi had traveled to Afghanistan. In Afghanistan, he met Khalid al-Mihdhar. They joined the Muslims in Bosnia to fight against the Serbian Bosnians in 1995. Then with his brother Salem al-Hazmi, al-Hazmi and al-Mihdhar returned to Afghanistan in time to fight with the Taliban against the Afghan Northern Alliance. Next, al-Hazmi traveled to Chechnya in 1998 to fight with the Chechen rebels. Returning to Saudi Arabia in early 1999, al-Hazmi decided to go to the United States with al-Mihdhar and his brother Salem al-Hazmi. They easily obtained visas.

By 1999 al-Hazmi had been recruited by al-Qaeda for a special mission. Original plans had called for him to become a pilot, but he lacked the necessary competency in English and the ability to pass pilot's training. He teamed with al-Mihdhar to provide logistical support for the September 11 plot. On September 11, 2001, al-Hazmi was part of the American Airlines Flight 77 hijacker team. He provided security while the airliner was crashed into the Pentagon.

See Also
American Airlines Flight 77; Mihdhar, Khalid al-; Pentagon Attack.

Suggested Reading
Terry McDermott, *Perfect Soldiers: The 9/11 Hijackers: Who They Were, Why They Did It* (New York: HarperCollins, 2005).

Homer, LeRoy Wilton Jr. (1965–2001)

LeRoy Homer was the first officer of United Airlines Flight 93, which crashed near Shanksville, Pennsylvania, on September 11, 2001. Captain Jason M. Dahl was the pilot on that fateful flight. Homer and Dahl tried to fight off the hijackers but were overpowered.

Homer had always wanted to be a pilot. He was born on August 27, 1965, and grew up in West Islip, on Long Island, New York. His parents had nine children but only two boys. At an early age, Homer dreamed of flying, and he started flight instruction at age fifteen. His first solo was at age sixteen. In 1983 Homer qualified for his private pilot's certificate. He attended high school in West Islip. Always a good student, Homer fulfilled a lifelong dream by entering the U. S. Air Force Academy on July 6, 1983. He rose to the cadet rank of captain in Cadet Squadron 31. He graduated from the U. S. Air Force Academy on May 27, 1987, and received a commission as a second lieutenant in the U.S. Air Force. His first assignment was flying Lockheed C-141B Starlifter out of McGuire Air Force Base in New Jersey. His duties required him to fly supplies into the war zones of Operations Desert Storm and Desert Shield. Later, he also flew missions in Somalia. Homer rose to the rank of captain before leaving the Air Force in 1995. He remained a member of the U.S. Air Force Reserve, serving as a flight instructor and recruiting officer. His duty in the reserves led to his promotion to the rank of major.

Shortly after leaving active duty in the Air Force, Homer found a position as a pilot with United Airlines. He joined United Airlines in May 1995. His first assignment was as second officer on the Boeing 727. In 1996, he was promoted to first officer on the Boeing 757/767. Homer married Melodie Thorpe, a Canadian native, on May 24, 1998, and they had one daughter. They lived in Marlton, New Jersey.

On September 11, 2001, United Airlines Flight 93 took off from Newark International Airport, headed for San Francisco International Airport with no hint of trouble. On board was a team of hijackers led by Ziad Jarrah. Not long after the aircraft reached its designated flight height, the hijackers invaded the cockpit and gained control of the aircraft. Both Homer and Dahl were overpowered, and they may have been incapacitated or killed. When the passengers learned that the hijackers were on a suicide mission, they tried to regain control of the cockpit and almost succeeded. Realizing that danger, Jarrah crashed the aircraft in a field near Shanksville, Pennsylvania, killing all aboard.

Homer has received many honors since his death. He had always been well-liked both in the military and in civilian life, so tributes to him have flooded in. A memorial service was held in Hamilton, Ontario, and in Trenton, New Jersey. The Congress of Racial Equality (CORE) honored him, and he received the Dr. Martin Luther King, Jr. Award. In his honor, the LeRoy W. Homer Jr. Foundation has been established to provide financial support and encouragement to young people with an interest in aviation, to pursue professional training leading to certification as a private pilot.

See Also
Dahl, Jason Matthew; Jarrah, Ziad Samir; United Airlines Flight 93

Suggested Reading
Johanna Huden, "Kin Recall Tragic United Pilot," *New York Post* (September 21, 2001), p. 16; Marshall Wilson, "Widow of United Co-Pilot Retraces Fatal Sept. 11 Flight," *San Francisco Chronicle* (January 19, 2002), p. A8.

I

Ielpi, Lee (1944–)

Lee Ielpi is a retired firefighter who has become a leader in the September 11 families movement since losing his son at the World Trade Center complex on September 11. As of 2001, he had retired after twenty-six years in the New York City Fire Department (FDNY). Nineteen of those years had been with the Rescue 2 company. At the time of his retirement, Ielpi was one of the most highly decorated firemen in the history of the FDNY.

Ielpi had always wanted to be a firefighter. He was born in 1944 in Great Neck, New York. After high school, Ielpi joined the Great Neck Vigilant Fire Department in 1963. Within a few years he was promoted to chief of that fire department. In 1968 Ielpi was drafted into the U.S. Army, and he served a tour of duty in Vietnam with the 2nd Battalion, 28th Infantry, 1st Infantry Division. While in Vietnam, he was a member of a reconnaissance unit and earned several medals for bravery under fire. Leaving the army in 1970, Ielpi immediately joined the FDNY. For the first seven years, he worked in the Brownsville station of Brooklyn, New York. Then, in 1977, he became a member of the elite Rescue 2 company. By his retirement Ielpi had earned twenty-four citations for exemplary service, including a Class B Ribbon of Honor for service beyond the call of duty.

Ielpi lost his eldest son on September 11, 2001, at the World Trade Center complex. Ielpi had married before beginning his military duty, and he and his wife had two sons and two daughters. In 2001 both sons were firefighters with the FDNY. His eldest son, Jonathan Ielpi, was a firefighter in Squad 288 in Queens. Jonathan's squad responded to the World Trade Center attack by racing to the scene. The squad was busy evacuating people from the south tower when the building collapsed. Jonathan and six members of his squad died.

Ielpi arrived at the World Trade Center complex shortly after the collapse of the twin towers. He spent the next three months working in the debris trying to recover bodies and hoping to find his son's body. Jonathan's body was found on December 11, 2001, and his funeral was held on December 27, 2001. During those months Ielpi became an expert on the recovery process. When the mayor's office decided to reduce the number of firefighters and police working at the site,

Ielpi was one of the spokespersons who negotiated a compromise keeping more firefighters and police at the site looking for bodies or remains.

Ielpi has slowly become one of the leaders of the September 11 families movement. He has not been one of the more vocal leaders, but he has maintained contact with the other leaders of the movement. When the 9/11 Commission wanted a tour of Ground Zero at the World Trade Center, Ielpi gave the tour. Ielpi then helped start the September 11th Families Association. This group has served as an umbrella organization for the families, and its headquarters is at a building across the street from the World Trade Center complex site. He has also been active in the controversy over what type of buildings will be built on the site and what kind of memorial for the victims will be on the site. Much of his energy has been devoted to serving as the "ambassador for the dead," taking trips around the country to talk to school and community groups about September 11.

See Also

Firefighters at Ground Zero; World Trade Center, September 11

Suggested Reading

Mike Dillon, "The Persistence of Memory," *Pittsburgh Post-Gazette* (March 16, 2003), p. B2; Muriel Dobbin, "Sept. 11 Families Still Linked by Loss," *Sacramento Bee* (August 9, 2004), p. A1; Mike Littwin, "Father of Fallen Firefighter Wages War Against Complacency," *Rocky Mountain News* [Denver] (September 11, 2006), p. 2S; Patrice O'Shaughnessy, "Witness to Devastation: Retired Firefighter, Vietnam Vet Went to Find Son—and Stayed," *Daily News* [New York] (May 27, 2002), p. 5; Dennis Smith, *Report from Ground Zero* (New York: Viking, 2002).

Lee Ielpi, a retired New York City firefighter, pauses near the site of the New York World Trade Center disaster, where he volunteered in the recovery effort, December 1, 2001. (AP IMAGES/Mark Lennihan.)

Lee Ielpi's Comments at the End of the Search

People have been building up the last day to be a horrible day. I have other things . . . . I don't know what others will do. I set a goal on the second day, when I realized this wasn't going to turn out very good. The main goal was to find my son, and others. I walked in the shoes of these people, of the civilians at home, then I was blessed we could bring Jon [his son] home and bring him to bed. How could I not come back to try to find others?

Quoted in Patrice O'Shaughnessy, "Retired Firefighter, Vietnam Vet Went to Find Son—And Stayed," *Daily News* [New York] (May 27, 2002), p. 5.

Immigration and Naturalization Services (INS)

The Immigration and Naturalization Services (INS) had the legal responsibility to monitor entrance of foreigners into the United States, and in the case of the September 11 conspirators, it failed miserably. All of the September 11 conspirators had little trouble entering the United States, despite doctored passports and false statements on visa applications. Most of the hijackers were from Saudi Arabia, where there was an express approval program for visas to the United States.

The exception to this ease in entering the United States was the case of Jose Melendez-Perez. He was an immigration inspector at Orlando International Airport when, on August 4, 2001, he interviewed a Saudi national by the name of Mohamed al-Katani. Melendez-Perez questioned al-Katani through an Arabic translator, and he became suspicious of al-Katani's conduct and answers. When Melendez-Perez tried to put al-Katani's answers under oath, al-Katani refused. After consulting with his supervisor, Melendez-Perez denied al-Katani entry and had him placed on an airliner back to Saudi Arabia. Melendez-Perez had risked his job by rejecting al-Katani because instructions had come down that Saudis were to receive special treatment. Evidence surfaced later indicating that Mohamed Atta was waiting for him at the Orlando International Airport. Staff at the 9/11 Commission have surmised that al-Katani was to be the twentieth hijacker. Al-Katani was later captured in Afghanistan, and he has been held at the Guantánamo Bay Detention Camp as an enemy combatant.

Part of the reason the INS was so ineffectual was that it was not actively looking for possible terrorists. To the INS leadership immigration was an economic issue—how many immigrants could be admitted and what impact they would have on the American economy. Also, it has long been noted, according to Daniel Benjamin and Steven Simon, that "the INS was considered the most poorly administered, underfunded, understaffed, and woefully disorganized part of the U.S. government." It had an antiquated paper system in which it could take an analyst almost two years to detect fraud, by which time the miscreant had disappeared into American cities. An effort had been made in the 1980s with the issuance of a *Red Book* to guide and train immigration and custom officials in the detection of fraudulent passports and visas, but the INS ceased printing it in 1992. The official explanation was that terrorists had obtained access to the book and could take countermeasures.

There was an attempt in the mid-1990s to build a system that could track foreign students. At the time there were approximately half a million international students in the United States, but no one knew who they were, where they were, and what their status was. The Department of Justice wanted a system that could track these students. Maurice Berez, a mid-level INS civil servant, formed a task force that devised a program called the Coordinated Interagency Partnership Regulating International Students (CIPRIS). This electronic system would require that student visa applications provide date of birth, nationality, parents' names, all overseas addresses, and detailed financial data. This information would then be shared with other governmental agencies and cross-checked. Schools would be required to report change of status of the international students. A pilot program of this system was started in Atlanta, Georgia, in April 1997 with twenty-one institutions, including Duke and Auburn universities. The pilot program was a resounding success.

But CIPRIS was never put into operation because it ran up against obstacles. What killed it was a combination of its cost and lobbying by colleges and universities. The INS executives balked at the $11 million price tag and wanted the institutions to collect from the international students a $100 fee. College and university administrators did not want to police international students and collect the fee. An education lobby called NAFSA: Association of International Educators hired a lobbyist to block the implementation of CIPRIS. He persuaded twenty-one senators to sign a letter against CIPRIS. The INS dropped the budget for CIPRIS from $11 million to $4 million, making it impossible to implement. Berez was removed from his position, and CIPRIS was reconfigured into a skeleton program and renamed SEVIS (Student and Exchange Information System). It was a passive database rather than one that did screening up front.

The loss of a tracking system meant that the INS continued in its inefficient ways with inadequate funding. The hijackers had no difficulties passing through the INS even though some came in on faulty visas and forged passports. Infringements of visa requirements were almost never noted. After September 11, officials of the INS admitted that the agency could not account for 314,000 foreigners ordered deported, and it had a backlog of over five million pending cases for legal residency. An example of the inefficiency in the tracking of international students was when the INS sent out notices six months after September 11 informing a flight school that Atta and al-Shehhi had been approved for student visas to study there. This incident was so embarrassing that several INS officials lost their jobs.

The INS's record was so poor that it was disbanded and its functions handed over to the Homeland Security Department. The INS and its 36,000 employees were broken into three pieces: Bureau of Immigration and Customs Enforcement, Bureau for Citizenship and Immigration Services, and the Bureau of Customs and Border Protection. A director has been appointed for each bureau, but there is no longer a single head of immigration functions, and this bothers some critics.

See Also
Atta, Mohamed el-Amir Awad el-Sayed; Shehhi, Marwan Yousef Muhammed Rashid Lekrab al-

Suggested Reading
Daniel Benjamin and Steven Simon, *The Age of Sacred Terror* (New York: Random House, 2002); Bob Graham, *Intelligence Matters: The CIA, the FBI, Saudi Arabia, and the Failure of America's War on Terror* (New York: Random House, 2004); Thomas H. Kean, Lee H. Hamilton, and Benjamin Rhodes, *Without Precedent: The Inside Story of the 9/11 Commission* (New York: Knopf, 2006); Gerald Posner, *Why America Slept: The Failure to Prevent 9/11* (New York: Ballantine Books, 2003); Michael Riley and Mike Soraghan, "INS Set to Join Homeland Security," *Denver Post* (March 2, 2003), p. B4; Steven Strasser, ed., *The 9/11 Investigations: Staff Reports of the 9/11 Commission; Excepts from the House-Senate Joint Inquiry Report on 9/11; Testimony from 14 Key Witnesses, Including Richard Clarke, George Tenet, and Condoleezza Rice* (New York: PublicAffairs, 2004); Susan B. Trento and Joseph J. Trento, *Unsafe at Any Altitude: Failed Terrorism Investigations, Scapegoating 9/11, and the Shocking Truth about Aviation Security Today* (Hanover, NH: Steerforth Press, 2006).

J

Jarrah, Ziad Samir (1975–2001)

Ziad Jarrah was another of the nineteen suicide skyjackers on September 11, 2001. He had been recruited by Ramzi bin al-Shibh at al-Quds Mosque. Less religious than the other members of the Hamburg Cell, Jarrah still joined the September 11 conspiracy. He was the hijackers' pilot on United Airlines Flight 93.

Jarrah came from a prosperous Lebanese family. He was born on May 11, 1975, in Beirut, Lebanon, into a wealthy and influential family. His father held a high-ranking post in the Lebanese social security system, and his mother taught school. Although the family lived in a prosperous area of Beirut, the Lebanese civil war that began in 1975 made this Sunni neighborhood less than secure. Jarrah attended the best private Christian schools in Beirut, but he was never more than an indifferent student. His family claimed that he was more interested in girls than his studies. He flunked his high school finals and only graduated two years later. Members of his family were secular Muslims who paid little attention to religion. After finishing his schooling, the family sent him to study biochemistry in Greifswald, Germany, in the spring of 1996. His parents subsidized his education by sending him at least $2,000 dollars a month. In Germany, Jarrah met Aysel Sengün, a young Turkish student studying dental medicine, and they became a couple.

Jarrah was a happy-go-lucky person until he returned to Lebanon for a winter break in 1997. He returned with a much more serious outlook on life, and he began to have trouble with his girlfriend. Jarrah wanted her to conform to a more traditional Muslim form of behavior. Searching for a career, Jarrah decided to study aeronautical engineering at Hamburg University of Applied Science. Jarrah joined the al-Quds Mosque in Hamburg, and he became a militant Islamist. Bin al-Shibh was his chief contact at the al-Quds Mosque, and Jarrah had little contact with Mohamed Atta. Jarrah was never an active member of the Hamburg Cell, but he shared most of its orientation. As religion became a more important part of his life, his relationship with his girlfriend deteriorated to the point that she was unable to understand him. They still intended to be married at a future time.

Jarrah was a follower, not a leader, in the September 11 plot. In some respects, he was the weak link among the leaders of the plot. He was intelligent enough to pass the qualifying tests as a pilot, but he lacked some of the other characteristics of a dedicated terrorist, such as ruthlessness. An American psychological profile pointed out character flaws: "indecisive and impulsive as well as immature, unstable, and unprofessional." Nevertheless, he trained at an al-Qaeda camp beginning in November 1999 along with Mohamed Atta. He was with Atta and Marwan al-Shehhi when they met and talked with Osama bin Laden in Kandahar. It was at this time that bin Laden asked them to swear allegiance to him and to be part of a suicide mission. Jarrah agreed with the others to do both. He then received a briefing from Mohammad Atef, the military chief of al-Qaeda, on the general outlines of the September 11 operation. Jarrah returned to Germany with the others to prepare for their mission.

Jarrah entered the United States on June 27, 2000, on a Delta flight from Munich. He trained at the Florida Flight Training Center in Venice, Florida. His flight instructor considered him an average pilot who needed more training to become a proficient pilot. Jarrah left the school without a commercial pilot's license. In an October 2000 note Jarrah wrote about his longing for paradise.

In January 2001 Jarrah returned to Germany. Then, in April 2001, Jarrah was back in the United States, living in Hollywood, Florida. While there, Jarrah took martial arts lessons at the U.S. 1 Fitness Club, working with Bert Rodriguez. Rodriguez held eight black belts in the martial arts, and he considered Jarrah a good student. Jarrah made one last trip to Germany to see his girlfriend,

> **Note of Ziad Jarrah**
>
> I come to you with men who love the death just as you love life. . . . The Mujahideen give their money for the weapons, food, and journeys to win and to die for Allah's cause, but the unhappy ones will be killed. Oh, the smell of paradise is rising.
>
> Quoted in Terry McDermott, *Perfect Soldiers: The 9/11 Hijackers: Who They Were, Why They Did It* (New York: HarperCollins, 2005), p. 88.

leaving on July 25 and returning on August 4. Later in August 2001, Jarrah moved to an apartment in Lauderdale-by-the-Sea. While still in Germany, Jarrah had received notification that he had qualified for a commercial license to fly single-engine aircraft. After his return from Germany, Jarrah began to study the manuals on flying Boeing 757 and 767 aircraft. In the weeks before September 11, Jarrah lived with Ahmed al-Haznawi. Throughout late August and September, Jarrah traveled frequently from south Florida to the Washington, D.C., area. On September 7, 2001, Jarrah made a flight from Ft. Lauderdale to Newark, New Jersey, on Continental Airlines with al-Haznawi. Jarrah reappeared in the Washington, D.C., area when he received a speeding ticket on Interstate 95 in Maryland. Jarrah and two of his fellow conspirators checked in at the Newark Airport Marriott soon after midnight on September 11. Before boarding United Airlines, Jarrah made a last phone call to Aysel Sengün in Germany.

Jarrah was the leader and pilot of the hijack team of United Airlines Flight 93. Team members had some trouble passing through security at Dulles International Airport, but they all made it. Once in the air, the hijackers seized control of the aircraft. Jarrah assumed the role of pilot. He began turning the aircraft around to head to the Washington, D.C., area. There were only three hijackers to control the crew and passengers. Soon passengers learned through cell phone calls that the aircraft was to be used as a flying bomb. They revolted and attempted to regain control of the plane. When it became apparent that the hijackers were about to be overpowered by the passengers, Jarrah crashed the aircraft into the ground near Shanksville, Pennsylvania. Jarrah followed instructions to destroy the aircraft if the mission did not have a chance of success.

See Also
Atta, Mohamed el-Amir Awad el-Sayed; Hamburg Cell; Quds Mosque, al-; United Airlines Flight 93

Suggested Reading
Richard Bernstein, *Out of the Blue: The Story of September 11, 2001, from Jihad to Ground Zero* (New York: Times Books, 2002); Jere Longman, *Among the Heroes: United Flight 93 and the Passengers and Crew Who Fought Back* (New York: Perennial, 2003); Terry McDermott, *Perfect Soldiers: The 9/11 Hijackers: Who They Were, Why They Did It* (New York: HarperCollins, 2005).

Jersey Girls

The Jersey Girls were four widows of the World Trade Center complex disaster on September 11 who formed an alliance to find out the truth of why it happened. They were dissatisfied with the official version that it could not have been prevented and the failure of the Senate-House Joint Committee on Intelligence to ferret out the truth because of roadblocks put out by the Bush administration. Kristen Breitweiser served as the unofficial spokesperson of the Jersey Girls, but the other three, Patty Casazza, Lorie Van Auken, and Mindy Keinberg, were just as vocal and determined to find out the truth. Each had lost her husband at the World Trade Center complex. Three of the husbands had worked at Cantor Fitzgerald in the north tower in an area above the airliner crash where there was not a chance for escape. Before September 11, none of them were acquainted with each other. The group was also bipartisan, with Breitweiser and Casazza having voted for George W. Bush in 2000 and Van Auken and Kleinberg having voted for Al Gore.

The Jersey Girls' determination to find the truth about September 11 led to the creation of the 9/11 Commission. Their attitude was that because the U.S. government had taken away the right to sue and hold people accountable in a court of law with the Victim's Compensation Fund, they would fight for accountability in a nonpolitical, independent blue-ribbon panel. Almost daily the four women haunted the halls of Congress, approaching politicians and demanding an accounting. One witness has described them as crying, pleading, and cajoling to persuade representatives and senators to act. They were also active in placing pressure on the White House through appearances on television and radio talk shows. Exactly what happened and accountability were their key points. When it looked like the 9/11 Commission was finally going to happen, the Jersey Girls then concentrated on the composition of the commission. The White House selected Henry Kissinger to be chair of the commission. This selection made the Jersey Girls uneasy. They confronted Kissinger and demanded that he disclose the names of his consulting firm's clients. When the Senate concurred, Kissinger resigned from the commission. In the meantime, the Jersey Girls began to lobby the White House to name former New Jersey governor Thomas Kean as Kissinger's replacement. The Jersey Girls were familiar with Kean and valued his impartiality and limited ties to the Bush administration.

As soon as the 9/11 Commission began to function, the Jersey Girls joined the Family Steering Committee. This group of twelve individuals, eleven women and one man, was a loose confederation of representatives from the major families of 9/11 organizations. Its goal was to keep the 9/11 Commission on the straight and narrow path of finding out the truth and making sure that the White House and government agencies cooperated. This determination led to monitoring of the progress of the commission and to constant calls to its co-chair Thomas Kean.

The merger with the Family Steering Committee ended the independence of the Jersey Girls until the Family Steering Group disbanded soon after the issuance of the commission's report. Throughout the fourteen-month ordeal of the 9/11 Commission, however, the Jersey Girls continued to play an active role within the Family Steering Committee. They were particularly effective in pressuring the Bush adminis-tration to allow Condoleezza Rice to testify in public before the 9/11 Commission. When the White House initially refused, the Jersey Girls and the rest of the Family Steering Group walked out in silent protest. They were back when Rice finally testified.

> **Thomas Kean's Comments on the Influence of the Jersey Girls**
>
> They call me all of the time. They monitor us, they follow our progress, they've supplied us with some of the best questions we've asked. I doubt very much if we would be in existence without them.
>
> Quoted in Sheryl Gay Stolberg, "9/11 Widows Skillfully Applied the Power of a Question: Why?" *New York Times* (April 1, 2004), p. A1.

The Jersey Girls criticized parts of the *9/11 Commission Report* for its vagueness, but in the end they supported it. Along with the others, the Jersey Girls protested against blacking out of sections of the report. Notwithstanding this reservation, their next task was to put pressure on the Bush administration to implement the provisions of the *9/11 Commission Report*. This pressure caused conservative backers of the Bush administration to coordinate an attack on the motives of the Jersey Girls. They interpreted the actions of the Jersey Girls as evidence that they were backing the candidacy of John Kerry. The attacks from conservative Republicans were vicious enough that the Jersey Girls did begin to campaign for John Kerry's presidential run. Breitweiser was particularly active although she had been a Republican before September 11. It was their disillusionment with the Bush administration and their belief that it tried to sabotage the 9/11 Commission that turned them to the Democra-tic Party.

The Jersey Girls have maintained a high profile in the intervening years since September 11. Most of their political activities have centered around lobbying for homeland-security improvement. They also participated in a documentary film titled *911: Press for Truth,* which appeared in early September 2006. But their actions and their criticisms of the Bush administration have continued to bother extreme right-wing conservatives. In President Bush's second term, the most vicious attack on them was by the right-wing writer Ann Coulter. In her 2007 book *Godless: The Church of Liberalism,* Coulter characterized the Jersey Girls in the following terms: "These broads are millionaires, lionized on TV and in articles about them, reveling in their status as celebrities." She then added, "I've never seen people enjoying their husbands' deaths so much." These tasteless remarks led the Jersey Girls to respond with a statement (see sidebar).

Reply of the Jersey Girls to Attack by Ann Coulter

Contrary to Ms. Coulter's statements, there was no joy in watching men that we loved burn alive. There was no happiness in telling our children that their fathers were never coming home again. We adored these men and miss them every day.

Quoted in Gene Lyons, "Coulter's Latest Smear Tactic Backfires," *Arkansas Democrat-Gazette* (June 14, 2006), p. 1.

See Also
Family Steering Committee; Kean, Thomas Howard; National Commission on Terrorist Attacks upon the United States; Victims' Compensation Fund

Suggested Reading
Kristen Breitweiser, *Wake-Up Call: The Political Education of a 9/11 Widow* (New York: Warner Books, 2006); Gene Lyons, "Coulter's Latest Smear Tactic Backfires," *Arkansas Democratic-Gazette* (June 14, 2006), p. 1; Ernest R. May, ed., *The 9/11 Report with Related Documents* (Boston: Bedford, 2007); Dorothy Rabinowitz, "The 9/11/Widows," *Wall Street Journal* (April 14, 2004), p. A14; Sheryl Gay Stolberg, "9/11 Widows Skillfully Applied the Power of a Question: Why?" *New York Times* (April 1, 2004), p. 1.

Joint Inquiry Committee. *See* Senate Select Committee on Intelligence and the House Permanent Select Committee on Intelligence Joint Inquiry into the Terrorist Attacks of September 11

Joint Terrorism Task Force
New York City's Joint Terrorism Task Force (JTTF) was a joint New York City Police Department (NYPD) and FBI effort to combat the domestic terrorism threat to New York City. It was formed in 1980 in the midst of a terrorist campaign by Puerto Rican nationalists, after it became apparent that better cooperation between the NYPD and the FBI was necessary. The original plan was for a unit of ten FBI agents and ten New York City police detectives, but over the years the size of the unit expanded. In 1990, Neil Herman, an FBI agent, assumed control of the JTTF.

The early focus of the JTTF was domestic terrorism. Besides Puerto Rican nationalists, the agents of the JTTF were involved in the investigation of the black nationalist group called the New Afrikan Freedom Fighters (NAFF). The acquittal of the eight defendants in a conspiracy trial angered members of the task force.

Another important case was the assassination of Israeli extremist Meir Kahane by Islamist El Sayyid Nosair. Members of the JTTF had monitored paramilitary training by militants before the assassination. Shortly after the assassination, the JTTF was shut out of the case and lost access to sixteen boxes of intelligence information.

In the early 1990s the JTTF recruited a Muslim agent. Emad Salem, a former Egyptian army officer, penetrated the al-Kifah Refugee Center militant circle. There he heard about a possible bomb plot against a dozen Jewish targets. The problem was that elements in the JTTF had reservations about Salem. He was simply too good to be true. Salem kept reporting about a bomb plot, but the details were vague. His handlers wanted Salem to wear a wire, but he refused to compromise himself. After his refusal, the JTTF let him go in July 1991. His parting remark was "Don't call me when the bombs go off." He had been their best access to Islamist militants in the New York City area, but the agents were more interested in winning a court case than in gathering intelligence.

The JTTF had more to worry about than terrorist plots. In the summer of 1992, the head of the New York City's Criminal Division tried to transfer the functions of the JTTF to urban gang cases, saying, "Terrorism is dead." It took the 1993 World Trade Center Bombing to change this attitude.

In the meantime, the JTTF had recruited another informant. Garret Wilson, a black former U.S. Army veteran, was the new source of information. He had been contacted by the Islamists for paramilitary training. Although Wilson was not in the inner circle of the 1993 World Trade Center plot, he heard strange things that he reported to the JTTF. But about when the agents were getting close to the plot, a bureaucrat became nervous and closed the investigation.

The 1993 World Trade Center bombing made the unit begin to study international terrorism as well as domestic terrorism. Members of the JTTF were part of the 700 investigating agents assigned to the World Trade Center bombing. Within weeks the JTTF team had arrested or identified all of the World Trade Center bombers. Now with more resources, the JTTF began to investigate other militants. Emad Salem was rehired, and the team sent him in to investigate the doings in the al-Kifah Mosque. There he learned that Abdel-Rahman was instigating a plot to assassinate Egypt President Hosni Mubarak during a New York visit in April 1993. Because of questions of his safety, Mubarak canceled his New York City visit. The JTTF became heavily involved in the investigation of the United Airlines Flight 800 Crash off the coast of the United States. Agents of the JFFT spent seventeen months investigating the explosion and crash. It finally took a series of computer simulations to prove that the explosion had been an accident, not a terrorist attack. This investigation consumed most of the JTTF's attention at a time when it needed to be investigating potential terrorism conspiracies.

The members of the JTTF had no knowledge of the September 11 plot before it was carried out. They had been suspicious of increased al-Qaeda activity in the United States and were busy investigating leads. New York City was a prime target of any terrorist conspiracy. Then a CIA agent presented the JTTF staff with photos of possible terrorists on June 11, 2001, and he asked for information about them. After identifying the individuals in the photos, the CIA agent refused to give out any further information, infuriating the JTTF agents. The JTTF agents became even more suspicious when they received the news that two prominent al-Qaeda operatives had been operating for more than a year in San Diego, California—Khalid al-Mihdhar and Nawaf al-Hazmi. They had participated in a meeting of al-Qaeda leaders in 2001. A formal request for more information was made to the FBI, but the staff of the JTTF did not receive the information until after September 11. Like the rest of the nation, the members of the JTTF watched with horror the events of September 11.

See Also

Bush Administration; Clinton Administration; Federal Bureau of Investigation; Hazmi, Nawaf bin Muhammad Salim al-; Mihdhar, Khalid al-; World Trade Center Bombing (1993)

Suggested Reading

John Miller, Michael Stone, and Chris Mitchell, *The Cell: Inside the 9/11 Plot and Why the FBI and CIA Failed to Stop It* (New York: Hyperion, 2002); Timothy Naftali, *Blind Spot: The Secret History of American Counterterrorism* (New York: Basic Books, 2005).

Jones, Steven E. (1949–)

Steven Jones is a former physics professor at Brigham Young University who has become one of the leaders of the conspiracy theorists about the events on September 11, 2001. His earlier work as a physicist had been with cold fusion, and he was able to escape the debacle of that research without much damage to his scientific reputation. Jones was active in other physic projects when he turned his attention to the physics of falling buildings. His nineteen-page paper titled "Why Indeed Did the WTC Buildings Collapse?" at a departmental seminar at Brigham Young University became his introduction to the controversy of a U.S. government conspiracy on September 11.

Jones had a traditional academic career. He was born on March 25, 1949. His family was Mormon, and he was raised in that faith. His family lived in Bellevue, Washington, and he graduated from Bellevue High School in 1967. Jones then attended Brigham Young University where he earned a BA in physics, magna cum laude, in 1973. His PhD in physics, in 1978, came from Vanderbilt University. After postdoctoral research at Cornell University and the Los Alamos Meson Physics Facility, he became a senior engineering specialist at the Idaho National Engineering Laboratory in Idaho Falls, Idaho, in 1979, remaining there until 1985. In 1989 Jones became the associate director at the Brigham Young University Center for Fusion Studies, and he remained in this position until 1994. In the meantime, he became a tenured professor in the Department of Physics and Astronomy at Brigham Young University.

Jones's early-career research on cold nuclear fusion landed him in a rivalry with Stanley Pons and Martin Fleischmann over cold fusion possibilities. Jones's more modest findings avoided much of the controversy when it became apparent that cold fusion did not work because of alpha-muon sticking losses. His research, however, was rejected for experimental error. After leaving cold fusion, Jones turned to other research areas, including metal-catalyzed fusion. Besides physics research, Jones as a life-long Mormon was interested in archaeology and the Book of Mormon. Although mostly apolitical, he was a Republican voter and a supporter of President George W. Bush. His political attitude changed after September 11, 2001.

Jones's life as a tenured professor at Brigham Young became more difficult after he joined the 9/11 conspiracy movement. Although he had no expertise in the building sciences, Jones decided that the collapse of the twin towers and Seven World Trade Center building defied the laws of physics. In a departmental seminar at Brigham Young University on September 22, 2005, Jones presented the outlines of a paper that would become "Why Indeed Did the WTC Buildings Collapse?" His thesis was the buildings could not have pancaked like they did from explosions and fires of airliner crashes. Instead, Jones suggested that it would have taken controlled demolitions in the buildings to produce such a collapse. In his eyes the culprits were rogue agents working in the U.S. government. A revised edition of this paper appeared in a book edited by David Ray Griffin and Peter Dale Scott titled *9/11 and American Empire: Intellectuals Speak Out.*

This paper and his subsequent charges of a U.S. government conspiracy made Jones a controversial figure at Brigham Young University. Soon after his presentation, members of the university's engineering department began questioning his conclusions. This questioning was soon followed by similar criticism from the faculty of the College of Physical and Mathematical Sciences and the faculty of structural engineering. Nearly a year after his Jones's presentation of his thesis, Brigham Young University's administration placed Jones on paid leave on September 7, 2006. Jones then announced his retirement from the university on October 20, 2006.

Since his retirement from Brigham Young University, Jones has devoted his energies to the 9/11 conspiracy movement. He was a co-founder with James H. Fetzer, a former philosophy professor at the University of Minnesota at Duluth, of Scholars for 9/11 Truth. This alliance disintegrated almost a year later as Fetzer became enamored by some of the more outlandish conspiracy theories, such as those that featured mini-nukes or high-energy weapons. Jones wanted to keep the conspiracy theories more scientific. This disagreement and others led Jones to separate from the Scholars for 9/11 Truth on December 5, 2006, and start his own organization—Scholars for 9/11 Truth and Justice. He also became the co-editor of the *Journal of 9/11 Studies,* which publishes articles about 9/11 conspiracy theories.

Criticism of Jones's analysis has come mostly from structural engineers. A report by the National Institute of Standards and Technology (NIST) contradicted Jones's thesis by stating that high-temperature fires started by jet fuel caused the buildings' out columns to collapse. Moreover, after the collapse of the twin towers, the New York Fire Department allowed the Seven World Trade Center building to burn and subsequently collapse because there was nothing the firefighters could have done to prevent it. Despite contradictory testimony, Jones continues to hold to his thesis.

See Also

Conspiracy Theories; Fetzer, James H.; Griffin, David Ray; Scholars for 9/11 Truth

Suggested Reading

John Gravois, "Professors of Paranoia? Academics Give a Scholarly Stamp to 9/11 Conspiracy Theories," *Chronicle of Higher Education* 52.42 (June 23, 2006), p. A10; Peter McKnight, "Attempts to Make Sense of Senseless Acts," *Vancouver Sun* (September 16, 2006), p. C5.

Judge, Mychal (1933–2001)

Father Mychal Judge was a Franciscan priest serving as the chaplain for the New York City Fire Department (FDNY) who died serving others on September 11, 2001. He was born on May 11, 1933, in Brooklyn, New York, into an Irish immigrant family from County Leitrim. His birth name was Robert Emmett Judge. When he was only six years old, his father died from a lingering illness. Judge took jobs as a boy to help support his mother and two sisters. Judge entered the Franciscan order in 1954, and he attended St. Bonaventure College, graduating in 1957. He was ordained a priest in 1961. His assignment was to serve as the pastor of St. Joseph's parish in East Rutherford, New Jersey, and then at St. Joseph's parish in West Milford, New Jersey. Judge showed an early interest in firefighting. After other assignments at Siena College in Loudonville, New York, and St. Francis of Assisi, he became a fire chaplain in 1992.

Father Judge took his responsibilities as fire chaplain seriously. He always carried a pager and responded to calls throughout the city regardless of the time and circumstances. At the scene of fires, he was seen counseling people in need. He was also active in consoling family members at the hospital. Judge also performed masses at FDNY ceremonies. While performing these duties, Judge became a beloved figure in the fire department. Part of his popularity was that although he talked about his love for Jesus, he was never judgmental or unfairly critical of anyone. Judge was open about his gay sexuality, but few if any of the firefighters he served cared.

Father Judge's Philosophy of Firefighting

Good days, bad days, up days, down days, sad days, happy days, but never a boring day on this job. You do what God has called you to do. You show up, you put one foot in front of another, you get on the rig, you go, and you do the job, which is a mystery, and a surprise. You have no idea when you get on that rig—no matter how big the call, no matter how small—you have no idea what God is calling you to.

Quoted in Thomas Von Essen with Matt Murray, *Strong of Heart: Life and Death in the Fire Department of New York* (New York: ReganBooks, 2002), p. 5.

On two occasions before his death, Father Judge received national attention. The first was his support for the victims of AIDS. Long before it was acceptable to give help to AIDS victims, Father Judge was active, even though he had opposition from within the Catholic Church. Many members of the church hierarchy were uncomfortable with Father Judge because he was gay.

Father Judge's second venture onto the national headlines was his role in comforting the families of the victims of TWA Flight 800 off Long Island, New York, in 1996. This aircraft had exploded in midair, killing all of the 230 crew and passengers. Despite lengthy investigations, the exact nature of the explosion is still a subject of dispute. After conducting masses for the victims, he spent time counseling the families regardless of their denominations.

Father Judge was serving as the chaplain to the New York Fire Department on September 11, 2001. He was a gregarious man who enjoyed being a chaplain and loved publicity. Father Judge had been an alcoholic, but he had avoided drink for over twenty years as an active member of Alcoholics Anonymous (AA). As soon as he heard about the World Trade Center incident, Father Judge dashed to the World Trade Center to render aid to the victims. He began giving last rites to those dying. While giving the last rites to a firefighter named Daniel Suhr, Father Judge was struck by falling debris. Shortly afterward, Father Judge entered the lobby of the North Tower of the World Trade Center. Debris from the collapse of the South Tower of the World Trade Center hit him, killing him instantly. His body was removed later by the firefighters with great dignity. There is a picture of firefighters and a policeman carrying his body out, and this picture has received the title "American Pieta." They respected his courage in administering the last rites for the victims of September 11 in the face of danger. Father Judge was buried on September 15, 2001, at Holy Sepulchre Cemetery in Totowa, New Jersey.

Twin Sister's Commentary on the Death of Mychal Judge

I truly believe this was a moment my brother had been working towards all of his life. This is how he wanted to die, with his fire fighters around him trying to help in a disaster. His was a glorious death. I don't know how people manage to do these things. I do know my brother loved to pray. We used to joke about it all the time. This was his life. Images like that picture make a hero and that is what my brother was—a hero.

Chris Hughes, "The Brave Chaplain: My Hero Twin," *Mirror* [New York] (September 18, 2001), p. 7.

Since his death, Father Judge has become a controversial figure because there is a growing campaign to make him a saint. His conduct at the World Trade Center has led to a growing mythology. For a candidate to qualify for sainthood, five years must have passed since his or her death, and at least two miracles must be attributed to the candidate. Several people have claimed that their prayers to Father Judge produced miracles. The archdiocese of New York has left it up to the Franciscan order to advance his sainthood, but the leaders of the Franciscan order say they will not press it because he was a good friar but should not be set apart. The fact that Father Judge was gay is a complicating factor.

See Also
Firefighters at Ground Zero; World Trade Center, September 11

Suggested Reading
Dale Brazao and Kevin Coombs, "Father Mike Died Doing His Duty; Father Mike Loved Life, Loved Souls," *Toronto* Star (September 16, 2001), p. A1; Charisse Jones, "The Making of St. Mychal," *USA Today* (February 20, 2003), p. 1A; Dennis Smith, *Report from Ground Zero* (New York: Viking, 2002); Daniel J. Wakin, "Killed on 9/11, Fire

---

Candidacy of Mychal Judge for Sainthood

Yet it is Judge's contradictions, as well as his compassion, that make him appealing to so many. He was a recovering alcoholic who sported a shamrock tattoo on his behind. He loved to spin yarns and was ever ready with a joke. The Brooklyn native wore his brown Franciscan robe on the hottest days of summer, always remembered a widow's birthday and wasn't above tweaking church officials he found to be pretentious or hypocritical.

Charisse Jone, "The Making of St. Mychal," *USA Today* (February 20, 2003), p. 1A.

Mychal Judge, a chaplain with the New York City Fire Department, stands at the shore before a service where 230 candles were lit for the victims of TWA Flight 800 on July 17, 2000, at Smith Point Park in Shirley, New York. (AP IMAGES/Ed Betz.)

Chaplain Becomes Larger Than Life," *New York Times* (September 27, 2002), p. A1; Thomas Von Essen with Matt Murray, *Strong of Heart: Life and Death in the Fire Department of New York* (New York: ReganBooks, 2002).

Justification for the September 11 Suicide Mission

The most difficult aspect of the September 11 attacks for Americans to understand was the use of suicide as a weapon. Nineteen young men bonded together to hijack four American commercial aircraft and crash them into preselected targets. They had no regard for their safety or for anybody else. Each had received at least basic training at al-Qaeda camps to prepare for such a mission. An important part of this training was religious instruction that prepared them for what they called a martyrdom mission.

The religious justification for suicide missions is controversial among Muslim religious authorities. Both opponents and proponents refer to the religious teachings of the Prophet Mohammad as stated in the Koran or to the sayings of the Prophet in the hadiths. Personal suicide is not a part of Muslim religious practice, and this is reflected in the low personal suicide rate in the Muslim world. On the other hand, suicide undertaken as part of jihad, or holy war, is where it becomes controversial.

Jihad has two meanings in Muslim theology. Foremost, jihad means a personal struggle to adhere to the precepts of being a Muslim. The other meaning of jihad is war against the enemies of Islam. Again there are two meanings to this concept. There is jihad that aggressively wages war for the faith. This was the type of jihad that the Muslim successors to the Prophet Mohammad waged in the expansionary period of its history. Then there is defensive jihad, which exists when the Islamic world is attacked by outsiders. According to this concept, it is the obligation of every able-bodied Muslim to participate in war against an invader. Islamist groups consider the presence of Israel in the Middle East as part of an invasion of the Muslim world. Because the United States is an ally of Israel and has a presence in the Middle East, it is also considered a partner in this invasion. Al-Qaeda and other Islamist groups maintain that the war against Israel and the United States is a continuation of the war between the West and the Muslim world that dates back to the Crusades in the Middle Ages.

What Is Jihad?

Jihad literally means "to struggle." In the military sense it is meant in the context, "to struggle against oppression." Jihad is therefore an act to liberate people from the oppression of tyrants. Jihad is not illegal acts against innocent people. When tabloid journalism mistakenly informs the masses that Jihad is "to commit illegal acts of terror," they are revealing the lack of their unprofessional approach to the subject.

Interpretation of Jihad from the Azzam Web site, which advocates Jihad against the West, from Adam Parfrey, ed., *Extreme Islam: Anti-American Propaganda of Muslim Fundamentalism* (Los Angeles: Feral House, 2001), p. 266.

Suicide as a political weapon has a history in the Muslim world. The most famous historical cases of suicide used as a political weapon were those carried out by the assassins of the Ismaeli Shiite sect of Hassan ibn Sabbah, who established the Ismaeli Assassins in the Middle Ages (1034–1255), and they carried out suicide missions against Muslim Sunnis and Christian Crusaders. After the collapse of this sect, there were sporadic suicide missions mostly against European colonial targets. Only in the early 1980s did the use of suicide as a weapon reappear in the Middle East. It has appeared elsewhere mostly in association with the Tamil Tigers in Sri Lanka. The first incident of a suicide mission in the Middle East in modern times was by the Shiite Amal organization when a suicide bomber drove a car with explosives into the Iraq Embassy in Beirut on December 15, 1981, killing sixty-one people. Hezbollah (the Party of God) in Lebanon borrowed this tactic and has used it with lethal effect against American and Israeli targets. Later, both the Palestinian Islamic Jihad and Hamas began depending on suicide bombers for use against the Israelis. The military wing of al-Fatah, the al-Aqsa Martyrs' Brigade, has also resorted to the use of suicide bombers.

Noting the effectiveness of suicide bombers, al-Qaeda's leadership adopted the practice. Suicide bombing is considered an effective weapon in a war in which one side is so much stronger militarily than the other. Besides its lethal impact, a suicide bombing has the element of surprise. The suicide bomber is able to get close to the target before he or she detonates the bomb. Al-Qaeda leaders claim that it is the most successful tactic in inflicting damage and at the same time the least costly in terms of loss of its operatives. This belief is reinforced by the fact that suicide attacks claim ten to fifteen times the casualties of any other terrorist operation.

At training camps in Afghanistan, candidates were appraised for the characteristics necessary to recruit for a martyrdom mission. Candidates had to be religious and of strong character. The members of the Hamburg Cell were ideal candidates because of their strong religious views, language expertise, and ability to adapt to Western society without arousing suspicion. Once a candidate had been selected, he underwent specialized training for the mission. For those on the September 11 mission, this meant concentrating on hijacking a commercial aircraft in flight. Those selected to be pilots were given leadership training and sent to the United States for pilot training. Other candidates received different training for different missions.

> **Interpretation of Suicide Terrorism**
>
> "Suicide terrorism" is the most aggressive form of terrorism, pursuing coercion even at the expense of angering not only the target community but neutral audiences as well. What distinguishes a suicide terrorist is the attacker does not expect to survive the mission and often employs a method of attack (such as a car bomb, suicide vest, or ramming an airplane into a building) that requires his or her death in order to succeed. In essence, suicide terrorists kill others at the same time that they kill themselves.
>
> Robert A. Pape, *Dying to Win: The Strategic Logic of Suicide Terrorism* (New York: Random House, 2005), p. 10.

See Also

Hamburg Cell; Qaeda, al-

See Document

Document #7

Suggested Reading

Abdel Bari Atwan, *The Secret History of al Qaeda* (Berkeley: University of California Press, 2006); Robert A. Pape, *Dying to Win: The Strategic Logic of Suicide Terrorism* (New York: Random House, 2005); Barry Rubin and Judith Colp Rubin, eds., *Anti-American Terrorism and the Middle East: A Documentary Reader* (New York: Oxford University Press, 2002).

K

Kean, Thomas Howard (1935–)
Thomas H. Kean was the chair of the 9/11 Commission that convened to study the events of September 11, 2001. He was a well-respected Republican politician from New Jersey whose moderate views and popularity in the Republican Party led to his appointment as 9/11 Commission chair.

Kean spent his entire political career in New Jersey. He was born on April 21, 1935, in New York City. With his father having served as a Member of Congress, and his grandfather as a U.S. senator, Kean's family had a long history in New Jersey politics. Kean's early education began at St. Mark's School in Southborough, Massachusetts. He then attended Princeton University and later earned a master's degree from the Teachers College, Columbia University. His early career was as a teacher of history and government. When Kean decided to run for public office, he first won election to the New Jersey General Assembly in 1967, and became New Jersey House Speaker for a year in 1972. He aspired to higher office but was unsuccessful in winning the Republic nomination for New Jersey Governor in 1977. Kean was more successful in 1981, and was elected the forty-eighth governor of New Jersey. His term as governor lasted until 1990. Kean proved hugely popular in office, and he made New Jersey a two-party state. Kean left politics to become president of Drew University in Madison, New Jersey. He continued to head the small liberal arts university until 2005.

President Bush appointed Kean chair of the 9/11 Commission because of Kean's reputation as a consensus builder. He earned this reputation through service on various national foreign policy boards under the administrations of George H. W. Bush, Bill Clinton, and George W. Bush. President George W. Bush turned to him after Henry Kissinger resigned as chair of the 9/11 Commission. Perhaps Kean's most important decision on the 9/11 Commission was to make former U.S. Representative Lee Hamilton (D-IN) co-chair. Making the commission bipartisan increased its credibility. Commissioners made all decisions as a group, and met with the media as a team. This bipartisan approach helped make the 9/11 Commission work.

The 9/11 Commission was a massive undertaking. It had to organize itself in record time because its mandate was only for eighteen months, and its initial budget of $3 million was inadequate. There were also conflicting political agendas from various parties outside the commission. Besides pressure from the political side, Kean and the 9/11 Commission had to withstand pressure from the Family Steering Committee. As the process moved forward Kean and Hamilton because frustrated with repeated misstatements by Pentagon and FAA officials. Some of these frustrations have appeared in their book *Without Precedent: The Inside Story of the 9/11 Commission*. The 9/11 Commission issued its final report, the *9/11 Commission Report*, on July 22, 2004.

The 9/11 Commission has had to withstand considerable criticism then and now. Members and staff did not have the luxury of unlimited time, and members also had to withstand criticism for the political orientation of some of their staff. Philip D. Zelikow, the Commission's Staff Director, had extensive contacts with the Bush administration. Kean has tried to answer most of the criticisms. In turn, Kean's participation in the ABC TV miniseries *The Path to 9/11* has been criticized for the show's anti-Clinton bias.

Kean is now in semiretirement. His main occupation is as chairman of the board of the Robert Wood Johnson Foundation, a foundation that specializes in health and health care. He and his wife live in Bedminster Township, New Jersey. Kean keeps his hand in politics by writing a weekly column for the Newark, New Jersey, *Star-Ledger* newspaper. His income is supplemented by service on several corporate boards of directors. Kean was active in supporting his son, Tom Kean Jr., in his unsuccessful 2006 campaign for governor of New Jersey.

Reasons Thomas Kean Accepted the Post of Chair of the 9/11 Commission

It's hard to say no when the president of the U.S. asks you to do something—although I've said no before. I knew a lot of people who died on September 11, and lost some good friends. This is an area where many people commute to work in New York—the train only takes 40 minutes to reach the station directly under the Twin Towers. Almost a third of those killed, some 700, were from New Jersey. In the communities around here there were funerals for months.

Interview of Thomas Kean in Steven Knipp, "Without Fear or Favour," *South China Morning Post* (January 17, 2005), p. 16.

Comment by 9/11 Commission Member Richard Ben-Veniste

Tom Kean is a man of enormous good humor and noblesse oblige. His personal charm has played no small role in the cohesiveness and camaraderie that has developed among the members of the commission.

Richard Ben-Veniste quoted by Linton Weeks, "An Indelible Day; On 9/11, University President Thomas Kean Had No Idea How Much His Life Would Change," *Washington Post* (June 16, 2004), p. C1.

See Also

Family Steering Committee; Hamilton, Lee H.; National Commission on Terrorist Attacks upon the United States

Suggested Reading

David T. Cook, "Thomas Kean and Lee Hamilton," *Christian Science Monitor* (December 6, 2005), p. 25; Thomas H. Kean, Lee H. Hamilton, and Benjamin Rhodes, *Without Precedent: The Inside Story of the 9/11 Commission* (New York: Knopf, 2006); Dana Milbank,

"With 9/11 Film, Kean Finds Tough Critic in Hamilton," *Washington Post* (September 12, 2006), p. A2; Philip Shenon, "9/11 Commission Says U.S. Agencies Slow Its Inquiry," *New York Times* (July 9, 2003), p. A1.

Kerik, Bernard Bailey (1955–)

Bernard Kerik was the Police Commissioner of the City of New York on September 11, 2001. He was a long-time political ally of Mayor Rudolph Giuliani. His actions at the World Trade Center on September 11 elevated him, along with Giuliani, to the national limelight.

Kerik had an unusual background. He was born on September 4, 1955, in Paterson, New Jersey. His mother was a prostitute, and his father deserted him when he was only two years old. He was raised by a violent stepfather with a criminal record. He had trouble in school, often getting into fights. Kerik finally dropped out of high school. He later earned a GED and a mail-order bachelor's degree from Empire State College. In his autobiography Kerik states that his violent tendencies were leading to a life of crime until he joined the U.S. Army. Kerik became a military policeman, serving in Korea and then with the 18th Airborne Corps at Fort Bragg, North Carolina. His passion was martial arts, and he earned a black belt at age eighteen. After leaving the Army, he worked at security assignments for the Saudi royal family between 1982 and 1984. Returning to the United States, Kerik joined the Passaic County Sheriff's Office, where he held a number of jobs. Kerik's career took off when he took a job with the New York City Police Department. His first assignment was working undercover for the anticrime and narcotics units in Harlem, Spanish Harlem, and Washington Heights. His successes led to his selection for the U.S. Justice Department's New York Drug Enforcement Task Force. During his duty as a uniformed and plainclothes officer, Kerik earned thirty medals for meritorious and heroic service, including the department's Medal for Valor. On January 1, 1998, he was appointed Commissioner of the New York City Department of Correction. Kerik earned praise for improving the safety of the city's jail system, and improving the morale of the guards. Kerik became the fortieth Police Commissioner of the City of New York on August 21, 2000, appointed by Mayor Rudolph Giuliani. Kerik had responsibility for a uniformed force of more than 41,000 officers, and a civilian force of more than 14,500. He had a reputation as "a tough-talking, sometimes coarse, law enforcer who rarely stood on ceremony," and as one interested in shaking up the status quo. He was considered a tough boss who was willing to fire subordinates whom he considered to be slackers. Kerik was also known to be reluctant to cooperate with the FBI.

Kerik was in charge of the New York City Police Department on September 11. He was taking a shower in his office at 1 Police Plaza when he was informed about the aircraft that hit the North Tower. He immediately headed for the World Trade Center, where he took charge of police operations. Kerik was there when the second aircraft crashed into the South Tower. By this time Mayor Giuliani had made an appearance at the World Trade Center. Communications equipment failed, and coordination between police and firefighters was lacking. Both Giuliani and Kerik survived the collapse of the towers, but they were at risk from falling debris. They made it out of the area and established a new communication center.

Over the next few months Kerik worked to rebuild the New York Police Department (NYPD). The loss of twenty-seven police officers on September 11 was debilitating to the department. Kerik spent the next four months working to build the department back to pre–September 11 standards and to improve morale. Mayor Giuliani and Kerik worked hand in hand to restore New York City to normalcy. They both received considerable media attention for their efforts.

Kerik retired from the Police Commissioner's job at the end of Mayor Giuliani's tenure in office. He worked for awhile as a partner in Giuliani's consulting firm, Giuliani Partners, until President George W. Bush sent him to Iraq to create an Iraqi police force after the invasion. His role there turned out to be controversial: his stay was short, and he was not effective. Returning to the United States, he served on the board of directors of Taser International, manufacturer of stun guns used by police departments. He used his stock options as a director to sell $5.8 million of Taser stock.

Kerik's performance on September 11, 2001, came under scrutiny by the 9/11 Commission. Commissioners criticized Kerik and the NYPD for their performance on September 11. They cited the long-running rivalry between the police and firefighters for having led to failures in command and control and for communication problems. Kerik countered by calling the criticism Monday morning quarterbacking.

Kerik tried to stay out of the limelight until President George W. Bush nominated him for the position of Secretary of Homeland Security on December 3, 2004. Rudolph Giuliani had pressed the White House to select Kerik for this post. A problem arose in the failure of the Bush administration to have Kerik vetted properly; when they did review his background, they found financial and moral problems. His financial picture was clouded by suspicions of illegality. On the moral side, there was evidence

> **Criticism of Kerik for Failure of Leadership**
>
> A prominent Republican member of the September 11 Commission, former Navy Secretary John F. Lehman, sharply criticized Kerik and former Fire Commissioner Thomas Van Essen for failures of leadership during the terrorist attacks, saying that rivalry between the departments hampered rescue efforts. The command and control of their departments, Lehman said, were "not worthy of the Boy Scouts." Kerik heatedly disputed the charge.
>
> Michael Powell and Dan Eggen, "A Tough Cop Tempered by 9/11 and Iraq," *Washington Post* (December 4, 2004), p. A1.

of adultery involving more than one woman. When it became apparent that Kerik could not survive the confirmation process, Kerik withdrew from consideration as Secretary of Homeland Security, citing an illegal immigrant nanny he had hired for whom he failed to pay taxes. Soon afterward Kerik also quit the Giuliani Partnership.

Since 2004 Kerik has been in and out of legal trouble. Federal and state authorities began to investigate his various financial transactions. After leaving Giuliani Partners, he formed his own security firm, the Kerik Group. In July 2006 he pleaded guilty to conflict-of-interest charges for accepting $165,000 in gifts from a mob-linked construction firm that was seeking business with the city. Kerik was ordered to pay $221,000 in fines and fees and faced a misdemeanor charge for failing to inform city ethics regulators about a $28,000 loan from a real estate developer in 2002. In September 2006 Kerik became embroiled in an illegal wiretapping case involving a woman who wanted evidence of her husband's

Former New York City Police Commissioner Bernard Kerik exits the Bronx supreme court June 30, 2006, in New York a year and a half after his Homeland Security nomination sank over ethics questions. Kerik pleaded guilty to charges of accepting tens of thousands of dollars in gifts while a top city official. (AP IMAGES/Louis Lanzano.)

adultery. Since then federal authorities have investigated him for violating federal tax laws. They tried to persuade Kerik in March 2007 to plead to the charges and serve two years in prison, but he turned the offer down.

See Also
Giuliani, Rudolph William Lewis "Rudy" III; World Trade Center, September 11

See Document
Document #14

Suggested Reading
Mike Allen and Peter Baker, "On Kerik Nomination, White House Missed Red Flags," *Washington Post* (December 15, 2004), p. A4; Arnaud de Borchgrave, "Bernard Kerik, a Life," *Pittsburgh Tribune Review* (December 8, 2004), p. 1; Russ Buettner and William K. Rashbaum, "Kerik Is Again a Figure in an Official Investigation," *New York Times* (September 28, 2006), p. B6; Dennis Buffa, Murray Weiss, and Todd Venezia, "Bernie— From a Hero to a Zero," *New York Post* (July 1, 2006), p. 8; Elisabeth Bumiller and Erick Lipton, "Kerik's Position Was Untenable, Bush Aide Says," *New York Times* (December 12, 2004), p. 1; Kevin Flynn et al., "A Street Cop's Rise from High School Dropout to Cabinet Nominee," *New York Times* (December 3, 2004), p. A26; Stephanie Gaskell, Jennifer Fermino, and Andy Soltis, "Heroes Rage at WTC Probe," *New York Post* (May 19, 2004), p. 6; John Solomon and Matthew Mosk, "Ex-Partner of Giuliani May Face Charges," *Washington Post* (March 31, 2007), p. A1.

Kifah Refugee Center, al-

The al-Kifah Refugee Center in Brooklyn, New York, was the center of militant Islamist plots against the United States in the 1990s. It had been founded in 1987 by Abdullah Azzam during one of his periodic visits to the United States in the 1980s. As the flagship of approximately forty al-Kifah Refugee Centers in the United States, it was housed in a three-story building on Atlanta Avenue above the Fu King Chinese Restaurant and near the al-Faroog Mosque. Mustafa Shalabi,

Egyptian and an electrical engineer by training, had been selected by Azzam to head the Brooklyn refugee center. Shalabi had been arrested in Egypt in the aftermath of the assassination of President Anwar Sadat in 1981, and immigrated to the United States soon after his release from prison. He was an admirer of Azzam and followed his instructions loyally.

The mission of the refugee center was to raise funds for the establishment of a purified Islamic state in Afghanistan. Shalabi was a strong fundraiser, so soon money was flowing from the refugee center to Afghanistan and Pakistan. Although Shalabi was a militant Islamist, he was not a terrorist. The benefit of Shalabi's close ties to Azzam ended with the latter's assassination in 1989. In the meantime, there had developed a more militant wing at the refugee center that wanted to bring jihad (holy war) to the United States.

The political situation at the al-Kifah Refugee Center changed dramatically after the arrival of Abdul Rahman. The blind Egyptian imam had great prestige in the Islamist world. His arrival in the United States in 1990 was greeted with open arms by both Shalabi and the militants. Shalabi leased a house for him in the Bay Ridge area of Brooklyn. At first Abdul Rahman sided with Shalabi, but in a matter of months he changed sides. The source of contention was money and how to spend it. Shalabi wanted to continue giving funds to build an Islamist state in Afghanistan, but the militants were eager to use the money for terrorist operations in the United States. Suddenly Abdul Rahman began calling Shalabi a bad Muslim. Shalabi realized that he had lost out in the power struggle with Abdul Rahman, and he prepared to return to Egypt. Soon after Abdul Rahman changed sides Shalabi was mysteriously murdered. The events surrounding his murder on February 26, 1991, are so murky that no one has been charged in his death.

With Shalabi out of the way, the militants had control of al-Kifah Refugee Center. Abdul Rahman began to quietly issue a series of fatwas (religious rulings) declaring war on the United States. The militants began to consider a series of plots. Some of the plots were unreasonable, but after recruiting Ramzi Yousef the militants settled on bombing the World Trade Center. The arrest and conviction of key members of the al-Kifah Refugee Center did not end the plotting. Soon another plot was instigated, which involved the bombing of key tunnels, the United Nations building, and the FBI headquarters in New York City. This plot was infiltrated by a Muslim agent, Emad Salem, of the New York City Joint Terrorism Task Force, and the participants were arrested before the bomb could be built.

After the arrest of Abdul Rahman and the militants of the al-Kifah Refugee Center, the plots stopped coming out of the center. Al-Qaeda leaders observed how dangerous it was to conduct a terrorist campaign out of a refugee center. The nineteen suicide bombers made certain to avoid mosques, service centers, and any outward signs that they were devoted Muslims. In this way the plotters attempted to blend into the American scene.

See Also

Nosair, El Sayyid; World Trade Center Bombing (1993)

Suggested Reading

John Miller, Michael Stone, and Chris Mitchell, *The Cell: Inside the 9/11 Plot, and Why the FBI and CIA Failed to Stop It* (New York: Hyperion, 2002); Gerald Posner, *Why America Slept: The Failure to Prevent 9/11* (New York: Ballantine Books, 2003).

Kuala Lumpur Meeting

The Kuala Lumpur Meeting was a planning meeting of eighteen terrorists that took place in Kuala Lumpur, Malaysia, on January 5, 2000. This meeting was one of convenience because it allowed mid-level al-Qaeda operatives a chance to review their upcoming operations. They also wanted to explore possible operations in South Asia.

Even before the meeting, the National Security Agency (NSA) had intercepted communications indicating that such a gathering would take place. Late in 1999 the agency began intercepting communications between Nawaf and Salem al-Hazmi in Karachi, Pakistan, and Khalid al-Mihdhar in Yemen. These intercepts came from the telephone of a prominent Yemeni family—the Hada family—who had marriage ties to al-Qaeda member Khalid al-Mihdhar. From these intercepts the NSA learned there would be a major meeting of al-Qaeda operatives in Kuala Lumpur. Yazid Sufaat, a former Malaysian army captain and successful Malaysian businessman academically trained in biochemistry in Great Britain and the United States, provided his weekend retreat at the Bandar Sungai Long condominium complex outside Kuala Lumpur for the meeting. Exactly what was discussed at this gathering is unknown, but from informants it is known that planning occurred for the attack on the USS *Cole*, and there was discussion of using aircraft as weaponry, possibly in South Asia. Khallad bin Atash and Muhammad Omar al-Harazi, operational chiefs of the attack on the USS *Cole* on October 12, 2000, were in attendance. Representing the September 11 plot were Ramzi bin al-Shibh, al-Mihdhar, and Nawaf al-Hazmi.

Once American authorities learned of the meeting, they requested that Malaysian security officials photograph the attendees and bug the condo. Bugging was impossible because of the constant coming and going of the participants, but Malaysia's security service—the Special Branch—took photographs. Two photos came to have special importance—those of Khalid al-Mihdhar and Nawaf al-Hazmi. Both were Saudi citizens with combat experience in Bosnia and training at al-Qaeda camps in Afghanistan. Although al-Mihdhar and al-Hazmi were known al-Qaeda operatives, they left Kuala Lumpur and entered the United States without incident. They were eligible to be put on a watch list to prevent their entry, but the CIA neglected to do so. This inaction proved to be a monumental mistake, for al-Mihdhar and al-Hazmi were two of the nineteen suicide hijackers on September 11, 2001.

See Also

Bin al-Shibh, Ramzi; Hazmi, Nawaf bin Muhammad Salim al-; Mihdhar, Khalid al-; Qaeda, al-

See Document

Document #27

Suggested Reading

Bob Graham, *Intelligence Matters: The CIA, the FBI, Saudi Arabia, and the Failure of America's War on Terror* (New York: Random House, 2004); Peter Lance, *Triple Cross: How Bin Laden's Master Spy Penetrated the CIA, the Green Berets, and the FBI—And Why Patrick Fitzgerald Failed to Stop Him* (New York: ReganBooks, 2006); Terry McDermott, *Perfect Soldiers: The Hijackers: Who They Were, Why They Did It* (New York: HarperCollins, 2005); Steven Strasser (ed.), *The 9/11 Investigations; Staff Reports of the 9/11 Commission; Excerpts from the House-Senate Joint Inquiry Report on 9/11 Testimony from 14 Key Witnesses, Including Richard Clarke, George Tenet, and Condoleezza Rice* (New York: PublicAffairs, 2004).

L

Laden, Osama bin. *See* Bin Laden, Osama

Levin, Neil David (1955–2001)

Neil D. Levin, Executive Director of the Port Authority of New York and New Jersey, died at the World Trade Center complex on September 11, 2001. His position made him landlord of the World Trade Center complex, as well as operator of the New York City area's three major airports and its port facilities, bridges, tunnels, and the Port Authority Trans-Hudson (PATH) rapid transit system. Levin was a political appointee, and administering all these facilities was a difficult and demanding job.

Levin's training was as an economist. He was born in 1955 and raised in Atlantic Beach, New York. After graduation from high school, Levin attended Lafayette College, where he earned a bachelor's degree in economics. His next academic degree was an MBA from the C.W. Post Center of Long Island University's Graduate School of Business. Levin finished his academic training by earning a law degree from Hofstra University. In his first job he worked as counsel to the securities subcommittee of the U.S. Senate Banking Committee, where he worked closely with Senator Alfonse M. D'Amato. Part of his job involved helping to draft the Insider Trading Sanctions Act of 1984. He spent seven years as chair of the Federal Home Loan Bank Board of New York, and then joined Goldman Sachs & Company, where he became a vice president after two years with the company.

Levin's close ties with Republican politicians in New York advanced his career. Governor George Pataki appointed Levin New York State Superintendent of Banks. This position gave him oversight responsibility for 4,500 banks, thrifts, and other financial institutions in the state of New York. Governor Pataki later appointed Levin superintendent of the State Insurance Department and head of the Commission on the Recovery of Holocaust Victims' Assets.

The Port Authority of New York and New Jersey was Levin's next assignment. Some controversy had surrounded his predecessor, but when New York Governor Pataki and New Jersey Governor Donald DiFrancesco jointly appointed Levin

Executive Director in spring 2001, there was no controversy. Levin had earned a reputation as consensus maker, which enabled him to function smoothly with other politicians. His relationship with Mayor Giuliani was particularly important. It did not hurt that Levin had married Christine Ann Ferer in May 1996. She was an NBC broadcast journalist, and a public personality in her own right.

On September 11, 2001, Levin was caught in the wrong place at the wrong time, like so many other victims of the day. His office was on the sixty-fourth floor of the North Tower of the World Trade Center complex. Although American Airlines Flight 11 hit the tower higher than this floor, Levin was in a breakfast meeting with Fred V. Morrone, the Port Authority's police superintendent, in the Windows on the World Restaurant on the 107th floor of the North Tower. Levin was trapped, like all of those on floors above where the plane crashed. His wife frantically tried to reach him, but without success. There was no chance of escape, and Levin and Morrone evidently died when the North Tower collapsed. Levin's body has never been found.

Levin's wife has become active in the families of September 11 movement. New York Mayor Michael Bloomberg appointed her to a position of liaison with the families who are victims of September 11, placing her in the middle of the family groups' criticism of the mayor's office. Governor Pataki honored Levin by naming a program of the State University of New York the Neil D. Levin Graduate Institute of International Relations and Commerce.

See Also
American Airlines Flight 11; Giuliani, Rudolf William Louis "Rudy" III; Port Authority of New York and New Jersey

Suggested Reading
Ronald Smothers, "Pataki Names State Official as Port Authority's Chief," *New York Times* (March 31, 2001), p. B6; Edward Wyatt, "Neil Levin, Executive Director of Bistate Port Authority, 46," *New York Times* (September 22, 2001), p. A5.

Lewin, Daniel M. (1970–2001)

Daniel M. Lewin was the first victim of the terrorist plot on September 11, 2001. He was born in 1970 in Denver, Colorado, but lived as a teenager in Jerusalem, Israel, after the family moved there in 1984. Because he held both American and Israeli citizenship, he frequently moved between the two countries. Lewin served his four-year Israeli military obligation as an officer in the Israeli Defense Forces elite counterterrorist unit, Sayeret Matkal. He also graduated with BA and BS degrees in computer science and mathematics from Technion University in Haifa, Israel. His first job was with IBM's research laboratory in Haifa, where he worked on development of the Genesys system, a processor verification tool. In 1996, he entered Massachusetts Institute of Technology (MIT) as a graduate student. After receiving a master's degree in 1997, he began collaborating on special projects with Professor F. Thomson Leighton. Together they devised innovative algorithms for optimizing the Internet. In 1998 they founded the Internet company Akamai Technologies. Lewin was chief technical officer and a member of the board of Akamai Technologies, and his financial interests in the company made him a multimillionaire. He lived in Brookline, Massachusetts, with his wife and two children. At the time of his death he was a PhD candidate in the Algorithms groups at MIT's Laboratory for Computer Science.

Lewin was a passenger on American Airlines Flight 11 that boarded at Logan International Airport bound for Los Angeles International Airport. His seat was 9B, in the first-class section of the aircraft. Shortly before 8:17 a.m. the skyjacking team led by Mohamed Atta attacked the flight attendants in First Class. Lewin evidently reacted to the situation but before he could intervene, Satam al-Suqami, a member of the skyjacking team seated in 10B, fatally stabbed him. (The hijack team may have identified him as a possible air marshal.) Betty Ann Ong, a flight attendant, reported in a phone call to Amy Sweeny at Logan International Airport that a passenger in seat 9B had had his throat cut by a passenger in seat 10B at approximately 8:20 a.m. An FAA memo later suggested that Lewin had been shot, but this information is probably in error because there were no reports of gunshot by Ong. In any event, Lewin was probably the first victim of the September 11 attack, unless one of the flight attendants died before him. Since his death his company, Akamai Technologies, has prospered from its position as an Internet music enabler.

> **Growing Prominence of Daniel Lewin**
>
> Lewin was recently named one of the 25 most influential Chief Technology Officers by InfoWorld, and ranked seventh in the Power 100 list of the *Enterprise Systems Journal*. Having risen to such prominence in the IT industry in just three years, Lewin's was in every way a career cut short in its prime. He was studying for a PhD at MIT at the time of his death. In private life Lewin lived in Brookline, Massachusetts, and his pastimes were devoted to the pursuit of speed—motorcycling, fast cars, and skiing.
>
> Martin Campbell-Kelly, "Lewin: 'A Better Internet'," *Independent* [London] (September 14, 2001), p. 6.

See Also
American Airlines Flight 11; Ong, Betty Ann

Suggested Reading
Martin Campbell-Kelly, "Terror in America—Obituary: Daniel Lewin," *Independent* [London] (September 14, 2001), p. 6; Richard Sisk and Monique el-Faizy, "First Victim Died a Hero on Flt. 11," *Daily News* (July 24, 2004), p. 7.

M

Marrs, Jim (1943–)

Jim Marrs is a freelance journalist and a veteran conspiracy theorist who has joined the ranks of those claiming that a U.S. government conspiracy led to the September 11 attacks. Marrs first became famous because of his involvement in the investigations surrounding the John F. Kennedy assassination. His book, *Crossfire: The Plot That Killed Kennedy*, appeared in 1989 and served as the basis for Oliver Stone's movie *JFK*, for which Marrs served as an advisor. Marrs has spent most of his journalistic career as an investigative journalist. He was born on December 5, 1943, in Fort Worth, Texas. His father sold structural steel for a St. Louis company. Marrs attended public schools in Fort Worth and showed an early interest in journalism. He entered North Texas State University and graduated with a BA in journalism in 1966, after which he joined the U.S. Army. After leaving the military in 1968, he worked as a police reporter and general assignments reporter for the *Fort Worth Star-Telegram*. Marrs took a leave of absence to travel to Vietnam with a Fourth Army intelligence unit. After returning to the *Fort Worth Star-Telegram*, he worked as a military and aerospace writer. He was also a graduate student for two years at Texas Tech in Lubbock, Texas.

Marrs gained a national reputation as a leading critic of the official version of the assassination of John F. Kennedy in 1963. After interviews with witnesses, Marrs was convinced that the Warren Commission was a government cover-up. He left the *Fort Worth Star-Telegram* in 1970 to work full-time on his investigation and concluded that Lee Harvey Oswald, commonly thought to be the assassin of Kennedy, had been set up by the U.S. government and killed before he could expose the plot. *Crossfire* became a nonfiction bestseller. Since 1976, Marrs has taught a course at the University of Texas at Arlington about the events surrounding the Kennedy assassination. Beginning in 1980, he has devoted his energies to freelance writing and public relations consulting, as well as dabbling in the publishing of a weekly newspaper.

Marrs' next big project was a study of a secret government project involving a psychic phenomenon known as "remote viewing." He spent nearly three years researching, only to have his publishing company cancel the book in 1995. Two months afterward, the CIA announced the program, and information about it appeared in the *Washington Post*. This development was a keen disappointment to Marrs, but he posted his manuscript, *PSI Spies*, to the Internet via his Web site.

Marrs next turned his attention to unidentified flying objects (UFOs). After several years of research, his book, entitled *Alien Agenda,* was published by HarperCollins in May 1997. In this book, he recounted the history of UFO sightings and the response to them from the U.S. government. This book also received national exposure, becoming the bestselling UFO book to date. Marrs appeared as a speaker at several UFO-related national conventions and at other public affairs. He also began teaching a course about UFOs at the University of Texas at Arlington.

Marrs's interest in conspiracies produced another book, published in 2000 by HarperCollins: *Rule by Secrecy: The Hidden History That Connects the Trilateral Commission, the Freemasons, and the Great Pyramids.* He attempted to tie modern secret societies to those of ancient times—the so-called "ancient mysteries." This book also sold well, reaching the *New York Times* Best Seller List.

It did not take Marrs long to suspect a U.S. government conspiracy surrounding the events of September 11, 2001. The ineptitude of the agencies of the U.S. government was so dramatic that it has made for a field day for conspiracy theorists worldwide. In 2003, Marrs produced a book entitled *The War on Freedom* (which has since appeared under the title *The Terror Conspiracy: Deception, 9/11 and the Loss of Liberty*), in which he examined the various actions of the U.S. government with a view to proving a conspiracy that allowed the events of September 11 to happen. Marrs, who has been busily promulgating his thesis throughout the nation, has also been active in the Scholars for 9/11 Truth.

See Also
Conspiracy Theories; Fetzer, James H.; Scholars for 9/11 Truth

Suggested Reading
Jonathan Curiel, "The Conspiracy to Rewrite 9/11," *San Francisco Chronicle* (September 3, 2006), p. E1; Adam Harvey, "The Big Lie," *Sunday Mail* [South Australia] (September 10, 2006), p. 46; Ted Mahar, "Who Shot JFK?" *Oregonian* [Portland] (December 20, 1991), p. 6; Jim Marrs, *The Terror Conspiracy: Deception, 9/11, and the Loss of Liberty* (New York: Disinformation, 2006).

Mazza, Kathy (1955–2001)

Kathy Mazza, a captain in the Port Authority Police Department and the first female commanding officer of the Port Authority Police Academy, was one of two woman police officers to die while evacuating people from the World Trade Center on September 11, 2001. Mazza, a late recruit to the Port Authority police, was nevertheless rapidly promoted, becoming one of two female captains in the Port Authority Police Department.

Mazza's first career was in nursing. Born in 1955, in Massapequa, New York, she was the only girl among three brothers. After high school, Mazza attended Nassau Community College, earning a nursing degree. For the next ten years, she worked as a cardiothoracic nurse at the Long Island Jewish Hospital in Queens and at St. Francis Hospital in Roslyn, New York. In 1985, she married Christopher Dolosh, an officer in the New York City Police Department's 25th precinct. They lived in South Farmingdale, New York. In 1987 she decided to change professions by enrolling in the Port Authority Police Academy.

Mazza's career in the Port Authority Police Department prospered. After a tour of duty at JFK Airport in New York City, she was promoted to sergeant. After a year in the central police pool, she returned to JFK Airport for six more years. Her career was briefly interrupted when she underwent open-heart surgery to correct a quarter-sized hole in her heart in 1992, but this was only a temporary lull in her upward climb in the hierarchy of the Port Authority Police Department. In December 1998, Mazza became a lieutenant and assumed command of the Staten Island Bridges and New Jersey Marine Terminals. In April 2000, she was promoted to captain, making her one of two female captains out of fourteen. She took advantage of her installation as commander of the Port Authority Police Academy to institute a program teaching life-saving techniques that has saved at least sixteen lives to date.

Kathy Mazza's Drive for Excellence

Kathy was such a shining star. They couldn't deny her, and she wasn't going to back down. She wasn't going to go away quietly and be satisfied with being passed over. She knew that as a female in law enforcement, you have to give at least 150 percent to gain the respect and acknowledgment of your colleagues. Kathy was always willing to do that. She worked incredibly hard, and she earned every promotion.

Comment from Jessica Gotthold, Port Authority Police Officer, quoted in Susan Hagen and Mary Carouba, *Women at Ground Zero: Stories of Courage and Compassion* (New York: Alpha Books, 2002), p. 305.

Mazza volunteered to help at the World Trade Center complex during the September 11 emergency. She had been at the Jersey City headquarters of the Port Authority police when the attack occurred and left with five others to respond to the emergency. Mazza and her crew helped evacuate people from the North Tower. From the position of the bodies, it is evident that the five of them—Mazza, Lt. Robert D. Cirri, Chief James A. Romito, Officer James W. Parham, and Officer Stephen Huczko—were trying to evacuate a woman in a rescue chair even after the South Tower had collapsed. They were found sixty feet below ground on February 9, 2002.

Mazza's family established the Kathy Mazza Memorial Fund for Pediatric Cardiology at Saint Francis Hospital in her honor, and in 2003 the Town of Oyster Bay, Long Island, dedicated the Captain Kathy Mazza Park to her memory and heroism.

See Also
Port Authority of New York and New Jersey

Suggested Reading
Larry Celona, Mark Stamey, Farrah Weinstein, and Adam Miller, "3 Who Died as They Had Lived: Helping," *New York Post* (November 18, 2001), p. 18; Susan Hagen and Mary Carouba, *Women at Ground Zero: Stories of Courage and Compassion* (New York: Alpha Books, 2002); Eric Lipton, "For 5 Officers, Apparent Last Heroic Act," *New York Times* (February 11, 2002), p. B3; Michael Thier, "A Female Captain in Policing's Male World," *Newsday* [New York] (September 21, 2001), p. 1.

Merino, Yamel (1976–2001)

Yamel Merino was a young emergency medical technician (EMT) killed by the collapse of the South Tower of the World Trade Center complex on September 11,

2001. The twenty-four-year-old was one of the three women who died attempting to aid the victims of the terrorist attack.

Merino was a single parent who was resolved to be a success. She was born on October 21, 1976, and raised in Yonkers, New York. Her schooling was interrupted by the birth of a son when she was sixteen years of age, but she studied and received her general equivalency diploma. In June 1997, at age twenty, she started working at Metrocare, an ambulance company. Although she loved her job, her ultimate goal was to become a nurse. Much of the time her job in the ambulance company required her to transport the elderly and the handicapped—but she had time to be a fervent New York Mets fan.

> **Recollection of the Yamel Merino's Personality**
>
> Yamel Merino had a soft, sweet voice and a gentle smile, yet she could be as strong as a bull. She had to lift heavy patients onto gurneys in her job as an emergency medical technician. She knew her job was dangerous. Every night, she prayed for God to protect her 8-year-old son, whom she was raising on her own.
>
> Diane Cardwell et al., "Parties, Love Notes and Other Small Memories That Now Loom Large," *New York Times* (September 18, 2001), p. B10.

Merino was one of the first emergency medical technicians to arrive at the World Trade Center complex. Her assignment was working in a triage area at the Marriott Hotel, across the street from the twin towers. Witnesses report that she was last seen calming hysterical survivors before the South Tower collapsed on her. Her body was found on September 12. Merino was the youngest female rescue worker to be killed and was among the first buried. Her funeral was heavily attended. Because Merino was employed by a private company instead of a municipal employee, her family was ineligible for the financial support received by FDNY and NYPD employees after September 11.

See Also
Casualties of September 11

Suggested Reading
Diane Cardwell et al., "Parties, Love Notes and Other Small Memories That Now Loom Large," *New York Times* (September 18, 2001), p. B10; Susan Hagen and Mary Carouba, *Women at Ground Zero: Stories of Courage and Compassion* (New York: Alpha Books, 2002), pp. 293–298; Ian O'Connor, "EMT Answered Call to Be a Hero Daily," *USA Today* (September 10, 2002), p. 3C.

Meyssan, Thierry (1957–)

Thierry Meyssan is a French left-wing journalist and intellectual who has become a leading proponent of the view that the U.S. government was part of a conspiracy surrounding the events of September 11. He believes that right-wing elements within the U.S. government threatened President George W. Bush with a coup d'état unless he increased military spending and went to war against Afghanistan and Iraq. Meyssan added that these right-wingers also initiated a media campaign against Osama bin Laden to mask their conspiracy.

Meyssan, who was born on May 18, 1957, rebelled against his traditionalist Catholic family by becoming a left-wing freethinker. He attended Catholic schools and for a time was a theology student, but his rebellion against his family's political views led him into left-wing politics. In 1989 he founded Project Ornicar to

French author Thierry Meyssan holds his book, *9–11: The Big Lie*, in this March 19, 2002, photo, taken in Paris. (AP IMAGES/Michel Euler, File.)

oppose discrimination against homosexuals. In March 1994 Meyssan formed the Voltaire Network (*Réseau Voltaire*) as a platform from which to attack the French right wing and the Catholic Church. Casting himself as a free-thinker along the lines of Voltaire, Meyssan made the secret Catholic organization Opus Dei a special target. Also in 1994, Meyssan became National Secretary of the Radical Party of the Left (*Parti radical de gauche*). He was active in working in political campaigns—during Bernard Tapie's try for election to the European Parliament in 1994 and during deputy Christiane Taubira's candidacy in the 2002 French presidential election. Meyssan was also active in the National Committee of Vigilance Against the Extreme Right (*Comité national de vigilance contre l'estrême droite*) from 1996 until 1999, when he became head of the Radical Anti-Prohibitionist Coordination (*Coordination radical anti-prohibitionniste*), a group resolved to fight organized crime and the drug trade.

Meyssan had already built a reputation in French left-wing circles when he published his book, *The Big Lie* (*l'Effroyable imposture*), asserting that parts of the U.S. government had orchestrated the events of September 11. The book appeared in 2002 and became an immediate bestseller in France, within months selling over 200,000 copies. Its popularity corresponded to the growing anti-Americanism among French citizens who increasingly feared the political intentions of the United States.

In his book, Meyssan makes a number of charges about September 11 that seem difficult to correlate with the facts. He asserts that a right-wing cabal organized the attacks on September 11 to force President George W. Bush to build military strength for an invasion of Afghanistan and Iraq. He believes that members of this plot, rather than al-Qaeda operatives, crashed the airliners into the World Trade Center complex, but he has alternated between blaming a truck bomb and a guided missile for the damage to the Pentagon. He has also claimed that Osama bin Laden was a stooge of the CIA who could be easily blamed for the attacks. He wrote that Muslims could not have crashed the aircraft, because the Koran forbids suicide.

However, Meyssan has never traveled to the United States and did not interview any witnesses. He has dismissed witnesses out of hand because of his belief that they are part of the conspiracy. His evidence came from photographs and data gathered by other conspiracy theorists on the Internet. An eyewitness to the crash, James S. Robbins—a contributing editor to the *National Review*—replied to Meyssan by calling his ideas an affront to any reasoning person (see sidebar).

Despite its popularity in France, Meyssan's book has

Reaction of September 11 Eyewitness James S. Robbins to Meyssan's Theories

So, of course, I take it personally when a half-wit like Meyssan comes along saying [the airliner crash into the Pentagon] did not happen. And he is so evidently at war with reality that one is tempted not to waste time with him. His ideas are obviously foolish, easily disproved, an affront to any reasoning person. It would be easy to ignore him. But that would be a mistake. . . . Allowing the extremists to go unchallenged only encourages them. . . . When such ideas are allowed to stand, they take root among the impressionable and those predisposed to think the worst. And especially now that communications technology has made it possible to give global reach to the bizarre and archive it forever, it is essential for men and women of reason resolutely to counter the delusions of the fringe element. I was there. I saw it. That is my entire rebuttal.

James S. Robbins, "9/11 Denial," *National Review* (April 9, 2002), p. 1.

---

been panned by French critics. Two French investigative journalists, Guillaume Dasquie and Jean Guisnel, have written *L'Effroyable mensonge* (*The Terrible Lie*) that counters all of Meyssan's points about September 11. In researching their book, they traveled to the United States and interviewed witnesses to disprove Meyssan's assertions.

Meyssan has paid little attention to the negative publicity for his book, which has now been translated into English for American and British audiences. He is continuing to advance his conspiracy theories in another book, *The Pentagate* (*Le Pentagate*).

See Also
Conspiracy Theories; Pentagon Attack

Suggested Reading
Max Berley, "The French Disconnection," *Pittsburgh Post-Gazette* [Pennsylvania] (April 14, 2002), p. E1; Stephen Goode, "What's behind the Hatred of America?" *Insight on the News* (January 19, 2004), p. 39; John Lichfield, "Delusions of Ground Zero: Thierry Meyssan with a Copy of His Discredited Book," *Independent* [London] (July 22, 2002), p. 7; Alan Riding, "Sept. 11 as Right-Wing U.S. Plot: Conspiracy Theory Sells in France," *New York Times* (June 22, 2002), p. A1; James S. Robbins, "9/11 Denial," *National Review* (April 9, 2002), p. 1.

Mihdhar, Khalid al- (1975–2001)

Khalid al-Mihdhar was one the hijackers of Flight 77, which crashed into the Pentagon on September 11, 2001. He was an early recruit to the September 11 plot and was intended to be one of the pilots. His ineptness and poor English skills kept him from any role as a pilot, but he continued to serve in a support role. Al-Mihdhar was an early convert to militant Islamism. Born on May 16, 1975, in Mecca, Saudi Arabia, he completed a rudimentary education and became an active Islamist. As a teenager, he traveled to Afghanistan in 1993 and then with his friend Nawaf al-Hazmi joined Muslim fighters in Bosnia in their war against Bosnian Serbs. In 1996 al-Mihdhar moved back to Afghanistan with the al-Hazmi brothers in time to fight with the Taliban against the Afghan Northern Alliance. In 1997 he joined the Chechen rebels in Chechyna in their fight against the Russian army. By 1998 he had become a part of al-Qaeda and returned to Afghanistan for training at a special al-Qaeda training camp at Mes Aynak. In early 1999 he returned to Saudi Arabia, and on April 7, 1999, he obtained a U.S. visa through the U.S. Consulate in Jeddah, Saudi Arabia. In late 1999 the Saudi government placed al-Mihdhar on a Saudi terror watch list, and then–Saudi Intelligence Minister Prince Turki al Faisal warned the CIA about both al-Mihdhar and al-Hazmi. By that time, both lived in San Diego, California, a region where they had arrived in November 1999.

Sometime in early 1999, al-Mihdhar was recruited to the September 11 plot by Mohamed Atta. On January 5, 2000, he attended the three-day conference of al-Qaeda supporters in Kuala Lumpur, Malaysia, where the outline of the September 11 plot was discussed. He and al-Hazmi returned to the United States on January 15, 2000, arriving in Los Angeles, where they met the Saudi Omar al-Bayoumi, who directed them to the large Muslim community in San Diego, California. Al-Bayoumi found them an apartment and helped them settle in. Because neither al-Mihdhar nor al-Hazmi spoke English, they made no attempt to make contact with anyone outside their own Muslim community. Later, they moved to another apartment in the home of a retired literature professor Abdussattar Shaikh—who, unbeknownst to them, was an informer for the FBI.

Al-Mihdhar's Aptitude for Piloting

[Fred] Sorbi gave [Kalid al-Mihdhar and Nawaf al-Hazmi] introductory lessons in one of his small Piper Cherokees, each taking a turn at the controls for about an hour. "We took them up to show them how the airplane flies," said Sorbi. On approach to the runway at the end of the flight, Sorbi said, one of the men—he couldn't remember which—grew extremely frightened and started praying aloud, calling out to Allah as the other man piloted the small plane toward the landing strip. Sorbi advised them to delay further lessons: "We told them to go to college and learn to speak English if they wanted to become pilots. They said they were."

Terry McDermott, *Perfect Soldiers: The 9/11 Hijackers: Who They Were, Why They Did It* (New York: HarperCollins, 2005), p. 192.

Al-Mihdhar's role was to learn to become a pilot. He tried to learn to fly small aircraft at San Diego's Montgomery Field. But both al-Mihdhar and al-Hazmi proved such poor students that their instructor told them to go to college and learn English, which meant that other pilots had to be trained. Al-Mihdhar instead became the recruiter for the muscle part of the operation. In June 2000, he headed back to the Middle East for an extended stay. On June 10, 2001, he traveled to Saudi Arabia, where he finalized plans for the emigration of the final twelve members of the plot. To do this, he traveled extensively throughout the Middle East, Southeast Asia, and

Afghanistan. Despite his suspicious activity, al-Mihdhar was able to return to the U.S. on July 4, 2001, on the Visa Express Program. In August 2001 he moved to Laurel, Maryland.

On September 10, 2001, al-Mihdhar and two associates traveled to Herndon, Virginia, where they stayed at a Marriott Residence Inn, preparing for the mission the next day. Early on the morning of September 11, al-Mihdhar and four others boarded American Airlines flight 77, where he provided much of the protection for the hijacking team's pilot until the airliner crashed into the west wing of the Pentagon.

See Also
Hazmi, Nawaf bin Muhammad Salim al-; Pentagon Attack

See Document
Document #1

Suggested Reading
Bob Graham, *Intelligence Matters: The CIA, the FBI, Saudi Arabia, and the Failure of America's War on Terror* (New York: Random House, 2004); Terry McDermott, *Perfect Soldiers: The 9/11 Hijackers: Who They Were, Why They Did It* (New York: HarperCollins, 2005).

Millennium Plots

Leaders of al-Qaeda planned for a series of terrorist operations to take place on or around January 1, 2000. At least three plots surfaced during investigations in the months and weeks before the millennium. Khalid Sheikh Mohammad has claimed credit for planning and financing these plots, whose targets were in three different places—Amman, Jordan; Los Angeles, California; and, Aden, Yemen. Fortunately, none of the plots were carried out—but the news clearly indicated that al-Qaeda's leadership was busy concocting plots to the detriment of the United States. Al-Qaeda operatives had planned to bomb the Radisson Hotel in Amman, along with Christian tourist sites in and around the city on January 1, 2000, hoping to kill as many Americans as possible. Jordanian authorities, however, learned of the plot and raided the terrorists' bomb factory, which was hidden in an upper-middle-class residence. The terrorists had planned to use poisons and other improvised devices to increase the casualties of their attacks, planning to disperse hydrogen cyanide in a downtown Amman movie theater. News of this plot reached American officials in the middle of 1999.

The terrorists also plotted to plant a large bomb at the Los Angeles International Airport, a plan that originated in Canada among Muslim militants there. Ahmed Ressam tried to smuggle the explosives from Canada to the United States through the British Columbia–Washington Ferry Entry Point. An alert U.S. Customs Officer, Diana Dean, suspicious of Ressam's nervousness, pulled him over and had begun to check the vehicle when Ressam made a break. Dean and fellow customs officers soon captured him, and an examination of his vehicle revealed a large quantity of explosives and a map of the Los Angeles International Airport. American authorities believed that Ressam would have received assistance from al-Qaeda members in the Los Angeles area, but no proof of this has surfaced.

Finally, the terrorists planned a marine bombing intended to sink the destroyer USS *The Sullivans* at its berth in the port of Aden, Yemen. Al-Qaeda operatives overloaded a small boat with explosives, to the point of sinking, and nothing remained but to cancel the operation. Because of the covert nature of this operation—and because of its failure—American authorities did not learn about this plot until much later, after the attack on the USS *Cole*.

See Also
Qaeda, al-; Ressam, Ahmed

Suggested Reading
Vernon Loeb, "Planned Jan. 2000 Attacks Failed or Were Thwarted; Plot Targeted U.S., Jordan, American Warship, Official Says," *Washington Post* (December 24, 2000), p. A2.

Mohamed, Ali Abdel Saoud (1952–)

American authorities first began to understand Osama bin Laden's role in the Islamist movement after questioning Ali Mohamed. Until the mid-1990s, authorities believed bin Laden to be a secondary character acting mostly as a "money man." Mohamed was a professional soldier and Islamist who then served as a sergeant in the U.S. Army.

Mohamed's entire career has been associated in one way or another with the military. He was born in 1952 in Kafr el-Sheikh, near Alexandria, Egypt. His father was a professional soldier, and Mohamed followed in his footsteps. He attended the Military Academy in Cairo and then enrolled in the University of Alexandria, where he earned a master's degree in psychology in 1980. He joined the Egyptian Army as an officer in 1971, and his abilities as a linguist allowed him rapid promotion as an intelligence specialist in the Egyptian Special Forces. In that capacity Mohamed participated in the 1973 Yom Kippur War against Israel. In 1981 he underwent Green Beret training at Ft. Bragg, North Carolina.

At the same time that his military career prospered, Mohamed became a militant Islamist. Religious since childhood, he was attracted to the extremist Islamist side of Islam. His spiritual mentor was Abdel Rahman, and he made contact with elements in the Islamist extremist terrorist group Egyptian Islamic Jihad. Members of this group and of Mohamed's military unit assassinated Egyptian President Anwar Sadat in 1981. Although Mohamed approved of the assassination, he was not implicated in the plot because he was then stationed at Ft. Bragg. Later, Mohamed's association with religious and political extremists led to his dismissal from the Egyptian army in 1984. Bitter about his forced dismissal at the rank of major, he reached out to Ayman al-Zawahiri and his Egyptian Islamic Jihad for support, swearing an Islamic oath of allegiance (*bayat*) to al-Zawahiri and the Egyptian Islamic Jihad.

After working as a security advisor to Egypt Airlines and, briefly, as an operative of the CIA, Mohamed immigrated to the United States in 1986. During his service as a CIA operative in Lebanon, he confessed to being a CIA agent in his contacts with Hezbollah, an incident that caused his name to be placed on a State Department Watch List. Nevertheless, Mohamed had little trouble obtaining a visa to the United States and arrived in New York City on a TWA aircraft on September 6, 1985.

Once in the United States, Mohamed lived in Santa Clara, California, and soon married an older American woman. He was unemployed for several months before landing a security officer job with American Protective Services of Sunnyvale,

California. One of his first actions was to set up an Islamist cell with the help of recruit Khalid Dahab, but his goal was to join the U.S. Army. In August 1986, Mohamed volunteered for military duty. Basic training was at Ft. Jackson, South Carolina. The army then assigned him to Ft. Bragg, where he served as a supply sergeant until he was appointed assistant lecturer on Islamic culture and politics at the JFK Special Operations Warfare School. During his off-duty hours in the military, he studied for a PhD in Islamic Studies. His views were controversial, and in 1987 he decided that he wanted to fight against the Soviets in Afghanistan. Mohamed took a thirty-day leave to travel to Afghanistan to train mujahideen fighters. While in Afghanistan, he led several patrols against Soviet forces. Mohamed's commanding officer at Ft. Bragg, Lieutenant Colonel Robert Anderson, became so concerned with Mohamed's political views and his unauthorized trip to Afghanistan that he filed two intelligence reports on him—reports that were somehow lost in the military's bureaucracy.

After returning to the United States, Mohamed moved closer to the militants at the al-Kifah Mosque. On weekends, he trained volunteers in military tactics at sites in Brooklyn and New Jersey. Mohammed copied maps and training manuals and used these resources to write the multivolume terrorist manual used by al-Qaeda. He also wrote and translated the contents of a 180-page manual entitled *Military Studies in the Jihad against the Tyrants.* Mohamed had become increasingly close to Abdel Rahman and el Sayyid Nosair. He taught Nosair field-survival tactics and weapons handling. Nosair used these lessons to assassinate the Israeli extremist Rabbi Meir Kahane. Mohamed decided to leave the army and received an honorable discharge in November 1989. That same year, Mohamed became an American citizen. He also started a leather import–export business that served as cover for his frequent trips to the Middle East. By the early 1990s, he had become familiar with—and contacted—both Ayman al-Zawahiri (former head of the Egyptian Islamic Jihad and second-in-command in al-Qaeda) and Osama bin Laden. He handled security arrangements for bin Laden's transfer from Sudan to Afghanistan. After Mohamed's return to the United States, he was al-Qaeda's only open operative in the country. In 1992 he returned to Afghanistan, where he gave weapons instruction and intelligence training to al-Qaeda trainees.

> **Confession of Ali Mohamed in October 2000**
>
> I was involved in the [Egyptian] Islamic Jihad organization and the Islamic Jihad organization had a very close link to al Qaeda. And the objective of all this, just to attack any Western target in the Middle East, to force Western countries to pull out from the Middle East, based on the Marine [barracks] explosion in Beirut [in 1983].
>
> Quoted in Peter L. Bergen, *The Osama bin Laden I Know: An Oral History of al Qaeda's Leader* (New York: Free Press, 2006), p. 143.

In the spring of 1993, an FBI field agent interviewed Mohamed, who told him all about Osama bin Laden's plans to overthrow the Saudi regime and rid the Middle East of foreigners. The agent informed his FBI superiors about Mohamed and bin Laden, but nothing happened. Mohamed continued to perform small missions for al-Qaeda around the world. On one mission in 1995, he scouted targets in Nairobi, Kenya, and advised that the American embassy was the best target. Returning to the United States, Mohamed moved with his wife to Sacramento, California, in 1997 and found a job with Valley Media, a wholesaler of recorded music and videos, as a computer network support specialist. Throughout the 1990s, Mohamed remained a triple agent working for both al-Qaeda and the FBI but kept his allegiance with al-Qaeda. In 1998 the FBI decided to arrest Mohamed for lying to the FBI. After his arrest on November 4, 1998, he was reluctant to cooperate with the FBI. Even threats to send him back to Egypt, where he had been sentenced to death in absentia in the spring of 1999, did not persuade him to cooperate. Finally, in October 2000, Mohamed began to cooperate with the FBI, confessing his role in the African embassy bombings. In return, the FBI promised Mohamed to refrain from pursuing the death penalty or life in prison in future court trials. He has never been sentenced despite pleading guilty to five counts of conspiracy to kill, kidnap, and maim Americans both in the United States and abroad, as well as to the destruction of American property both in the United States and abroad. Since his cooperation, Mohamed has been held in protective custody in a Florida prison.

See Also
Abdel Rahman, Sheikh Omar; Bin Laden, Osama; Kifah Refugee Center, al-; Qaeda, al-; Zawahiri, Ayman al-

Suggested Reading
Richard Bernstein, *Out of the Blue: The Story of September 11, 2001, from Jihad to Ground Zero* (New York: Times Books, 2002); Peter Lance, *Triple Cross: How Bin Laden's Master Spy Penetrated the CIA, the Green Berets, and the FBI—And Why Patrick Fitzgerald Failed to Stop Him* (New York: ReganBooks, 2006); John Miller, Michael Stone, and Chris Mitchell, *The Cell: Inside the 9/11 Plot, and Why the FBI and CIA Failed to Stop It* (New York: Hyperion, 2002); Lawrence Wright, *The Looming Tower: Al-Qaeda and the Road to 9/11* (New York: Knopf, 2006).

Mohammed, Khalid Sheikh (1965–)

Khalid Sheikh Mohammed was the operational chief for the planning for the September 11 operation. He had been active in extremist Islamist activities with his nephew Ramzi Yousef before and after the 1993 World Trade Center bombing, but it was his role as instigator of the September 11 plot that made him notorious. Until his capture in Pakistan, he rivaled Osama bin Laden as the United States' "public enemy number one."

Mohammed came from a family with strong religious and political views. He was born on April 24, 1965, in the Fahaheel neighborhood of Budu Camp, Kuwait. His father was a Muslim cleric from the Pakistani province of Baluchistan. Because of the citizenship rules of Kuwait, the family remained as guest workers instead of Kuwaiti citizens. The young Mohammed grew up in Kuwait resenting his inferior status. Mohammed was a good student and excelled in science. His father died before he graduated high school, and his elder brothers assumed responsibility for his care. Because both brothers had strong political views, they guided his political orientation, which eventually led him to join the Muslim Brotherhood at age 16. He graduated from Fahaheel Secondary School in 1983, and his brothers decided to send Mohammed to the United States to further his education. Mohammed traveled to the United States in 1983 to study mechanical engineering at Chowan College, a Baptist school in Murfreesboro, North Carolina. After a short stay there, Mohammed transferred to North Carolina Agricultural and Technical State University in Greensboro, North Carolina (now University of North Carolina—Greensboro). At both schools, Mohammed remained aloof from American students and American society. Most of his contacts were with other students from Arab countries. After graduating in 1986 with a degree in mechanical engineering, Mohammed traveled to Pakistan to join the mujahideen in fighting Soviets in Afghanistan. His older brother Zahed Sheikh Mohammed was head of a Kuwaiti charity, the Committee for Islamic Appeal (*Lajnat al Dawa al Islamia,* or LDI), in Peshawar, Pakistan. His other brother worked for Abdul Rasool Sayyaf's newspaper in Peshawar. For a time, Mohammed taught engineering at a local university. The three brothers worked together with Abdullah Azzam, Sayyaf, and Gulbaddin Hekmatyar to determine the strategy of the Afghan resistance. Mohammed's war experiences in Afghanistan changed his life, especially after he lost a brother, Abed Sheikh Mohammed, in the fighting late during the war, at the Battle of Jalalabad. Mohammed became secretary to the Afghan warlord Sayyaf and, through him, made the acquaintance of Osama bin Laden and other Islamist leaders.

After the end of the Afghan-Soviet war in 1989, Mohammed stayed in Pakistan, where he devoted his activities to operations run against the West. When the political situation in Afghanistan deteriorated for Islamist militants, Mohammed looked elsewhere for employment. The conflict in Bosnia attracted him, and he fought with the mujahideen there in 1992. During these years, Mohammed held a number of jobs before ultimately working for the Qatari government as an engineer in its electricity headquarters. His first involvement in a major terrorist operation was with his nephew, Ramzi Ahmed Yousef. His role in the planning of the February 26, 1993, bombing of the World Trade Center in New York City is still mostly conjecture, but it is known that he sent Yousef $660 to help build the bomb. This bombing, however, proved a disappointment. Although it caused many casualties, it failed to cause the collapse of the twin towers or kill the hoped-for thousands. After Yousef returned to Karachi, Pakistan, he met with Mohammed. It was at one of these meetings in 1993 that Yousef and his friend, Abdul Hakim Murad, suggested a way to attack the United States. Murad, who had earned a commercial pilot license at an American commercial pilot school, proposed packing a small airplane full of explosives and dive-bombing into the Pentagon or the headquarters of the Central Intelligence Agency. Mohammed quizzed Murad about details of pilot training and the ways that such an operation might be carried out. Nothing was done at that time, but Mohammed later used this information in the September 11 plot.

Later in 1993 Mohammed contacted Hambali, the operation chief of the Indonesian Islamist terrorist group Gama'a Islamiyya. Mohammed and Yousef traveled to the Philippines to work on a plan, Project Bojinka, that envisaged the bombing of a dozen U.S. commercial aircraft over the Pacific during a two-day period. He also worked with Yousef to plan the assassination of Pope John Paul II during his visit to the Philippines, but a chemical mishap caused by Yousef ended this attempt. Mohammed returned to Pakistan, where he kept in touch with

Yousef. Only after Yousef was captured in 1995 did Mohammed begin to make separate plans for terrorist operations, one of which was the use of commercial aircraft as terrorist weapons. However, he needed allies before undertaking such a massive operation.

American intelligence was slow to realize the importance of Mohammed in the terrorist world even as he traveled throughout the Muslim world making contacts. Evidence obtained in Yousef's apartment in Manila indicated Mohammed's association with Yousef, but nothing else was known. Beginning in 1993, Mohammed lived in Doha, Qatar, working at the Ministry of Electricity and Water. In his spare time, Mohammed raised money for terrorist groups. Enough evidence about his participation in Yousef's activities existed that a New York grand jury issued a secret indictment against him in January 1996. Although American authorities tried to persuade Qatari officials to extradite Mohammed, the Qatar government was reluctant to do so. Efforts to mount a seizure operation were hindered by a lack of commitment on the part of the American military, the CIA, and the FBI. Eventually a half-hearted effort was made by the FBI, but Mohammed was long gone, warned by his friend Abdullah ibn Khalid, the minister of religious affairs in Qatar, that the Americans were looking for him.

Mohammed began cooperating with al-Qaeda in 1996. Bin Laden invited him to join al-Qaeda's military committee under Mohammad Atef. Mohammed was to swear loyalty (*bayat*) to bin Laden and to al-Qaeda, bringing with him connections to the Middle East and South Asia, as well as plans to attack the United States. He met with bin Laden and Atef, al-Qaeda's military commander, at bin Laden's Tora Bora mountain refuge in 1996, where Mohammed presented to them a variety of terrorist schemes, the most promising of which was the use of commercial airliners as flying bombs to use against targets in the United States. Yet, though bin Laden asked Mohammed to join al-Qaeda, Mohammed turned him down, wishing to retain his autonomy. Despite this, Mohammed developed a close working relationship with al-Qaeda. Mohammed needed al-Qaeda to supply money and martyrs for his operations even as he supplied the planning, but bin Laden was noncommittal about the plan until 1998, when he proposed that the four leaders of the plane hijackings should be two Saudis—Khalid al-Mihdhar and Nawaf al-Hazmi—and two Yemenis—Walid Mohammed bin Attash and Abu Bara al-Yemeni. This plan, however, fell apart when the two Yemenis were unable to obtain American visas. At this time, no need existed for pilots—something that soon changed. This

---

Relationship of Khalid Sheikh Mohammed and Osama bin Laden

It doesn't surprise me [that Khalid Sheikh Mohammed organized 9/11]. It's not exactly bin Laden's territory. He's not very fond of details, looking at details. He's the enigma; he's the chairman of the company, so to speak. He is the symbol of the organization. He would still need people like Khalid Sheikh Mohammed to be advising him on certain operations, and Khalid Sheikh Mohammed would, in turn, need people to execute things.

Comment by Yosri Fouda after talking with Khalid Sheikh Mohammed, quoted in Peter L. Bergen, *The Osama bin Laden I Know: An Oral History of al Qaeda's Leader* (New York: Free Press, 2006), p. 303.

change of plans led to the later recruitment of Mohamed Atta, Ziad Jarrah, and Marwan al-Shehhi from the Hamburg Cell. At this time American intelligence had no idea of the extent of Mohammed's growing contacts with al-Qaeda, but the FBI was offering a $2 million reward for his capture because of his role in the Manila plot.

Shortly after his 1996 meeting with bin Laden, Mohammed began recruiting operatives for a future suicide mission. His liaison with al-Qaeda's leadership was Ramzi bin al-Shibh. He briefed bin Laden and the leadership of al-Qaeda orally on his final plan for a suicide mission using commercial aircraft sometime in 1998 or 1999. By this time, Mohammed, who had sworn a loyalty oath to bin Laden, had been integrated into al-Qaeda's leadership hierarchy. Recruits for the mission were trained at the Afghan al-Matar Training Complex, where Abu Turab al-Urduni, a Jordanian trainer, taught them how to hijack planes, disarm air marshals, and use explosives. Mohammed confessed in a June 2002 interview with the Muslim journalist Yosri Fouda that the operation in the United States had been planned two-and-a-half years before it took place.

> **Khalid Sheik Mohammed Confesses to His Role in the 9/11 Attacks**
>
> About two and a half years prior to the holy raids on Washington and New York the military committee held [a] meeting during which we decided to start planning for a martyrdom operation inside America. As we were discussing targets, we first thought of striking a couple of nuclear facilities but decided against it for fear it would go out of control. The attacks were designed to cause as many deaths as possible and havoc and to be a big slap for America on American soil.
>
> Quoted in Yosri Fouda and Nick Fielding, *Masterminds of Terror: The Truth Behind the Most Devastating Terrorist Attack the World Has Ever Seen* (New York: Arcade, 2003), p. 114.

Mohammed's original plan included the hijacking of ten aircraft and the destruction of ten targets but was ultimately reduced to four. Once the operatives were selected and Mohamed Atta had been picked and briefed as mission leader, Mohammed watched from behind the scenes.

After September 11, Mohammed knew that he was a marked man. He eluded capture for nearly two-and-a-half years. Considerable investigation was required by American authorities before they realized just how important Mohammed was to the planning of September 11; but once his importance was realized, his capture was only a matter of time. On March 1, 2003, a joint team of Pakistani and American agents arrested Mohammed in Rawalpindi, Pakistan, seizing his computer, cell phones, and documents. For more than two-and-a-half years, American authorities held him at a remote prison site in Pakistan, where he was interrogated about his role in al-Qaeda and in the September 11 attacks. In September 2006 Mohammed was transferred to the Guantánamo Bay Detainment Camp. In early March 2007 the Bush administration announced that he and thirteen others would appear before military courts to determine whether or not they were enemy combatants, after which enemy combatants would appear before a military tribunal. Before the proceedings, it was reported that Mohammed had been increasingly forthcoming about his role in the September 11 plot. His confessions included myriad plots—most of which were never carried out or were failures. At his hearing at the Combatant Status Review Tribunal

Hearing on March 10, 2007, Mohammed stated that he had been the organizer of the September 11 plot, justifying it as part of a war between the Islamist world and the United States. Mohammed also confessed to complicity in many other plots, among which were the 1993 World Trade Center bombing and the killing of the Jewish journalist Daniel Pearl in Pakistan, in which he claimed personal involvement only, stating that it was not related to his al-Qaeda activities. Although his open confession of participation in these terrorist acts equated to a guilty plea, Mohammed simultaneously claimed that he had been tortured. His fate is still to be determined.

See Also
Atta, Mohamed el-Amir Awad el-Sayed; Bin al-Shibh, Ramzi; Bin Laden, Osama; Guantánamo Bay Detainment Camp; World Trade Center Bombing (1993); World Trade Center, September 11; Yousef, Ramzi Ahmed

See Document
Document #42

Suggested Reading
Dan Eggen, "9/11 Report Says Plotter Saw Self as Superterrorist," *Washington Post* (July 27, 2004), p. A1; Yosri Fouda and Nick Fielding, *Masterminds of Terror: The Truth Behind the Most Devastating Terrorist Attack the World Has Ever Seen* (New York: Arcade, 2003); Terry McDermott, *Perfect Soldiers: The 9/11 Hijackers: Who They Were, Why They Did It* (New York: HarperCollins, 2005); Peter Lange, *1000 Years for Revenge: International Terrorism and the FBI: The Untold Story* (New York: ReganBooks, 2003); Warren Richey, "The Self-Portrait of an Al Qaeda Leader," *Christian Science Monitor* (March 16, 2007), p. 1; Andy Soltis, "'I Did 9/11 from A to Z'-Qaeda Big's Evil Boasts & Slay-Plot Shockers at Gitmo Trial," *New York Post* (March 15, 2007), p. 8.

Motassadeq, Mounir el- (1974–)
Mounir el-Motassadeq was a member of the Hamburg Cell, the leaders of which participated in the September 11, 2001, attacks in the United States. He was not one of the leaders of the cell, but he provided material support for its planning and for its operations in Germany. Despite evidence to the contrary, el-Motassadeq has maintained his innocence, claiming that no terrorist organization existed in Hamburg.

Little is known about el-Motassadeq's personal background. He was born on April 3, 1974, in Marrakesh, Morocco. His father was an affluent doctor. After graduating from a Moroccan secondary school with distinction, el-Motassadeq decided to study electrical engineering at German schools and moved to Münster, Germany, in 1993, where he studied German. During this time, he married a Belarus woman, with whom he later had a son. He was fluent enough in German to be accepted into the electrical engineering program at the Technical University of Hamburg-Harburg. In addition to his studies, el-Motassadeq became active at the al-Quds Mosque. Soon after he arrived in Hamburg, he became acquainted with Mohamed Atta, with whom he prayed at both the university and the mosque. Often el-Motassadeq and Atta ate together; according to witnesses, they discussed religion and politics.

Much of the evidence linking el-Motassadeq with the Hamburg Cell and the September 11 plot is circumstantial. His close association with Atta and Ramzi bin al-Shibh is suspicious in itself, but in May 2000 he flew to Afghanistan. El-

Motassadeq spent three weeks at the al-Qaeda training camp near Kandahar, Afghanistan. A witness at the camp has stated that he attended a session at which Osama bin Laden spoke. Earlier he had covered for Atta, bin al-Shibh, Ziad Jarrah, and Marwan al-Shehhi when they made their trip to Afghanistan for al-Qaeda training. El-Motassadeq was a signatory for Atta's will and held power of attorney over al-Shibh's bank account, making his denial of any knowledge of the September 11 plot dubious. Although he covered for his friends in Germany while they trained as pilots and sent them funds in the weeks before September 11, he did not flee Germany before September 11 as bin al-Shibh did. Reports have surfaced that bin al-Shibh stated under interrogation that el-Motassadeq was not part of the September 11 plot; but, after weeks of surveillance by German authorities, el-Motassadeq was arrested on November 28, 2001.

The ambiguity of el-Motassadeq's relationship with the Hamburg Cell has complicated the conviction of el-Motassadeq of a crime difficult to prove in German courts. The German legal system protects individual rights even more strictly than the American system. In February 2003, during his first trial, el-Motassadeq was convicted of over 3,000 counts of accessory to the murders on September 11, 2001. A German panel of judges sentenced him to a fifteen-year prison term, but an appeals court overturned the verdict as unproven because the United States had refused to allow a key witness to testify—the only surviving leader of the Hamburg Cell, Ramzi bin al-Shibh. El-Motassadeq was retried for his membership in a terrorist organization and convicted again in August 2005 and sentenced to seven years, but an appeals court also overturned this conviction. On February 7, 2006, Germany's Federal Constitutional Court ordered an early release of el-Motassadeq, claiming an absence of proof that he had been informed about the September 11 plot. El-Motassadeq was released shortly thereafter, but the Federal Supreme Court rejected his appeals and ruled that sufficient evidence existed to prove that he was aware of the hijacking scheme. The court held him guilty of accessory in 246 counts of murder for those killed on the hijacked aircrafts. On January 8, 2007, el-Motassadeq received a sentence of fifteen years from the State Supreme Court in Hamburg, and his lawyers continue to draft appeals on his behalf. In the meantime, however, he remains in prison.

See Also
Atta, Mohamed el-Amir Awad el-Sayed; Bin al-Shibh, Ramzi; Hamburg Cell; Jarrah, Ziad Samir; Shehhi, Marwan Yousef Muhammed Rashid Lekrab al-

Suggested Reading
Richard Bernstein, "German Court Convicts Man of Qaeda Ties," *New York Times* (August 20, 2005), p. A6; Desmond Butler, "Trial in Germany; Friend of Hijacker Admits to Training in Afghanistan," *New York Times* (October 23, 2002), p. A11; Peter Finn, "Germany Makes Its First Sept. 11 Arrest," *Washington Post* (November 29, 2001); Mark Landler, "9/11 Associate Is Sentenced in Germany to 15 Years," *New York Times* (January 9, 2007), p. A10; Anton Notz, Deborah Steinborn, and Hugh Williamson, "Guilty of Terrorism," *Financial Times* [London] (February 20, 2003), p. 15.

Moussaoui, Zacarias (1968–)
Zacarias Moussaoui has become infamous as the so-called "twentieth member" of the suicide hijacking mission of September 11, 2001. He was born on May 30,

1968, in St.-Jean-de-Luz, near Narbonne, France, to Moroccan parents. His father was a successful tiler, and his mother worked in a variety of menial jobs until finding a position in the French postal system. Moussaoui's parents divorced when he was only three years old, and his mother raised him along with his older brother and two older sisters. She continued to bring up her children in France, but their upbringing was secular. During Moussaoui's youth, his family moved around France—first to a resort in the Dordogne and then to Mulhouse in Alsace before finally settling down in Narbonne. While in Mulhouse, the children spent a year in an orphanage run by the local Social Services Department. Moussaoui and his mother did not get along and had frequent and furious arguments. Things became so serious that Moussaoui left home in 1986. A good student, he easily passed his vocational baccalaureate. After passing entrance exams, he opted to study mechanical and electrical engineering at a school in Perpignon. His French girlfriend, Fanny, followed him, and they lived together. Moussaoui transferred to the University of Montpellier's Economic and Social Administration program, but he had begun to tire of school when the Persian Gulf War broke out in 1991.

The plight of Iraqi civilians and Palestinians concerned Moussaoui, and he became increasingly interested in politics. He had experienced racism in France, and his sympathy for Muslim causes was increasing. While at the University of Montpellier, he came into contact with Muslim students advocating extremist Islamist views. He made a six-month visit to London in 1992, but his stay in England proved disillusioning when he found British society intolerant and class-ridden. This experience, however, did not prevent him from returning to England, where he stayed for the next three years. He attended the South Bank University in London, studying international business. Moussaoui earned his degree in 1995 and he moved back to Montpellier. Some time during his stay in England, Moussaoui became converted to the Wahhabi strain of Islam by the militant Islamic teacher Abu Qatada, who ran a religious community, the Four Feathers, near Baker Street in London. His behavior during visits to France and Morocco alarmed his family. Soon after his conversion, al-Qaeda recruiters convinced him to join al-Qaeda.

> **Moussaoui's Brother Describes the Process of Recruitment by Al-Qaeda**
>
> First, they pick out young people who, one way or another, have been estranged from their families. These young people, with no adult to guide them, are cut off from strong moral anchors. The chaotic personal and family history of Zacarias fits the pattern perfectly.
>
> Abd Samad Moussaoui with Florence Bouquillat, *Zacarias, My Brother: The Making of a Terrorist* (New York: Seven Stories Press, 2003), pp. 114–115.

Between 1995 and 2001, Moussaoui's association with al-Qaeda became even closer. He received training in Afghanistan at al-Qaeda's Khaldan camp in 1998, at the same time as Mohamed Atta. Moussaoui's trainers found him enthusiastic but questioned his stability. Moussaoui was finally recruited for a future suicide mission, but little evidence exists to show that it was the September 11 plot. The al-Qaeda leadership had other plans for him, and he wanted to work on a Boeing 747 simulator, unlike the hijackers of the September 11 bombings, who trained exclusively on 757 and 767 simulators. Moussaoui's friend, Hussein al-Attas, described him "as the kind of man who believed it was acceptable to kill civilians who harmed Muslims and that he approved of the 'martyrs' who did just that."

Moussaoui entered the United States in hopes of becoming a pilot. He arrived at Chicago's O'Hare Airport on February 23, 2001, with a ninety-day visa. Within days of his arrival, he began learning to fly small aircraft at the Airman Flight School in Norman, Oklahoma. He became frustrated by his lack of progress after failing the written examination, for which he blamed inexperienced instructors at the school. After looking at other pilot schools, Moussaoui contacted the Pan Am International Flight Academy in Eagan, Minnesota, near Minneapolis, hoping to learn how to fly the huge Boeing 747-400. After only a few days of training in mid-August, the school's instructors became suspicious of Moussaoui, who showed more interest in flying than in taking off or landing. He also inquired about the protocols used for communicating with flight towers, asked about cockpit doors, and wondered how much damage a fully loaded 747 could do. After a meeting of the instructors, one volunteered to contact a friend in the Minneapolis FBI field office. Instead, the call went to FBI Special Agent Harry Samit, a U.S. Navy aviation veteran and small-engine pilot who was immediately suspicious of Moussaoui.

The Minneapolis FBI field office was part of the Joint Terrorism Task Force (JTTF) system, and a brief investigation showed that his visa was "out of status," having expired on May 22, 2001. This led the INS (Immigration and Naturalization Service) agent in the JTTF to authorize the arrest of Moussaoui on August 16, 2001. Moussaoui refused to allow the FBI agents to search his belongings but agreed to allow them to be taken to the local INS building. Because of Moussaoui's French citizenship, the FBI requested information concerning him from French authorities, who deemed Moussaoui dangerous and conveyed this to the FBI office in Minneapolis.

The Minneapolis FBI agents wanted a search warrant to examine Moussaoui's belongings—in particular, his laptop—but ran into difficulties at FBI headquarters in Washington, D.C. Two types of search warrants are possible—standard criminal search warrants and Foreign Intelligence Surveillance Act (FISA) search warrants, which are issued by a secret Foreign Intelligence Surveillance Court (FISC). FBI headquarters found insufficient cause for a criminal warrant. The agents' request for a FISA court warrant was denied because he was not affiliated with a recognized terrorist group, even though Moussaoui had contacts with Chechen rebels and close ties to al-Qaeda.

The political climate changed after September 11, and Moussaoui became a key target for retribution. American federal prosecutors charged Moussaoui with capital crimes, accusing him of six acts: preparing acts of terrorism, conspiracy to hijack an aircraft, destruction of an aircraft, use of weapons of mass destruction, murder of American officials, and destruction of property—even though Moussaoui had been in jail for twenty-five days when the events of September 11 occurred. Moreover, doubt still lingered about Moussaoui's role in the September 11 plot. The FBI had difficulty in proving that had Moussaoui cooperated, the September 11 attacks could have been prevented.

Nevertheless, Attorney General John Ashcroft insisted that the Justice Department seek the death penalty. Opposition to this position arose within the Justice Department, because a death sentence would make plea bargaining impossible. Although Moussaoui had information about al-Qaeda, no attempt was made to extract it from him.

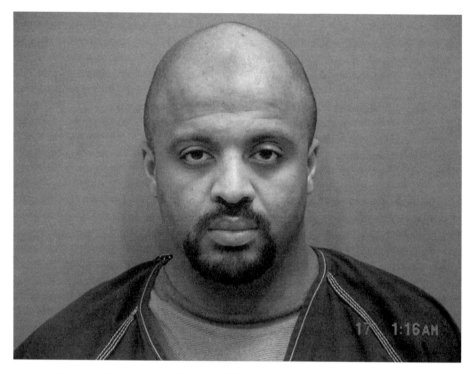

Zacarias Moussaoui in an August 17, 2001, file photo provided by the Carver County, MN, sheriff's department. (AP IMAGES/Carver County Sheriff's Department, File.)

The trial was a national event. Moussaoui's irrational behavior and sudden guilty plea created even more controversy. It became apparent that Moussaoui *wanted* to be martyred. During the sentencing, prosecutors argued for the death sentence, but a dubious jury handed him a life sentence without chance of parole instead, reflecting Moussaoui's role as an al-Qaeda operative who intended to commit acts of terror rather than any action he might have taken. Moussaoui is now serving his sentence at a federal maximum-security prison.

See Also
Federal Bureau of Investigation; Qaeda, al-

See Documents
Document #30; Document #40

Suggested Reading
Bob Graham, *Intelligence Matters: The CIA, the FBI, Saudi Arabia, and the Failure of America's War on Terror* (New York: Random House, 2004); Seymour M. Hersh, *Chain of Command: The Road from 9/11 to Abu Ghraib* (New York: HarperCollins, 2004); Seymour M. Hersh, "The Twentieth Man: Has the Justice Department Mishandled the Case against Zacharias? *New Yorker* (September 30, 2002), p. 56; Joint Inquiry into Intelligence Community Activities before and after the Terrorist Attacks of September 11, 2001, *Hearings Before the Select Committee on Intelligence U.S. Senate and the Permanent Select Committee on Intelligence House of Representatives* (Washington, DC: U.S. Government Printing Office, 2004), vol. 2; Abd Samar Moussaoui with Florence Bouquillat, *Zacarias, My Brother: The Making of a Terrorist* (New York: Seven Stories Press, 2003).

Murad, Abdul Hakim Ali Hashim (1968–)

Abdul Hakim Murad was a coconspirator of Ramzi Yousef in Operation Bojinka. He suggested to Yousef and Khalid Sheikh Mohammed that a commercial aircraft would be a good terrorist weapon. This advice was based on his experience obtaining a pilot's license in the United States.

Murad wanted to become a commercial pilot. He was born on January 4, 1968, in Kuwait, but his father was from Pakistan and worked as a crane operator for a petroleum company in Kuwait. After graduating from high school in al-Jery, Kuwait, Murad pursued his dream of becoming a commercial pilot by attending the Emirates Flying School in Dubai, United Arab Emirates. He then traveled to the United States to train at various commercial pilot schools—Alpha Tango in Gern Stages, Texas; Richmore Flying School in Schenectady, New York; Coastal Aviation in New Bern, North Carolina; and California Aeronautical Institute in Red Bluff, California. Murad obtained his FAA multiengine license from Coastal Aviation on June 6, 1992.

Murad returned to the Middle East in July 1992. Soon after his arrival in Pakistan, Yousef contacted him. Murad helped Yousef plan the assassination of Benazir Bhutto, but the bomb exploded prematurely, wounding Yousef. When Yousef transferred his operations to the Philippines, Murad followed him. Yousef's uncle, Khalid Sheikh Mohammed, also joined them. Sometime during this period, Murad began to discuss with Yousef and Mohammed a scheme to hijack commercial aircraft and use them as flying missiles. Murad, who had the piloting skills the others lacked, talked about the need to train pilots for such a mission. In the meantime, Yousef was engaged in a plot to assassinate the Pope and to launch Operation Bojinka. These plans were in the process of implementation when the chemical accident at the Josepha apartment ended them. Yousef sent Murad back to pick up his laptop computer, but in doing so Murad was arrested by the police.

After capturing him, the Philippine police interrogated Murad. Murad was reluctant to cooperate until Colonel Rodolfo Mendoza, the commander of the Philippine National Police's Special Investigations Group, began his interrogation. Under pressure, Murad identified Yousef as his coconspirator, later mentioning a plan to hijack commercial airliners and crash them into targets like the Pentagon, or nuclear facilities. Other possible targets identified by Murad were the Transamerica Tower in San Francisco, the Sears Tower in Chicago, the World Trade Center in New York City, and the White House. Philippine police told American authorities about the plans to turn commercial aircraft into flying bombs in 1995. Murad's mission was to fly his aircraft into CIA headquarters in Langley, Virginia.

For whatever reason, American authorities ignored Murad's tale. In fact, the FBI later claimed that it

> **Murad's Scheme for a Suicide Hijacking**
>
> The Philippine report on [Murad's] hijacking proposal conveyed the simplicity of his idea: "What subject have in his mind is that he will board any commercial aircraft pretending to be an ordinary passenger. Then he will hijack said aircraft, control its cockpit and dive it into CIA Headquarters. There will be no bomb or any other explosive that he will use in its execution. It is, simply a suicidal mission that he is very much willing to execute. That all he need is to be able to board the aircraft with a pistol so that he could execute the hijacking."
>
> Terry McDermott, *Perfect Soldiers: The 9/11 Hijackers: Who They Were, Why They Did It* (New York: HarperCollins, 2005), p. 167.

had never heard of the plot. This denial came as the interrogation material from Murad became available. After being extradited from the Philippines, Murad is now serving a life sentence in an American federal prison.

See Also
Mohammed, Khalid Sheikh; Yousef, Ramzi Ahmed

See Document
Document #26

Suggested Reading
Peter Lance, *Triple Cross: How Bin Laden's Master Spy Penetrated the CIA, the Green Berets, and the FBI—And Why Patrick Fitzgerald Failed to Stop Him* (New York: Regan, 2006); Terry McDermott, *Perfect Soldiers: The 9/11 Hijackers: Who They Were, Why They Did It* (New York: HarperCollins, 2005).

N

National Commission on Terrorist Attacks upon the United States
The creation of an independent commission to inquire into all aspects of the 9/11
attacks was prompted because of the stark limitations of earlier congressional
inquiries. Congress's Joint Inquiry on Intelligence had outlined serious deficiencies in governmental intelligence-gathering and interagency cooperation, but the
White House had refused to turn over documents to the investigators, citing constitutional separation of powers. Senator John McCain described the process as
"slow-walked and stonewalled." A more in-depth inquiry into the policy miscal-
culations of the Bush and Clinton administrations engendered partisanship and
found Republicans and Democrats attacking the other party's administration. The
best way to mitigate such issues was to create an independent, bipartisan commission having unlimited access to all documents and officials.

However, conflicting interests caused delays in forming such a commission. The
Bush administration was reluctant to support such a commission, fearing that it
would concentrate chiefly on mistakes made during the Bush administration.
Democrats feared a witch hunt for errors made during the Clinton administration.
Intense pressure from the families of those killed during the attacks finally forced
the creation of the commission. The survivors of the dead made it plain to all
involved that they wanted an immediate investigation of the events surrounding
September 11, but it was not until fourteen months after the attacks that the 9/11
Commission was announced. The National Commission on Terrorist Attacks
upon the United States, or the 9/11 Commission, received a mandate from the
President of the United States and the U.S. Congress to investigate the facts and
circumstances of the attacks on the United States that occurred on September 11,
2001. Legislative authority for this commission was given by Public Law 107-306,
signed by President Bush on November 27, 2002. The five Republicans and five
Democrats selected for this commission were a matter of some controversy. President Bush selected Henry Kissinger, once Nixon's Secretary of State, to chair the
committee, and Senator Tom Daschle appointed George Mitchell, former Senate
majority leader and chief negotiator of the Northern Ireland Peace Accords, as
vice-chair.

These appointees soon encountered political difficulties. The families of the victims confronted Kissinger about his consulting firm's clients, some of whom were suspected to be Saudis and even, possibly, the Bin Laden family. Responding to pressure, the Senate Ethics Committee ruled that the members of the commission had to abide by congressional rules on the disclosure of possible conflicts of interest, which meant that Kissinger had to disclose his entire client list. He was unwilling to do so and resigned from the commission. Mitchell encountered the same problem with the client list of his law firm, so he, too, resigned from the commission. President Bush then turned to the well-respected former Governor of New Jersey, Thomas H. Kean, and Senator Tom Daschle to former Indiana congressman Lee H. Hamilton. Neither Kean nor Hamilton had prior dealings with each other, but they soon began to work together.

The final members of the commission were Thomas H. Kean (chair), Lee H. Hamilton (vice-chair), Richard Ben-Veniste, Fred F. Fielding, Slade Gorton, Max Cleland, John F. Lehman, Timothy J. Roemer, and James R. Thompson. Midway in the commission's deliberations, Cleland left the commission for a government job and was replaced by Bob Kerrey. In the interests of bipartisanship, Kean made Hamilton co-chair.

The families of the victims maintained the momentum behind the creation of the 9/11 Commission, championing its subpoena powers by lobbying members of Congress and even the White House. These representatives formed the twelve-member Family Steering Committee (FSC). Members of the FSC came mainly from four organizations: Families of September 11, Voices of September 11th, the Skyscraper Safety Campaign, and September 11th Advocates. Soon after the creation of the 9/11 Commission, representatives from the Family Steering Committee met with Kean and Hamilton to express their desire for the commission to move swiftly and aggressively. They presented to Kean and Hamilton a document entitled *September 11 Inquiry: Questions to Be Answered,* which consisted of fifty-seven questions about 9/11 that reflected their greatest desire: accountability.

Almost immediately the 9/11 Commission began to work with Philip Zelikow, who had a reputation as a presidential historian and who was the director of the Miller Center of Public Affairs at the University of Virginia. Zelikow's Republican connections included work on the National Security Council of President George H. W. Bush and on the transition team of the National Security Council of President George W. Bush. His coauthorship of a book with Condoleezza Rice on German unification, as well as his relationship with Stephen Hadley, the National Security Advisor, made Democratic commissioners leery of him. Members of the Family Steering Group were also unhappy with his selection and petitioned to have him removed. Both Kean and Hamilton, however, had confidence in his integrity, and he stayed. Zelikow became the mainstay of the 9/11 investigation, supervising the 80-person staff and playing a major decision-making role.

Much criticism was also directed at the composition of the 9/11 staff, at least half of which was drawn from the agencies the commission was tasked to investigate. This raised worries that evidence would be looked at in lights that would exonerate agencies and people implicated. Some critics have maintained that the evidence was "cherry-picked" to produce a portrayal that sat well with investigators. Again members of the Family Steering group complained, but to no avail. Even Kean and Hamilton expected the 9/11 Commission to fail in its mission,

realizing that the odds of its success were low because the political stakes were so high. Both
Republicans and Democrats lined
up together to find fault as part
of a commission expected to
operate on a rigid, unrealistic
timeline with inadequate funds.

Although the 9/11 Commis-
sion had broad subpoena powers, it used these judiciously and
only against those unwilling or
unable to produce necessary
documents. The most notorious
offenders were the Federal Aviation Administration (FAA) and the North
American Aerospace Defense Command (NORAD), both of which were so
reluctant to produce documents regarding the events of September 11 that the
commission was forced to subpoena documents from them. Both agencies
compiled with the subpoenas, which also acted as a warning to the White House
to produce its own documents when required.

> **Reasons Why the 9/11 Commission Would Fail**
>
> Both of us [Kean and Hamilton] were aware of grum-
> bling around Washington that the 9/11 Commission was
> doomed—if not designed to fail: the commission would
> splinter down partisan lines; lose its credibility by leaking
> classified information; be denied the necessary access to
> do its job; or alienate the 9/11 families who had fought
> on behalf of its creation.
>
> Thomas H. Kean, Lee H. Hamilton, and Benjamin Rhodes,
> *Without Precedent: The Inside Story of the 9/11 Commission*
> (New York: Knopf, 2006), p. 15.

In its analysis of the failures to detect the September 11 conspiracy, the 9/11
Commission listed four contributing factors: (1) a "failure of imagination" to even
conceive of the possibility of such an operation, (2) a "failure of capabilities" that
allowed al-Qaeda to operate in the United States despite agencies designed to prevent just such activity, (3) a "failure of management" by national security leaders
whose agencies neither shared information nor collaborated in their activities, and
(4) a "failure of policy" by both the Clinton and Bush administrations to priori-
tize counterterrorism.

The 9/11 Commission not only criticized the failures leading to September 11
but also made a series of recommendations. Among these recommendations were
a National Counterterrorism Center, a national intelligence director, the reform of
congressional oversight of national security, reform within the FBI, more trans-
parent levels of information sharing between government agencies, and smoother
transitions between presidential administrations. It did recognize, however, that
not all of its recommendations would find approval both in the White House and
in Congress.

In the course of the commission's investigations, members of the commission
and its staff reviewed 2.5 million documents and interviewed more than 1,200
individuals in ten countries. Nineteen days of public hearings and the testimony of
160 witnesses informed its investigation, but from the beginning, the commission
was under pressure to achieve its objectives in a short time. Its request for an
extension was greeted with little enthusiasm because the report would be produced too near to the 2004 presidential election. An extension of two months was
granted, but still too little time remained to answer all the questions posed.

Despite its attempts at thoroughness, the 9/11 Commission has been subjected
to severe criticism both from the inside and the outside. One of the criticisms has
to do with the Able Danger controversy. Then-Congressman Curt Weldon
charged that the commission ignored Able Danger and its alleged identification of

Mohamed Atta before September 11, but Kean and Hamilton have replied that Able Danger was brought to the commission's attention late in its deliberations. Both the commissioners and the staff concluded that none of the Able Danger materials indicated any knowledge of Atta—despite the meeting of the commission's executive director, Zelikow, with Lieutenant Colonel Shaffer at Bagram Air Base in Afghanistan in late 2003, at which time Shaffer informed Zelikow of the findings of Able Danger.

See Also

Able Danger; American Airlines Flight 11; American Airlines Flight 77; Atta, Mohamed el-Amir Awad el-Sayed; Pentagon Attack; United Airlines Flight 93; United Airlines Flight 175; World Trade Center, September 11

See Documents

Document #31; Document #34; Document #36

Suggested Reading

Thomas H. Kean and Lee H. Hamilton, *Without Precedent: The Inside Story of the 9/11 Commission* (New York: Knopf, 2006); Ernest R. May, ed., *The 9/11 Report with Related Documents* (Boston: Bedford, 2007); Steven Strasser, ed., *The 9/11 Investigations: Staff Reports of the 9/11 Commission; Excerpts from the House-Senate Joint Inquiry Report on 9/11; Testimony from 14 Key Witnesses, Including Richard Clarke, George Tenet, and Condoleezza Rice* (New York: PublicAffairs, 2004).

National Security Agency (NSA)

The National Security Agency is the U.S. government's electronic spy service. When President Harry Truman created this agency to consolidate the government's code-breaking activities, the NSA's mandate included the surveillance of both domestic and international communications, something that changed when Congress passed the Foreign Intelligence Surveillance Act (FISA) in 1978, requiring search warrants from the FISA court before NSA domestic wiretaps in cases of national security. Until September 11, 2001, the primary mission of the NSA was the surveillance of international communications.

The head of the National Security Agency was Air Force General Michael Hayden, who was director of the NSA from March 1999 to April 2005—the longest in the history of the agency. Officially, his boss was George Tenet, head of the CIA, but in reality the NSA was an independent agency answering to the President more than to the CIA.

Exploiting the capabilities of today's supercomputers, the National Security Agency has learned to deal with a massive amount of intelligence-related information. International intelligence-gathering has been hidden under the codename Echelon. As reported by James Risen, the NSA has recruited personnel who were "technicians, math and linguistic geeks, and military and civilians who were bureaucratic conformists." In 1990, in its greatest success, it stole every Soviet code machine and manual.

The National Security Agency began to target the communications of al-Qaeda leaders in the late 1990s. At that time, al-Qaeda leaders used communication systems that the NSA could monitor by using satellites and other signals technologies, as it did to transmissions from an al-Qaeda logistics center in Yemen in 1998. After word leaked out in an article in the *Washington Times* that the NSA had this capability, al-Qaeda leaders stopped using satellite cell phones and e-mail.

Since then, all of al-Qaeda's communication has been in code. A problem developed in the late 1990s that affected the NSA's ability to handle its normal volume of data. The NSA's computer system, which was becoming outdated, crashed for four days in January 2000. The required upgrades cost $1 billion and were not totally in place by September 11, 2001. Even today, the NSA's attempts to overhaul its badly dated computer system have not been successful.

As the volume of al-Qaeda traffic went up, ominous conversations about "Zero Hour" made NSA and CIA analysts nervous. George Tenet, director of the CIA, warned the Bush administration that something big was going to happen—perhaps even in the United States. He communicated this to Condoleezza Rice in a meeting on July 10, 2001, but nothing came of it. Later, General Hayden was forced to explain before Congressional committees why a key intercept on September 10, 2001, regarding something big scheduled for September 11, was not translated until September 12.

Within weeks of September 11, the NSA received permission from the Bush administration to start the controversial "terrorist surveillance program." This program required that at least on one side of the phone call be from outside the United States and that there be probable cause to believe the person on the other side to be associated with al-Qaeda or another terrorist group. The president had to reauthorize this program every forty-five days, something he has faithfully done. Budgetary increases have enlarged the project's funds from about $4 billion pre-September 11 to $8 billion in 2007. What has made this surveillance program especially controversial is the loose interpretation that has included far more phone calls than the authorization explicitly allows. Soon after September 11, all telephone companies were submitting to pressure from the NSA. This circumvention of the Foreign Intelligence Surveillance Act (FISA) and the Foreign Intelligence Surveillance Courts (FISC) came to an end in 2007 when the Bush administration promised to use a more systemic approach to intelligence-gathering from telephone communications.

See Also
Central Intelligence Agency; Foreign Intelligence Surveillance Act of 1978; Qaeda, al-; Tenet, George

Suggested Reading
Bob Barr, "Privacy . . . Now the Guard? Approve a Rollback of Bush's Power," *Atlanta Journal-Constitution* (May 2, 2007), p. 15A; Siobhan Gorman, "Management Shortcomings Seen at NSA," *Baltimore Sun* (May 6, 2007), p. 1A; Bob Graham, *Intelligence Matters: The CIA, the FBI, Saudi Arabia, and the Failure of America's War on Terror* (New York: Random House, 2004); James Risen, *State of War: The Secret History of the CIA and the Bush Administration* (New York: Free Press, 2006); Bob Woodward, *State of Denial* (New York: Simon and Schuster, 2006).

Naudet Documentary on 9/11
The Naudet brothers' documentary film on the events of September 11, 2001, was an accidental product, but it is the most accurate portrayal of the events of that day. Jules and Gédéon Naudet, who were filming a documentary about a rookie fireman's experiences in New York City's fire department, were on location filming with Engine 7 Company, Ladder 1 Company of the Fire Department of New York City (FDNY) on the morning of September 11. Jules Naudet was riding with

Battalion Chief Joseph Pfeifer to check out a gas leak when the American Airlines Flight 11 flew overhead. Naudet turned his camera in time to record the aircraft crashing into the North Tower. Pfeifer allowed Naudet to record the rescue operations until it became too dangerous. Meanwhile Gédéon was back at the fire house filming the reactions of the firefighters as they prepared to head to the World Trade Center complex. He then followed the firefighters to the World Trade Center complex to film their ordeal. They were filming when the South and North Towers collapsed. Together they filmed 180 minutes, much of it considered too graphic for public consumption. The footage includes jumpers landing and a screaming woman burning from aviation fuel that poured down an elevator shaft. It also captures the removal of chaplain Mychal Judge's body. Naudet and Gédéon received permission to film both the rescue attempts and the subsequent hunt for bodies.

The Naudet brothers turned their footage into a documentary with the assistance of retired New York City firefighter James Hanlon as codirector. CBS aired the film, titled simply *9/11*, commercial-free on March 10, 2002, narrated by actor Robert De Niro. It has since been shown by CBS several times. Normally the film would have had to be edited because of the use of profanity by the participants, but a federal appeals court granted a temporary halt to the Federal Communications Commission's enforcement of its indecency rules. This film has been studied by law enforcement authorities trying to understand the sequence of events of September 11.

> **Reason Why Naudet Brothers Censored Their Documentary**
>
> It is a story about a firehouse and the men in the firehouse, going through their daily lives, and, after Sept. 11, surviving this. It's not a story about death or what happened. It's a tribute.
>
> Quoted in Lisa de Moraes, "CBS's Controversial Date with Destiny; Network Defends Airing '9/11' Special with Scenes inside the Trade Center," *Washington Post* (March 9, 2002), p. C1.

See Also
Firefighters at Ground Zero; Judge, Mychal

Suggested Reading
Paul J. Gough, "9/11 Documentary Update exposes CBS to Indecency Laws," *Ottawa Citizen* [Canada] (August 11, 2006), p. D7; Renee Peck, "On Sept. 11, Two French Filmmakers Were Shooting a Documentary about New York City Firefighters When the Unthinkable Happened," *Times-Picayune* [New Orleans] (March 9, 2002), p. 1; David Usborne Top, "The Brothers Who Made Ground Zero, the Movie," *Independent* [London] (February 8, 2002), p. 7.

New York City Landmarks Bombing Conspiracy

The New York City Landmarks Bombing Conspiracy was another attempt to attack the United States that followed the 1993 World Trade Center bombing. Sheikh Omar Abdel Rahman was the spiritual leader of this plot, but the actual work was done by his followers at the al-Kifah Refugee Center. The leaders were Ibrahim Siddig Ali, Mohammed Salah, Fares Kallafal, and Emad Salem. Almost immediately after the bombing of the World Trade Center on February 26, 1993, the conspirators began planning a series of bombings of New York City landmarks. By May 1993 they had selected four targets—the FBI Building, the United

Nations, and the Lincoln and Holland tunnels. The plotters considered the George Washington Bridge, but they lacked the know-how to bring it down.

The conspirators then began building bombs, renting a workspace at 139-01 90th Avenue, Jamaica, Queens. Although they had selected four targets, they intended to build three large bombs. Because they lacked the bomb-making expertise of World Trade Center bomber Ramzi Yousef, they tested their bomb components constantly. However, an undercover agent had disclosed the nature of their plot to the Joint Terrorism Task Force (JTTF) from its beginning. Emad Salem, a former Egyptian military officer, carried a wire for the JTTF that recorded the conversations of the plotters. Salem acted as the chief bomb maker for the conspiracy. Some of the taped recordings implicated Abdel Rahman. These taps allowed the JTTF to keep abreast of the progress of the terrorists in building the bombs. The terrorists were busy doing just that when JTTF agents raided the bomb-making facility and arrested eight men. Most of the conspirators were caught red-handed. Clement R. Hampton-El and Victor Alvarez were arrested later. A few days later the JTTF agents arrested Abdel Rahman.

The trial of the twelve members of the conspiracy began in June 1995. In addition to those arrested earlier, El Sayyid Nosair, the assassin of Rabbi Meir Kahane, was the twelfth defendant. Siddig Ali turned state's evidence and implicated the other conspirators. The defendants were convicted of forty-eight of the fifty counts on October 1, 1995. Abdel Rahman and Nosair received life sentences in solitary confinement without chance of parole, and the other defendants garnered sentences ranging from twenty-five to fifty-seven years. This trial ended the second attempt to launch a bombing campaign in the United States by Islamist terrorists.

See Also
Abdel Rahman, Sheikh Omar; Joint Terrorism Task Force; Nosair, El Sayyid; World Trade Center Bombing (1993); Yousef, Ramzi Ahmed

Suggested Reading
J. Bowyer Bell, *Murders on the Nile: The World Trade Center and Global Terror* (San Francisco: Encounter Books, 2003); Gerald Posner, *Why America Slept: The Failure to Prevent 9/11* (New York: Ballantine Books, 2003); Daniel Benjamin and Steven Simon, *The Age of Sacred Terror* (New York: Random House, 2004).

New York City Police Department (NYPD)

The New York City Police Department responded en masse to the attacks of September 11, 2001. Police worked to rescue and evacuate those trapped in the World Trade Center complex and in doing so suffered their greatest casualties. They also tried to control traffic around the complex, with mixed levels of success. One major problem was the lack of coordination between the police and the firefighters, two departments that have traditionally had poor relations. Both police and firefighters tended to act independently, without coordinating with the other agency. Much of the bad feelings arose from the Fire Department of New York (FDNY) belief that the NYPD was a political favorite, receiving more funds and personnel. Whatever the reason, the hostility between the two departments hindered operations at the World Trade Center complex on September 11.

Failures in the communication system also hindered the activities of the police. The radios refused to work around the World Trade Center, and what communication systems did work were soon overwhelmed by traffic. Police and others had to use cell phones to call family members and establish communications.

Casualties, lower among police than among the firefighters, were nevertheless high. Police lost 23 officers, including one woman. This loss paled beside that of the firefighters of the FDNY, but police losses were severe enough to cause a crisis of confidence. A demoralized police force had to be returned to normal police duties, a task that was the responsibility of Police Commissioner Kerik—who was generally successful. Kerik left office in January 2002, leaving much still to be done to reestablish the morale of the police of the NYPD. Later, when the 9/11 Commission questioned New York firefighters and police about their conduct on September 11, Kerik and the police became defensive, charging that the commission was unfairly second-guessing their actions.

See Also
Firefighters at Ground Zero; Kerik, Bernard Bailey

Suggested Reading
Peter Lange, *1000 Years for Revenge: International Terrorism and the FBI: The Untold Story* (New York: ReganBooks, 2003); Patrice O'Shaughnessy, "Painful Days for Cops Who Won't Give Up," *Daily New* [New York] (December 16, 2001), p. 28; Dennis Smith, *Report from Ground Zero* (New York: Viking, 2002).

9/11 Commission. *See* National Commission on Terrorist Attacks upon the United States

Nineteen Martyrs
In the Muslim world, the participants in the attacks on September 11, 2001, have been characterized as the Nineteen Martyrs. These nineteen young men are revered throughout much of the Middle East, where it is believed that by giving up their lives they weakened the hated power of the United States. Yet, several of the participants' families have denied that their sons were capable of such an act, and some of the families accuse the CIA of having them killed. Moreover, the identities of all but the leaders of the operation are in doubt. Reports have surfaced that some of them had entered the United States on false passports, and their names may never be known. Regardless of these problems, the nineteen hijackers sought and found martyrdom, their apparent motivation the threat they believed the United States posed to Islam. They differed in the intensity of their religious beliefs, but they were united in their worldview, believing that the West had been corrupted by greed, sin, and selfishness. In contrast, they believed the Islamic world to be an oasis of faith threatened by the West—in particular, the United States. Fifteen of the nineteen hailed from Saudi Arabia. They were sons of well-to-do families, and most were well-educated. Their fathers' occupations ranged from supermarket owners to tribal princes.

The members of the September 11 plot arrived in the United States at different times. Mohamed Atta and the other designated pilots arrived earliest for their pilot training and served as mentors of the later arrivals. Those later arrivals entered the United States from Dubai between March and June 2001, traveling in small groups and landing at four different airports to allay suspicion. Although they arrived in the United States knowing they were part of a martyrdom mission, for reasons of operational security they were not given the details of their mission.

The plan called for more than twenty hijackers, but at least six of the men selected for the mission were unable to obtain visas to enter the United States. In all, the nineteen terrorists entered and reentered the United States thirty-three times—most of that activity on the part of the four pilots. They flew back to Europe to consult with al-Qaeda leaders on the progress of the mission, as well as on personal business.

The leader of the nineteen was Atta, who was assisted by Marwan al-Shehhi, Hani Hanjour, and Ziad Jarrah. These individuals were also the pilots of the four hijacked aircraft: Atta of American Airlines Flight 11, al-Shehhi of United Airlines Flight 175, Hanjour of American Airlines Flight 77, and Jarrah of United Airlines Flight 93. The pilots bought tickets for flights on Boeing 757s and 767s, because learning to fly these more modern models was much easier than learning to fly older aircraft. The pilots trained on simulators. Takeoffs and landings were difficult, but actually flying was relatively easy. The flight control systems made the aircraft responsive and made normal flight easy. The leadership of the plot took at least twelve intercontinental flights to check on security and plan for takeovers.

The secondary leaders of the plot were Nawaf al-Hazmi and Khalid al-Mihdhar. They had originally been selected to be pilots, but their lack of English and limited education made them poor choices. Their responsibilities then became providing logistical support. The remainders of the hijackers were muscle men sent over to the United States later, most of them from Saudi Arabia.

The thirteen muscle men had been trained to hijack aircraft and provide physical support for the pilots. At al-Qaeda camps in Afghanistan, they were trained in hand-to-hand combat and taught how to assault a commercial airliner's cockpit area, giving no quarter to crew or passengers.

Each of the muscle men was assigned to a team. American Airlines Flight 11 carried Abdul Aziz al-Omari, Wail al-Shehri, Waleed al-Shehri, and Satam al-Suqami. The team on United Airlines Flight 175 was assigned Fayez Rashid Banihammad, Ahmed al-Ghamdi, Hamza al-Ghamdi, and Mohammad al-Shehri. American Airlines Flight 77 carried Salem al-Hazmi and Majed Moqued. The United Airlines Flight 93 team received Saeed al-Ghamdi, Ahmed al-Haznawi and Ahmed al-Na'ami.

> **Osama bin Laden's Comments about the Hijackers, from a Videotape Made in November 2001**
>
> The brothers, who conducted the operation, all they knew was that they have a martyrdom operation and we asked each of them to go to America but they didn't know anything about the operation, not even one letter. But they were trained and we did not reveal the operation to them until they are there and just before they boarded the planes. Those who were trained to fly didn't know the others.
>
> Stefan Aust et al., *Inside 9–11: What Really Happened* (New York: St. Martin's Press, 2001), p. 320.

In the week before September 11, the hijackers moved around the Eastern coast trying to avoid suspicion. They enrolled at local gyms to maintain their physical shape. In the meantime, Atta and the other leaders were traveling the country on commercial airliners noting weaknesses in security. Atta's choice of Tuesday, September 11, 2001, was based on their research, which led them to consider that date the best for a successful hijacking.

Because the nineteen knew their mission to be one of martyrdom, each selected a name that honored an important person or event from the Golden Age of Islam,

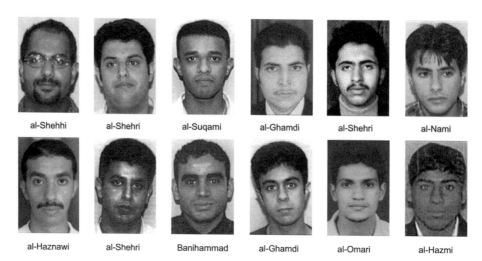

al-Shehhi   al-Shehri   al-Suqami   al-Ghamdi   al-Shehri   al-Nami

al-Haznawi   al-Shehri   Banihammad   al-Ghamdi   al-Omari   al-Hazmi

Twelve of the nineteen 9/11 hijackers are shown in this photo combo. In the top row, from left to right, are Marwan al-Shehhi, Waleed al-Shehri, Satam al-Suqami, Hamza al-Ghamdi, Mohammad al-Shehri, and Ahmed al-Na'ami. In the bottom row, left to right, are Ahmed al-Haznawi, Wail al-Shehri, Fayez Banihammad, Saeed al-Ghamdi, Abdul Aziz al-Omari, and Salem al-Hazmi. (AP IMAGES/Files.)

the decades that followed the death of the Prophet Muhammad. Each name was recognizable in the Muslim world and chosen for maximum mass appeal. Several made videotapes of their confessions of faith before leaving the Middle East. After their deaths, these videotapes were broadcast over the Internet. The mission and the publicity surrounding the nineteen martyrs themselves made them popular figures throughout much of the Muslim world.

On the morning of September 11, each team proceeded to its assigned airport, passing through security with only minimal interference. Each team member carried box cutters, utility knives, and chemical sprays. Both box cutters and chemical sprays were prohibited items. Teams had been divided into two groups: cockpit assault and passenger security. Two members of each team, including the designated pilot, were assigned to the cockpit assault unit and had seats near the cockpit door in the first-class section. The others were seated at the rear of the first-class section to provide security from the crew and the passengers, keeping them from interfering in the hijacking. Anyone who stood in their way was either to be killed or incapacitated.

The goal of the hijackers was to seize control of the aircraft within fifteen minutes after takeoff. This goal was accomplished on American Airlines Flight 11, American Airlines Flight 77, and United Airlines Flight 175, but not on United Airlines Flight 93. Delay in seizing the aircraft, exacerbated by the time it took to reverse the aircraft's course, allowed the passengers and crew to organize resistance against the terrorists. This aircraft crashed rather than completing its mission. In the eyes of Osama bin Laden and al-Qaeda's leadership, the mission remained a complete success. Each year since September 11, 2001, celebrations have been held across the world honoring the nineteen martyrs. Many in the Muslim world have perceived the events of September 11 as a just response to what they consider the many transgressions of the United States against the Muslim world. Others, less certain, have feared an American backlash. The celebrations have been widely reported in the press and, despite official and public disapproval of these celebrations, continue to take place. But not all Muslims approve of the September 11 attacks and the actions of the nineteen hijackers.

Majority of Muslims Disapproved of the September 11 Attacks

In the Gallup poll of nine Muslim countries, perhaps more important for judging hatred of the U.S. is the question about the 9/11 attacks. A surprisingly large 67 percent of Muslims said the 9/11 attacks were morally unjustified.

Clark McCauley, "Understanding the 9/11 Perpetrators: Crazy, Lost in Hate, or Martyred," in N. Matuszak, ed., *History Behind the Headlines: The Origin of Ethnic Conflicts Worldwide*, vol. 5 (New York: Gale Publishing Group, 2002), p. 277.

See Also
American Airlines Flight 11; American Airlines Flight 77; Atta, Mohamed el-Amir Awad el-Sayed; United Airlines Flight 93; United Airlines Flight 175; World Trade Center

See Documents
Document #6; Document #7; Document #13

Suggested Reading
Terry McDermott, *Perfect Soldiers: The 9/11 Hijackers; Who They Were, Why They Did It* (New York: HarperCollins, 2005); Steven Strasser, *The 9/11 Investigations: Staff Reports of the 9/11 Commission; Excerpts from the House-Senate Joint Inquiry Report on 9/11; Testimony from 14 Key Witnesses, Including Richard Clarke, George Tenet, and Condoleezza Rice* (New York: PublicAffairs, 2004).

North American Aerospace Defense Command (NORAD)

The North American Aerospace Defense Command (NORAD) has the military responsibility to defend the continental United States from enemy attacks, but on September 11, 2001, it failed to do so. NORAD's mission includes defending the United States from foreign bombers or ballistic missiles, but civilian aircraft were not a part of this mission. On September 11, NORAD's radars were mostly directed outward to detect attacks from abroad. Because the Federal Aviation Administration (FAA) was responsible for domestic aviation, NORAD depended on information from the FAA, but the FAA was not a part of the infrastructure of defense against foreign attack. This black hole of responsibility meant that both NORAD and the FAA lacked protocols for dealing with a scenario such as that surrounding the events of September 11.

The lack of protocols did not mean that no Standard Operating Procedures (SOP) existed between the FAA and NORAD. In the event of a hijacking the FAA was responsible to inform the Pentagon's National Military Command Center (NMCC), which would then seek approval from the Secretary of Defense for military assistance in the hijacking. Upon the Secretary's approval, NORAD would receive orders to scramble a flight of jets with orders to find the aircraft and monitor it from a distance of five miles, at no time interfering with the hijacking. No guidelines were in place for dealing with a hijacking meant to end in a suicidal crash. Only a presidential order could be given to shoot down an American commercial aircraft—an order that had to be relayed through the chain of command.

Because of a lack of coordination and information between NORAD and the Federal Aviation Administration (FAA), the actions of NORAD turned into a morass of errors on September 11. On that date NORAD had fourteen National Guard jets on standby throughout the country. Complicating the situation, NORAD was conducting three war games on September 11. One of the war games was with NEADS (Northeast Air Defense Sector), which diminished the number of fighter jet flights available. FAA officials disregarded SOP and contacted NORAD directly. NORAD's Northeast Air Defense Sector (NEADS) scrambled two F-15s from Otis Air Force Base in Massachusetts at 8:46 a.m., but the pilots had only a vague notion of their mission. They were vectored toward military-controlled airspace off Long Island. Within seconds of their takeoff, American Airlines Flight 11 crashed into the North Tower of the World Trade Center complex. Eight minutes before the F-15s arrived in New York City at 9:10 a.m., United Airlines Flight 175 crashed into the South Tower of the World Trade complex. The jets' slowness in arriving indicates that they had not traveled at their maximum speed, but even if they had arrived sooner, they had no orders to intercept the hijacked aircraft. It is uncertain just what they could have done to prevent the second crash. Much the same can be said about the two jets of the 177th Flight Wing of the New Jersey Air National Guard in Atlantic City, New Jersey, which, though available, were never called to assist.

By 9:00 a.m. it had become apparent that the hijacking plot involved more commercial airliners. At 9:24 a flight of F-16s of the National Guard's 119th Fighter Wing was scrambled from Langley Air Force Base in Virginia, tasked with protecting the Washington, D.C., area after a report that American Airlines Flight 11 was heading in that direction. Flight 11, however, had crashed into the North Tower forty minutes before. Lacking accurate information, the pilots of the F-15s and F-16s tried to keep visual contact with possible hijacked aircraft. Exactly what these pilots would have done if ordered to intercept a hijacked aircraft is unknown. Their orders were to "identify type and tail numbers of the hijacked aircraft"—nothing more.

Orders to intercept and possibly shoot down a hijacked aircraft had to be authorized by President George W. Bush. Both the F-15s and F-16s had full combat loads, but the pilots had no direct orders to do anything but intercept. President Bush was in Sarasota, Florida, and Vice President Dick Cheney was in Washington, D.C. Cheney contacted President Bush and received authorization from him to shoot down hijacked aircraft shortly after 10:00 a.m. This order did not reach NORAD until 10:31—much too late to do anything. American Airlines Flight 77 had already crashed into the Pentagon at 9:37. It was known by the FAA at this time, however, that hijackers had seized United Airlines Flight 93, and that this airliner might be headed toward the Washington, D.C., area. For some reason, this information was not transmitted by the FAA to the Pentagon's National Military Command Center. The NMCC did not learn that United Airlines Flight 93 had been hijacked until after it had crashed, informed at last by the Secret Service.

The shoot-down order authorization was sent to NORAD at 10:31 a.m., but the 9/11 Commission reported that this order never reached the F-15 or F-16 pilots. It came to be a moot point, because by the time this order would have reached the pilots, it was already too late. United Airlines Flight 93 had crashed near Shanksville, Pennsylvania at 10:03 a.m. Shooting down an American commercial airliner would have been a traumatic experience for the pilots, even with a presidential order authorizing it. It is doubtful whether the pilots would have done so, especially if over heavily populated areas.

The confusion on September 11 extended into NORAD's record-keeping about the events of September 11. So many contradictory accounts came out of NORAD that the 9/11 Commission staff had difficulty finding out just what had happened. NORAD's leadership has been particularly defensive about its conduct on September 11, and so many discrepancies have appeared in its records that conspiracy theorists have used NORAD as an example of government complicity in the attacks. In fact, NORAD depended on the FAA for information, some of which proved to be inaccurate and belated. As the 9/11 Commission pointed out, the military had "nine minutes' notice that American Airlines Flight 11 had been hijacked; two minutes' notice that an unidentified aircraft, American 77, was headed toward Washington, and no notice at all about United Airlines 175 or 93." The military, which depends heavily on contingency plans, had no contingency plan available to help NORAD

Problems with the FAA and NORAD Timelines
Indeed, many of the families' most detailed and frequently asked questions dealt with the FAA and NORAD. As it became apparent that FAA and NORAD officials had been inaccurate—if not untruthful—in making public statements, including in testimony before Congress and the 9/11 Commission, the families became more upset. The notion that they were not being told the truth fed their mistrust of the government, and nearly aligned some of them with the conspiracy theorists.

Thomas H. Kean, Lee H. Hamilton, and Benjamin Rhodes, *Without Precedent: The Inside Story of the 9/11 Commission* (New York: Knopf, 2006), p. 260. |

handle hijackers determined to use commercial aircraft on suicide missions. Because NORAD was operating in the dark, it failed much as any other agency in the government on that fateful day.

See Also
American Airlines Flight 11; American Airlines Flight 77; National Commission on Terrorist Attacks upon the United States; United Airlines Flight 93; United Airlines Flight 93

See Document
Document #35

Suggested Reading
Thomas H. Kean, Lee H. Hamilton, and Benjamin Rhodes, *Without Precedent: The Inside Story of the 9/11 Commission* (New York: Knopf, 2006); Glenn J. Kashurba, *Quiet Courage: The Definitive Account of Flight 93 and Its Aftermath* (Somerset, PA: SAJ Publishing, 2006); Peter Lance, *Triple Cross: How Bin Laden's Master Spy Penetrated the CIA, the Green Berets, and the FBI—And Why Patrick Fitzgerald Failed to Stop Him* (New York: ReganBooks, 2006).

Nosair, El Sayyid (1955–)

The first case of Islamist extremism in the United States was the assassination of the Israeli extremist politician Meir Kahane on November 5, 1990, by El Sayyid Nosair. Nosair stalked Kahane for several days before shooting him twice on a New York City street. He then escaped in a taxi. After a policeman accosted him, the two exchanged shots, and Nosair received a severe wound to the neck.

Nosair had a relatively normal upbringing. Born in 1955 at Port Said, Egypt, he was displaced along with his family during the Six Days War with Israel in 1967. Nosair spent his adolescent years in Cairo, Egypt, where his academic achievements led to his graduation with a degree in industrial design and engineering from the Helwan University Faculty of Applied Arts. In July 1981, Nosair decided to immigrate to the United States. His first residence was in Pittsburgh, Pennsylvania, where he found work as a diamond cutter. Despite his distaste for the United States, he married an American woman who had recently converted to Islam. After Nosair lost his job as a diamond cutter because of a dispute with his employer, he held a variety of jobs, but none so prestigious or lucrative. Nosair decided to move his family to New York City.

Nosair had previously held moderate Islamic views, but after his move to New York City he became more militant. His religious home was al-Farooq Mosque in Brooklyn, which was affiliated with al-Kifah Refugee Center. At al-Kifah, Nosair became enamored with the jihadist philosophy of Abdullah Azzam. Nosair wanted to go to Afghanistan in 1987 to fight against the Soviets, but he lacked the funds to do so. Instead, he joined others in paramilitary training. Many of his compatriots were later to participate in the 1993 World Trade Center Bombing. Nosair also became an admirer of Abdul Rahman, the blind Egyptian religious leader and militant terrorist. With Abdul Rahman's blessings from Egypt, Nosair formed a terrorist cell. Now working as a janitor, Nosair began to consider schemes that ranged from assassinations to bombings. He threw a grenade at Mikhail Gorbachev when the Soviet Premier visited New York City on December 8, 1989—but it failed to explode. In April 1990 he exploded a crude bomb in a gay bar, causing minor injuries. After Abdul Rahman arrived in the United States in May 1990, Nosair received more direction, as well as instructions on weapon use given by Ali Abdel Saoud Mohamed, who drew from his service in the Egyptian and American armed forces.

> **Explanation for the Assassination of Meir Kahane**
>
> El-Sayyid Nosair was sure he had changed the course of history. He believed this because of his bizarre reading of Israeli politics. Kahane was a Brooklyn rabbi who founded the Jewish Defense League and then immigrated to Israel and established the Kach party, which was banned from his country's parliament in 1988 because of its blatant racism—the group advocated, for example, the expulsion of Arabs from Israel and the Occupied Territories. Yet Nosair was convinced that Kahane was destined to be the leader of the Jewish state and a force in global affairs; "They were preparing him to dominate, to be the prime minister someday," he would later say. "They were preparing him despite their assertion that they reject his agenda and that he is a racist."
>
> Daniel Benjamin and Steven Simon, *The Age of Sacred Terror* (New York: Random House, 2002), p. 4.

Nosair decided to assassinate Meir Kahane. Kahane was an Israeli extremist, but Nosair believed that one day Kahane would be the leader of the Jewish state—and thus that his death would advance the Palestinian cause. He began stalking Kahane, looking for an opportunity to shoot him. When the opportunity arose, Nosair shot Kahane three times. After the assassination, the New York District Attorney's office assumed jurisdiction of the case. The FBI turned over sixteen boxes of information gathered in a search of Nosair's apartment to the Manhattan District Attorney's office, but the boxes promptly disappeared. The New York City Joint Terrorism Task Force became interested in the case because of its domestic terrorism aspects, but the FBI agents and New York City police detectives of the JTTF were removed from the case. The Nosair case was botched from its beginning. Nosair was charged with simple murder rather than participation in a conspiracy. The New York Police Department's Chief of Detectives, Joseph Borelli, refused to classify Kahane's assassination as a political assassination, instead calling Nosair a "lone deranged gunman" despite evidence to the contrary. Kahane, though a victim, did not inspire sympathy. The case then took a strange turn; William Kunstler, the well-known defense lawyer, handled Nosair's defense, and Nosair was convicted of shooting two people after the assassination—but not of causing Kahane's death. He was sentenced to seven and a half to twenty-two and a half years in prison. The lightness of his sentence caused great celebration in the Muslim community and convinced Islamist militants that the United States was merely a paper tiger.

From his prison cell, Nosair has continued to advocate violence against the United States. Several of the 1993 World Trade Center Bombing conspirators visited Nosair in prison to confirm their plans. He constantly advocated terrorist projects, many of which were designed for his compatriots to break him out of prison. After government officials became aware of his activities and his participation in the 1993 World Trade Center Bombing, a subsequent trial sentenced him to life in prison.

See Also

Abdel Rahman, Sheikh Omar; Mohamed, Ali Abdel Saoud; World Trade Center Bombing (1993)

Suggested Reading

Daniel Benjamin and Steven Simon, *The Age of Sacred Terror* (New York: Random House, 2002); Peter Lange, *1000 Years for Revenge: International Terrorism and the FBI—the Untold Story* (New York: ReganBooks, 2003); John Miller, Michael Stone, and Chris Mitchell, *The Cell: Inside the 9/11 Plot, and Why the FBI and CIA Failed to Stop It* (New York: Hyperion, 2002).

O

Office of Emergency Management (OEM)

The Office of Emergency Management is New York City's disaster management team, but during and after the September 11 attacks on the World Trade Center it ceased to function effectively—not because of lack of planning or preparedness, but because its headquarters was located in the World Trade Center complex and neutralized in the attacks.

A similar type of organization had been set up by the then-Mayor of New York City, David N. Dinkins, in 1990, under the name Aviation Emergency Preparedness Working Group (AEPWG), intended to handle emergencies after aircraft crashes. Representatives from the Fire Department, Police Department, Emergency Medical Services, and other agencies served in this group. A report from the AEPWG recommended that the various agencies practice working together and stated that they needed a single radio frequency that commanders of the agencies could share during emergencies. After several drills, the group was disbanded in 1994 when Rudolph W. Giuliani became the new mayor and established the Office of Emergency Management.

The Office of Emergency Management was to serve as the command-and-control center during large-scale emergencies. Its offices were on the twenty-third floor in Seven WTC, a forty-seven-story building on the north side of the complex. This post had been made bomb-resistant and bulletproof and had been reinforced to be able to withstand hurricanes. It also had a reserve of thirty days of food and water. The OEM operated on a twenty-four-hour schedule and was responsible for coordinating the sixty-eight city, state, and federal agencies, as well as the city's fire and police departments. Personnel monitored all emergency radio frequencies, and the center had a state-of-the-art communication system.

Despite its support from the mayor's office, the Office of Emergency Management never had enough political clout to force cooperation between the Fire Department of New York (FDNY) and the New York City Police Department (NYPD), even though this lack of cooperation had been one of the reasons for founding the OEM. Despite the reminder of the 1993 World Trade Bombing, the rivalry and distrust between the two departments remained high. Instead of bickering, they refused to communicate, exacerbating the situation by using different radio frequencies. This utter inability to communicate interdepartmentally greatly hindered evacuation operations on September 11.

The airliner crashes into the North and South Towers destroyed the ability of the Office of Emergency Management to operate. When the first aircraft hit the North Tower, it made the elaborate communications system at the Office of Emergency Management's headquarters in Seven World Trade Center (7 WTC) useless. Throughout the course of the evacuations and the final collapse of the twin towers, the Office of Emergency Management was effectively out of the loop. Cut off from the OEM, firefighters and police operated without coordination. Moreover, the damage to the twin towers extended to 7 WTC, requiring the offices of the OEM to be evacuated. Later that evening, 7 WTC collapsed as well.

As soon as possible, the Office of Emergency Management reestablished its command-and-control headquarters in a warehouse at one of the harbor piers in Manhattan. By setting up its bank of computers and establishing communications with other government agencies, the OEM was able to participate in the decision-making during the World Trade Center cleanup, readying itself for any future emergencies.

After September 11, controversy arose over who had located the Office of Emergency Management in the World Trade Center complex. The then-Director of the Office of Emergency Management, Jerome M. Hauer, had recommended a site in Brooklyn, but Rudy Giuliani wanted it in Manhattan. Hauer, with the advice the mayor's aides, selected the World Trade Center complex. Fingerpointing about the decision has led to bitter exchanges among those who were in power at the time.

See Also
Giuliani, Rudolph William Louis "Rudy" III; World Trade Center, September 11

Suggested Reading
David W. Ausmus, *In the Midst of Chaos: My 30 Days at Ground Zero* (Victoria, Canada: Trafford, 2004); J. Bowyer Bell, *Murders on the Nile: The World Trade Center and Global Terror* (San Francisco: Encounter Books, 2003); Jim Dwyer and Kevin Flynn, *102 Minutes: The Untold Story of the Fight to Survive inside the Twin Towers* (New York: Times Books, 2005).

Ogonowski, John (1951–2001)

John Ogonowski was the pilot of American Airlines Flight 11, which al-Qaeda hijackers crashed into the North Tower of the World Trade Center complex on September 11, 2001. A veteran pilot with twenty-three years of experience flying for American Airlines, he was a member in good standing with the Allied Pilot Association (APA), and his reputation as a good pilot had led to his promotion to the rank of captain in 1989, as well as his assignment to fly the prestigious Boston–Los Angeles route.

Ogonowski had spent his entire life flying. He was born in 1951 in Lowell, Massachusetts. His father was a truck driver and farmer. Ogonowski's entire education took place in Lowell, where he attended St. Stanislaus Elementary School and Keith Academy. After high school, he entered Lowell Technical Institute, graduating in 1972 with a BSc in nuclear engineering. While in college, he joined the U.S. Air Force (USAF) Reserve Officers' Training Corps (ROTC). After graduating, he entered the U.S. Air Force and graduated from flight school in Texas.

Assigned to an Air Force Base in Charleston, South Carolina, he flew C-141s to and from Vietnam. After leaving the U.S. Air Force at the rank of captain in 1978, Ogonowski found a job flying commercial aircraft for American Airlines—and a wife who was a flight attendant.

Ogonowski's passion for flight was matched by his love of farming. He lived on the 150-acre White Gate Farm in Dracut, Massachusetts, with his wife and three daughters. Ogonowski was a passionate farmer and raised hay, corn, pumpkins, blueberries, and peaches on his farm. In 1998, Ogonowski became active on behalf of immigrant Cambodian farmers as part of the New Entry Sustainable Farming Project. He gave the immigrants access to some of his land and even prepared it for them, rarely collecting the rent they owed him. Ogonowski was also active in the Dracut Land Trust, working to preserve farming land in the Dracut area.

Ogonowski's role in the events of September 11, 2001, is unclear, because too few survivors remained to tell the tale. He left his farm before 6:00 a.m. in his GMC pickup to travel the thirty-five miles to Logan International Airport. It was a routine takeoff and everything went fine until about fifteen minutes into the flight. His last contact with air traffic controllers was an order to climb to 35,000 feet. Shortly after this change in altitude, the hijackers, under the command of Mohamed Atta, seized control of the aircraft, killing one of the passengers, Daniel M. Lewin, to forestall any resistance. The airline industries' standard operating procedure (SOP) was for crews not to resist hijackers and to discourage passengers from doing so. Consequently, the hijackers met with no opposition. It is thought that Ogonowski hit a button allowing him to communicate via radio without afterward taking his hands from the controls, making air traffic controllers privy to conversations in the cockpit. At this time, a statement was made by one of the hijackers that other planes were involved, but nothing could be done by Ogonowski, who had been neutralized by the hijackers before they crashed the airliner into the North Tower of the World Trade Center complex.

Ogonowski had been a well-liked figure in Dracut. A living memorial to his life was established when the Dracut Land Trust, with aid from the federal government, purchased a thirty-three-acre plot of land that Ogonowski had once farmed, restricting it for solely agricultural purposes. Some of the land will be made available to immigrant farmers who participate in the New Entry Sustainable Farm Project.

See Also
American Airlines Flight 11; Atta, Mohamed el-Amir Awad el-Sayed

Suggested Reading
Richard Bernstein, *Out of the Blue: The Story of September 11, 2001, from Jihad to Ground Zero* (New York: Times Books, 2002); John Ingold, "American Airlines Flight 11: Ordinary Lives Intersect on Celebrity-Studded Flight," *Denver Post* (September 16, 2001), p. A10; Christine McConville, "Pilot's Dream, His Memory Preserved," *Boston Globe* (November 30, 2003), p. 1.

Olson, Barbara (1955–2001)

Barbara Olson was a conservative American television commentator who was a passenger on American Airlines Flight 77 when it crashed into the Pentagon. She had worked for FOX News and other media outlets. Her presence on American

Airlines Flight 77 was the result of her presence at the taping of Bill Maher's program *Politically Incorrect.*

Before becoming a political commentator, Olson was a lawyer. She was born on December 27, 1955, in Houston, Texas, as Barbara Kay Bracher. After graduating from Waltrip High School in Houston, she attended the University of Saint Thomas, where she earned a Bachelor of Arts degree. Her first career, as a professional ballet dancer, took her to Houston, New York, and San Francisco. She then worked in Hollywood as an assistant to the actor Stacy Keach before deciding to go to law school. She obtained a law degree from Yeshiva University's Benjamin N. Cardozo School of Law and worked for three years for the Washington, D.C., law firm Wilmer Cutler and Pickering. Next, she served as an assistant U.S. attorney for the District of Columbia from 1992 to 1995, specializing in the prosecution of drug cases.

By the mid-1990s, Olson became more involved in politics. She was the Chief Investigative Counsel for the House of Representatives Government Reform Committee. Later, Olson served as a staff lawyer for Senate Minority Whip Don Nickles. In both of these positions, she investigated cases of misconduct by President Clinton and Hillary Rodham Clinton. Her national profile rose when she became a TV commentator. In 1997 she married Theodore Olson, who later became the United States Solicitor General for the Bush administration.

Based on her earlier investigations Olson made the Clintons a special target. A self-styled Reagan conservative, she began attacking them in her commentaries, outlining her views in frequent appearances on FOX News. She also published two books criticizing the Clinton administration: *Hell to Pay: The Unfolding Story of Hillary Rodham Clinton* and *The Final Days: The Last, Desperate Abuses of Power by the Clinton White House.*

Soon after the hijacking, Olson contacted her husband by cell phone and described what was going on. Her description of how passengers and crew were herded to the rear of the aircraft by the hijackers, who were armed with knives and box cutters, was the first indication of how the other hijacking had

---

Barbara Olson and Her Attacks on the Clintons

In fact, if there was, as Hillary Clinton famously claimed, a "massive right-wing conspiracy" against her husband, Olson was at the heart of it. She was in charge of another Scaife investment, the "Arkansas Project" at the right-wing magazine *The American Spectator*, an investigation of the various (mostly unproven) allegations against the Clintons that are collectively known as "Whitewater," named after a contested Clinton real-estate deal. However, Olson vigorously denies any suggestions of conspiracy.

Godfrey Hodgson, "Olson: Partying and Politicking," *Independent* [London] (September 14, 2001), p. 6.

Olson's Actions on September 11

When, on Tuesday, hijackers took over American Airlines flight 77 from Washington to Los Angeles, on which she was a passenger, Olson coolly locked herself in the lavatory and speed-dialed her husband at his office a mile or so away and told him what had happened, speaking to him only seconds before the plane plunged into the Pentagon. She was only on the fatal flight because she had delayed her trip to be with her husband on his birthday.

Godfrey Hodgson, "Olson: Partying and Politicking," *Independent* [London] (September 14, 2001), p. 6.

occurred. Her husband contacted others and informed them of the hijacking. Contact was reestablished with Barbara Olson, who wanted to know what she should do, but there was nothing that she could do and she died when the plane crashed into the Pentagon.

See Also
American Airlines Flight 77; Pentagon Attack

Suggested Reading
Neil A. Lewis, "Solicitor General Got 2 Calls from Wife on Doomed Plane," *New York Times* (September 12, 2001), p. A19; Peter Worthington, "She's Still the Clintons' Nemesis," *Toronto Sun* (December 21, 2001), p. 16.

O'Neill, John (1952–2001)

John O'Neill was the former FBI counterterrorist expert who warned the FBI about a possible terrorist attack on the United States. His counterterrorism experience led him to suspect that al-Qaeda was conspiring to commit a terrorist act— probably in New York City. Because of this belief, he began a job at the World Trade Center on September 10, 2001.

O'Neill spent most of his career as a FBI agent. He was born on February 6, 1952, at Atlantic City, New Jersey, where his parents ran a small taxi business. After graduating from high school, he joined the FBI as a fingerprint technician and attended American University, from which he graduated in 1974. He studied government and law enforcement at the university's School of Justice and then enrolled in the MSc program at George Washington University, studying forensic science. In 1976, upon his graduation, he entered the FBI training program in pursuit of his childhood ambition to become a FBI agent. His training took place at the FBI's Quantico training facility in Virginia. His first assignment was with the Baltimore Office, where his work led to rapid promotion, culminating in his July 1991 assignment to the Chicago field office. O'Neill had built a solid reputation as an aggressive, effective FBI agent. In Chicago, he and his field agents attacked and ultimately ended the reign of notorious street gangs.

Outbursts of violence in anti-abortion protests led the FBI to pick O'Neill in 1994 to head a task force investigating such violence, called the Task Force on Violence Against Abortion Providers Conspiracy (VAAPCON). This task force was directed to find a nationwide conspiracy, but when no such conspiracy was found, it was disbanded.

In November 1994 O'Neill was promoted to chief of counterterrorism in FBI headquarters. His first action was the coordination of the arrest of Ramzi Yousef, the 1993 bomber of the World Trade Center, in Islamabad, Pakistan. He acted on a tip from Richard Clarke, President Clinton's national coordinator for counterterrorism, claiming that Yousef had been sighted. Over the course of three days, O'Neill coordinated the capture of Yousef and his transportation to the United States. Among other investigations that O'Neill participated in was that of the bombing at the Khobar Towers in Saudi Arabia. On March 9, 1995, O'Neill warned his FBI supervisors that Osama bin Laden was becoming the greatest threat to the United States, but his warning was for the most part ignored.

In December 1996 O'Neill received another promotion—this time to special agent in charge of the National Security Division in the FBI's New York City office, where he was in charge of about 400 agents. O'Neill joined New York

City's Joint Terrorism Task Force in the middle of its investigation of the explosion and crash of United Airlines Flight 800. He was able to persuade the investigators to conduct computer simulations that ultimately showed the explosion to be an accident rather than a terrorist act.

O'Neill became convinced as early as 1997 that militant terrorist groups were preparing a major terrorist attack in the United States. He said as much in a 1997 conference held in Chicago and attended by agents from the FBI and CIA, arguing that members of Islamic fundamentalist groups in the United States were fully capable of carrying out a major terrorist attack, having the necessary support infrastructure to do so. O'Neill believed it was his job to ferret out these groups and expose them before they carried out their plots.

In 2000 he had attended a conference in Miami, Florida. O'Neill left a briefcase with sensitive material about suspected terrorist operations in the United States in a conference room when he made a brief phone call. During his absence, the briefcase disappeared. It was recovered several hours later, but O'Neill had to withstand a series of investigations from the FBI's Office of Professional Responsibility. On October 12, 2000, al-Qaeda operatives using a boat filled with explosives attacked the American destroyer USS *Cole* in Aden harbor, Yemen. O'Neill received the assignment to assemble a team and investigate the attack. He immediately ran into opposition from Barbara Bodine, the U.S. Ambassador to Yemen. She wanted to be in charge of the investigation, and she desired limited FBI—or any other outside—intervention. Even worse, Yemeni authorities put obstacles in the way of O'Neill's team. After a month, he and his team left Aden, frustrated by the lack of support they had received from Bodine and the Yemeni government. He believed the suspects to be al-Qaeda operatives, but the Yemeni government would not allow access to them. Bodine had him declared persona non grata, refusing to allow him to return to Yemen.

O'Neill returned to the United States empty-handed and decided that his career in the FBI was over. In spring 2000 he had already been passed over for the position of assistant director in charge of the New York field office. His habit of stating his strongly held opinions had won him enemies in the FBI hierarchy. After looking around, he took a job in the private sector, working as the Director of Security at the World Trade Center.

O'Neill started his new job on September 10. Based on his experience as a terrorism expert, he believed that something bad was going to happen soon in

---

Personality of John O'Neill and How It Affected His Job

After all, [O'Neill] had devoted his life to integrating his professional and personal lives—his "day job" and his "night job"—into a cohesive force that would help him accomplish his missions. He had performed his job as an FBI agent with flair and panache, but he wanted to be remembered as a serious and successful law enforcement agent, not someone known merely for stylish eccentricity, or more seriously, for a careless breach of protocol. Yet O'Neill was both: he was a serious and successful—even prescient—law enforcement, and he was also a flawed man who led a tangled personal life, a complex figure whose unorthodox approach to his job and miscues led to his exit from the FBI, his one great love.

Murray Weiss, *The Man Who Warned America: The Life and Death of John O'Neill, the FBI's Embattled Counterterror Warrior* (New York: ReganBooks, 2003), pp. 389–390.

New York City. At a dinner party on the evening of September 10, O'Neill made a prediction that a terrorist attack would hit the New York City area in the near future. He was on duty at the World Trade Center Complex on the morning of September 11. His immediate reaction was to help rescue people first at the North Tower and later at the South Tower. O'Neill disappeared when the South Tower collapsed. His body was found on September 21 under twelve feet of debris. It was discovered that he had died from blows to the skull and chest. O'Neill was buried on September 28, 2001, in Atlantic City, New Jersey.

See Also
Bin Laden, Osama; Clarke, Richard A.; Joint Terrorism Task Force; Qaeda, al-; World Trade Center; Yousef, Ramzi Ahmed

Suggested Reading
John Miller, Michael Stone, and Chris Mitchell, *The Cell: Inside the 9/11 Plot, and Why the FBI and CIA Failed to Stop It* (New York: Hyperion, 2002); Murray Weiss, *The Man Who Warned America: The Life and Death of John O'Neill, the FBI's Embattled Counterterror Warrior* (New York: ReganBooks, 2003).

Ong, Betty Ann (1956–2001)

Betty Ong was a Chinese American flight attendant on American Airlines Flight 11 who first reported the tactics of the hijackers to authorities on the outside. She was a veteran flight attendant, and the flight to San Francisco always took her home. Her reporting of the tactics of the hijackers has proven helpful in understanding how they took over the aircraft.

Ong's family and home were in San Francisco's Chinatown. She was born on February 5, 1956, in San Francisco, into a well-respected Chinese American family. Her family owned and operated a specialty grocery store in San Francisco. Soon after her graduation from George Washington High School, Ong took a job as a flight attendant with American Airlines, a position in which she spent fourteen years. Most of her assignments were as a purser on the Boston-to-Los Angeles flights, and she moved to Massachusetts.

> **Thomas Kean Describes Betty Ong's Heroism**
>
> With the assistance of her fellow crew members, Betty was able to provide us with vital information that would later prove crucial to the investigation. Betty's selfless acts of courage and determination may have saved the lives of many others. She provided important information which ultimately led to the closing of our nation's airspace for the first time in its history.
>
> Steven Knipp, "An Angel's Last Call," *South China Morning Post* (August 14, 2004), p. 14.

Shortly after the hijackers seized the aircraft, Ong obtained a phone and contacted an American Airlines agent. She contacted Vanessa Minter, an American Airlines agent in North Carolina, who opened up a conference call with Nydia Gonzales in Dallas, Texas. In the next twenty-three minutes Ong gave a detailed description of the hijackers. She estimated there to be three or four hijackers, all of Middle Eastern origin. Her identification of the seat numbers allowed the FBI to learn the names, addresses, and passport details of the hijackers. Ong also reported that passenger Daniel M. Lewin had been killed and that at least one flight attendant was dead as well. She was also certain that the hijackers had neutralized or killed the pilot—John Ogonowski. Ong continued to describe the situation until the aircraft crashed into the North Tower of the World Trade Center complex. Since then there have been several celebrations of her life and her courage.

See Also

American Airlines Flight 11; Lewin, Daniel M.; Ogonowski, John

Suggested Reading

Cicero A. Estrella, "Heroine of 9/11 Gets Her Due; Chinatown Honors Flight Attendant," *San Francisco Chronicle* (September 22, 2004), p. B1; Stephen Kiehl, "'I Think We're Getting Hijacked,'" *Baltimore Sun* (September 10, 2006), p. 1A; Steven Knipp, "An Angel's Last Call," *South China Morning Post* (August 14, 2004), p. 14.

Operation Bojinka

Operation Bojinka was the first plan by terrorists to attack commercial aircraft. The name Bojinka is Serbo-Croatian for "big bang," or "explosion." Ramzi Yousef conceived of the plan to blow up eleven U.S. commercial aircraft with the help of his friend Abdul Hakim Murad. Yousef had discussed such a plan earlier with his friend, who knew something about commercial aircraft after receiving a commercial pilot's license from a pilot training school in the United States. There were four members of the Bojinka cell: Yousef, Murad, Khalid Sheikh Mohammed, and Wali Khan Amin Shah. Funds for the operation came from al-Qaeda sources. Mohammed Jamal Khalifa, brother-in-law to Osama bin Laden, was the contact man for funding.

Yousef, a skilled bomb maker, built a liquid bomb timed to detonate using a Casio watch timer. He decided to experiment with such a bomb, exploding it at the Greenbelt Theater in Manila. It worked, but only a few moviegoers were even slightly injured. His next experiment took place on a commercial aircraft, Philippines Airline Flight 434 from Manila to Cebu City in the southern Philippines. Yousef planted his liquid bomb underneath a passenger seat and left the plane when it landed. The bomb exploded on the next stage of the flight, killing a 24-year-old Japanese engineer, Haruki Ikegami. The force of the explosion blasted a small hole in the 747's floor, but it also severed the aileron cables that controlled the plane's flaps. Despite the damage, the pilot managed to control the plane to a safe landing at Naha Airport in Okinawa. Yousef called the Associated Press and claimed responsibility in the name of the Islamist terrorist group Abu Sayyaf.

Yousef's original scheme was to target eleven American commercial aircraft, and he had the necessary type of bomb. He knew that he had to build a more powerful bomb. After studying Boeing 747 blueprints, Yousef decided that the bombs needed to be placed in a seat above the central fuel tank, adjacent to the wing. The resulting explosion would ignite the fuel,

> **Bomb Found by Philippine Police**
>
> "The guys in the bomb squad had never seen an explosive like this before," says [former Philippine police officer] Fariscal. Neither had many U.S. investigators. "The particularly evil genius of this device was that it was virtually undetectable by airport security measures," says Vincent Cannistraro, the former head of the CIA's counter-terrorism centre.
>
> Matthew Brzezinski, "Operation Bojinka's Bombshell," *Toronto Star* (January 2, 2002), p. 6.

destroying the aircraft in the ensuing explosion. Yousef began to gather the chemicals he needed to make his new, stronger bomb.

A chemical accident in a Manila apartment ended the plot. While mixing chemicals in the sixth floor in the Josefa Building on President Quirino Avenue, Yousef produced a mixture that suddenly produced flame and black smoke. Both Yousef and Murad fled the apartment when the Manila Fire Department arrived. In their haste to leave, they left Yousef's laptop computer, manuals, and computer files behind. Yousef persuaded Murad to attempt to recover the laptop and other materials from the apartment, but Philippine police suddenly arrived and arrested him. Yousef watched Murad's arrest and immediately flew to Pakistan. Later, Pakistani authorities arrested him for his role in the 1993 World Trade Center Bombing.

Besides leading to the idea of attacking American commercial aircraft carriers, Operation Bojinka expanded Khalid Sheikh Mohammed's idea of using commercial aircraft as weapons. Murad mentioned this concept to Mohammed, because it was so easy for anyone to obtain commercial pilot training in the United States. Mohammed, who had contacts with al-Qaeda's leadership, was able to persuade Osama Bin Laden to finance the plot, but the idea of commercial aircraft as a terrorist weapon goes back to Yousef's Operation Bojinka.

See Also
Bin Laden, Osama; Mohammed, Khalid Sheikh; Murad, Abdul Hakim Ali Hashim; Yousef, Ramzi Ahmed

See Document
Document #26

Suggested Reading
Daniel Benjamin and Steven Simon, *The Age of Sacred Terror* (New York: Random House, 2004); Peter Lange, *1000 Years for Revenge: International Terrorism and the FBI: The Untold Story* (New York: ReganBooks, 2003); Simon Reeve, *The New Jackals: Ramzi Yousef, Osama bin Laden and the Future of Terrorism* (Boston: Northeastern University Press, 1999)

Occupational Safety and Heath Agency (OSHA)

The federal Occupational Safety and Heath Agency arrived at the site of the World Trade Center complex on September 12, 2001. The OSHA office in World Trade Center Building 6 had been destroyed along with the rest of the buildings in the complex. OSHA employees faced many of the dangers of the others at the World Trade Center complex, but all were successfully evacuated. Much like others at the site, OSHA employees had helped the injured to treatment centers and searched for survivors. When the South and North Towers collapsed, they, too, had to run for their lives. Official OSHA activity began on September 12, 2001.

Difficulty of Using Respirators

It was impossible to dig with a respirator on. It was extremely hot, and none of us had our masks on. I was inhaling all that stuff because they were passing buckets over my head and all this stuff was falling on me and the dust was being kicked up. One guy looked down at me and said, "You should put your mask on." But the mask just didn't matter to me at that point. That may sound very foolish, but it wasn't my health that mattered. It was getting the people out that mattered the most.

Comment by Police Officer Patty Lucci, quoted in Susan Hagen and Mary Carouba, *Women at Ground Zero: Stories of Courage and Compassion* (New York: Alpha Books, 2002), p. 157.

A worker uses a cutting torch while an excavator claws at debris at the site of the terrorist attacks on New York's World Trade Center, Monday, December 3, 2001. (AP IMAGES/Richard Drew.)

OSHA monitors workplace safety. Individuals working on the debris pile at the World Trade Center site performed dangerous jobs. Sharp metal objects, unstable footing, dust, smoke, and fires all posed danger to rescuers. OSHA officials had consulting powers but not enforcement powers; they could point out dangerous situations but had no authority to do anything but verbalize their concerns. Nevertheless, 1,000 OSHA agents appeared at the World Trade Center site during the cleanup.

OSHA provided equipment support, distributing more than 113,000 respirators from September 13, 2001, to February 6, 2002, 4,000 of which were made available during the first few weeks after the attacks. But OSHA workers had difficulty convincing those working at the site to use respirators. OSHA agents found that the firefighters were the most reluctant of all to use the respirators (although they were not alone), objecting that their sense of smell was vital to locating some the remains. OSHA reported that fewer than 45 percent of Ground Zero workers wore respirators.

OSHA's main responsibility was monitoring air samples. Its agents took 3,600 bulk and air samples looking for metals, asbestos, silica, and other air-borne compounds. Despite these efforts, the air around the World Trade Center site remained toxic. Most OSHA tests check for the existence of individual compounds, but the air at the World Trade Center was a chemical soup.

See Also

Cleanup Operations at Ground Zero; Firefighters at Ground Zero

Suggested Reading

Graham Rayman, "9/11 Five Years Later; Still More Blame amid Lasting Pain," *Newsday* [New York] (September 9, 2006), p. A6; Susan Q. Stranahan, "The Health of Ground Zero," *Milwaukee Journal Sentinel* (January 24, 2002), p. 11A.

P

The Path to 9/11 (TV Miniseries)

The Path to 9/11 was a two-part TV miniseries that appeared on ABC on September 10 and 11, 2006. This Walt Disney production dramatized the 1993 World Trade Center Bombing in New York City and the conspiracy that led to the events of September 11, 2001. Prerelease publicity focused on the failure of the Clinton administration to deal with the threat of Osama bin Laden and al-Qaeda and claimed that the screenplay had been based on the conclusions of the 9/11 Commission Report. It touted former Governor Thomas H. Kean, the chairman of the 9/11 Commission, as a senior consultant to the miniseries. Other sources for the screenplay were John Miller, Michael Stone, and Chris Mitchell, authors of *The Cell: Inside the 9/11 Plot, and Why the FBI and CIA Failed to Stop It* (2002). Despite these claims of authenticity, members of the 9/11 Commission and members of the Clinton administration were critical of what they called distortions in the miniseries. They also asserted that the writer and producer, Cyrus Nowrasteh, a politically conservative Iranian American Muslim, held anti-Clinton views.

The production did attract talented people. This five-hour docudrama had a budget of $40 million. Its producers were Hans Propper and Cyrus Nowrasteh and its director David L. Cunningham. Nowrasteh also wrote the screenplay. Harvey Keitel played the leading character, John O'Neill (the former FBI counterterrorist expert who was employed as Security Director of the World Trade Center complex when he perished in the attack). Other key players were Katy Selverstone as Nancy Floyd; Shaun Taub as Emad Salem; Michael Benyaer as Khalid Sheikh Mohammed; and a host of other actors and actresses who assumed the roles of Madeleine Albright, Barbara Boudine, Condoleezza Rice, George Tenet, and Richard Clarke, among others.

See Also

Bin Laden, Osama; National Commission on Terrorist Attacks upon the United States; O'Neill, John; World Trade Center, September 11

Suggested Reading

Scott Collins and Tina Daunt, "ABC Stands by Its 9/11 Story—Almost," *Los Angeles Times* (September 9, 2006), p. A1; Melanie McFarland, "Shaky Ground, Fudged Facts Put 'Path to 9/11' on a Slippery Slope," *Seattle Post-Intelligencer* (September 9, 2006), p. C1; Frazier Moore, "What Can We Learn from ABC's Folly?" *Associated Press Financial Wire* (September 12, 2006), p. 1; Edward Wyatt and Laura M. Holson, "A Show That Trumpeted History but Led to Confusion," *New York Times* (September 18, 2006), p. C1.

Patriot Act. *See* USA PATRIOT Act

Pavel Hlava Video

Pavel Hlava, a Czech immigrant construction worker, made a videotape of American Airlines Flight 11 and United Airlines Flight 77 approaching and crashing into the North and South Towers of the World Trade Center on September 11, 2001. On the morning of that day, Hlava was trying out his new video camera in the passenger seat of a Ford Explorer SUV in Brooklyn near the Brooklyn-Battery Tunnel. He wanted to capture the New York City environment for his friends and relatives back in the Czech Republic. By accident, he recorded Flight 11 as it struck the North Tower of the World Trade Center, unaware at the time that he was recording the event. Later, he accidentally recorded the crash of United Airlines Flight 77 into the South Tower.

What the Camera Saw on September 11

They did not even see the pale fleck of the airplane streak across the corner of the video camera's field of view at 8:46 a.m. But the camera, pointed at the twin towers of the World Trade Center from the passenger seat of a sport utility vehicle in Brooklyn near the Brooklyn-Battery Tunnel to Manhattan, kept rolling when the plane disappeared for an instant and then a silent, billowing cloud of smoke and dust slowly emerged from the north tower, as if it had sprung a mysterious kind of leak. . . . The camera pointed upward, zoomed in and out, and then, with a roar in the background that built to a piercing screech, it locked on the tarrying image of the second plane as it soared, like some awful bird of prey, almost straight overhead, banking steeply, and blasted into the south tower.

James Glanz, "Rare Tape Shows Each Jet Hitting Tower," *New York Times* (September 9, 2003), p. A1.

Hlava was unaware of the importance of his videos until almost two weeks later. He had made the tapes in order to make postcards to send back to the Czech Republic. His inability to speak English also confused the situation. Several times Hlava and his brother attempted to sell the tape privately both in New York City and in the Czech Republic, but their lack of English and no understanding of the new media prevented a sell. The existence of the tape was first made public when a friend of Mr. Hlava's wife traded a copy of the tape to another Czech immigrant for a bar tab at a pub in Ridgewood, Queens. It was only after a woman told a freelance news photographer, Walter Karling, that the tape was brought to the attention of the *New York Times*. By this time almost two years had gone by. In December 2003, Hlava returned to the Czech Republic.

See Also
American Airlines Flight 11; World Trade Center, September 11

Suggested Reading
James Glanz, "Two Years Later: Images; A Rare View of Sept. 11, Overlooked," *New York Times* (September 7, 2003), p. 1; Karen Matthews, "Newly Surfaced Tape Might Help 9/11 Investigators," *Gazette* [Montreal] (September 8, 2003), p. A21.

Pentagon Attack

The attack on September 11, 2001, damaged the west side of the Pentagon and caused heavy loss of life. As the headquarters of the United States Department of Defense, the Pentagon was an obvious target in any type of hostilities including terrorist acts. It is considered the world's largest office building. The building is huge, covering twenty-nine acres. Ten numbered corridors provide 17.5 miles of hallways. Although the building was built to house as many as 50,000 military and civilian personnel, on September 11, 2001, it had approximately 18,000 employees, as well as about 2,000 non-defense support personnel, working there. The building was built between 1941 and 1943, during World War II. Its unique construction incorporates five concentric rings named A, B, C, D, and E, from the inner ring facing the courtyard (A) to the outermost ring (E).

Five terrorists seized American Airlines Flight 77 as it traveled from Dulles International Airport (outside Washington, D.C.) to Los Angeles, California. Instead, they crashed it into the Pentagon. The five hijackers—Hani Hanjour, Nawaf al-Hazmi, Salem al-Hazmi, Khalid al-Mihdhar, and Majed Moqued—had little trouble passing through the Dulles checkpoint with weapons, which they subsequently used to take over the aircraft. Once seated in the first-class section, they seized control of the aircraft shortly after takeoff. As air traffic controllers at Dulles tried to regain contact with the airliner, the hijackers redirected the aircraft toward the Washington, D.C., area. A request was made to a U.S. Air Force transport for a visual sighting, and the pilot replied that he had the airliner in sight. An air traffic controller asked the C-130 pilot, Lt. Col. Steve O'Brien, to monitor the airliner. He reported that the airliner was moving low and fast, and then he watched it crash into the west side of the Pentagon. The flight hit at first-floor level and penetrated three of the five rings of that section of the Pentagon.

The personnel at the Pentagon had no warning of the approaching aircraft. Many of the Pentagon workers were watching news footage on TV of the attacks on the World Trade Center complex. Several of the survivors remarked later how they talked about how vulnerable the Pentagon was to a similar type of attack. Suddenly there was a tremendous explosion. Those not killed or injured in the original explosion had to face fire and reduced visibility from the smoke. Most of those working in the Pentagon were evacuated, but those trapped in the West side of the building were unable to escape.

First Minutes at the Pentagon

It felt like a train was going underneath us. There was a series of explosions, or at least noises that sounded like explosions. While the plane was skidding across the first floor, it was knocking out the support columns, which made explosion-like sounds. Any time a column went down, that opened a hole in the floor, which offered a gateway for the ball of fire to go through. We lost 22 coworkers in our area because of that. It was basically one fireball, but it was like an octopus with tentacles, reaching for any avenue of approach, as we call it in the military. The aircraft had 20,000 gallons of fuel, so the fireball was powerful. We all recognize in our area, those of us who worked on the second floor, that we are fortunate to be alive. It was by the grace of God that we survived. If it hadn't been for the extra precautions they took, like the blast-proof window and coating the floors with Teflon-like material, more would have died, including me.

Testimony of Army Lt. Col. Victor Correa, quoted in Dean E. Murphy, *September 11: An Oral History* (New York: Doubleday, 2002), p. 231

The key to survival was finding a safe route out of the building. Most of the rescues of the trapped or incapacitated took place in the first half-hour after the attack. Both military personnel and civilians aided hundred of individuals badly shaken or injured. This help enabled many people to escape the building, keeping the casualty rate relatively low. Once firefighters and other professional rescue people arrived, they began to discourage active participation by nonprofessionals because it was simply too dangerous entering a building where there were still fires and structural collapses.

Firefighting teams from the Arlington County Fire Department and other area fire departments responded to the emergency as soon as they heard the news. News of the attack came to the Arlington County Emergency Communications Center (ECC), which began broadcasting the news of the attack to various agencies and fire departments. On arriving at the Pentagon, the firefighters began fighting the fire and rescuing some of those who were trapped. Many of those rescued were severely burned. Although firefighting at the Pentagon was much easier than at the World Trade Center complex because of the Pentagon's fewer number of floors, difficulties were caused by the high-temperature fire caused by burning aviation fuel. It took firefighters nearly five hours to put out the fire feeding on the aviation fuel and the burning building. As soon as the fire and smoke subsided, a general search for survivors took place. There were no survivors. Because many of the offices on the west side were undergoing renovation, the number of casualties was lower than would have been if the offices had been occupied. The blast and fire killed 128 Pentagon personnel, as well as the crew and passengers of Flight 77.

A video image made available by the Pentagon on May 16, 2006, shows an explosion after American Airlines Flight 77 crashed into the Pentagon on September 11. (AP IMAGES/Pentagon.)

The evacuation process and fire fighting had several interruptions because of warnings about possible other airliner attacks. Most serious of these warnings concerned United Airlines Flight 93 approaching the Washington, D.C., area. At each warning the Pentagon had to be evacuated. Despite these interruptions, by the end of the day on September 12 the fires had been contained.

It took ten days after the attack for all human remains to be removed from the Pentagon. A body-recovery team of one or more FBI agents, one or two FEMA representatives, a photographer, and a four-body carrier unit from the 3rd Infantry Regiment (Old Guard) looked for remains. Each body or body part was photographed at the site. Later, cadaver-sniffing dogs were brought in to help the body-recovery teams.

See Also
American Airlines Flight 77; Hazmi, Nawaf bin Muhammad Salim al-; Mihdhar, Khalid al-; Pentagon Attack

See Document
Document #15

Suggested Reading
Richard Bernstein, *Out of the Blue: The Story of September 11, 2001, from Jihad to Ground Zero* (New York: Times Books, 2002); Alfred Goldberg et al., *Pentagon 9/11* (Washington, DC: Historical Office, Office of the Secretary of Defense, 2007); Michael Hedges, "Workers at Pentagon Recount Horrific Scene," *Houston Chronicle* (September 12, 2001), p. A22.

Phoenix Memo

The Phoenix Memo was an attempt by FBI field agent Kenneth Williams of the Phoenix FBI Field Office to warn FBI headquarters of a suspiciously large number of Middle Eastern males studying to become commercial pilots. His memo noted an "inordinate number of individuals of investigative interest" attending aviation training in Arizona. He believed that this might be part of "an effort to establish a cadre of individuals in civil aviation, who would be in position to conduct terrorist activity in the future." Williams also suspected that some of these pilot trainees had connections with al-Qaeda. Williams was right. One of the ten trainees of whom he was most suspicious had contacts with Hani Hanjour. Williams sent the memo to individuals in the Usama Bin Ladin Unit (UBLU) and the Radical Fundamentalist Unit (RFU) within the Counterterrorism Division at FBI headquarters and to several FBI special agents in the New York City field office.

Williams was a rookie FBI agent most of whose previous experience was with the San Diego Police Department and its SWAT team. He had become the counterterrorism expert in the Phoenix Field Office, but most of the attention was directed toward fighting the drug trade. In the middle of his investigation of Middle Eastern flight students, he received a six-month assignment to a high-profile arson case. This delayed his sending of the memo until after the end of the arson case.

Williams recommended in his memo that the FBI investigate the 3,000 or so commercial pilot schools for possible al-Qaeda operations. This undertaking would have been on a massive scale and would have overloaded the FBI field offices with little chance of FBI offices receiving any credit for their labor. Despite this failing, such an investigation might have identified some of the September 11 plotters and prevented the events of September 11. The problem was that this memo fell into a bureaucratic black hole, and no agent assumed responsibility for it.

The memo appeared at FBI headquarters on July 10, 2001, and elicited little interest. Nor was there any interest in it at the New York City Field Office's Joint Terrorism Task Force (JTTF). Agents in the New York City Field Office knew that Middle Eastern flight students were common, and they also knew many of the students were affiliated with al-Qaeda. These agents reasoned that Bin Laden needed pilots to transport goods and personnel in Afghanistan. Personnel at FBI Headquarters let the memo sit a week before deciding what to do with it. The FBI had a system where communications and memoranda were classified as a lead, meaning that the office sending a communication can request that the receiving office or officers take some follow-up action or conduct additional investigation. The lead was filed by the receiving office without notifying the officers' superiors of its existence. Finally, on July 30, 2001, the memo was assigned to an Intelligence Assistant (IA) in the Radical Fundamentalist Unit. This agent decided that the memo belonged to the Usama Bin Ladin Unit. She was able to persuade a UBLU agent to take charge of the memo. This agent discussed the issue with colleagues over the legality of the proposal and whether it raised profiling issues. On August 7, 2001, the agents in the RFU and UBLU closed the file. They briefly considered assigning the Phoenix Memo to a headquarters analysis unit but decided against it.

> **What Happened to the Phoenix Memo**
>
> It was reviewed by midlevel supervisors, who headed the agency's bin Laden and Islamic extremist counterterrorism units. But the officials said the memorandum was never sent to top F.B.I. managers, including Thomas J. Pickard, who was acting director in the summer of 2001 before Mr. Mueller took over early in September. Other senior officials were unaware of the memorandum before Sept. 11, including Michael Rolince, who managed the bureau's international terrorism unit, and Dale Watson, his superior, the officials said.
>
> David Johnston and Don Van Natta Jr., "The F.B.I. Memo: Ashcroft Learned of Agent's Alert Just after 9/11," *New York Times* (May 21, 2002), p. A1.

This inaction remained hidden within FBI Headquarters until the Joint Committee on Intelligence's investigators learned of its existence. Several of the participants then disclosed what had happened. This failure to respond to a warning was a black mark on FBI Headquarters for its lack of action to this warning. Some of the FBI's field investigators became unhappy because no one in FBI Headquarters was held responsible for this lapse of judgment.

See Also
Federal Bureau of Investigation; Joint Terrorism Task Force; Pilot Training for September 11

See Document
Document #29

Suggested Reading
Bob Graham, *Intelligence Matters: The CIA, the FBI, Saudi Arabia, and the Failure of America's War on Terror* (New York: Random House, 2004); Joint Inquiry into Intelligence Community Activities before and after the Terrorist Attacks of September 11, 2001, *Hearings before the Select Committee on Intelligence U.S. Senate and the Permanent Select Committee on Intelligence House of Representatives*, vol. 2 (Washington, DC: U.S. Government

Printing Office, 2004); Don Van Natta Jr. and David Johnston, "Anti-U.S. Views at Pilot Schools Prompted Agent's Alert," *New York Times* (May 22, 2002), p. 22; Jim Yardley and Jo Thomas, "For Agent in Phoenix, the Cause of Many Frustrations Extended to His Own Office," *New York Times* (June 19, 2002), p. 18.

Pilot Training for September 11

The key to the terrorist conspiracy of September 11 was pilot training. Khalid Sheikh Mohammed's original plan, as presented to Osama bin Laden and the other leaders of al-Qaeda in mid-1996, envisaged the use of aircraft as flying bombs. Mohammed's nephew, Ramzi Yousef, had proved in the 1993 World Trade Center bombing in New York City that no bomb delivered by conventional means could cause enough damage to destroy a complex as large as the World Trade Center. The use of an aircraft as a flying bomb meant that the aircraft had to be large enough to carry a huge load of aviation fuel. The only candidates for such a mission were the aircraft flown by commercial airlines. Mohammed and his planners knew that seizing a commercial aircraft was possible, but the big problem was flying the aircraft to the target. Al-Qaeda knew that it could recruit intelligent, educated, and highly motivated suicide bombers, but training a handful of them to fly commercial aircraft was beyond them. Al-Qaeda was forced to send a select group of al-Qaeda operatives to the United States and enroll them into commercial pilot training schools. Such training was expensive—about $30,000 per person—but al-Qaeda had the necessary funds available. An additional risk that nevertheless had to be taken was the exposure of operatives to the attention of American authorities both on entry into the United States and during their stay in the country.

The United States has a thriving commercial pilot training industry. In 2000 around 3,000 commercial flight schools operated under the auspices of the National Air Transportation Association (NATS). These schools were located around the country, often in remote areas, operating from local airstrips and often training their students in airplane hangers—about 70,000 students annually, before September 11, 2001. Local interest in pilot training is steady, but some of the more ambitious schools actively recruited students from foreign countries. These schools had an agreement with the Immigration and Naturalization Service (INS) that allowed foreign students to enter the United States on the highly coveted I-20M immigration forms designed to help foreign students acquire visas to enter the United States as vocational students. Foreign students have flocked to the United States because a commercial pilot license in Europe or the Middle East would cost as much as $100,000 to earn in contrast to $30,000 in the United States. In Florida's 220 commercial pilot training schools in 2000, 27 percent of the students were international students.

It was easy for al-Qaeda to send a handful of its operatives to receive commercial pilot training. These operatives trained in at least ten schools—from the Sorbi Flying Club in San Diego, California, to the Freeway Airport in Bowie, Maryland. After investigating the Airmen Flight School in Norman, Oklahoma in July 2000 and finding it unsatisfactory, Mohamed Atta and Marwan al-Shehhi trained together at two Florida schools—Huffman Aviation in Venice, Florida, and Jones Aviation Flying Service at the Sarasota-Bradenton International Airport. After rejection by a flight instructor at the Jones Aviation Flying Service, they received most of their pilot training from Huffman Aviation. After Atta and al-Shehhi received their commercial pilot licenses in December 2000, they began renting small aircraft to fly up and down the East Coast. It was on one such trip, on December 26, 2000, that Atta abandoned his rented aircraft on the taxiway at a Miami Airport after its engine sputtered before takeoff. The Federal Aviation Agency (FAA) complained about this but did nothing about it. In January 2001, Atta and al-Shehhi took even more flying lessons at the flight school at Gwinnet County Airport, near Atlanta, Georgia.

The other pilots trained at different schools. Several of them raised the suspicions of their flight instructors because of their apparent indifference to takeoffs and landings. All they seemed to be interested in was flying aircraft. This apparent disinterest made these pilots-in-training poor candidates for commercial pilots. Only one of the hijackers, Hani Hanjour, had ambitions to be a commercial pilot, but he was so poor a pilot that no commercial aviation company would hire him. Frustrated in his ambition to be a pilot, he joined the ranks of the hijackers.

The pilot flight schools have fallen on hard times after September 11, hurt by a combination of security-related red tape, diminished enrollment, and the stigma of association with the 9/11 hijackers. Florida and its pilot schools have suffered the most, but the hard times have affected the entire country.

Blame for the 9/11 Hijackers and Pilot Training

"We never recovered," said Mr. [Terry] Fensome, whose school has 30 students now, down from the 60 before the attacks, though none of the hijackers trained at Pelican [Flight Training Center]. "The idea that the flight schools were to blame for this was totally off the wall, and it hurt us a lot." At least 50 of the state's flight schools have closed since 9/11, most of them mom-and-pop operations that could not survive the drop in business and rising costs. The number of foreign students has plummeted, flight school owners say, because of tough new immigration rules, the battered aviation industry and a general fear of bias since 9/11.

Abby Goodnough, "Hard Times Are Plaguing Flight Schools in Florida," *New York Times* (September 14, 2002), p. 20.

See Also
Atta, Mohamed el-Amir Awad el-Sayed; Hanjour, Hani Saleh Husan; Shehhi, Marwan Yousef Muhammed Rashid Lekrab al-

Suggested Reading
Steve Fainaru and Peter Whoriskey, "Hijack Suspects Tried Many Flight Schools," *Washington Post* (September 19, 2001), p. A15; David Hirschman, "I Didn't See Evil," *Atlanta Journal-Constitution* (January 27, 2002), p. 1A; Barry Klein, Thomas C. Tobin, and Kathryn Wexler, "Florida Flight Schools Decry Rush to Regulate after Attacks," *St. Petersburg Times* [Florida] (September 24, 2001), p. 1A; Aaron Sharockman, "9/11 Hijackers Practiced Here," *St. Petersburg Times* [Florida] (March 31, 2006), p. 1A.

Port Authority of New York and New Jersey

The Port Authority of New York and New Jersey and its police force, the Port Authority Police Department (PAPD), suffered heavily on September 11. In 1921 the states of New York and New Jersey created an independent agency, the Port Authority of New York and New Jersey, to oversee the harbors. Throughout the 1930s and 1940s the Port Authority's authority increased to include the administration of the Holland and Lincoln Tunnels, as well as of various bridges. It also built the World Trade Center complex in the 1960s and 1970s. The Port Authority owned the World Trade Center complex until June 2001, when Larry Silverstein leased it. But by September 11 the Port Authority still had its agencies in fifteen floors in the North Tower.

The Port Authority Police Department provided security for the Port Authority of New York and New Jersey's various responsibilities. It had been formed in 1928 by recruiting forty men to police the bridges to Staten Island. Headquartered in Jersey City, New Jersey, it supervises individual operating units, each of which has its own commander. Over the years, the PAPD grew until, in 2001, it had 1,100 police officers. This police force was responsible for three airports, two tunnels, four bridges, the PATH Subway System, two interstate bus terminals, and marine cargo terminals in both New York and New Jersey, as well as the World Trade Center complex.

Port Authority police were on duty on September 11. They responded to the emergency and worked beside the firefighters of the Fire Department of New York City and the officers of the New York City Police Department to evacuate the North Tower and South Tower. Thirty-seven members of the PAPD were killed on September 11, including Superintendent of Police Fred Marrone, Chief of Police James Romito, Inspector Anthony Infante, Captain Kathy Mazza, and a number of Emergency Service Unit officers. Thirty-eight Port Authority civilian employees also died, including Neil Levin, executive director of the Port Authority.

The first problem of the rescue and recovery phase of September 11 surfaced when the Port Authority police were ignored by the FDNY and the NYPD. Both the firefighters and police were busy establishing their areas of responsibility, and during the early hours the PAPD police were unable to communicate with either. It took a while before the PAPD was accepted by the other departments. Later, however, because the PAPD police knew the ins and outs of the World Trade Center complex, the Port Authority police became equal partners with the firefighters and city police.

See Also
Firefighters at Ground Zero; Mazza, Kathy; New York City Police Department; World Trade Center, September 11

Suggested Reading
Susan Hagen and Mary Carouba, *Women at Ground Zero: Stories of Courage and Compassion* (New York: Alpha, 2002); William Keegan Jr. and Bart Davis, *Closure: The Untold Story of the Ground Zero Recovery Mission* (New York: Touchstone Book, 2006).

Predator
The Predator is a medium-altitude, long-range, unmanned aerial vehicle used by the CIA and the U.S. Air Force as an antiterrorist weapon. Developed by the U.S. Air Force in the 1990s for long-range reconnaissance missions, it is about the size of a small SUV and is powered by a 101-horsepower propeller-driven engine that gives it a top speed of 135 miles per hour. It holds enough fuel to travel 400 nautical miles (460 miles). Its ability to orbit an area gives it an advantage over other, faster reconnaissance aircraft. When equipped with a pair of Hellfire antitank missiles, it also becomes an effective, lethal weapon. The Hellfire missile is an air-to-ground missile about five-and-a-half feet long that weighs just over 100 pounds and can be fired from attack helicopters and the Predator.

The Predator is remotely controlled. A team of three—a pilot and two sensor operators—operate the Predator from a ground-control station that can be thousands of miles away. Controls for the system resemble those used in ultrasophisticated model aircraft and advanced video games. It has a TV camera, an infrared camera, and a system that enables it to penetrate smoke and clouds.

The Predator has great potential for use against terrorists—particularly in remote areas—but its development was slowed by interagency gridlock. Both the CIA and the U.S. Air Force wanted to gain control of the Predator program. Leaders of the CIA envisaged it as a counterterrorism weapon, but the U.S. Air Force saw it as a reconnaissance asset. This infighting hindered the development of the program. Early versions of the Predator were used in Bosnia, and it was finally sent to Afghanistan in September 2000. President Clinton authorized its use in Afghanistan to hunt down Osama bin Laden. Unfortunately, soon after it arrived in Afghanistan, one of the Predators crashed. It was suspected that news of its capabilities, or the possible capture of one of the aircraft, caused the Predator program to be shelved for improvements. Despite its obvious capabilities for neutralizing leaders of al-Qaeda, the Predator program remained shut down until after September 11.

Revival of political fighting between the CIA and the U.S. Air Force caused most of the delay. The CIA still wanted to use the Predator as a weapon, and the Air Force insisted that it be chiefly restricted to reconnaissance missions. The addition of the Hellfire antitank missile system sacrificed the Predator's ability to see through smoke and cloud. There was also argument about who would pay the $1 million price for each Predator. The Bush administration finally ruled that the Department of Defense would pay for them, ending this part of the controversy.

The effectiveness of the Predator was proved when it killed key al-Qaeda leaders in Afghanistan and Yemen. A Predator-fired missile also killed senior al-Qaeda officials, including Mohammad Atef, in the early stages of the overthrow of the Taliban regime. Slow communications when seeking approval for a strike saved Omar and most of the Taliban from a Predator attack on October 7, 2001. Then, in October 2002, a Predator launched its Hellfire missiles at a car carrying Abu Ali al-Harithi and Ahmed Hijazi, as well as four other al-Qaeda operatives, on a road in Marib province, Yemen. Al-Harithi had been part of the plot to attack the USS *Cole* in October 2000. A National Security Agency communications satellite intercepted a phone call from al-Harithi, and the Predator tracked the car before launching its missile. The car was destroyed with all its passengers, except one who escaped. This was exactly the type of mission the CIA had envisaged for the Predator system.

Despite this success, the Predator program has come under the operational control of the U.S. Air Force after a decision made by the Bush administration. The CIA selects the target, but after the Predator is in flight, operational control is turned over to Air Force personnel in the United States. The job of completing a Predator's mission requires a task force of about 55 people to pilot the aircraft, check sensors, monitor communications, and manage the mission. Besides these personnel requirements, the Predator needs enough equipment for its ground control station that the equipment has to be hauled around by a C-130 transport aircraft. Despite this heavy logistical load, the use of the Predator has been common in fighting the Iraq insurgency. The Predator was at first used in Iraq chiefly

The unmanned Predator B taxis back to its hangar in El Mirage, California, on September 6, 2001, after a test flight over the Mojave Desert. (AP IMAGES/Doug Benc.)

in its reconnaissance mode, but this has changed as fighting against insurgents has intensified.

In 2002 a new version of the Predator, Predator B, appeared in the inventory of the U.S. military. Predator B is a larger model than its predecessor and has a more powerful jet engine. It lacks some of the loitering capability of the Predator, but it can fly twice as high and is much faster. Because it can carry a heavier armament package, the Predator B is more a hunter-killer than its earlier model. The U.S. Air Force has used both the Predator and the Predator B in Iraq.

See Also
Bin Laden, Osama; Bush Administration; Central Intelligence Agency

Suggested Reading
Bruce V. Bigelow, "Predator, Part II: Spy Plane's New Version is Bigger, Better, More Capable," *San Diego Union-Tribune* (August 27, 2002), p. C1; Richard A. Clarke, *Against All Enemies: Inside America's War on Terror* (New York: Free Press, 2004); Mick Farren, *CIA: Secrets of "The Company,"* (New York: Barnes and Noble, 2003); Mark Huband and Mark Odell, "Unmanned Weapon Makes Its Mark in Yemeni Sea of Sand," *Financial Times* [London] (November 6, 2002), p. 24; Judith Miller and Eric Schmitt, "Ugly Duckling Turns Out to Be Formidable in the Air," *New York Times* (November 23, 2001), p. B1; Walter Pincus, "Predator to See More Combat," *Washington Post* (March 22, 2005), p. A3; Thomas E. Ricks, "U.S. Arms Unmanned Aircraft," *Washington Post* (October 18, 2001), p. A1; Winn L. Rosch, "Unmanned Vehicles, Crews Await War," *Plain Dealer* [Cleveland, OH] (February 13, 2003), p. C2; Richard Sisk, "Hellfire Homed in on Terrorist's Cell Phone," *Daily News* [New York] (November 20, 2002), p. 28.

Q

Qaeda, al-

Al-Qaeda is the umbrella terrorist organization that planned and carried out the attacks of September 11, 2001. Osama bin Laden formed al-Qaeda in May 1988, near the end of the Afghan–Soviet War, from the Mujahideen Services Bureau. The idea for an organization to coordinate Islamist activities came from bin Laden's mentor, Abdullah Azzam. An organizational meeting on August 11, 1988, and another on August 20, finalized plans. In November 1988, the existence of al-Qaeda was formally announced. From its beginning, al-Qaeda had an organizational structure consisting of four committees: military, religious, financial, and media. A consulting council headed by bin Laden oversaw the organization.

Al-Qaeda's Operational Principle

Al Qaeda pursues a method or principle that calls for "centralization of decision and decentralization of execution." The decision was made centrally, but the method of attack and execution was the duty of field commanders. . . . The planning for the *Cole* operation was carried out by the people [on the ground]. The idea was formed and the target was set and then it was referred to a higher military control committee in al Qaeda called the Military Affairs Committee, which does not plan, but gives the green light, the support, and the funds for these operations. But, the planning, execution, and method of attack were all undertaken by field commanders in the operations field.

Peter L. Bergen, *The Osama bin Laden I Know: An Oral History of al Qaeda's Leader* (New York: Free Press, 2006), p. 253.

Leadership with al-Qaeda is highly selective. Only about two hundred individuals have sworn loyalty (*bayat*) to bin Laden and provide the leadership cadre. Empty leadership positions caused by deaths and captures are filled by highly motivated subordinates. These leaders have extensive contacts in the Islamist world and communicate via the Internet.

Bin Laden recruited a large number of Afghan fighters into al-Qaeda at the end of the Afghan–Soviet War. Many of these recruits headed back to their native countries, where they formed indigenous terrorist groups. Among the more prominent groups affiliated with al-Qaeda are Abu Sayyaf (the Sword of God, the

Philippines), the Armed Islamic Group (the GIA, Algeria), Hezbollah (the Party of God, Lebanon), the Islamic Group (Egypt), Hamas (Palestine), the Islamic Jihad (Egypt), Gama'a Islamiyya (Indonesia), and the Moro Islamic Liberation Front (MILF, Philippines), along with at least twenty-two additional groups.

Al-Qaeda believes in training its operatives in basic combat skills. An estimated 10,000 to 110,000 trainees have trained in al-Qaeda camps from 1989 to 2001. Probably about 30,000 have graduated during that period. About 3,000 trainees were assessed as capable of advanced training for terrorist operations. Graduates of these camps retain their affiliation with al-Qaeda when they go elsewhere.

Al-Qaeda established various training camps in Afghanistan and Pakistan in the 1990s. Most of the instructors were Egyptians and had previous experience in the military or in security forces. After the loss of Afghanistan as a base, several of these camps were transferred to remote areas in Pakistan to join the Pakistani camps already there.

Instructors at the camps issue a training manual to the trainees that emphasizes teamwork, willing submission to leaders, and, above all, secrecy. Among its recommendations are that apartment living arrangements during a mission should be in groups of three. The manual also recommends that martyrdom missions have at least four targets for greatest effect.

Only a select few of the trainees were deemed worthy of a martyrdom mission. Psychological profiling was conducted by the instructors to select those most worthy. The best candidates were those who were highly religious and well-educated. A graduate of the al-Masada Training Camp, Hasan Abd-Rabbuh al-Suraghi, put it another way, stating that instructors looked for candidates who were "young, zealous, obedient, and [had] a weak character that obeys instructions without question." The instructors had no difficulty finding volunteers.

Western terrorist analysts have been confused over the extent of al-Qaeda's control over these groups. The only consensus is that al-Qaeda has been able to establish a degree of coordination among its member groups. Rohan Gunaratna, a Sri Lankan and a former research fellow at the Centre for the Study of Terrorism and Political Violence at University of St. Andrews in Scotland, has described al-Qaeda as "a secret, almost virtual

---

How Al-Qaeda Instructors Select Those for Special Missions, According to an Early Member of Al-Qaeda

The majority of the instructors were Egyptians who were paid their salaries by bin Ladin. It seems that these instructors, who used to work in Azzam's camps before he was assassinated, had past experience in the Egyptian army or security organs. During the training period, there were some Egyptians whose task was to screen the young men well. They looked for certain specific qualifications among these young men. The most important criteria were that the ones who are chosen should be young, zealous, obedient, and with a weak character that obeys instructions without question. This period of scrutiny went on for one to two weeks in closed and guarded locations which were accessible only to al Qaeda. Sometimes, only very few were selected and were asked whether they wanted to join. If these accepted to join, they were asked to leave and bid farewell to their families and then to return for higher training in the camps on specialized military curricula (preparatory level, middle level, and final level).

Peter L. Bergen, *The Osama bin Laden I Know: An Oral History of al Qaeda's Leader* (New York: Free Press, 2006) p. 84.

organization, one that denies its own existence in order to remain in the shadows."

Al-Qaeda is a selective organization that rigidly oversees the selection of its members to carry out operations. It recruits only the most talented and motivated candidates, who then earn a modest salary of about $200 a month; those with great responsibilities may receive up to $300. Before the loss of Afghanistan in late 2001, al-Qaeda had trained more than 5,000 operatives in a dozen training camps to carry out terrorist operations. Recruits were processed through main training camps before being sent to various locations for specialized training. About fifty-five possible training locations existed.

Besides specialized training, political and religious instruction also took place. Osama bin Laden made regular visits to the camps, where he gave lectures and pep talks. He also held personal talks with those selected for special operations. Bin Laden met with Mohamed Atta, Marwan al-Shehhi, and Ziad Jarrah when they arrived for training in Afghanistan. Because of al-Qaeda's high prestige in the Muslim world, there are many Arabs—probably as many as 100,000—who are willing to join al-Qaeda if invited. This highly selective system is used to make operations resistant to foreign intelligence services penetration. Those agents who

---

Qualification for Membership in Al-Qaeda

1. Islam: The member of the Organization must be Moslem. . . .
2. Commitment to the Organization's Ideology: This commitment frees the Organization's members from conceptional [*sic*] problems. . . .
3. Maturity: The requirements of military work are numerous, and a minor cannot perform them. . . .
4. Sacrifice: He [the member] has to be willing to do the work and undergo martyrdom for the purpose of achieving the goal and establishing the religion of the majestic Allah on earth.
5. Listening and Obedience: In the military, this is known today as discipline. . . .
6. Keeping Secrets and Concealing Information: [This secrecy should be used] even with the closest people, for deceiving the enemies is not easy. . . .
7. Free of Illness: The Military Organization's member must fulfill this important requirement. . . .
8. Patience: [The member] should have plenty of patience for [enduring] afflictions if he is overcome by the enemies. . . .
9. Tranquility and "Unflappability": [The member] should have a calm personality that allows him to endure psychological traumas such as those involving bloodshed, murder, arrest, imprisonment, and reverse psychological traumas such as killing one or all of his Organization's comrades. . . .
10. Intelligence and Insight. . . .
11. Caution and Prudence. . . .
12. Truthfulness and Counsel. . . .
13. Ability to Observe and Analyze. . . .
14. Ability to Act, Change Positions and Conceal Oneself. . . .

Stefan Aust et al., *Inside 9-11: What Really Happened* (New York: St. Martin's Press, 2001), pp. 267–272.

have attempted to penetrate al-Qaeda are killed when discovered or even suspected. In 2002 al-Qaeda had operatives active in fifty-five countries.

Financial support for al-Qaeda comes from a variety of sources. In the early years bin Laden used his personal fortune of between $30 and $35 million to support many of al-Qaeda's operations, but after leaving Sudan his personal fortune diminished, and other sources of income had to be developed. Other significant sources of funding have come from Islamic nongovernmental organizations (NGOs), such as Islamic charities and foundations. After the attacks on September 11, 2001, western authorities attacked these NGOs, and a considerable amount of funding for al-Qaeda suddenly dried up. For a time financial support came from state sponsors—Afghanistan, Iran, and Sudan—but these sources of funding have also mostly ceased.

Al-Qaeda has conducted operations in a systematic way. It developed operations by using three types of operatives. Local militants were recruited for groundwork but had no knowledge of the details of a plan. Sleepers were sent to live and work in the area long before the operation. Finally, al-Qaeda specialists and martyrs were brought in at the final stages of the mission. Once the mission was accomplished, the survivors were to go underground again. This was the type of operation that al-Qaeda carried out in the African embassy bombings. Al-Qaeda planners, however, were flexible and willing to improvise in case conditions changed.

> **Ineptness of Some of Al-Qaeda's Operations**
>
> One underappreciated aspect of Al Qaeda operations was how crude many of them were. Intelligence analysts sometimes cited the plans' complexity and sophistication, as if blowing up buildings or boats or vehicles was high-end science. In fact, many Al Qaeda plots have been marked by the haphazardness of their design and execution. Over the years, many of the plots seemed hare-brained at worst, ill-conceived at best, pursued by ill-equipped and unprepared, inept men. Some were almost comical in their haplessness: boats sank, cars crashed, bombs blew up too soon. Some of the men virtually delivered themselves to police. The gross ineptitude of the execution often disguised the gravity of the intent, and hid, also, the steadfastness of the plotters. Whatever else they did, they did not go away.
>
> Terry McDermott, *Perfect Soldiers: The 9/11 Hijackers: Who They Were, Why They Did It* (New York: HarperCollins, 2005), pp. 174–175.

Al-Qaeda's first terrorist operation took place in 1992. This was the bombing of a hotel in Aden, Yemen, on December 29, 1992, that barely missed its targeted U.S. troops. On June 26, 1995, an al-Qaeda–led group attempted to assassinate Egyptian President Hosni Mubarak as he visited Addis Ababa, Ethiopia. Al-Qaeda cooperated with an Iranian group in a June 25, 1996, truck bombing outside the Khobar Towers in Dharhran, Saudi Arabia, that killed nineteen U.S. servicemen and wounded five hundred others. Its next operation was the bombing of the U.S. embassies in Nairobi, Kenya, and Dar es Salaam, Tanzania, on August 7, 1998, killing 234 people. A suicide bombing of the American warship USS *Cole* on October 5, 2000, killed seventeen sailors and wounded thirty-nine others. All of these attacks paled beside the havoc of the al-Qaeda–led suicide attacks on the World Trade Center's twin towers and on the Pentagon on September 11, 2001.

The collapse of the Taliban in Afghanistan in the autumn of 2001 was a serious blow to al-Qaeda's future operations. It lost its main base for the training of its operatives, as well as a secure staging area. Another important loss was al-Qaeda's military operations chief, Mohammad Atef. He was the victim of a Predator strike in the early days of the attack on the Taliban in Afghanistan. The survival of bin Laden and his second-in-command, al-Zawahiri, has allowed al-Qaeda to reestablish operations outside of Afghanistan, although on a much more limited basis. Because of its decentralized command structure, al-Qaeda has been able to recover some of its strike capability by entrusting operations to subordinate groups. Despite this, al-Qaeda has been put on the defensive, forced to pursue operations prematurely or send operatives underground as sleepers for future operations. Western intelligence and security forces continue to consider al-Qaeda a major threat, poised to strike at any time and anywhere with any type of weapon, from biological to nuclear.

Since 2003 al-Qaeda military forces have been fighting alongside Taliban forces in Afghanistan. Because bin Laden was aware in advance of the September 11 attacks, he began distributing al-Qaeda's fighting assets throughout Afghanistan so that al-Qaeda forces could survive the onslaught of American retaliation. It took the American military the three weeks until October 7, 2001, to begin offensive operations against the Taliban and al-Qaeda. During this interval, al-Qaeda dismantled its forces in Afghanistan and sent most of them into Pakistan and other central Asian countries. Most of the battles during the Northern Alliance takeover of Afghanistan—such as those at Tora Bora and Shahi Kowt—were delaying actions designed to allow al-Qaeda forces time to escape into Pakistan.

Besides fighting and planning future operations, al-Qaeda has become increasingly active on the Internet, where it contacts its operatives and recruits sympathizers. *Al-Neda* and *al-Ansar* have been the two most prominent Web sites for al-Qaeda. Information provided on these Web sites by al-Qaeda members gives justification for al-Qaeda operations. Western intelligence services have tried, with only limited success, to close down these Web sites.

Al-Qaeda and Taliban forces have made a military comeback since 2003. From secure bases in Afghanistan and Pakistan, military operations have been launched without fear of detection. The Afghan government has had to depend on NATO forces for security, but parts of Afghanistan have fallen into the hands of the al-Qaeda–Taliban alliance.

The loss of Afghanistan as a training and staging area has hindered al-Qaeda's terrorist operations. Immediately after the loss of its training camps, al-Qaeda's leadership began to look for alternate sites. An unlikely replacement has been Europe. An underground railroad of recruits for al-Qaeda has been set up from the Middle East to Germany and Great Britain. Both Germany and Great Britain have been more tolerant in their laws against suspected terrorists, although both have tightened their laws since September 11. After receiving training, many al-Qaeda recruits have returned to the Middle East and been smuggled into Iraq to join the Sunni resistance to the American occupation of Iraq, and to fight Iraq's Shiites.

See Also

Azzam, Sheikh Abdullah Yussuf; bin Laden, Osama; Taliban; World Trade Center, September 11; Zawahiri, Ayman al-

See Documents:

Document #5; Document #6

Suggested Reading

Jane Corbin, *Al Qaeda: In Search of the Terror Network* (New York: Thunder's Mouth Press, 2002); Rohan Gunaratna, *Inside Al Qaeda: Global Network of Terror* (New York: Columbia University Press, 2002); Hamdi A. Hassan, *Al-Qaeda: The Background of the Pursuit for Global Jihad* (Stockholm: Almqvist and Wiksell International, 2004); Lawrence Wright, *The Looming Tower: Al-Qaeda and the Road to 9/11* (New York: Knopf, 2006).

Quds Mosque, al-

Al-Quds Mosque was the mosque in Hamburg, Germany, where leaders of the September 11 attack worshiped and planned the attack. It was located in a poorer section of Hamburg on Steindamm Street. The mosque was situated above a body building gym near Hamburg's central railway station. This location, close to cheap transportation, made it attractive to expatriate Muslims. Al-Quds was one of the few Arab Sunni mosques; most of others in Hamburg were Shiite or Turkish Sunni. It was small, holding at most 150 people at prayer time. These small mosques were good places for Islamist extremists to cultivate and recruit members.

> **Attraction of Radical Mosques for Young Muslims**
>
> The reasons that young immigrants turn to fundamentalist Islam while in Europe are many. In most cases, radical mosques played a key role in their conversion. Some, like Shadi Abdallah, turned to the mosque simply because it offered the cheapest meals. Once there, they become fascinated with radical sermons and caught up in terrorist activities. Others begin going to the mosque out of homesickness. Many consider it more a social center than a place of worship. Nevertheless, after hearing the fiery words of local radicals, some change.
>
> Lorenzo Vidino, *Al Qaeda in Europe: The New Battleground of International Jihad* (Amherst, NY: Prometheus Books, 2006), p. 44.

Al-Quds was an extremist mosque because of the preaching of its leading cleric, Mohammed al-Fazazi. The founders of the mosque had been Moroccans, and most of its clerics were Moroccans—including al-Fazazi. He preached there constantly. Al-Fazazi believed Western civilization was the enemy of the Muslim world, and he believed in martyrdom. He was quoted in 2000 as saying that "who[ever] participates in the war against Islam with ideas or thoughts or a song or a television show to befoul Islam is an infidel on war footing that shall be killed, no matter if it's a man, a woman, or a child." It was these ideas that attracted Mohamed Atta to Islamist extremism and later to al-Qaeda. Al-Fazazi spent considerable time with the young men in his congregation talking with them about jihad, holy war, and martyrdom. Later, al-Fazazi's involvement in bombings in Morocco and Spain landed him a 30-year prison sentence in Morocco.

The al-Quds Mosque remained a place where it was possible to recruit others susceptible to the appeal of al-Fazazi and, later, al-Qaeda. Atta taught religious classes at al-Quds Mosque, but his hard-line position alienated all but those who thought as he. All of the members of the Hamburg Cell were recruited at the al-Quds Mosque, including Marwan al-Shehhi, Ramzi bin al-Shibh, and still others.

See Also

Atta, Mohamed el-Amir Awad el-Sayed; Bin al-Shibh, Ramzi; Hamburg Cell

Suggested Reading
Jane Corbin, *Al-Qaeda: The Terror Network That Threatens the World* (New York: Thunder's Mouth Press, 2002); Terry McDermott, *Perfect Soldiers: The 9/11 Hijackers: Who They Were, Why They Did It* (New York: HarperCollins, 2005); Lorenzo Vidino, *Al Qaeda in Europe: The New Battleground of International Jihad* (Amherst, NY: Prometheus Books, 2006).

R

Rendition

Rendition has been a successful but controversial way to fight terrorism. This program is run by the CIA but has been approved by both President Clinton and President George W. Bush. There are two forms of rendition: ordinary rendition and extraordinary rendition. Ordinary rendition occurs when a terrorist suspect is captured in a foreign country and then turned over to the United States. The individual is then transported to the United States or held at a foreign site for interrogation. Extraordinary rendition is the turning over of a suspected terrorist to a third-party country for detainment and questioning. Often the suspect is wanted by that country for past offenses or crimes. The first use of ordinary rendition was in 1986 by the Reagan administration after the suicide bombings in Beirut, Lebanon. Fawaz Yunis had participated in a hijacking of a Jordanian aircraft in 1985, during which three Americans had been killed. FBI agents and U.S. Navy SEALs seized him in a boat off the Lebanese coast.

Rendition as a policy lay dormant until the rise of terrorism in the early 1990s. One such rendition involved the capture of Ramzi Yousef and his transportation to the United States. There was a need for rules to standardize rendition. Michael Scheuer, then the head of the Alex Station in the CIA, drew up the guidelines for a new rendition program in 1996, and he ran the rendition program for forty months. President Clinton signed off on this program. Intent of the rendition program was to dismantle and disrupt the al-Qaeda network and detain Islamic terrorists. Because the Clinton administration and the FBI did not want the captives brought to the United States where the legal process protected them too much, the CIA focused on al-Qaeda suspects who were wanted in a third country. In the early years, most of the extraordinary renditions were to Egypt, where tougher methods were used on interrogations.

The CIA has always been nervous about rendition. It has justified it with the contention that when Allied governments had intelligence on terrorists that could not be used in a court of law, sometimes rendition was the only way to neutralize the terrorists. For renditions the CIA used paramilitary officers organized into teams and under the supervision of a CIA handler.

The rendition program has been effective, but it includes the danger that the information gathered is tainted by torture. Moreover, international law prohibits the forced return of any person, regardless of the crime, to a foreign location where that person would be subject to torture or mistreatment. Michael Scheuer has maintained that he warned the lawyers and policymakers about the dangers of turning over al-Qaeda suspects to foreign countries.

Michael Scheuer on Rendition

Well, several senior C.I.A. officers, myself included, were confident that common sense would elude that bunch (non-C.I.A. officials), so we told them—again and again and again. Each time a decision to do a rendition was made, we reminded the lawyers and policy makers that Egypt was Egypt, and that Jimmy Stewart never starred in a movie called "Mr. Smith Goes to Cairo." They usually listened, nodded, and then inserted a legal nicety by insisting that each country to which the agency delivered a detainee would have to pledge it would treat him according to the rules of its own legal system.

Michael Scheuer, "A Fine Rendition," *New York Times* (March 11, 2005), p. A23.

In the Bush administration, the CIA continues to handle rendition cases. Whereas rendition cases were infrequent in the Clinton administration, they became numerous in the Bush administration. Approximately 100 suspected al-Qaeda operatives have been captured and turned over to foreign governments for interrogation since 1996. Most of the rendition cases, however, have taken place since September 11, 2001. In recent years a white Gulfstream V jet has been used to move prisoners around to various countries. Egypt, Afghanistan, and Syria have been popular destinations, but at least fourteen European states have known what was going on and have cooperated with the United States. Several Eastern European states even housed CIA detention centers.

Former CIA Agent Bob Baer on Rendition Destinations and Possible Fates

If you want them to be tortured, you send them [suspected terrorists] to Syria. If you want someone to disappear—never to see them again—you send them to Egypt.

Quoted in Lila Rajiva, "The Torture-Go-Round: The CIA's Rendition Flights to Secret Prisons," *Counterpunch* (December 5, 2005), p. 4.

In one blatant case, two Egyptians were seized in Sweden and sent to Egypt. Ahmed Agiza and Muhammed al-Zery were radical Islamists, and they had sought political asylum in Sweden. On December 18, 2001, American agents seized both of them and placed them on a Gulfstream jet bound for Cairo, Egypt. The Swedish government cooperated after its representatives had been assured that Agiza and al-Zery would not be tortured. Once it was learned that both Agiza and al-Zery had been tortured, there was a major political outcry in Sweden against the Swedish government and the United States. Egyptian authorities determined that al-Zery had no contacts with terrorists, and he was released from prison in October 2003. Agiza was less lucky because he had been a member of Egyptian Islamic Jihad and close to its leader Ayman al-Zawahiri. An Egyptian court sentenced Agiza to twenty-five years in prison.

Rendition has become more controversial since the backfire of several rendition cases. The first such case was that of the radical Islamist cleric Abu Omar. His full name is Hassan Osama Nasr, and he lived in Milan, Italy, in political refugee status. Omar had been under investigation for terrorism-related activities and support of al-Qaeda when the CIA, with the assistance of the Italian security personnel, seized him off the streets of Milan on February 17, 2002. He was taken to a NATO base near Aviano, Italy, and then flown to Egypt on February 18. There Omar was offered a deal to be an informant. After he refused, Omar was sent to a prison where he claims that he was tortured. Italian authorities became incensed over this rendition, and a judge charged twenty-five American CIA operatives and two Italian security officers with abduction. The Italian government has decided not to request extradition of the CIA operatives, but the affair has damaged American and Italian relations.

Two other cases of rendition have caused unrest among allies. One was that of Maher Arar, a Canadian citizen from Ottawa and a software engineer. Arar was changing planes in JFK Airport in New York from an American Airlines flight from Zurich, Switzerland, on September 26, 2002, when U.S. authorities detained him. They were acting on inaccurate information given to them by the Royal Mounted Canadian Police (RMCP) that Arar was a member of al-Qaeda. After interrogation and a stay at the Metropolitan Detention Center, he was flown to Jordan on October 8, 2002. CIA operatives then transferred him to Syria. In Syria, he was imprisoned, and he was intensively interrogated for nearly a year. It took an intervention by the Canadian government to win Arar's release after ten and a half months in October 2003. Since then, Arar has been seeking to sue both the American and the Canadian government.

Another case was the December 2003 rendition of Khalid el-Masri, a German citizen. El-Masri was born in Kuwait but raised in Lebanon. In 1985 he immigrated to Germany, where he became a German citizen in 1994. He took a vacation in Skopje, Macedonia, but he was arrested at the Macedonian border on December 31, 2003, because his name resembled that of Khalid al-Masri, the mentor of the al-Qaeda Hamburg Cell. CIA agents took him into custody on January 23, 2004, shortly after Macedonian officials had released him. He was sent to Afghanistan where he was tortured during lengthy interrogations. El-Masri went on a hunger strike for twenty-seven days in the confinement camp. American officials determined that he had been wrongfully detained, and he was released on May 28, 2004. He was dumped on a desolate road in Albania without an apology or funds to return home. German authorities have initiated legal proceedings against CIA officials for their handling of el-Masri.

These cases of torture have been verified, and they have made rendition a difficult policy to justify. Most of the rendition cases came the first two years after September 11, and there have been fewer of them recently. Political fallout, however, continues both at home and among our allies.

See Also
Bush Administration; Clinton Administration

See Document
Document #24

Suggested Reading
Tyler Drumheller and Elaine Monaghan, *On the Brink: An Insider's Account of How the White House Compromised American Intelligence* (New York: Carroll and Graf, 2006); Roy Eccleston, "CIA 'Renditions' in Tune with Habib Claim of Abuse in Egypt," *Australian*

(February 14, 2005), p. 17; Stephen Grey and Ian Cobain, "From Secret Prisons to Turning a Blind Eye: Europe's Role in Rendition," *Guardian* [London] (June 7, 2006), p. 1; Michael Scheuer, "A Fine Rendition," *New York Times* (March 11, 2005), p. A23; Craig Whitlock, "In Letter, Radical Cleric Details CIA Abduction, Egyptian Torture," *Washington Post* (November 10, 2006), p. A23; Tracy Wilkinson, "Details Emerge in Cleric's Abduction," *Los Angeles Times* (January 10, 2007), p. A4.

Rescorla, Cyril Richard (Rick) (1939–2001)

One of the unsung participants on September 11, 2001, was Rick Rescorla. He was the vice president of security for Morgan Stanley in the South Tower of the World Trade Center. Part of his job was to conduct security drills for Morgan Stanley. After arriving at his office at 7:00 a.m. on the forty-fourth floor of the South Tower, he was present when American Airlines 11 crashed into the North Tower. Rescorla spent the remainder of his life helping evacuate Morgan Stanley's 2,600 employees from the South Tower.

Most of Rescorla's life was in the military. He was born in 1939 in Hayle, Cornwall, England, and raised by his grandparents. His grandfather worked at the local power plant, and his grandmother was a housewife. He had a normal childhood and soon became a competitive rugby player. He did well in school, but the family lacked the funds to send him to a university. As soon as he finished schooling at Penzance County Grammar School at age eighteen, he joined the British Army in 1957, serving in an intelligence unit. His tour of duty took him to Cyprus where he fought against the Greek terrorist group EOKA. Upon leaving the British Army, he found a job as a colonial policeman in Northern Rhodesia. It was here that Rescorla met Dan Hill, an American veteran of the U.S. Army. They became lifelong friends.

Rescorla decided to immigrate to the United States in 1963. He contacted his friend Dan Hill. Once in the states, he joined the U.S. Army. After attending Officer Candidate School (OCS) and obtaining a commission as a second lieutenant, he was sent to South Vietnam as a rifle platoon leader. He was assigned to Company B, 1st Battalion, 7th Cavalry, 1st Cavalry Division (Airmobile), where he saw combat in the Ia Drang Valley under then Lieutenant Colonel Harold G. Moore. Rescorla became a battlefield legend in his unit for his bravery, and he earned the nickname "Hard Core." When the going got toughest, Rescorla would start singing Cornish songs in a baritone voice, settling everybody down. He earned a Silver Star, Bronze Stars for Valor and Meritorious Service, and a Purple Heart for a wound.

After the Vietnam War, Rescorla returned to the states. He attended the University of Oklahoma on the GI Bill. In 1967 he became an American citizen. After graduating with bachelor's and master's degrees in literature, he went on to earn a law degree, also at the University of Oklahoma. Shortly after law school, in 1972, he married. Rescorla briefly taught criminal justice at the University of South Carolina Law School. He also remained first in the Oklahoma National Guard and then in the Army Reserve, from which he retired as a colonel in 1989. Next, he turned to corporate security. His first corporate security job was with Continental Illinois National Bank and Trust Company in Chicago. He then moved to New York City to take a job with Dean Witter at the World Trade Center. After Dean Witter merged with Morgan Stanley, Rescorla was promoted to executive vice president in charge of security.

Rescorla was always concerned about the lack of security at the World Trade Center complex. After studying the security situation at the World Trade Center, Rescorla made a series of recommendations to tighten security, but these recommendations were ignored. He and fellow consultant Dan Hill were concerned about the underground garage entrances, but their warning was ignored. They proved to be right when the 1993 World Trade Center bombing took place. Rescorla believed that other terrorists would target the World Trade Center complex as well. He even

> **Complex Personality of Rick Rescorla**
>
> Rescorla was also a passionate and complex man, a writer and a lawyer, as well as a blood-streaked warrior and six-figure security expert. At his home in suburban Morristown, N.J., he carved wooden ducks, frequented craft fairs, took playwriting classes. He wrote romantic poetry to his second wife, Susan, and renewed their vows after just one year of marriage. "He was a song-and-dance man," she says. He was a weeper, too. He liked to quote Shakespeare and Tennyson and Byron—and Elvis and Burt Lancaster. He was a film buff, history buff, pottery buff—"pretty much any kind of buff you can be," says his daughter, Kim. He liked to point his Lincoln Mark VIII in random directions and see where it would take him.
>
> Michael Grunwald, "On September 11, Rick Rescorla Died as He Lived: Like a Hero," *Washington Post* (October 28, 2001), p. F1.

envisaged that terrorists might hijack a cargo plane and load it with explosives, chemicals, or biological weapons before flying the aircraft into the World Trade Center complex or some other monumental building. It was even possible that the aircraft might have a small nuclear weapon. Based on these suspicions, Rescorla recommended that Morgan Stanley move someplace more secure and in a building only several stories high.

When nothing came of his recommendations, Rescorla began tightening security. He conducted fire and evacuation drills every other month. These drills were not popular. Rescorla also implemented a policy of the employees obeying his and his staff's announcements rather than those of the Port Authority.

Rescorla died on September 11, 2001, while evacuating Morgan Stanley people from the South Tower. Immediately after the first plane plowed into the North Tower, he began evacuating people from the South Tower. Rescorla ignored instructions for everybody to stay where they were. Rescorla believed that the North Tower might collapse. Soon afterward,

> **Response of Rick Rescorla When Told Not to Evacuate South Tower**
>
> The dumb sons of bitches told me not to evacuate. They said it's just Building One. I told them I'm getting my people the [expletive] out of here.
>
> Words of Dan Hill, quoted in Michael Grunwald, "On September 11, Rick Rescorla Died as He Lived: Like a Hero," *Washington Post* (October 28, 2001), p. F1.

another aircraft crashed into the South Tower. Rescorla made it plain to everyone that he would evacuate only when everybody else had been evacuated. He went back into the South Tower to search for stragglers. His actions meant that Morgan Stanley lost only six of its employees on September 11. While he was hunting for stragglers, the tower collapsed, killing him. His body has never been recovered. Rescorla had earlier told his wife that if she ever wanted a memorial to him, he would be okay with a plaque at a nearby bird sanctuary called the Raptors, to be placed on two American eagle cages. This plaque is his memorial. His wife had the following words engraved on them after his name and dates: "Just like the eagle, you have spread your wings, and soared into eternity."

See Also
World Trade Center, September 11; World Trade Center Bombing (1993)

Suggested Reading
Richard Bernstein, *Out of the Blue: The Story of September 11, 2001, from Jihad to Ground Zero* (New York: Times Books, 2002); Michael Grunwald, "Tower of Courage; On September 11, Rick Rescorla Died as He Lived: Like a Hero," *Washington Post* (October 28, 2001), p. F1; James B. Stewart, *Heart of a Soldier: A Story of Love, Heroism, and September 11th* (New York: Simon & Schuster, 2002); Jonathan Yardley, "A Hero's Tale," *Washington Post* (September 8, 2002), p. T2.

Ressam, Ahmed (1967–)

Ahmed Ressam became infamous as the al-Qaeda operative who was part of a plot to bomb the Los Angeles International Airport on January 1, 2000. For this reason Ressam earned the name as the "Millennium Bomber." Although this attempt failed, it was an indicator that al-Qaeda was actively plotting against the United States.

Ressam had a difficult childhood. He was born on May 19, 1967, in the town of Bou Ismail, Algeria. His father was a veteran of the Algerian War of Independence from France, and he worked as a government chauffeur. Ressam was the eldest of seven children. He was an active child and a good student. At age sixteen, however, a long-festering ulcer led him to have medical treatment and an operation in Paris. During this time, Ressam fell behind on his schoolwork, and even after repeating a year of school, he failed his final exam. This failure meant that he was ineligible to attend a university. Ressam applied for jobs with the Algerian police and security forces, but he was turned down. Unable to find meaningful employment, Ressam began working in a small café that his father had opened. In the meantime, he lived a secular life, drinking wine, smoking hashish, and dating girls. Political conditions in Algeria deteriorated in the early 1990s with open warfare between the military-controlled government and the radical Islamist Islamic Front for Salvation. Ressam decided that there was no future in Algeria, so he left for France.

Ressam arrived in Marseilles, France, on September 5, 1992, and his thirty-day visa soon expired. After obtaining a false French passport under the name Nasser Ressam, he traveled to Corsica where he worked at odd jobs, mostly picking grapes and oranges. On November 8, 1993, French authorities arrested him in Ajaccio, Corsica, and charged him with immigration violations. Facing a March 1994 hearing and probable deportation to Algeria, Ressam fled to Canada.

Ressam arrived in Montreal, Canada, on February 20, 1994. An immigration agent spotted the false passport and detained him. Ressam claimed political asylum to avoid deportation to Algeria. His insisted that the Algerian police had arrested him for selling firearms to a terrorist and had tortured him. Ressam was released on bond and told to have a lawyer represent him at a March 28, 1994, hearing. In the meantime, Ressam lived off welfare from the Canadian government. Even after missing the March court date, Ressam was able to remain in Canada. Ressam began attending the Assuna Annabawiyah Mosque, where he ran into young men engaged in small-time criminal activity. To supplement his income, Ressam turned to small-scale crime. He was arrested once for shoplifting and then for pick-pocketing, but in both instances he received only fines and probation. His stealing of identifications and passports led him to an al-Qaeda operative, Fateh Kemal, who bought them from Ressam. Kemal used the proceeds from these crimes to support al-Qaeda's operations both in Canada and in the Middle East.

In 1996 an al-Qaeda leader in Canada recruited Ressam for training as an al-Qaeda operative. Ressam had made many contacts among Algerians in Canada. It was noted by Hal Bernton that these were disaffected young men who spent their time "playing soccer, smoking cigarettes, and decrying the corrupt culture of their new country while simultaneously exploiting its generous immigration and welfare laws." Ressam developed a working relationship with members of the Algerian terrorist group Armed Islamic Group (GIA), and this group also had ties with al-Qaeda. Abderraouf Hannachi recruited Ressam to train at an al-Qaeda training camp in Afghanistan. On March 17, 1998, Ressam traveled to Peshawar, Pakistan, where he met Abu Zubaydah, the head of al-Qaeda's training program. After three weeks in Peshawar, Ressam headed to the Khalden training camp in Afghanistan. There he met Zacarias Moussaoui. Ressam and about thirty Algeri-ans were placed under the command of Abu Doha, an Algerian who lived in Lon-don. After a stay at the Darunta Training Camp for learning bomb construction, Ressam returned to Canada after eleven months in Afghanistan. His travel back to Canada took him through the Los Angeles International Airport. Ressam took the time to scout out the best places to plant a large bomb. He also returned to Mon-treal with $12,000, a bomb-making manual, and a supply of hexamine, a booster material for explosives.

Ressam's return to Canada had been easy, but the other members of his cell were detained elsewhere. These other members were to be the leaders of the cell, and their absence meant Ressam had to take a leadership role. He began to recruit others into his cell. Those recruited were Abdelmajid Dahoumane, Mohktar Haouari, and Abdelghani Meskini, but none of them had received any al-Qaeda training. Using a stolen Royal Bank Visa card, Ressam and his cell began planning to build a bomb. His target was the Los Angeles International Airport, and the decision was made to place the bomb near a crowded security checkpoint for max-imum casualties. In November 1999 the cell began the actual construction of the bomb in Vancouver, British Columbia. After the bomb was built, the decision was made that only Ressam would transport the bomb because it was thought that cus-toms officers would be more reluctant to pull over a lone driver.

Ressam started transporting the bomb on December 14, 1999. He took the M.V. Coho Ferry from Victoria, British Columbia, to Port Angeles, Washington. Customs inspector Diana Dean became suspicious about how Ressam was behav-ing. A close inspection found ingredients for a bomb in the spare-tire compart-ment. Ressam made a break for it but was soon captured. For a while, the custom agents had no idea that the materials they had found were intended for a highly sensitive bomb.

What Ressam did not know was that he and his cell had been under investiga-tion by the Canadian Security and Intelligence Service (CSIS) since 1996. CSIS agents knew of his connections to the Algerian terrorist group Armed Islamic Group (GIA) and later al-Qaeda. Their surveillance of Ressam and his cell led these agents to conclude that they were relatively harmless. Even when a French terrorist expert, Jean-Louis Bruguiere, insisted that Canadian authorities arrest Ressam and his compatriots, the CSIS was slow to respond. What the CSIS did not know was that Ressam had been building a bomb to use in the United States.

After his arrest, Ressam cooperated with American authorities to reduce his prison sentence. In a four-week trial in the U.S. District Court in Los Angeles, Ressam was convicted on April 6, 2001, of conspiracy to commit an international terrorist act, explosives smuggling, and lying to customs officials among the nine counts with which he was charged. With the prospects of a prison sentence of 130 years, Ressam decided to cooperate for a reduced sentence. His information was used in the briefing paper titled "Bin Laden Determined to Strike in the U.S.," which President George W. Bush received on August 6, 2001. He also gave valuable information about al-Qaeda and some of its operatives. Ressam began to have doubts about cooperating in 2004 and stopped communicating with authorities. On July 27, 2005, U.S. District Judge John Coughenour sentenced Ressam to twenty-two years in prison. The U.S. prosecutor appealed the sentence as too lenient, and the Ninth U.S. Circuit Court of Appeals panel ruled in January 2007 against one of the nine felony convictions of Ahmed Ressam. This was the count involving the use of false documents while transporting explosives. Ressam's final sentence is still in adjudication.

Joel Cohen (right) of the Department of Homeland Security stands next to a giant monitor displaying Ahmed Ressam (left) at the Los Angeles Joint Regional Intelligence Center in Norwalk, California, in 2006. Ressam was convicted of trying to mount a bombing of Los Angeles International Airport in California to coincide with the millennium celebrations held in 2000. (AP IMAGES/Nick Ut.)

See Also
Millennium Plots; Moussaoui, Zacarias; al-Qaeda; Zubaydah, Abu

Suggested Reading
Hal Bernton et al., "Chapter 2: The Fountainhead," *Seattle Times* (June 23, 2002), p. A14; Hal Bernton et al., "Chapter 4: Sneaking In," *Seattle Times* (June 24, 2002), p. A5; Hal Bernton et al., "Chapter 7: Joining Jihad," *Seattle Times* (June 27, 2002), p. A8; Hal Bernton et al., "Chapter 8: Going to Camp," *Seattle Times* (June 28, 2002), p. A12; Hal Bernton et al., "Chapter 10: The Mission," *Seattle Times* (June 30, 2002), p. A10; Hal Bernton et al., "Chapter 11: The Ticking Bomb," *Seattle Times* (July 1, 2002), p. A6; Hal Bernton et al., "Chapter 12: The Crossing," *Seattle Times* (July 2, 2002), p. A6; Ian Mulgrew, "Ressam Gets 22 Years in Prison," *Gazette* [Montreal] (July 28, 2005), p. A1; Marc Sageman, *Understanding Terror Networks* (Philadelphia: University of Pennsylvania Press, 2004); Michelle Shephard, "Dossier Reveals Secrets of Forming Al Qaeda Cell," *Toronto Star* (April 25, 2005), p. A12; Paul Shukovsky, "Terrorist Ahmed Ressam Is Sentenced but U.S. Judge Lashes Out at Bush Policies on Suspects," *Seattle Post-Intelligencer* (July 28, 2005), p. A1.

Rowley, Coleen (1954–)

Coleen Rowley is the FBI agent from the Minneapolis field office who clashed with FBI headquarters over the handling of Zacarias Moussaoui's case. She was the principal legal advisor to the Minneapolis field office. She has been outspoken in her belief that the mishandling of the Moussaoui case by FBI headquarters contributed to the success of the terrorists on September 11.

Rowley spent twenty-four years in the FBI. She was born December 20, 1954, and raised in a small town in northeast Iowa. After high school, she attended Wartburg College in Waverly, Iowa. She graduated summa cum laude in 1977 with a degree in French. Her next decision was to enter the College of Law at the University of Iowa, from which she received a JD in 1980. Shortly thereafter, Rowley passed the Iowa bar exam. Her career choice was to become a FBI agent. After passing through the training at Quantico, Rowley was appointed a special agent with the FBI in January 1981. Her first assignment was in the Omaha, Nebraska, field office, but she soon was sent to the Jackson, Mississippi, field office. In 1984 Rowley was assigned to the New York field office, where she spent six years and specialized in organized crime. Because of her expertise in French, she received an assignment with the U.S. embassy in Paris, France, and later at the consulate in Montreal, Canada. Rowley received a promotion and an assignment to the Minneapolis field office as the chief legal adviser in 1990.

Rowley's chief claim to fame was her attack on FBI headquarters for the mishandling of the Moussaoui case. Special agent Harry Samit received a communication from personnel at the Eagan flight school that they believed Moussaoui might be attending their school to train for a terrorist attack. Moussaoui was arrested on a visa problem, but the agents at the Minneapolis office wanted a warrant to gain access to more information. Counterterrorism supervisors David Frasca and Michael Maltbie rejected the warrant requests. Bureau lawyers then turned down the Foreign Intelligence Surveillance Act (FISA) warrant request. Nothing was done, despite the growing frustration of the special agents at the Minneapolis field office, until after September 11. Rowley's frustration came to a head.

Rowley reacted negatively to the statement by the director of the FBI that an investigation of Moussaoui would not have prevented September 11. Her

Rowley's Response to Not Receiving Information about the Phoenix Memo

Although I agree it's very doubtful that the full scope of the tragedy could have been prevented, it's at least possible we could have gotten lucky and uncovered one or two more of the terrorists in flight training prior to Sept. 11, just as Moussaoui was discovered, after making contact with his flight instructors.

Quoted in Dan Eggen, "Agent Claims FBI Supervisor Thwarted Probe," *Washington Post* (May 27, 2002), p. A1.

response was a thirteen-page letter that she sent to Mueller on May 21, 2002, in which she outlined the failures of FBI leadership on the Moussaoui case. Rowley accused these FBI leaders of effectively "deliberately sabotaging" the Moussaoui investigation. She indicated that certain facts had been "omitted, downplayed, glossed over, and/or mischaracterized in an effort to avoid or minimize personal and/or institutional embarrassment on the part of the FBI and/or even perhaps for improper political reasons." Rowley criticized FBI headquarters of careerism, and she was indignant that those blocking the Moussaoui case and other terrorist cases were being promoted. Because Rowley knew that this letter

FBI Agent Coleen Rowley of the Minneapolis FBI field office testifies before the Senate Judiciary Committee in 2002 at the Capitol in Washington. (AP IMAGES/Joe Marquette.)

was dynamite, she asked for whistle-blower protection against retaliation. At first Mueller kept the letter secret, but word got out. Rowley became an overnight sensation.

Rowley received an invitation to testify before the Senate Judiciary Committee in June 2002. The Moussaoui case was off-limits, but she talked about the weaknesses of the FBI organization. She was critical that it took eight layers of bureaucracy before reaching the director. Another aspect of the FBI found lacking was its inadequate computer system. Despite assurances that there would be no retaliation from Mueller, Rowley knew that her FBI career was at an end. She retired from the FBI in 2004 after twenty-four years of service.

Rowley decided to run for political office in Minnesota. Her residence was in Apple Valley, Minnesota. She opted to run against incumbent representative John Kline for the Second Congressional District of Minnesota seat in the U.S. House of Representative in the November 2006 election. Rowley ran on an anti–Iraq War platform. Despite her popularity, she lost to Kline in the election.

See Also
Federal Bureau of Investigation; Moussaoui, Zacarias; Samit, Harry

See Document
Document #30

Suggested Reading
Dan Eggen, "Agent Claims FBI Supervisor Thwarted Probe," *Washington Post* (May 27, 2002), p. A1; Greg Gordon, "Rowley Explains Criticisms," *Star Tribune* [Minneapolis] (June 7, 2002), p. 1A; Susan Milligan, "FBI Whistle-Blower," *The Boston Globe* (June 7, 2002), p. A33; Richard Gid Powers, *Broken: The Troubled Past and Uncertain Future of the FBI* (New York: Free Press, 2004); Robert Russo, "FBI Likened to Little Shop of Horrors," *Gazette* [Montreal] (June 7, 2002), p. B1.

S

Samit, Harry

Harry Samit is an FBI agent who attempted to warn the FBI and other U.S. agencies about the terrorist threat of Zacarias Moussaoui's pilot training. He had served as a U.S. Navy naval aviator and as a naval intelligence officer before joining the FBI. The FBI assigned him to the FBI field office in Minneapolis, Minnesota. After joining the FBI, he earned his small aircraft pilot license. Samit had been in the FBI for only about two years in the summer of 2001, but he was assigned to Squad 5 in the Joint Terrorism Task Force (JTTF) to investigate terrorism. It was at this time that Samit received a tip about the erratic behavior of a Middle Eastern student at the Pam Am International Flight Academy in Eagan, Minnesota, near Minneapolis.

Samit conducted an investigation with the assistance of an INS agent attached to the JTTF. They ended up arresting Moussaoui on a visa violation. Clancy Provost, a certified flight instructor at the Pan-Am International Flight Academy, had become suspicious about what was motivating Moussaoui to fly a jumbo jet— in particular, Moussaoui's inquiries about cockpit doors and damage that a fully loaded Boeing 747 could inflict in a crash. It was also noted that Moussaoui was more interested in flying the aircraft than in takeoffs and landings. In addition, the Pan Am International Flight Academy catered to advanced pilots working for commercial airlines flying Boeing 747, Boeing 757, and Boeing 767, and Moussaoui had limited flying time and no small aircraft license.

Samit arrested Moussaoui on August 16, 2001, but his attempts to obtain a criminal search warrant and then a FISA court warrant were denied by FBI headquarters. FBI headquarters opposed a criminal warrant on the grounds that it might hinder a FISA court warrant. Samit's immediate supervisor, Greg Jones, tried to help him, but without success. Samit sent a twenty-six-page memo on August 20, 2001, citing that Moussaoui had been training on Boeing 747 flight simulators and had bought a pair of small knives, leading him to believe that Moussaoui was a terrorist bent on hijacking an airliner. This document arrived at FBI headquarters, but it never made it up the FBI's chain of command. The vital information linking Moussaoui to the Chechen rebels and their connection with al-Qaeda in the FISA application was removed by the FBI's deputy counsel, thus killing the application. The head of the CIA, George Tenet, did receive a briefing based on FBI information about Islamic fundamentalists learning to fly, but not about Moussaoui. Samit also sent an e-mail to the FBI's bin Laden unit, but he did not receive a response before September 11, 2001.

Becoming frustrated by the FBI, Samit tried to notify the FAA by memo of the possible threat of an attempt to hijack an airliner. Again FBI headquarters censored the memo. Still determined to communicate his suspicions, Samit talked with a Minneapolis FAA official, but nothing came of the contact. Much as others in the Minneapolis office, Samit became increasingly bitter, but he refused to attack the FBI directly as his colleague Colleen Rowley did.

Samit even informed the CIA's Counterterrorism Center about the Moussaoui case. The CIA reacted with enthusiasm about linking Moussaoui with other intelligence information. FBI headquarters, however, reacted negatively to the CIA's receiving this information. Samit was rebuked for making this contact.

> ### Information about Moussaoui
>
> Special Agent Harry Samit, under cross-examination as Moussaoui's death-penalty trial . . . acknowledged that French intelligence advised the FBI 12 days before the attacks that Moussaoui was "very dangerous." The partially declassified French cable of Aug. 30, 2001, also said Moussaoui had been indoctrinated by Islamic extremists and had been in Afghanistan. But despite those red flags, Samit said, a request for a special national security warrant to search Moussaoui's belongings was—like earlier ones—shot down by headquarters supervisor Michael Maltbie and his boss, David Frasca. He said Maltbie had voiced concerns that an inadequately documented warrant request would hurt his career. Samit said headquarters went so far as to delete from one warrant request information from French intelligence that linked the leader of a Chechen rebel group with whom Moussaoui had associated to al-Qaida leader Osama bin Laden. Headquarters then said Minneapolis agents had failed to tie Moussaoui to an international terror group.
>
> Greg Gordon, "Moussaoui Alerts Ignored, Agent Says," *San Francisco Bee* (March 21, 2006), p. A1.

Orders came down from FBI headquarters that the Minneapolis field office could contact others only through headquarters.

Samit did go along with the scheme to deport Moussaoui to France where French intelligence would then search his belongings and communicate their findings back to the FBI. Unfortunately, this plan was to be implemented on September 10, 2001. This scheme meant that news of the search would arrive back to the FBI sometime late on September 11 or September 12. Events on September 11 ended this initiative. After September 11, there was no problem obtaining a criminal warrant for Samit. The search found some incriminating evidence, and the most important was the telephone number of Ramzi bin al-Shibh, one of the leaders of the Hamburg Cell.

In his testimony at the Moussaoui trial in 2006, Samit gave his version of the Moussaoui case. He also blasted his superiors at FBI headquarters. He went so far as to accuse them of "criminal negligence, obstruction, and careerism."

See Also
Bin al-Shibh, Ramzi; Federal Bureau of Investigation (FBI); Moussaoui, Zacarias; Rowley, Coleen; Tenet, George

See Documents
Document #30; Document #40

Suggested Reading
Greg Gordon, "Terror Timeline Connects the Dots," *Star Tribune* [Minneapolis] (June 4, 2006), p. 16A; Neil A. Lewis, "F.B.I. Agent Testifies Superiors Didn't Pursue Moussaoui Case," *New York Times* (March 21, 2006), p. A12; Jerry Markon and Timothy Dwyer, "FBI Was Warned about Moussaoui," *Washington Post* (March 21, 2006), p. A1; Richard Gid Powers, *Broken: The Troubled Past and Uncertain Future of the FBI* (New York: Free Press, 2004); Richard A. Serrano, "Agent Faults FBI on 9/11," *Los Angeles Times* (March 21, 2006), p. A1; Richard A. Serrano, "9/11 Trial Reveals Troubles Then, and Ahead," *Los Angeles Times* (March 26, 2006), p. A5.

Saracini, Victor J. (1950–2001)

Victor Saracini was the captain of the United Airlines Flight 175 that hijackers seized on September 11, 2001, and flew into the South Tower of the World Trade Center. He had worked as an airline pilot for United Airlines for sixteen years at the time of his death. At the time of the crash, Saracini was either dead or incapacitated.

Saracini made a success of himself after a slow start. He was born on August 29, 1950, and raised in Atlantic City, New Jersey. After dropping out of high school, Saracini worked a variety of jobs before applying to study at the New Mexico Institute of Mining and Technology. He graduated in 1975 with a bachelor of general studies degree. His next career move was attending the Naval Aviation Officer Candidate School. Saracini successfully completed naval aviation training and became a naval pilot. He was commissioned as an ensign in December 1975. He served on S-3A anti-submarine warfare aircraft aboard the aircraft carrier U.S.S. Saratoga. His active-duty service ended in 1980, but he remained in the Naval Reserve at Naval Air Station Willow Grove, Pennsylvania, until 1985. Saracini attained the rank of lieutenant and served as a crewmember on a Lockheed P-3 Orion aircraft. After leaving the navy, Saracini worked as a flight instructor at Louisiana Tech University during the years 1980–82. It was at Louisiana Tech that he met and later married his wife—Ellen Saracini. He worked at flying corporate and commercial aircraft until he was able to find a pilot job with United Airlines in 1985. Saracini and his wife had two daughters: Kirsten and Brielle.

Saracini had no expectation of trouble on September 11, 2001, when his United Airlines Flight 175 left Logan International Airport in Boston, Massachusetts, for Los Angeles International Airport. His first hint of trouble was when the air traffic controllers asked him if he could see American Airlines Flight 11. Saracini acknowledged that he could see that aircraft, and he was warned to maintain distance from that aircraft. Sometime around 8:47 a.m., the al-Qaeda hijack team used knives and mace to subdue the pilots and crew. It has been surmised that at this time the hijackers killed Saracini and his copilot, Michael Horrocks. The new pilot was Marwan al-Shehhi, and he turned the aircraft around, directing it toward the New York City area. After lulling the passengers into thinking that the plane would land someplace safely and use them as hostages in negotiations, al-Shehhi crashed the aircraft into the South Tower of the World Trade Center complex. Everyone in the aircraft was instantly killed.

Saracini has been honored in various ways. Louisiana Tech has established a fellowship, the Victor J. Saracini Flight Scholarship. The Veterans Administration named an outpatient clinic north of Philadelphia after him—the Victor J. Saracini

Department of Veterans Affairs Outpatient Clinic. His wife has worked to establish a memorial—Garden of Reflection—at Memorial Park on Woodside Road in Lower Makefield, Pennsylvania. Finally, he was a dedicated member of the Air Line Pilots Association (ALPA), and this union has honored him.

See Also
United Airlines Flight 175

Suggested Reading
Chris English, "Saracini's Heart, Soul in Sept. 11 Memorial," *Bucks County Courier Times* [Pennsylvania] (May 29, 2005), p. 1.

Scheuer, Michael (1952?–)

Michael Scheuer was the head of the CIA's Counterterrorism Center's Alec Station during the early stages of the war between Osama bin Laden and the United States. He believed from the first that bin Laden constituted a clear and present danger to the United States, but he had difficulty persuading the leadership of the CIA and the Clinton administration about the threat. His strident attacks on those in the CIA and the Clinton administration who prevented the Alec Station from assassinating bin Laden led to his removal as head of the Alec Station in 1999, but he remained vocal on the issue. Since his resignation from the CIA in 2004, he has maintained a high profile by writing two books that castigate those who did not understand the threat of bin Laden and al-Qaeda.

Little is known about Scheuer's personal background. He was born sometime around 1952, but there is little information about where or about the details of his upbringing. As with most CIA agents, personal data are hard to come by. What is known is that Scheuer attended Canisius College in Buffalo, New York, graduating in 1974. He then obtained a master's degree from Niagara University in 1976. His final educational degree was a PhD from the University of Manitoba in 1986. Based on the fact that he served twenty-two years in the CIA and retired in 2004, Scheuer must have joined the CIA in 1982. Scheuer was never a field officer, but he worked as an analyst. Evidently he was good at analysis because in 1996 he was assigned to head the Osama bin Laden Unit in the Counterterrorism Center. This unit soon earned the name Alec Station after Scheuer's adopted son Alec.

Scheuer directed all of the assets of the Alec Station to find ways to neutralize bin Laden. In his three years as head of this unit, he became extremely frustrated in the failure of the Clinton administration to carry out operations to eliminate bin Laden as a threat. Scheuer made plain that collateral damage was acceptable to him if the operation captured or killed bin Laden. The Clinton administration, however, was leery of collateral damage. Another of Scheuer's assignments was drafting the provisions of the rendition process that was later authorized by President Clinton.

Scheuer has a pugnacious personality, and this led to personality conflicts with key people in government circles. He also had difficulty sharing information with the FBI. A personality conflict developed between him and John O'Neill, the counterterrorism expert with the FBI. O'Neill was just as aggressive as Scheuer, and they clashed. Both Scheuer and O'Neill kept material secret from the other agency. Scheuer's behavior became so aggressive that he was relieved as head of Alec Station in 1999. He stayed on in the CIA, and in September 2001 the CIA appointed him special advisor to the chief of Alec Station. He retained his position until he resigned from the CIA on November 12, 2004.

Since his retirement from the CIA, Scheuer has maintained a high profile as a critic of both the Clinton and Bush administrations' counterterrorism efforts. While still with the CIA, he wrote a book that gave the view of the United States from bin Laden's perspective titled *Through Our Enemies' Eyes: Osama bin Laden, Radical Islam, and the Future of the United States* (2003). The outline of this book had originally been written as an unclassified manual for counterterrorism officers, but Scheuer expanded it and received approval of the CIA to publish it. This book created so much controversy that the CIA has amended its policy, now prohibiting CIA agents from writing books while still employed. After his resignation from the CIA, Scheuer wrote another book, *Imperial Hubris: Why the West Is Losing the War on Terror* (2004). A lifelong Republican, Scheuer has been especially critical of President Clinton for not authorizing operations to neutralize bin Laden. He also attacked the American intelligence community for its failures of leadership. Finally, he was critical of the 9/11 Commission because of its failure to implicate and directly punish officials in the intelligence community who were negligent.

Scheuer has been actively spreading his views in the media. Besides drawing attention to intelligence failures before September 11, 2001, he has been critical of President Bush and his Iraq policies. It is Scheuer's contention that the American invasion and occupation of Iraq has not made the United States safer but rather has emboldened bin Laden, al-Qaeda groups, and other Muslim extremists. Scheuer laments that the Iraq war ended the hunt for bin Laden because he still constitutes a real threat. Although a frequent critic of the CIA, he also sometimes defends it from what he considers baseless charges.

Because elements in the CIA did not go along with the justification for the Iraq invasion, they have been punished. Alec Station's staff was reduced from twenty-five to only twelve. Most of the more experienced analysts were transferred to other positions. Then, in July 2006, the CIA shut down Alec Station with the explanation that the Islamist jihadist movement had diversified. Scheuer reacted to this closing by stating that this shutdown squandered ten years of expertise in the war on terror.

Scheuer's Views on the War on Terror

We are in danger of losing the war on terror. . . . The bin Laden unit was dismantled this summer, which Scheuer describes as an "appalling but not surprising example" of the CIA's distraction from its mission in Afghanistan and from the focus on snaring bin Laden. . . . Scheuer contends that important intelligence assets specifically spy planes, satellite imagery and intelligence analysts have been shifted away from Afghanistan to Iraq. He also emphasizes that the US military's reluctance to put troops on the ground in Afghanistan has plagued its efforts. . . . And he derides Washington's reliance on a conventional military response to a shadowy transnational enemy that will not be defeated by conventional means. "Americans have every right to ask how it is possible that we haven't killed or captured bin Laden. They should be questioning why we have almost 10 times the number of troops in Iraq. . . . I can understand if people are mad. They should be."

Quoted in Charles M. Sennott, "An Evasive Quarry, a Changing Mission," *Boston Globe* (September 12, 2006), p. A1.

Mike Scheuer, a twenty-two-year CIA veteran, and head of the CIA's Osama bin Laden unit until 1999, talks to the AP about the challenges of conducting the war against al-Qaeda, in an interview from his home in Falls Church, Virginia, in 2004. (AP IMAGES/J. Scott Applewhite.)

Scheuer has frequent opportunities to express his views. He has been employed as a news analyst for CBS News, commenting on counterterrorism issues. His affiliation with the Jamestown Foundation as its terrorism analyst has provided him with another forum. Much of his work at the Jamestown Foundation has been with its online publication *Global Terrorism Analysis*. Scheuer has also been active at scholarly conferences speaking on terrorism.

See Also
Alec Station; Bin Laden, Osama; Bush Administration; Central Intelligence Agency; Clinton Administration

Suggested Reading
Suzanne Goldenberg, "Agents Who Led Bin Laden Hunt Criticises CIA," *Guardian* [London] (July 8, 2006), p. 14; Greg Gordon, "Ex-CIA Official: Bush Plays into al-Qaeda's Hands," *Sacramento Bee* (November 20, 2004), p. A12; Eric Lichtblau, "Officer Denounces Agency and Sept. 11 Report," *New York Times* (August 17, 2004), p. A14; Dana Priest, "Former Chief of CIA's Bin Laden Unit Leaves," *Washington Post* (November 12, 2004), p. A4; Michael Scheuer, "A Fine Rendition," *New York Times* (March 11, 2005), p. A23; Lawrence Wright, *The Looming Tower: Al-Qaeda and the Road to 9/11* (New York: Knopf, 2006).

Scholars for 9/11 Truth
The Scholars for 9/11 Truth is an organization of academics and professionals who question the U.S. government's account of the events surrounding September 11, 2001. James H. Fetzer, a retired professor of philosophy from the University of

Minnesota at Duluth, and Steven E. Jones, a retired professor of physics from Brigham Young University, founded the Scholars for 9/11 Truth on December 15, 2005. Fetzer has remained as co-chair and webmaster of the group, but Jones left the group in December 2006. The original size of the group was around three hundred members, of which seventy-six were academics. Sixty-nine of them were in the humanities and social sciences. There were four physicists and three engineers. Critics have questioned the academic credentials of some of the members. Membership has fluctuated because there have been disagreements among members.

Although members hold various viewpoints, most members subscribe to the thesis that a coterie within the U.S. government planned and executed the attacks on September 11, 2001. They point out inconsistencies in the government's treatment. The most common belief is that the collapse of the World Trade Center complex is inconsistent with scientific facts unless controlled explosives were used. Many theorists propose thermal bombs were planted in the buildings. Witness accounts and the conclusion of such experts as firefighter Ray Downey are discounted. Downey was an expert on building collapses, and he predicted the collapse of the twin towers at the site shortly before losing his life there.

Leaders of the Scholars for 9/11 Truth have been active in disseminating their views, but divergent views have caused internal strains. Several members left the group because of the leadership's refusal to accept their arguments that no aircraft hit the World Trade Center complex. Even pictures showing the two aircraft hitting first the North Tower and then the South Tower combined with numerous eyewitness testimonies were not enough for them.

The most serious dissident was Steven E. Jones, a physicist at Brigham Young University before retirement. His argument was that the World Trade Center complex was destroyed by controlled demolitions on September 11. He stated that the physics did not work out and that the buildings could not collapse the way they did unless bombs were used. His controversial remarks and his activities as one of the founders and the co-chair of the Scholars for 9/11 Truth led Brigham Young University to place him on paid leave. He retired from the university on October 20, 2006. Jones began having doubts about Fetzer's claim about the U.S. government's possible use of mini-nukes, or high-energy weapons, against the World Trade Center. He resigned from the Scholars for 9/11 Truth on December 5, 2006. Shortly afterward, Jones started a new organization called Scholars for 9/11 Truth and Justice.

Now there are two organizations competing for the same audience. Of the two, the original group, still led by Fetzer, is more open to extreme theories about September 11. Jones's group has fewer adherents, but he is more careful about extreme claims. He also calls for more scientific research. Both organizations remain high-profile adherents to the idea of U.S. government misconduct on September 11. The problem for both groups is that recognized professionals in the scientific world have rejected their claims, and the groups lack the evidence necessary to overcome these objections.

See Also
Conspiracy Theories; Fetzer, James H.; Jones, Steven E.

Suggested Reading
Andrew Cline, "A Conspiracy against Us All," *National Review* (September 11, 2006), p. 1; Jonathan Curiel, "The Conspiracy to Rewrite 9/11; Conspiracy Theorists Insist the U.S.

Government, Not Terrorists, Staged the Devastating Attacks," *San Francisco Chronicle* (September 3, 2006), p. E1; John Gravois, "A Theory That Just Won't Die: Across America, a Small But Fanatical Cadre of Conspiracy-Minded Academics Believe the U.S. Government Engineered 9/11," *National Post* [Canada] (July 28, 2006), p. A14; Bob von Steinberg, "Some Look Back to 9/11 and See a U.S. Conspiracy," *Star Tribune* [Minneapolis] (September 6, 2006), p. 1A.

Senate Select Committee on Intelligence and the House Permanent Select Committee on Intelligence Joint Inquiry into the Terrorist Attacks of September 11

The Select Committee on Intelligence and the House Permanent Select Committee on Intelligence Joint Inquiry into the Terrorist Attacks of September 11 was the first attempt to study intelligence failures leading up to September 11. Robert Graham, chair of the Senate Select Committee on Intelligence, and Porter Goss, chair of the House Permanent Select Committee on Intelligence, agreed on the need for a joint committee of the two houses to study intelligence gathering before September 11. For the inquiry to be successful, they agreed that it had to be bipartisan, and it would need to have the full support of the congressional leadership and the White House. Despite assurances of support, the committee ran into opposition from the CIA, the FBI, and the White House. There was also little enthusiasm in Congress; it took Congress five months to announce the inquiry and another four months before the committee began to function.

The Joint Inquiry committee finally received its mandate in early 2002, and the co-chairmen Robert Graham and Porter Goss announced its beginning on February 14, 2002. It had a ten-month deadline to accomplish its task of evaluating the intelligence record before September 11, 2001. In the first months, the investigators for the Joint Inquiry began to compile evidence. Hearings began in June 2002. Those hearings in June, July, and the first half of September were held in closed sessions. In the second half of September, there were open hearings. Hearings in October alternated between open and closed. A final report of the Joint Inquiry appeared on December 10, 2002, but only 24 of the more than 800 pages were released to the public.

Eleanor Hill, a lawyer and former Pentagon inspector general, was the staff director for the committee. Hill had not been the first choice of the committee, but its first choice, L. Britt Snider, had run into difficulty because of his friendship with George Tenet, the director of the CIA. Hill was recommended by Sam Nunn, a former Georgia senator, to Senator Richard Shelby (R-AL). She was a partner in the law firm King and Spalding when she was offered the job working with the Joint Inquiry committee.

Hill's job was to supervise the creation of a variety of staff reports that pointed out intelligence gathering deficiencies. Her crew had to comb through the 150,000 pages of documents from the CIA, and a like number of documents from the FBI. Most of the difficulty was in obtaining access to the documents in the first place. Members of the staff also conducted intensive interviews and attended briefings.

Hill reported to the Joint Inquiry committee on all aspects of the intelligence picture before September 11. Among her reports to the committee was one on the FBI's failure to react to the Phoenix Memo and the refusal of FBI headquarters to authorize a search warrant for Zacarias Moussaoui's possessions. She also reported that the intelligence community had received at least twelve reports of possible terrorist attacks before September 11 but that nothing had been done about them.

A controversy developed when there was a leak of closed-session testimony from General Hayden about the National Security Agency (NSA). The testimony was about the fact that the NSA had intercepted two al-Qaeda messages on September 10, 2001, indicating that something would happen on September 11, but these fragmentary messages were not translated until September 12, 2001. Despite the classified nature of this material, first the *Washington Times* and then the Cable News Network (CNN) learned of it and publicized it widely. Other newspapers also picked up the story. This leak led Vice President Dick Cheney to attack the Joint Inquiry committee as the source of the leak. Cheney reprimanded both Goss and Graham by telephone. This incident produced negative publicity for the committee and led Goss and Graham to invite the FBI to investigate the leak. Nothing came of the investigation, but it gave critics of the committee more ammunition. It also further clouded an already tense relationship between the inquiry and the Bush administration.

Cooperation from the CIA and the FBI was minimal. Only four CIA witness testified, including George Tenet. None of the key FBI agents appeared before the committee. Senator Shelby complained about the lack of cooperation.

The Bush administration had doubts about the Joint Inquiry committee from the beginning, but it was more than unhappy about the final report. It wanted the final report to be a validation of its position that there was no way September 11 could have been avoided, meaning that no one was responsible. As soon as the White House realized the Joint Inquiry committee did not subscribe to this view, all cooperation ceased.

Officials of the White House worked to block the release of the full report, wanting instead to classify parts of the material retroactively. Consequently, the issuing of the full report was delayed, and significant parts of it were classified as secret. Most notable of the blacked-out sections was the section on Saudi citizens on American soil on September 11. Even the 9/11 Commission had difficulty gaining access to the full report, but in the end the full report came out.

Republican Senator Richard C. Shelby's Complaint about Lack of Cooperation

We've been assured by Vice President Richard B. Cheney that the administration—that means all the agencies, the CIA, NSA, FBI—would cooperate with this joint investigation. They're not cooperating fully.

Quoted in Joyce Howard Price, "Shelby Says FBI Was 'Asleep or Inept, or Both'," *Washington Times* (May 19, 2002), p. A1.

In the final analysis the failure to obtain key documents made the thirty-seven-member Joint Inquiry committee unhappy. The staff had reviewed almost 500,000 pages of documents from intelligence agencies and other sources. Approximately 300 interviews had been conducted, and 600 people had briefed them about intelligence matters. There had been thirteen closed sessions and nine public hearings.

Once the classified report was deposited on December 20, 2002, the battle began on the classified parts of the report. The first agency to look at it was the CIA. The CIA classified whole sections of the report, including material that had already appeared in the media. This wholesale reclassification was too much for the Joint Inquiry committee's staff. In a meeting with representatives from the CIA, the FBI, and the NSA, the staff went over the report page by page, reclaiming much of the material. The final obstacle was the White House, and its representatives wanted large parts of the report classified. The most notable section blacked out by the White House consisted of twenty-seven pages that dealt with the Saudi government's help given to the September 11 conspirators. White House representatives wanted the changes to the report to be hidden, but the final unclassified version of the report has those areas shaded in black. On July 24, 2003, the final unclassified report appeared.

Although there were gaps in the report because of documents that were never produced, the Joint Inquiry committee did document the failures of U.S. intelligence agencies. Both the CIA and the FBI received special criticism. The staff did uncover new information— the Phoenix Memo, the Moussaoui debacle, warnings about possible use of aircraft as weapons, failures to monitor known al-Qaeda operatives, and lack of coordination between CIA and FBI, to name only a few. Its most important recommendation was for the creation of a cabinet-level position, Director of National Intelligence, to coordinate all American intelligence agencies and their activities.

> **Senator Richard C. Shelby's Comment on the Responsibility of the FBI for Intelligence Failures**
>
> Asked who he believes was responsible for failing to understand the clues received before September 11 attacks, Mr. Shelby said: "I believe it is the FBI that's the responsible party. And I believe the FBI has failed the American people in that regard nothing was done on the information in that Phoenix memo. The FBI was either asleep or inept or both."
>
> Joyce Howard Price, "Shelby Says FBI Was 'Asleep or Inept, or Both'," *Washington Times* (May 19, 2002), p. A1.

See Also
Central Intelligence Agency; Moussaoui, Zacarias; Phoenix Memo

See Documents
Document #26; Document #27; Document #28; Document #29; Document #30

Suggested Reading
Mike Allen, "Bush Seeks to Restrict Hill Probes of Sept. 11," *Washington Post* (January 30, 2002), p. A4; Bill Gertz, *Breakdown: The Failure of American Intelligence to Defeat Global Terror*, rev. ed. (New York: Plume Books, 2003); Eric Lichtblau, "Report Details F.B.I.'s Failure on 2 Hijackers," *New York Times* (June 10, 2005), p. A1; John Prados, "Slow-Walked and Stonewalled," *Bulletin of the Atomic Scientists* 59.2 (March/April 2003), pp. 28–37; Dana Priest, "FBI Leak Probe Irks Lawmakers," *Washington Post* (August 2, 2002), p. A1; James Risen, "White House Drags Its Feet on Testifying at 9/11 Panel," *New York Times* (September 13, 2002), p. A12.

Shehhi, Marwan Yousef Muhammed Rashid Lekrab al- (1978–2001)

Marwan al-Shehhi was one of the key figures in the suicide hijacking of the American aircrafts on September 11, 2001. While attending school in Hamburg, al-Shehhi attended the al-Quds Mosque and joined the Islamist extremists in the Hamburg Cell. His friendship with Mohamed Atta and their sharing of a commitment to Islamist religious views made it easy for al-Shehhi to become a member of the September 11 conspiracy. He was the hijackers' pilot for the United Airlines

Flight 175 that crashed into the South Tower of the World Trade Center complex on September 11, 2001.

Al-Shehhi was raised in a religious environment. He was born on May 9, 1978, and raised in Ras al-Khaimah in the United Arab Emirates (UAE). Ras al-Khaimah was one of the poorest and most conservative of the emirates. The family was a member of the Shooh Bedouin tribe. His father was the person who called people to pray at the mosques (muezzin) in Ras al-Khaimah. Good grades allowed him to attend the Emirates al-Ain University. After finishing his schooling, al-Shehhi entered the UAE Army. Soon after he entered the military and reached the rank of sergeant, the army awarded him a scholarship to further his education in Germany. His goal was to study marine engineering. The government of the UAE gave him a scholarship of $2,000 monthly with a yearly bonus of $5,000. He entered into a German-language preparatory course in Bonn, which he passed in 1996. Next he enrolled at the University of Bonn, but his father's death in 1997 caused him to fail his coursework when he took an unofficial leave to return to the UAE. Returning to Germany, al-Shehhi passed the next course in 1997. He was an average student with little ambition. One of his teachers called him "aimless and immature."

By the time al-Shehhi returned to Germany, he was becoming increasingly militant in his religious views. Unhappy with the environment in Bonn, he petitioned the UAE Army to allow him to transfer his studies to the Technical University of Hamburg-Harburg. The strict religious environment at the al-Quds Mosque satisfied his new religiosity. His friendship with Atta only increased this tendency.

Marwan al-Shehhi's Religious Conviction

Shehhi never voiced the slightest doubts about his beliefs. He never spoke about women as anything other than potential marriage partners, and never spoke to them at all, unless compelled. There was nothing the least bit secular in his background. As one of the few Gulf Arabs in the Harburg group, and the son of a religiously trained father, Shehhi had more formal Islamic education, and had lived a stricter version of Islam his entire life, than the others.

Terry McDermott, *Perfect Soldiers: The 9/11 Hijackers: Who They Were, Why They Did It* (New York: HarperCollins, 2005), pp. 54–55.

By this time al-Shehhi's relationship with Atta had solidified, with Atta as the leader and al-Shehhi as a faithful follower. They had different personalities, with al-Shehhi playing the role of the "joker" and Atta the serious strategist. Despite his easy-going style, al-Shehhi was the acknowledged expert on Islamic scripture. Together with Ramzi Bin al-Shibh, the three were the heart and soul of the Hamburg Cell. The friends constantly debated how they could make a contribution to the Muslim cause. At first, they wanted to fight on the side of the Chechen rebels in Chechnya. But an al-Qaeda recruiter convinced them that joining al-Qaeda would be a better alternative to fighting in Chechnya. Al-Shehhi traveled with his friends to Afghanistan to train at al-Qaeda training camps.

Al-Shehhi left for Afghanistan in the fall of 1998 for training at the al-Qaeda Khalden camp. While in Kandahar, he—along with Mohamed Atta and Ziad Jarrah—met and talked with Osama bin Laden. Al-Shehhi, Atta, and Jarrah were recruited at this conversation for a special future martyrdom mission. Once they accepted the mission, Mohammad Atef outlined the basic outlines of the September 11 plot.

Returning to Germany, al-Shehhi joined with Atta and Ramzi in working at a warehouse, packing crates of computers for shipping. Never excited about his education, al-Shehhi stopped going to class, and the school dropped him as a student in December 2000.

Al-Shehhi became number two man behind Atta in the September 11 plot. He arrived in the United States separately from Atta, but they kept in touch. They trained together in Florida. Although al-Shehhi was never a skilled pilot, he was able to pilot United Airlines Flight 175 into the South Tower on September 11, 2001.

See Also
American Airlines Flight 11: Atta, Mohamed el-Amir Awad el-Sayed; Hamburg Cell; Bin al-Shibh, Ramzi; World Trade Center.

See Document
Document #13

Suggested Reading
Jane Corbin, *Al-Qaeda: The Terror Network That Threatens the World* (New York: Thunder Mouth's Press, 2002); Terry McDermott, *Perfect Soldiers: The 9/11 Hijackers: Who They Were, Why They Did It* (New York: HarperCollins, 2005); Stefan Aust et al., *Inside 9-11: What Really Happened* (New York: St. Martin's Press, 2001).

Smith, Moira (1963–2001)

Moira Smith was the only woman police officer in the New York City Police Department (NYPD) to die at the World Trade Center complex on September 11, 2001. She had been a police officer for thirteen years. Her husband was also a police officer. She died assisting those escaping from the South Tower just before the building collapsed.

Smith came to police work after a short career as a travel agent. She was born on February 14, 1963, in Brooklyn, New York. Her maiden name was Reddy. Both parents were Irish immigrants. She was popular in school. After graduation, she worked as a travel agent. Smith loved traveling, and her job gave her opportunities to do so. Then she decided to join the NYPD.

Smith spent the rest of her life in the police department. After joining the department on July 11, 1988, her first assignment was working in the Transit Police Department. Smith was awarded the Distinguished Duty Medal for her efforts in rescuing people from a derailed subway train on August 28, 1991. Smith decided to transfer from the Transit Police Department to regular police work. Her assignment was with the Thirteenth Precinct. She assumed her duties in the precinct in March 1996.

Smith's personal life was as satisfying as her police career. It was at the Transit Police Department that she met and married her husband—fellow police officer James Smith. They were both avid sports fans. Their marriage began in May 1998, and their daughter Patricia was born in July 1999. In September 2001 her husband was assigned to the police academy.

Smith died on September 11 helping evacuate people from the South Tower of the World Trade Center complex. She was on duty at the Thirteenth Precinct when the news arrived about an aircraft crash at the World Trade Center complex. Her first action was to rush to the scene of the emergency. There Smith gathered a number of people and took them to safety at her precinct. Smith then returned to the World

A photo of New York Police Officer Moira Smith, who died in the World Trade Center on September 11, is taped under her engraved name at the National Law Enforcement Officers Memorial in Washington on April 29, 2002. The names of Smith and eleven other law enforcement officers who died in the 9/11 attack are engraved on the memorial. (AP IMAGES/Kenneth Lambert.)

Trade Center complex to help evacuate more people. A photographer from the New York *Daily News* snapped a picture of her leading an injured man to safety from the South Tower. She had returned to the South Tower to help others when the South Tower collapsed, killing her. Several hundred people credited her for saving their lives.

It was not until March that the searchers were able to recover Smith's body. Smith was one of seven bodies found near the South Tower by searchers on March 20, 2002. Despite the fact that it was 4:00 a.m. when her body was found, an honor guard of police wrapped her in a U.S. flag and escorted her body through the wind and rain to the morgue.

Smith has received several honors for her heroism. A hero's salute was given to her at a 2002 Valentine's Day Mass at St. Patrick's Cathedral. The NYPD's Emerald Society Pipes and Drums escorted the family on this occasion. In a December 2002 awards ceremony, Moira Smith was awarded the NYPD's highest award for bravery—the Medal of Honor. Since then, a street has been named after her, and a ferry bears her name.

See Also
New York City Police Department

See Document
Document #14

Suggested Reading
Austin Fenner and Greg Gittrich, "7 More Bodies Found at WTC Site," *Daily News* [New York] (March 21, 2001), p. 3; Marianne Garvey, Mark Stamey, and Clemente Lisi, "Police Pay Tribute to Finest Heroine," *New York Post* (March 24, 2002), p. 17; Susan Hagen and Mary Carouba, *Women at Ground Zero: Stories of Courage and Compassion* (New York: Alpha Books, 2002); Michele McPhee, "Hero Given Last Salute: She Was Mom, Wife & Cop," *Daily News* [New York] (February 15, 2002),

---

Comment on Moira Smith's Performance as a Police Officer

I was always impressed with the way she did her job. She wasn't careless, but she never hesitated. She liked being out there with people, and she enjoyed the excitement. She was a good cop, and she knew how to handle people. What Moira did on September 11—and this is true for all the officers—wasn't a one-time thing. That's who Moira was. That was what she did every day. She wasn't reckless, but she never backed down.

Comment by Smith's husband, Jim Smith, quoted in Susan Hagen and Mary Carouba, *Women at Ground Zero: Stories of Courage and Compassion* (New York: Alpha Books, 2002), p. 311.

p. 8; Michele McPhee, "In His Girl's Face the Image of Her Lost Mom," *Daily News* [New York] (September 8, 2002), p. 15.

Swift Project

Within weeks of the events of September 11, 2001, the Bush administration launched a secret program to trace the financial records of people suspected of having ties to al-Qaeda. This secret project has been called the Swift Project. It was named after the Brussels banking consortium, Society for Worldwide Interbank Financial Telecommunication (SWIFT). The SWIFT serves as a gatekeeper for electronic transactions between 7,800 international institutions, and it is owned by a cooperative with more than 2,200 organizations. Every major commercial bank, brokerage house, fund manager, and stock exchange used its services.

The Bush administration entrusted the CIA and the U.S. Treasury Department to set up and run the Swift Project. Legal justification for the implementation of this project was the president's emergency economic powers. American agents used computer programs to wade through huge amounts of sensitive data from the transactions of SWIFT. Treasury officials have maintained then and now that the Swift Project was exempt from American laws restricting government access to private financial records because the cooperative was classified as a messaging service, not a bank or financial institution. This allowed the U.S. government to track money from a Saudi bank account of a suspected terrorist to a source in the United States, or elsewhere in the world. Evidently it was information of this type that allowed American officials to locate and capture Riduan Isamuddin Hambali, the operations chief of the Indonesian terrorist group Gama'a Islamiyya, in Thailand.

News of the Swift Project became public in 2006. It became identified with the surveillance of American citizens by the U.S. government. Despite considerable negative publicity, the Bush administration has continued to use the Swift Project to track the financial records of organizations and people suspected of giving money to al-Qaeda.

See Also
Bush Administration; Central Intelligence Agency

Suggested Reading
Bryan Bender, "Terrorist Funds-Tracking No Secret, Some Say," *Boston Globe* (June 28, 2006), p. 1; Dan Bilefsky, "Bank Consortium Faces Outcry on Data Transfer," *International Herald Tribune* (June 29, 2006), p. 4; Eric Lichtblau and James Risen, "Bank Data Sifted in Secret by U.S. to Block Terror," *New York Times* (June 23, 2006), p. 1; Josh Meyer and Greg Miller, "U.S. Secretly Tracks Global Bank Data," *Los Angeles Times* (June 23, 2006), p. 1; Sheryl Gay Stolberg and Eric Lichtblau, "Cheney Assails Press on Report on Bank Data," *New York Times* (June 24, 2006), p. 1.

T

Taliban

The first casualty of the American reaction to the September 11, 2001, attacks was the Taliban regime in Afghanistan. Mohammed Omar had founded the Taliban in the spring of 1994, and he remained its head until the Northern Alliance, with the assistance of the United States, overthrew the Taliban regime in late 2001. It was Omar's alliance with Osama bin Laden and the sponsorship of al-Qaeda training camps that led to the overthrow of the Taliban.

Omar founded the Taliban in the spring of 1994 in reaction to the feuding among Afghan warlords. He was born in 1959 into a poor Pashtun family in the small village of Nodeh near Kandahar, Afghanistan. His father was a landless peasant belonging to the Pashtun Hotak tribe of the Ghilzia branch of the Pashtuns. His early death left Omar in the hands of relatives. Omar studied at an Islamic school in Kandahar, but he never graduated from it. This failure to graduate did not prevent him from opening a madrasa (religious school) in Singhesar, a village near Kandahar.

> **Meaning of the Word *Taliban***
>
> The word "Taliban" literally means "students" in Arabic. However, in Persian this plural form of "talib" means "religious student." The word is merely applied to those who seek religious scholarship in traditional circles of learning, namely madrasahs. The students enrolled in theological and Islamic studies in modern universities are not called "talib."
>
> M. J. Gohari, *The Taliban: Ascent to Power* (Oxford: Oxford University Press, 1999), p. 31.

Shortly after fighting broke out between the Soviet army and the Afghans, Omar joined the mujahideen. He served in the ranks of the Younis Khalis' Brigade of the Islamic Party. Omar was in the middle of heavy fighting, and he suffered four wounds, including a shrapnel wound that caused the loss of his right eye. His combat experience and his wound increased his prestige among the Afghan Islamists because it proved that he had suffered for the Muslim cause. After the end of the war in 1989, Omar returned to his religious school.

Omar remained at his school until he became enraged by the conduct of an oppressive warlord who had raped two young women. He gathered a group of religious students (Taliban), and they hanged the warlord. Pakistani authorities in the Pakistani Inter-Services Intelligence (ISI) noted Omar's growing popularity among the Pashtuns after this act. They decided to give military aid to Omar and his Taliban forces. In the March 1996 council of Afghanistan's religious leaders at Kandahar, Omar was selected to be the head of the Taliban, or Commander of the Faithful. Using this religious authority, along with financial and military aid from Pakistan and Saudi Arabia, Omar and his Taliban forces were strong enough militarily on September 27, 1996, to seize Kabul and control most of Afghanistan.

After the triumph of the Taliban, Omar's strict interpretation of the Koran led him to institute the most severe religious restrictions on the Afghan population. The Taliban had difficulty ruling Afghanistan because its members preferred to focus on religion rather than politics or ways to run a government. Consequently, it was easy to turn to the Koran to rule. The Taliban regime issued a series of rules. Men were subjected to compulsory praying, and they were required to wear beards and turbans. Women lost all rights to hold jobs outside the home, and they could appear in public only when completely covered from head to foot and in the company of a male relative. Art, dancing, music, and television were forbidden. All secular education ended immediately, and boys were required to attend religious schools. Schooling for girls ended entirely. Criminals faced execution or mutilation for their crimes following the laws laid down in the Koran.

> **Explanation of the Taliban Movement by Vahid Mohdeh, a Former Taliban Official in the Afghan Foreign Ministry**
>
> The Taliban movement was not essentially political and its leaders were extremely religious individuals. In some instances such as with Mullah Omar, mystic inclinations were apparent. Many of them had no knowledge beyond a few religious books and their worldly perspective was limited to a couple of provinces in Afghanistan. Their understanding of political matters was completely auditory, the result of listening to radio news or talking with people. The majority of these leaders had no desire to study anything but the Holy Koran and religious texts.
>
> Peter L. Bergen, *The Osama bin Laden I Know: An Oral History of al Qaeda's Leader* (New York: Free Press, 2006), p. 163.

Omar had his Islamist Taliban regime firmly in control of most of Afghanistan, but his forces were still trying to defeat the anti-Taliban coalition of the Northern Alliance in the northern area of Afghanistan. For this the Taliban needed an ally, and bin Laden and al-Qaeda were available. Osama bin Laden had settled in Afghanistan in May 1996 after leaving the Sudan, and his al-Qaeda network had been placed at the disposal of the Taliban regime. To consolidate his relationship with the Taliban, bin Laden swore an oath of allegiance (*bayat*) to Mullah Omar. Al-Qaeda forces fought alongside Taliban forces in the war against the Northern Alliance. In return, the Taliban allowed bin Laden to build training camps to train al-Qaeda operatives.

Omar refused to hand bin Laden over to the United States after the September 11 attacks on the United States. The United States and its allies joined with the Northern Alliance in fighting against the Taliban. Despite the loss of its most important military leader in an al-Qaeda assassination of General Ahmed Shah Masoud, the Northern Alliance was able to overthrow the Taliban regime. Serious

Relationship between Taliban and Osama bin Laden as Described by a Pakistani Journalist

I think that Mullah Omar had a personal relationship with bin Laden. The majority of the Taliban leaders were against bin Laden and that is the reason that whenever I visited Afghanistan to interview bin Laden I was arrested by Taliban. I think that bin Laden was successful in telling Mullah Omar that "I'm fighting a religious war and this is a very important juncture of history and if you are going to surrender in front of the Americans, if you are going to accept the demand that I should be expelled from Afghanistan, you will humiliate the whole nation of Afghans in history." So that's why Mullah Omar was ready to sacrifice everything for Osama bin Laden. But the rest of the Taliban, they were saying that bin Laden is the biggest threat for the first ever Islamic government in modern times and if he is not forced to leave Afghanistan, then we will not be able to spread the world of God through our government. So actually there were two schools of thought in the Taliban and the majority of the Taliban leaders, they were against bin Laden.

Quoted in Peter L. Bergen, *The Osama bin Laden I Know: An Oral History of al Qaeda's Leader* (New York: Free Press, 2006), p. 236.

fighting near Kandahar forced Omar to leave the city on October 7, 2001. Omar remains a fugitive, probably hiding in the tribal lands of northwest Pakistan. His followers are still active in Afghanistan, hoping to restore the Taliban to power.

See Also
Bin Laden, Osama; Qaeda, al-; Zawahiri, Ayman al-

See Document
Document #20

Suggested Reading
Abdel Bari Atwan, *The Secret History of Al Qaeda* (Berkeley: University of California Press, 2006); M. J. Gohari, *The Taliban: Ascent to Power* (Oxford: Oxford University Press, 1999); Peter Marsden, *The Taliban: War and Religion in Afghanistan,* rev. ed. (London: Zed Books, 2002); Ahmed Rashid, *Taliban: Islam, Oil and the New Great Game in Central Asia* (London: Tauris, 2002).

Tenet, George (1953–)

George Tenet was the head of the CIA during the period leading up to and on September 11, 2001. He had been appointed head of the CIA by President Bill Clinton, and his mission had been to revitalize the organization. The CIA had experienced limited success with its two previous heads, leading to low morale and several key retirements. Tenet's background in congressional circles made him a good choice to repair damaged relations between the CIA and Congress.

Tenet came from a humble background. He was born on January 5, 1953, in Flushing, Queens, New York City. His father was a Greek immigrant, and his mother was an ethnic Greek who had fled Communist Albania. They ran a restaurant in Queens—the 20th Century Diner. Tenet was raised in Little Neck, Queens, where he attended Public School 94, Middle School 67, and Cardozo High School. After graduation from high school, Tenet entered Georgetown University, where he graduated in 1976 with a degree from the School of Foreign Service. Since then, he has been a devoted Georgetown basketball fan. He then earned a master's degree from the School of International Affairs at Columbia University in 1978.

Most of Tenet's professional life has been in government service. His first job was as the research director of the American Hellenic Institute. After three years there, he found a position working for Senator John Heinz of Pennsylvania. His next job was as a staff member of the Senate Select Committee on Intelligence (SSCI), and he then served as its staff director. It was his experience on the SSCI that led president-elect Bill Clinton to select him as a member of the national security transition team. After Clinton became president, Tenet was appointed senior director of intelligence programs at the National Security Council. He held this post from 1993 to 1995.

The Clinton administration decided that Tenet's next position should be in the CIA. Tenet was appointed deputy director of central intelligence in July 1995. He served in this post until the abrupt resignation of Deutch in 1996. During most of 1996 until U.S. Senate confirmed him as the director of central intelligence on July 1997, he served as the acting director. Tenet was a compromise candidate after President Clinton's first choice was rejected. The CIA was in disarray with budget cuts from Congress leading to severe personnel cuts. CIA personnel welcomed Tenet because it was known that he was an effective political operator, and the CIA needed to improve its image with Congress and other outsiders. Besides restoring relations with Congress and building morale, Tenet placed counterterrorism high on the CIA's agenda. He did so because of his increasing concern about the growing influence of Osama bin Laden and al-Qaeda.

Tenet's relationship with President Clinton was always tenuous. By the time Tenet was head of the CIA, Clinton was in serious trouble with the Republicans in Congress on a range of foreign policy and domestic issues. Intelligence matters were considered important but were low down on the agenda. Tenet rarely saw Clinton to give him briefings. Clinton relied on written intelligence summaries from the CIA. The terrorist incidents in 1998 and 1999 allowed Tenet to win President Clinton's attention, but Clinton still had reservations about trusting the CIA's intelligence. Steve Coll characterized Tenet's strength as his ability to "synthesize and organize the views of others." Clinton was more comfortable with intellectuals. At this time, Tenet's attention was divided between two concerns—

CIA Official L. Britt Snider's Appraisal of Tenet's Personality

I think he's always been a complex person. Ambitious, but never really a self-promoter. He never took himself too seriously, and he never sought the spotlight. While he's gregarious with people he knows, he actually seems rather shy around people he doesn't know. He's tough-minded but doesn't like to lock horns in controversies or turf battles if he can avoid them. He's fun to be around, but someone who's deadly serious about what he's doing.

Ronald Kessler, *The CIA at War: Inside the Secret Campaign against Terror* (New York: St. Martin's Griffin, 2003), p. 43.

Tenet's State of the CIA in the Late 1990s

The fact is that by the mid- to late 1990s American intelligence was in Chapter 11, and neither Congress nor the executive branch did much about it. Their attitude was that we could surge ahead when necessary to deal with challenges like terrorism. They provided neither the sustained funding required to deal with terrorism nor the resources needed to enable the recovery of the U.S. intelligence with the speed required.

George Tenet and Bill Harlow, *At the Center of the Storm: My Years at the CIA* (New York: HarperCollins, 2007), p. 108.

the proliferation of weapons of mass destruction and terrorism—with terrorism lower down on his agenda.

When George W. Bush's term began, Tenet was a holdover from a Democratic administration. In a briefing a week before Bush's inauguration, Tenet was able to establish a positive relationship with Bush with a series of intelligence briefings. He was able to impress the incoming president enough that he was retained as director of the CIA. In addition, the elder President Bush recommended that his son retain Tenet.

Several times Tenet warned Bush about the dangerous capabilities of Osama bin Laden and al-Qaeda. Bush and Tenet developed a strong professional relationship based on mutual respect. Every morning Tenet traveled to the White House to give President Bush an intelligence briefing. CIA's presidential briefer on the occasions when Tenet was unavailable or when President Bush traveled was Mike Morell, whose presence ensured that CIA intelligence briefings to President Bush could continue wherever the president was at any given time. In his and Morell's briefings, Tenet warned President Bush at least forty times about the possible danger from an al-Qaeda operation. Bush's reaction was that "the Clinton administration's response to bin Laden only confirmed that the U.S. would do little to go after him." Tenet's positive relationship with the president allowed him to survive the political fallout over the failure of the CIA to gather intelligence on the September 11 plot. Tenet was as surprised as the rest of the intelligence community about September 11, and he confessed as much in later remarks.

On the morning of September 11, 2001, Tenet was in Washington, D.C., having breakfast at the St. Regis Hotel with his friend and mentor, former senator David Boren, when he first learned of the events at the World Trade Center complex. His first comment to Boren was that this was probably a Bin Laden–al-Qaeda operation. He immediately launched an investigation into the hijackers. When the CIA began its investigation, there were some objections from the bureaucracy over privacy issues, but with some pressure the CIA was able to find out the names of the hijackers in short order.

After September 11, Tenet revamped the CIA's counterterrorism efforts. The Counterterrorism Center's staff increased from 340 to 1,500. Every lead about an al-Qaeda terrorist threat was followed up, and around 1,500 suspected al-Qaeda operatives were rounded up around the world in the next two years. President Bush gave Tenet a blank check in the pursuit of terrorists. They became even closer as Bush realized that Tenet's CIA was the only government agency that had any intelligence on bin Laden and al-Qaeda. This information was especially useful because Bush wanted to end bin Laden's sanctuary in Afghanistan even if this meant the overthrow of the Taliban regime. To this end, Bush defended the CIA from critics attacking it for its intelligence failures.

Tenet continued to be in President Bush's favor until the debacle over Iraq's alleged possession of weapons of mass destruction (WMDs). Although Tenet believed the invasion of Iraq was a mistaken policy, he went along after President Bush informed him in the fall of 2002 that war was inevitable. Despite this misgiving, prior to the invasion of Iraq by American and its allies, the CIA presented to President Bush evidence that Iraq had weapons of mass destruction—biological agents such as mustard gas and sarin. Tenet briefed Colin Powell, then secretary of state, on these weapons before Powell's speech before the United Nations on

February 5, 2002. The failure to find weapons of mass destruction was considered another intelligence blunder by the CIA. This time Tenet was seriously weakened because of the intelligence failure. Tenet remained head of the CIA until June 2, 2004, when President Bush accepted his resignation. The official reason for his resignation was a heart condition. His replacement was Porter Goss, former Republican congressman from Florida. Statements made by Goss and his initial appointments made it clear that Goss was coming to the CIA determined to make it loyal to the Bush administration.

Tenet had one of the longest tenures in history as head of the CIA. His seven-year term as CIA director was the second longest in American history. President Bush bestowed on Tenet the Presidential Medal of Freedom on December 14, 2004. Since then, Tenet has returned to his first love, Georgetown University, where he is a distinguished professor in the practice of diplomacy. His 2007 book, *At the Center of the Storm*, gives his defense of his tenure at the CIA. Tenet has also attacked the 2005 CIA inspector general's report on his responsibilities for the CIA's deficiencies before September 11.

Tenet's Response to the CIA's Inspector General's Report

Tenet said that the report is factually inaccurate and that it does not place his actions in the context of the times. In his statement, Tenet emphasized his repeated efforts to sound alarms about al-Qaeda before Congress and inside the White House in the months before the attacks.

Joby Warrick and Walter Pincus, "CIA Finds Holes in Pre-9/11 Work," *Washington Post* (August 22, 2007), p. A10.

See Also

Bush, George W.; Bush Administration; Central Intelligence Agency; Clinton Administration; Goss, Porter J.

Suggested Reading

Steve Coll, *Ghost Wars: The Secret History of the CIA, Afghanistan, and Bin Laden, From the Soviet Invasion to September 10, 2001* (New York: Penguin Books, 2004); Tyler Drumheller and Elaine Monaghan, *On the Brink: An Insider's Account of How the White House Compromised American Intelligence* (New York: Carroll and Graf, 2006); Ronald Kessler, *The CIA at War: Inside the Secret Campaign against Terror* (New York: St. Martin's Griffin, 2003); James Risen, *State of War: The Secret History of the CIA and the Bush Administration* (New York: Free Press, 2006); George Tenet and Bill Harlow, *At the Center of the Storm: My Years at the CIA* (New York: HarperCollins, 2007); Bob Woodward, *State of Denial* (New York: Simon and Schuster, 2006).

TIPOFF

TIPOFF is a U.S. State Department watch list, already in existence prior to September 11, 2001, designed to keep terrorists from obtaining visas to enter the United States. It also provided a way to tip off intelligence and law enforcement agencies about potential terrorists already in the United States. This watch list was established in 1987 by John Arriza, a U.S. State Department civil servant. Any agent of an American agency could send a name or a group of names to the State Department's Bureau of Intelligence and Research for inclusion on this list.

Before September 11, the U.S. State Department was the most active in contributing names to this list. In 2001 it had contributed more than 2,000 names. The second most active in contributing names was the CIA, with more than

FBI Director Robert Mueller (left) and CIA Director George Tenet (right) joke with one another on February 11, 2003, before testifying before the Senate Intelligence Committee in Washington. (AP IMAGES/Ron Edmonds.)

1,500 names. Other agencies added to the list, but the least active was the FBI. In 2001 the FBI added only 60 names to the list. By September 2001 there were approximately 60,000 names on the TIPOFF list.

The biggest weakness of TIPOFF was that the FAA did not participate because the airline industry opposed it. The FAA maintained a much smaller watch list. This FAA watch list had less than twenty names on it on September 11, 2001. The FAA's leadership maintained that it did not want to burden the commercial airline industry with having to deal with the huge TIPOFF watch list, which would cause delays and traveler inconvenience and cost money.

What was most striking about the al-Qaeda operatives on September 11 was that none of them were on the TIPOFF watch list. They had been able to gain access to the United States without arousing suspicion despite the fact that a CIA agent had been badgering German officials about the members of the Hamburg Cell and the fact that two known al-Qaeda operatives had attended the January 2000 Kuala Lumpur meeting.

> **Lack of Awareness at FAA about TIPOFF**
>
> The long-time chief of the FAA's civil aviation security division testified that he was not aware of the State Department's TIPOFF list of known and suspected terrorist (some 60,000 before 9/11) until he heard it mentioned during the Commission's January 26, 2004, public hearing. The FAA had access to some TIPOFF data, but apparently found it too difficult to use.
>
> *The 9/11 Commission Report: Final Report of the National Commission on Terrorist Attacks upon the United States* (New York: Norton, 2005), pp. 83–84.

Despite the defects of TIPOFF, the concept had enough merit that it survived the post–September 11 revamping of procedures and agencies. It has been expanded, and now the FBI contributes names. The FAA now both contributes to and uses the TIPOFF system.

See Also
Central Intelligence Agency; Federal Bureau of Investigation; Federal Aviation Administration (FAA); Qaeda, al-

Suggested Reading
Steven Strasser, ed., *The 9/11 Investigations; Staff Reports of the 9/11 Commission; Excerpts from the House-Senate Joint Inquiry Report on 9/11/ Testimony from 14 Key Witnesses, Including Richard Clarke, George Tenet, and Condoleezza Rice* (New York: PublicAffairs, 2004).

Transportation Security Administration

One of the first facts to come out of the investigations into September 11 was that the FAA had failed to provide the necessary airport security to prevent the September 11 attacks. Rather than reform the old system, a new agency, the Transportation Security Administration (TSA), was proposed to handle a revamped federal government security program. This new agency was to be housed in the Department of Transportation (DOT). Congress passed the Aviation and Transportation Security Act (ATSA) in record time, and President George W. Bush signed it into law on November 19, 2001. The new legislation made the TSA responsible for all screening issues, including hiring, testing, training, firing, and deploying screening personnel at all airports in the country. Congress gave the new agency deadlines in late November and December 2002 to come up with solutions to aviation security problems. All FAA records and personnel dealing with aviation security were turned over to the new agency.

Soon after its founding, the TSA began to run into trouble. Starting an agency almost from scratch is a daunting enough task, but other factors began to surface. First of all, passengers were skittish about flying after September 11. Then bureaucratic inefficiency, congressional political pressure, and complaints from the airline industry combined to hinder the new agency's mission. John W. Magaw, former head of the Secret Service, became the first head of the TSA. He hired law enforcement experts at senior levels instead of aviation security experts. Moreover, Magaw hired the senior management, paying them top salaries. Despite spending $6 billion in the agency's first six months, Magaw made few aviation security improvements. Criticism of the TSA became so intense that Magaw resigned in July 2002.

Magaw's replacement was Admiral James Loy, former head of the U.S. Coast Guard. He immediately began loosening security requirements in the interest of customer service. These actions made Loy popular with the airline industry, but it did little to improve aviation security. The Department of Transportation was no better at withstanding pressure from the airline industry than the FAA, and the TSA began to run out of money from its high salaries and lucrative outsourcing contacts to private companies.

Perception of the Reforms of the Aviation and Transportation Security Act

The Aviation and Transportation Security Act (ATSA) signed by President George W. Bush on November 19, 2001, promised a more seamless, sensible, and secure approach to protecting commercial aviation. Nevertheless, the view was held by many inside and outside of the industry that bad public policy and a lack of vision and leadership at the federal level delivered much less to the American people. Eighteen months after the 9/11 attacks, members of Congress, industry associations, independent experts, as well as most everyone else affected by the aviation sector were voicing loud concerns about the state of the new aviation security regimen.

Andrew R. Thomas, *Aviation Insecurity: The New Challenges of Air Travel* (Amherst, NY: Prometheus Books, 2003), p. 103.

The TSA had become a bloated agency. It had hired more than 70,000 employees at an annual cost of $8 billion. But the problem with this huge workforce was that tests of the screening system proved no more reliable and efficient than before September 11. The new system depended on eight layers in comparison to the three layers of redundancy to prevent or overcome hijackings. The new eight layers were (1) higher screening standards, (2) increased profiling, (3) better screening at checkpoints, (4) reinforced cockpit doors, (5) more air marshals, (6) armed pilots, (7) passenger and crew reaction, and (8) a shoot-down policy.

The problem with these new layers is that a competent and intelligent hijacker can shortchange these layers by simply waiting until the cockpit door is opened for some reason and then invade the cockpit. Once inside he can hide behind the improved cockpit doors and crash the aircraft before American fighter planes can shoot it down. This weakness in security has yet to be addressed.

Other security measures have also proven to be unsuccessful, including the explosives detection systems (EDA). The TSA has bought thousands of these machines at the cost of $1 million a piece. They are huge luggage-screening machines that use outdated X-ray technology. One major problem is that X-ray machines are incapable of detecting explosives. This technology has been described by Andrew R. Thomas, an expert in airline security, as "density-sensitive but chemically blind." None of these machines are capable of detecting an explosive, so it is left up to the operator to be suspicious about an item because of its shape or density.

Biometrics has been no more successful a tool. This technique uses technology to measure and analyze human body characteristics such as fingerprints, eye retinas, voice patterns, facial patterns, and hand measurement to authenticate people going into secure areas of the airport. It takes a scanning device, software that scans data into a database, and a database to hold the information. The problem is that biometrics does not work well because it is too easy to bypass. Tests of passengers and airport workers at Logan International Airport during a ninety-day period showed it was too easily fooled.

Another type of security that has serious faults is the Trusted Traveler Program. This system allows frequent flyers to undergo extensive background checks for clearance to allow the passengers to be issued a photo identification card for easy access through security. This idea has become popular in the commercial airline industry. But what if the wrong person obtained access to the Trusted Traveler Card? A terrorist or criminal who could obtain such a card would have open access to the aircraft with few restrictions.

Aviation experts are still concerned about aviation security. They distrust the new TSA for two essential reasons: its ties, much like the FAA, to the DOT's cozy relationship to the airline industry and the lack of leadership to improve aviation security in the TSA. Pressure from the airline industry to relax security standards is still intense. Next, the TSA has become so large and unwieldy that it moves at a glacial pace, and much of its security technology is outdated. In the opinion of many of these aviation experts, the new TSA is not much of an improvement on the FAA.

Aviation security is a thankless task, and it is easy to criticize it for its shortcomings. In its favor, the TSA has instituted a number of useful reforms helping to improve the screening system by better training of screeners and the acquisition of new technology. Also, the TSA leadership is much more alert to the dangers of terrorism.

See Also
Federal Aviation Administration (FAA)

Suggested Reading
Eric Lipton, "Scissors Ban on Airplanes Will Be Lifted Despite Critics," *New York Times* (December 3, 2005), p. A16; Alexandra Marks, "Well after 9/11, 'No Fly' Lists a Work in Progress," *Christian Science Monitor* (March 24, 2005), p. 2; Robert O'Harrow Jr. and Scott Higham, "TSA Airport Security Contract Examined for Fraud," *Washington Post* (July 1, 2005), p. A7; Robert O'Harrow Jr. and Scott Higham, "Post-9/11 Rush Mixed Politics with Security," *Washington Post* (December 25, 2005), p. A1; Andrew R, Thomas, *Aviation Insecurity: The New Challenges of Air Travel* (Amherst, NY: Prometheus Books, 2003).

U

United Airlines Flight 93

United Airlines Flight 93's Boeing 757-222 was the fourth aircraft hijacked by al-Qaeda hijackers on September 11, 2001. It took off from Newark International Airport at 8:43 a.m. bound for San Francisco International Airport. Normal flight time was six hours. The flight was nearly forty-five minutes late for its scheduled takeoff time of 8:01 a.m. On board were two pilots, Captain Jason M. Dahl and First Officer LeRoy Homer; a crew of five flight attendants; and thirty-seven passengers. It held 11,489 gallons of aviation fuel.

The hijack team had little difficulty passing security. Security checkpoints at Newark International Airport were operated by Argenbright Security under contract to United Airlines. Much as other airport security firms did, Argenbright conducted business at the pleasure of its contractor. Only two of the four hijackers had luggage and only one of them triggered the CAPPS (Computer-Assisted Passenger Prescreening System) process. Ahmed al-Haznawi's luggage was checked for explosives.

This hijack team was the smallest of the four. Ziad Jarrah was the team leader and designated pilot. He sat in first-class seat 1B, nearest to the cockpit door. Other members of the team, Saeed al-Ghamdi, Ahmed al-Haznawi, and Ahmed al-Na'ami, were in seats 3C, 3D, and 6B. Hijackers seized control of the aircraft at 9:28 a.m., just minutes after the pilot received a warning about possible cockpit invasions on the cockpit computer device ACARS (Aircraft Communications and Reporting System). The cockpit door was no obstacle, taking only about 150 pounds of pressure to knock down. In addition, the flight attendants had keys to the cockpit door—another means of access to the cockpit.

Exactly how the hijackers gained access to the cockpit will never be known, but they took control relatively easily. They probably took a key to the cockpit from the flight attendant in First Class. Within minutes of the assault, the hijackers had complete control of the aircraft. Both pilots were down—either killed or seriously incapacitated. Ahmed al-Haznawi, Saeed al-Ghamdi, and Ahmed al-Na'ami took turns controlling the thirty-three passengers and five flight attendants. Matters were complicated by having about a dozen passengers in the first-class section, with the rest seated in the back of the plane. Unlike the other teams, these hijackers were lenient on passenger discipline. After injuring one of the passengers, the hijackers controlled the others and the crew by threatening them with a bomb. To keep discontent down, they encouraged passengers and crew to contact their families by cell phone. Passengers made more than two dozen phone calls. This relaxed style came back to haunt the hijackers, for passengers who contacted family members learned that three other aircraft had been hijacked and had been turned into flying bombs.

As passengers began to realize there was no possibility of survival, plans circulated among some of the more aggressive men on board to attack the hijackers and regain control of the aircraft. By this time the passengers suspected that the hijackers had no bomb. About a dozen of them had experience in action sports, including football, rugby, and judo. Todd Beamer, Mark Bingham, Tom Burnett, Jeremy Glick, and several others decided to wait until the aircraft cleared populated areas to begin their attack. They were under no illusion about their probable fate, and showed extraordinary courage and compassion for others by waiting for the aircraft to fly over a rural area. They had other allies in CeeCee Ross-Lyles, one of the flight attendants, who was a former police officer; Rich Guadago, an enforcement officer with the California Fish and Wildlife Service; Linda Gronlund, a lawyer who had a brown belt in karate; and William Cashman, a former paratrooper with the 101st Airborne. Finally, Don Greene, vice president of Safe Flight Instrument Group, was a pilot with experience in single-engine aircraft, who could follow instructions to land the aircraft.

> **Passengers Realized That the Hijackers Were on a Suicide Mission**
>
> Evidence from mobile phone conversations made by the passengers suggests that they gradually became aware of what was unfolding in New York and Washington, where the three earlier hijacked planes slammed into the World Trade Centre and the Pentagon, and that they came to a decision to storm the cockpit and attempt to overpower the hijackers. One of the men, Todd Beamer, is said to have told his fellow passenger "Let's roll" before charging the flight deck.
>
> Andrew Gumbel, "Flight Recorder—The Final Conversation of Doomed Flight UA93," *Independent* [London] (November 17, 2001), p. 8.

The passengers waited for the opportunity. In the meantime, flight attendant Sandy Bradshaw started boiling water to be used against the hijackers. Sometime around 10:00 a.m. the passengers attacked the hijackers using a food tray container to smash into the cockpit area. Earlier the hijackers had all retreated into the cockpit area. A voice recording from the black box (cockpit data recorder) indicated the fierce nature of the struggle. For the next seven minutes the outcome was in doubt.

Jarrah was the pilot, and his contingency plan was to crash the aircraft if it seemed as though the hijackers would lose control of the plane. Evidently this is what happened, for the aircraft crashed upside down at a forty-five degree angle. It created a crater thirty feet or more in diameter. Because the plane crashed in a reclaimed mining area, the ground was relatively soft and the aircraft plunged deep into the ground. The fuel tanks exploded, leaving a blackened crater. Smoke from the explosion allowed local volunteer authorities to find the site soon after the crash. The crash was reported by numerous witnesses, and a visual inspection from

FBI investigators comb the crater left by United Airlines Flight 93, a Boeing 757, in Shanksville, Pennsylvania, about eighty miles southeast of Pittsburgh. FBI assistant agent in charge Roland Corvington said that more than 200 investigators were on the scene. (AP IMAGES/Gene J. Puskar.)

a passing unarmed Air National Guard C-130H cargo jet on a mission from Washington, D.C., to Minnesota confirmed the crash site.

The violence of the crash left no survivors. The black box was excavated fifteen feet into the crater, and the cockpit voice recorder was found twenty-five feet down. Only body parts were recovered. Sixty percent of the recovered remains were identified by a combination of fingerprint verification, dental records, and DNA analysis.

In commercial air disasters the National Transportation Safety Board (NTSB) handles investigations, but because this was a case of air piracy, the FBI assumed control although the Bureau of Alcohol, Tobacco, and Firearms; the NTSB; and the Pennsylvania State Police also assisted. Nothing could be done at the site, however, without the permission of the FBI. Early in the investigation two thousand people worked at the site daily.

The probable target of Flight 93 was the U.S. Capitol. Earlier meetings by al-Qaeda leaders had determined that the White House would present navigational problems. They had preferred that the White House be the target, but the Capitol was a target more easily recognized by inexperienced navigators.

See Also
Beamer, Todd Morgan; Bingham, Mark Kendall; Burnett, Thomas Edward; Dahl, Jason Matthew; Glick, Jeremy; Homer, LeRoy Wilton Jr.; Jarrah, Ziad Samir

See Document
Document #16

Suggested Reading
Stefan Aust et al., *Inside 9/11: What Really Happened* (New York: St. Martin's Press, 2001); Lisa Beamer and Ken Abraham, *Let's Roll! Ordinary People, Extraordinary Courage*

(Wheaton, IL: Tyndale House Publishers, 2002); Glenn J. Kashuba, *Quiet Courage: The Definitive Account of Flight 93 and Its Aftermath* (Somerset, PA: SAJ, 2006); Jere Longman, *Among the Heroes: United Flight 93 and the Passengers and Crew Who Fought Back* (New York: Perennial, 2003); 9/11 Commission, *The 9/11 Commission Report: Final Report of the National Commission on Terrorist Attack upon the United States* (New York: Norton, 2004); Susan B. Trento and Joseph J. Trento, *Unsafe at Any Altitude: Failed Terrorism Investigations, Scapegoating 9/11, and the Shocking Truth about Aviation Security Today* (Hanover, NH: Steerforth Press, 2006).

United Airlines Flight 175

Terrorists gained control of the Boeing 767-222 of United Airlines Fight 77 on September 11, 2001, and crashed it into the South Tower of the World Trade Center in New York City. Although this flight was scheduled to leave at 7:59 a.m., it left Logan International Airport at 8:15 a.m., with Los Angeles International Airport its destination. The pilots were Captain Victor Saracini, a fifty-one-year-old Navy veteran pilot, and the First Officer was Michael Horrocks. On board with the two pilots were seven flight attendants and fifty-six passengers. The plane held 23,980 gallons of aviation fuel. Shortly after takeoff, traffic controllers asked Saracini whether he could see American Airlines Flight 11. After he replied affirmatively, the pilots were ordered to maintain distance from the hijacked aircraft.

Among the fifty-six passengers on board were five members of an al-Qaeda terrorist team. The leader of this hijack team and its pilot was Marwan al-Shehhi. Other members of the team were Fayez Rashid Ahmed Hassan al-Qadi Banihammad, Ahmed al-Ghamdi, Hamza al-Ghamdi, and Mohand al-Shehri. The hijackers had little difficulty passing through security. The security checkpoint at Logan International Airport for United Airlines was staffed by personnel from Huntleigh USA. The hijackers had purchased tickets in the first-class section to be close to the cockpit. Much as in the takeover of American Airlines Flight 11, the terrorists organized themselves into sections: two were near the cockpit (in seats 2A and 2B), pilot al-Shehhi was in seat 6C, and the other two sat near the passenger section (in seats 9C and 9D).

The hijackers seized control of the aircraft sometime around 8:47 a.m. They used knives and Mace to subdue the pilots and crew, and then killed the pilots and at least one flight attendant. The hijackers then herded the crew and passengers toward the rear of the aircraft, assuring them everything would be okay. They lulled the passengers into thinking that the plane would land someplace safely and that the hijackers would use them as hostages in negotiations. Not all passengers accepted this argument (see sidebar). One passenger, Peter Hanson, called his father in Easton, Connecticut, and reported the hijackers' takeover. One of the flight attendants also reported the hijacking to the United Airlines office in San Francisco.

Message from Passenger Brian Sweeney to His Wife, Julie

Hey Jules, it's Brian. I'm on a plane and it's hijacked and it doesn't look good. I just wanted to let you know that I love you and I hope to see you again. If I don't, please have fun in life and live your life the best you can. Know that I love you and no matter what, I'll see you again.

Quoted in Greg B. Smith, "9/11 Voices Still Echoing," *Daily News* (March 25, 2002), p. 9.

United Flight 175 approaches the South Tower of the World Trade Center in this September 11, 2001, photo. (AP IMAGES, Carmen Taylor, File.)

Al-Shehhi turned the aircraft around and headed it toward the New York City area. Traffic controllers had lost contact with the plane. The passengers became concerned because of the aircraft's jerky movements. At this point some of the passengers considered storming the cockpit to regain control of the plane. They just did not have enough time. At 9:03 a.m. United Airlines Flight 175 slammed into the South Tower of the World Trade Center complex. The aircraft impacted between floors seventy-eight and eighty-four. Because the aircraft hit at greater speed than American Airlines Flight 11, it damaged the South Tower more severely than the North Tower had been. Consequently, the South Tower collapsed before the North Tower. There were no survivors on United Flight 175.

See Also
World Trade Center, September 11

Suggested Reading
Stefan Aust et al., *Inside 9/11: What Really Happened* (New York: St. Martin's Press, 2001); 9/11 Commission, *The 9/11 Commission Report: Final Report of the National Commission on Terrorist Attacks upon the United States* (New York: Norton, 2004).

United 93 (Film)

United 93 is a docudrama that attempts to chronicle events aboard United Airlines Flight 93 on September 11, 2001. British film director Paul Greengrass wrote and directed this docudrama. Greengrass is an experienced director. His previous credits include the acclaimed docudrama *Bloody Sunday,* which recreated the events of the 1972 massacre of Irish civil rights demonstrators by British troops in Northern Ireland, and the thriller *The Bourne Supremacy.* The first appearance of *United 93* was as a TV film titled *Flight 93,* broadcast on January 30, 2006, by the A&E Network. The network showed it several times during 2006. Greengrass then converted the film into a full-scale movie titled *United 93,* which premiered at the Tribeca Film Festival in New York City on April 26, 2006. Later that April, the movie made its appearance nationwide, receiving an R rating because of its language and violence, much to the displeasure of distributor Universal Pictures. Universal booked the film into 1,795 theaters, and it did well financially. Reviews of the movie were generally positive, with several film critics giving it a four-star rating.

The movie attempts to recreate the hijacking and the passengers' attempted takeover. It focuses on the activities of eight passengers—Todd Beamer, Mark Bingham, Tom Burnett, Jeremy Glick, Lauren Grancolas, Donald Greene, Nicole Miller, and Honor Elizabeth Wainio. After interviewing the families of the victims to learn personal details, Greengrass used unknown actors with physical characteristics similar to those on the aircraft. He even used airline employees in some of the roles. The movie hijackers were also unknowns. Four British men of Middle Eastern extraction—two Egyptians, one Moroccan, and one Iraqi—played the hijacker roles.

Greengrass tried to make the movie as realistic as possible. He found an out-of-service Boeing 757 and reconstructed it on London's Pinewood Studios soundstage. His camera operators used handheld cameras to create the aura of confusion and chaos. He relied on the conclusions of the *9/11 Commission Report,* cell phone transcripts, interviews, the cockpit black box recorder, and FAA and military records to make the dialogue as accurate as possible. Greengrass's goal was that the film have "a thriller's breathless quality but not seem exploitative or contrived." He believed the passengers' attempt to retake the aircraft to be heroic, but his feelings were more complex than this.

Paul Greengrass's Feelings about Passengers on United Airlines Flight 93

When I watch that film myself, I feel that . . . when they've reached the cockpit door, and they're wrestling with that guy, and it's the most brutal kind of struggle, I feel that's us today. And when they get through the door and they're wrestling for the controls of the plane with those guys, that feels like that's our tomorrow, if we're not careful.

Quoted in Desson Thomson, "For Paul Greengrass, a Connecting Flight," *Washington Post* (May 1, 2006), p. C1.

See Also
United Airlines Flight 93

See Document
Document #16

Suggested Readings
Joanna Connors, "No Risk in Telling Tale of 9/11 Flight: What Happened That Day Is Something That Belongs to Us All," *Plain Dealer* (April 30, 2006), p. J9; Roger Ebert, "Terror of the Moment: 'United 93' Avoids Clichés, Rolls with Reality of 9/11 Tension," *Chicago Sun Times* (April 28, 2006), p. NC28; Ethan Gilsdorf, "A Serious Man with a Serious Subject: 9/11," *Boston Globe* (April 28, 2006), p. D10; Jere Longman, "Filming Flight 93's Story, Trying to Define Heroics," *New York Times* (April 24, 2006), p. E1; Desson Thomson, "For Paul Greengrass, a Connecting Flight," *Washington Post* (May 1, 2006), p. C1; Tony Wong, "Chilling Seat for 9/11," *Toronto Star* (September 14, 2006), p. D12.

USA PATRIOT Act

One of the first post–September 11 legislative outcomes was adoption of the USA PATRIOT (Uniting and Strengthening America by Providing Appropriate Tools Required to Intercept and Obstruct Terrorism) Act. The intent of this legislation was to plug holes in domestic intelligence gathering considered to have developed over previous decades. The legislation was controversial because it dropped many of the safeguards that Americans had come to expect for protection against government interference in their private affairs.

The USA PATRIOT Act moved through Congress to the White House in a hurry. In an immediate reaction to the events of September 11, the USA PATRIOT Act was approved in the Senate on October 11, 2001, by a vote of 96 to 1. On October 12, 2001, the House of Representatives approved it with a vote of 337 to 79. The act became law when President George W. Bush signed it on October 26, 2001. Rarely has legislation moved through Congress and been signed into law with such speed. Critics have charged that adoption was too hasty, allowing the Department of Justice under Attorney General John Ashcroft to throw provisions defeated during the Clinton administration into a package passed with few Members of Congress thoroughly understanding it.

Provisions of the original act were controversial for having greatly expanded the power of government, with few checks and balances. The act expanded the range of crimes that could be tracked by government agencies using electronic surveillance. Federal authorities were granted authority to use "roving wiretaps" on any phone that a suspected terrorist might be expected to use. Law enforcement officers could now conduct searches of suspects without notifying them until later, a tactic that became known as a "sneak-and-peek" operation. This particular type of search had previously been used against organized crime figures and major drug dealers. Now FBI agents could obtain secret court orders to search such personal records as business, medical, library, and other files without probable cause in potential terrorism cases. The act made it a federal crime to harbor a terrorist. It also increased criminal penalties for a laundry list of offenses, ranging from conspiracy to commit terrorism to interference with a flight crew. Search warrants became easy to obtain in terrorist-related investigations. The Attorney General was authorized to detain foreign terrorism suspects for a full week without initiating any type of legal proceeding or having to show cause. Finally, the law provided for

Senator Patrick Leahy (D-VT) peers over President Bush's shoulder with his camera as the President signs the USA PATRIOT Act during a White House ceremony in October 2001. Standing behind the president, from left to right, are Senator Orrin Hatch (R-UT), Senator Patrick Leahy (D-VT), and Senator Harry Reid (D-NV). (AP IMAGES/Doug Mills.)

new financial and legal tools to end international money laundering. The only restriction on this law was that its surveillance and wiretap provisions were required to be renewed in 2005.

Critics of the USA PATRIOT Act have come from two ends of the political spectrum. Among the leading critics has been the American Civil Liberties Union (ACLU). From the other end of the spectrum, a second leading critic has been the oldest conservative grassroots lobbying organization in the country, the American Conservative Union (ACU). The ACLU's opposition is based on the argument that the law violates rights to privacy. In contrast, the ACU's opposition stems from its belief in the need to limit federal authority. Both organizations are hesitant about the use of anti-terrorism investigations to charge American citizens of crimes unrelated to terrorism. The PATRIOT Act has been used to investigate everything from murder to child pornography. Together the ACLU and ACU have lobbied to amend the USA PATRIOT Act to ensure protection for civil liberties.

Two other critics of the USA PATRIOT Act have been business interests and librarians. Business interests object to the act's anti–money-laundering provisions. These provisions were intended to prevent, detect, and prosecute money laundering and the financing of terrorism, and required banks and other financial institutions to establish programs to monitor financial activities. Fines and prison sentences are the penalties for noncompliance with money-laundering restrictions, and representatives of financial institutions have complained about the cost of compliance.

Librarians have challenged the right of FBI investigators to inspect library records, with the American Library Association having initiated several lawsuits against this provision. Besides objecting to the access given the FBI to inspect individuals' library records, librarians also oppose the act's prohibition against informing patrons that their records are the subject of a search. Most court fights to defeat the issuance of National Security Letters (the subpoenas for records, which do not require a judge's approval) have been unsuccessful, but the public's negative opinion of the practice has deterred the FBI from using it except in rare cases.

Supporters of the USA PATRIOT Act have maintained that its restrictions are necessary to fight the war against terrorism, and favor even greater restrictions if they prevent the conduct of terror operations on American soil. The act is required to be periodically renewed, and supporters consider it a necessity as long as terrorist threats continue.

Despite opposition to several of its provisions, the USA PATRIOT Act was renewed on March 7, 2006. With amendments to address a few objections to it, the act was approved in the Senate by a vote of 95 to 4, and in the House by 280 to 138. One amendment excluded libraries that function in a "traditional capacity" from having to furnish the records sought in a National Security Letter. Another amendment gave persons subpoenaed by the Foreign Intelligence Surveillance Act (FISA) Court the right to challenge the nondisclosure, or gag order, requirement of the subpoena. Finally, two of the act's provisions—the authority of the FBI to conduct roving wiretaps and the power of the government to seize business records with the FISA Court's approval—would be constrained by a four-year sunset requirement.

See Also
Bush Administration; Foreign Intelligence Surveillance Act of 1978

Suggested Reading
Charles Babington, "Congress Votes to Renew Patriot Act, with Changes," *Washington Post* (March 8, 2006), p. A3; Stewart A. Baker, *Patriot Debates: Experts Debate the USA Patriot Act* (New York: American Bar Association, 2005); Howard Ball and Mildred Vasan (eds.), *The USA Patriot Act: A Reference Handbook* (Santa Barbara, Calif.: ABC-CLIO, 2004); Amitai Etzioni, *How Patriotic Is the Patriot Act?* (New York: Routledge, 2004); Richard C. Leone and Greg Anriq (eds.), *The War on Our Freedoms: Civil Liberties in the Age of Terrorism* (New York: PublicAffairs, 2003); Paul Rush, "Patriot Act Forges Unlikely Alliance," *Insight on the News* (September 29, 2003), p. 26; John Yoo, *War By Other Means: An Insider's Account of the War on Terror* (New York: Atlantic Monthly Press, 2006).

V

Victims' Compensation Fund

The Victims' Compensation Fund (VCF) was a program allowing the government to partially compensate 9/11 victims with a monetary award. It covered both economic and noneconomic damages, and came in the aftermath of a $15 billion allocation from Congress to save the airline industry from bankruptcy. Members of Congress decided that it would not be prudent to assist the airline industry while ignoring the 9/11 families who had lost loved ones. Another reason for the VCF was to protect the airline companies from costly lawsuits. To do this, Congress set a cap of $1.6 million for each family. But this cap was later raised to cope with problems with the cap. In the final analysis the average award was $1.8 million.

Administrator of the Victim's Compensation Fund was attorney Kenneth Feinberg. Feinberg soon became unpopular with 9/11 families for having promised greater awards than were granted and for his slowness in responding to victims' families. He had an aggressive attitude, arguing that the 9/11 families should join the VCF because they could not sue any party other than the planners of the attacks, which enraged some of the families. Some of this criticism was unjust because he was in charge of a bureaucracy that took time to calculate awards. Feinberg served without pay, and was glad to return to private practice at the end of the process.

The victims' families were slow to sign up for the Fund. Part of their problem was in gauging whether it was wiser to sign up for the VCF than to privately pursue action in the courts. It soon became apparent that the families of those who died in the airliners were more likely to succeed in court than were the families of those who died on the ground. Action in court would be a long-term process with results uncertain, whereas the VCF offered almost immediate financial help with none of the uncertainty of the courts.

The families whose members had held higher-paying jobs were among the most unhappy with the Victims' Compensation Fund. Many of the victims in the twin towers had high-paying jobs that exceeded within five years the amount projected to be awarded. The families of victims of high net worth were initially awarded an amount equivalent to about ten cents on the dollar. Moreover, life insurance and pension payments counted against the final settlement. Finally, the VCF deducted Social Security payments to children in the final settlement. In the end the U.S. government made it plain that it was a take-it-or-leave-it proposition.

Because the Victims' Compensation Fund was financed by U.S. taxpayers, it became controversial. Many people attacked the 9/11 families for being greedy. This backlash caused much anguish among the families of the 9/11 victims. Some of the families became so angry that they attacked the VCF and Feinberg. When it became apparent that the lawyers were reluctant to press their claims after being pressured by leaders in the legal profession, some of the leaders of the 9/11 families movement began organizing a lobby group. The Jersey Girls—widows of those killed in the North Tower on September 11—were active in this movement.

> **Response to Charges of Greed by Kimi Bevin, Whose Husband Died on American Airlines Flight 93**
>
> The disputes became most bitter over accusations of greed on the part of the families of the dead. "How can people say it is greed? I have been left with a six-year-old daughter in a city where the cost of living is very high, and we are talking about less than three years of my husband's salary. Greed? I don't think so. I don't know how I am going to survive."
>
> Charles Laurence, "Envy over Cash for World Trade Center Victims," *Sunday Telegraph* [London] (September 8, 2002), p. 28.

The work of the Victims' Compensation Fund ended on its deadline of December 22, 2003. It paid out its first claim on August 22, 2002, and its final payment went out in early January 2005. More than $7 billion went to the survivors of 2,880 people who were killed and to 2,680 people who were injured in the attacks or rescue efforts that followed. Families of the people killed collected awards averaging more than $2 million, and the injured drew payouts averaging $400,000. It cost the government $86.9 million to administer the fund. Eighty families opted out of the VCF in order to privately sue the airlines and the FAA. Thirteen families chose to simply ignore the VCF altogether—from grief or for other reasons.

See Also
Jersey Girls

Suggested Reading
Kristen Breitweiser, *Wake-Up Call: The Political Education of a 9/11 Widow* (New York: Warner Books); David W. Chen, "Victims' Kin Find Fault with Overseer of 9/11 Fund," *New York Times* (November 13, 2002), p. B1; Martin Kasindorf, "9/11 Families Filing Claims as Deadline Nears," *USA Today* (December 19, 2003), p. 1; Martin Kasindorf, "Compensation Battles Inflict New Wounds on 9/11 Families," *USA Today* (January 19, 2004), p. 1A; Christopher Lee, "Report on Sept. 11 Fund Is Released," *Washington Post* (November 18, 2004), p. A3; Mark Mueller, "For Some, 9/11 Fund Is No Compensation," *Star-Ledger* [Newark, NJ] (November 21, 2004), p. 3.

Von Essen, Thomas (1945–)

Thomas Von Essen was the Fire Commissioner of the City of New York on September 11, 2001. The commissioner's job is a civilian position with no decision-making role at disaster scenes, but it is political in nature. It was Von Essen's job to advise the mayor, help with the media, and serve as liaison with other city agencies in the event of emergency. Most commissioners had little experience with firefighting, but Von Essen had been both a firefighter and head of one of the two firefighters unions. Rudy Giuliani had appointed him to be the thirtieth Fire Commissioner of the City of New York in 1996.

Von Essen came to firefighting indirectly. He was born in December 1945 in Queens, New York. His father was a New York City policeman in the 79th Precinct, and his mother was a housewife. The family lived in Ozone Park, a working-class neighborhood in Queens. Von Essen attended a Catholic grade school, Nativity of the Blessed Virgin Mary Catholic School. His good grades allowed him admittance to Bishop Loughlin High School in Brooklyn. But in high school Von Essen's grades began to suffer until he transferred into a public high school, John Adams High School. His grades improved slightly, and he graduated from high school. Von Essen then enrolled at St. Francis College in Brooklyn with the intent of studying accounting. He later married and had a baby girl. After serving two years in the U.S. Navy on submarines in the late 1960s, he decided to become a firefighter.

Von Essen became a member of the New York City Fire Department (FDNY) in 1970. He spent the next sixteen years working in Ladder Company 42 in the South Bronx. It was a period when the New York City area had numerous fires, and Von Essen became an experienced firefighter in record time. In 1981 he was made his house's union delegate to the Uniformed Firefighters Association (UFA), which then represented 8,700 firefighters. In the midst of his work as a firefighter, Von Essen graduated from St. Francis College in 1972 with a degree in economics. He followed by seeking a master's degree in education from the C. W. Post Campus of Long Island University. After obtaining a master's degree and certified teaching license, Von Essen briefly considered a teaching career before returning to firefighting. In 1983 he ran for the position of Bronx Trustee for the UFA and won. He was elected to the post of secretary of the UFA in 1984 and again in 1987.

After seven years in union administration, Von Essen returned to firefighting in 1990. However, firefighting was no longer exciting to him, and hard feelings from his union activities had surfaced. Von Essen took a leave of absence from firefighting and worked in real estate as assistant manager for the Mendik Company. This experience reinforced a decision to return to firefighting.

Von Essen decided to run for president of the Uniformed Firefighters Association in summer 1993. He won, and took office on August 1, 1993. Previous heads of the UFA had fought with New York City mayors over fire station closings and disputes over pay and working conditions. This all changed with the election of Mayor Rudolph Giuliani. Giuliani took over as mayor only a few months after Von Essen was elected president of the UFA. Von Essen had rallied the UFA behind Giuliani and against Mayor Dinkins. Although Giuliani appreciated the support from the UFA, he froze salaries for the next few years, making life difficult for Von Essen. In the meantime, Von Essen was able to build a good working relationship with then fire commissioner Howard Safir. When Safir was appointed police commissioner in 1986, Giuliani named Von Essen Fire Commissioner of New York City.

Von Essen was fire commissioner before and during the events of September 11, 2001. Early in his tenure he had used his post to concentrate on safety issues and training for firefighters. His good working relationship with the mayor helped him through several controversies. The most serious of these disputes concerned the installation of a new digital communication system. Unfortunately, this new communication system was delayed by malfunctions until after September 11, 2001.

Von Essen began his day on September 11, 2001, much like any other day. He was on his way to headquarters in Brooklyn when he and his driver noticed that there had been an explosion at the North Tower of the World Trade Center complex. Suddenly chatter on the fire department radio relayed that an airliner had crashed into the North Tower. His driver immediately took Von Essen to the World Trade Center complex, and he headed to the command post in the North Tower, where he found Chief Pete Ganci in charge of operations. By this time people were already jumping from the upper stories of the North Tower. Although all of the fire chiefs in the emergency command post were experienced firefighters, the lack of current information—the result of failure and overload of the communications system—hindered their decision making. When the second plane hit the South Tower the situation became truly grim. Fighting a fire and rescuing people from two high-rise buildings would be almost impossible. As more and more firefighters joined the fray, the scene became even more chaotic.

Since Von Essen had no command authority, he gathered information to pass on to Mayor Giuliani and his staff. At about this time Ray Downey, the head of Special Operations Command (SOC) and an expert on building collapse, remarked to him that the building they were in could collapse. The chiefs decided to move the command post, as it was becoming too dangerous in the lobby of the North Tower. Von Essen left the command post to report to Mayor Giuliani, and this action probably saved his life. While he was occupied looking for Giuliani, the South Tower collapsed. Once Von Essen found Giuliani he reported that the loss of firefighters, police, and civilians would be heavy. Then the North Tower suddenly collapsed and all was chaos. Von Essen stayed with Mayor Giuliani, and both of them began accepting help from any federal or state agency that offered it. Von Essen soon learned that his close friend, Father Mychal Judge, was dead, and that his friends Pete Ganci and Bill Feehan, Deputy Fire Commissioner, were missing and presumed dead. Feehan was a beloved member of the FDNY who had stayed on with the department past retirement age. A decision was made by the surviving fire chiefs to not fight the fire that had broken out at Seven World Trade Center because it was too dangerous to fight that fire in the unstable building.

In the aftermath of the destruction of the World Trade Center, Von Essen had to deal with a decimated fire department. What bothered Von Essen the most was that the most aggressive and skilled firefighters had been killed in the collapse of the twin towers. Moreover, many of the most experienced chiefs and captains had also been

> **Von Essen Explains Why So Many Senior Firefighters Lost Their Lives on September 11**
>
> It is the nature of our fire department, of our long-standing philosophy of aggressively attacking fires, that many of our leaders and many of the best, most able firefighters were the ones who were going to be lost. The fire department is the only place I know where the higher up a man moves, the greater the chance that he will place himself at risk. The best, most enthusiastic firefighters willingly expose themselves to the highest level of danger.
>
> Thomas Von Essen with Matt Murray, *Strong of Heart: Life and Death in the Fire Department of New York* (New York: Regan-Books, 2002), p. 52.

A worker passes by a fifty-eight-ton steel beam, the last remaining beam from the World Trade Center's South Tower, in this 2002 photo. The beam was spray-painted with the numbers of victims lost in the attacks: 37 Port Authority police, 23 New York police officers, and 343 New York firefighters. (AP IMAGES/Kathy Willens.)

killed. There were also the issues of morale and stress among the survivors, who had seen too many of their buddies killed or disappeared.

Von Essen remained the fire commissioner until the end of Giuliani's term of office on December 31, 2001. During that time, he had to weather firefighters' discontent over their reduction in force at Ground Zero in early November 2001. A compromise was eventually worked out, but Von Essen was subjected to severe criticism by both firefighters and families of firefighters. After leaving office Von Essen became a senior vice president with Giuliani's consulting business, Giuliani Partners.

See Also

Cleanup Operations at Ground Zero; Firefighters at Ground Zero

Suggested Reading

Al Baker, "Security; For Emergency Officials Touched by 9/11's Horrors, Fears of Creeping Complacency," *New York Times* (May 21, 2002), p. A17; Eunice Moscoso, "9/11 Hearing Heated; Communication Gap Called 'Scandal' as Victims' Families Grow Emotional," *Atlanta Journal-Constitution* (May 19, 2004), p. 1A; Thomas Von Essen with Matt Murray, *Strong of Heart: Life and Death in the Fire Department of New York* (New York: ReganBooks, 2002).

W

Wag the Dog (Movie)

The movie *Wag the Dog* had an impact on the Clinton administration's efforts to rally public support for the president's counterterrorism campaign against Osama bin Laden and al-Qaeda. The movie's story line involves a sex-obsessed U.S. president in the middle of a reelection campaign whose advisors stage a fake war in Albania to distract voters from the scandal. Dustin Hoffman and Robert DeNiro starred in this popular move, which appeared in December 1997. It bore enough resemblance to the true-life scandal involving President Clinton and White House intern Monica Lewinsky that it resonated politically among those hostile to Clinton. The national media also had a field day with the similarities between the movie and the conduct of President Clinton.

The Clinton administration's efforts to neutralize bin Laden led Republicans in Congress to suggest a comparison with the plot of *Wag the Dog*. This charge surfaced both in the media and among Republican congressmen after Tomahawk cruise missiles were fired into Afghanistan and Sudan on August 20, 1998. Investigative journalist Seymour Hersh went so far as to advance the "wag the dog" thesis to explain Clinton's actions in an article in the *New Yorker*. Soon

---

Mark Russell Led Pat Buchanan and Bill Press in This Song on CNN's *Crossfire*

If a woman gives you trouble or maybe two or three, and your explanation puts the public in a fog, no problem, pick that red phone up, it's an emergency, and go to war. It's been done before. It's "Wag the Dog."

"Wag the Dog." "Wag the Dog." Go to war, it's been done before, it's "Wag the Dog."

Well, no one will complain with a Hitler-like Hussein, and everyone will understand your war. An Afghanistan distraction from your problems and your pain, namely, Monica and Paula and God knows how many more.

"Wag the dog."

Quoted in Daniel Benjamin and Steven Simon, *The Age of Sacred Terror* (New York: Random House, 2002), p. 358.

Statement of Former Secretary of Defense William Cohen on the "Wag the Dog" Charge

I was prepared at that time and today to say I put my entire public career on the line to say that the President (Clinton) always acted specifically upon the recommendation of those of us who held the positions for responsibility to take military action, and at no time did he ever try to use it or manipulate it to serve his personal ends. And I think it's important to be clear because that "Wag the Dog" cynicism that was so virulent there I am afraid is coming back again, and I think we've got to do everything we can to stop engaging in the kind of self-flagellation and criticism, and challenging of motives of our respective presidents.

Quoted in Thomas H. Kean, Lee H. Hamilton, and Benjamin Rhodes, *Without Precedent: The Inside Story of the 9/11 Commission* (New York: Knopf, 2006), p. 160.

afterward it became a common theme broadcast by Clinton's critics, especially right-wing talk radio commentators and other cheerleaders of the "Get Clinton" campaign.

The charge of "wag the dog" made President Clinton and his advisors sensitive to any action that did not have an immediately successful outcome. In a practical sense this made any operation against bin Laden impossible. President Clinton believed that any operation against bin Laden would have to withstand scrutiny in the court of American public opinion. This restriction meant that capture or assassination plots had to avoid collateral damage and had to succeed.

See Also

Bin Laden, Osama; Qaeda, al-

Suggested Reading

David Benjamin and Steven Simon, *The Age of Sacred Terror* (New York: Random House, 2002); Richard A. Clarke, *Against All Enemies: Inside America's War on Terror* (New York: Free Press, 2004).

The Wall

"The Wall" was the term used to describe the FBI's barrier between intelligence gathering on one hand, and preparing for and prosecuting a criminal case, on the other. Promotions came to FBI agents who put together cases that led to the conviction of persons accused of criminal behavior. Intelligence gathering, on the other hand, led to information but not to convictions, and not to too much credit to the agents involved. The policy of the FBI before September 11, therefore, was to conduct intelligence gathering just to the point that the information gained could be used to prepare a case for trial. When a case reached the stage of preparation for trial, intelligence gathering stopped and restrictions were imposed against sharing information with other parts of the FBI and other government agencies. In theory, this restriction was enforced in order to ensure that the FBI played by the rules in gathering evidence in criminal cases. Additionally, Rule 6E of the Federal Rules of Criminal Procedure forbad the disclosure of grand jury material.

Although the Wall stood on legal justification, there were ways to skirt it in the interest of national security. However, FBI lawyers were reluctant to take chances, and the wall between intelligence gathering and criminal prosecution became more rigid. Guidelines for the Wall were further codified in a 1995 Justice Department memorandum issued during investigation of the 1993 World Trade Center bombing. This memorandum stated categorically that intelligence gathering and case preparation/prosecution must be kept separate. These guidelines were reconfirmed by the Justice Department in 2001. Despite this clear delineation between the two activities, the Clinton administration attempted to break down what it considered to be an artificial wall. Attorney General Janet Reno attempted at least once to achieve a more limited interpretation of Rule 6E, but FBI Director Louis Freeh opposed any changes and refused to allow revision of the rules of criminal procedure.

FBI agents found the Wall an insurmountable barrier in intelligence gathering, often protesting that it hindered their efforts to obtain intelligence on potential terrorist operations. The barriers of the Wall had kept FBI agents in the New York field office from gaining information about two of the September 11 hijackers—Khalid al-Mihdhar and Nawaf al-Hazmi—until it was too late. One FBI agent went so far as to send an e-mail to FBI headquarters in which he stated that "whatever has happened to this, someday someone will die and, wall or not, the public will not understand why we were not more effective in throwing every resource we had at certain problems."

The Senate and House Joint Inquiry Committee on Intelligence concluded in 2002 that in actuality a series of walls existed. Members of this committee were horrified to find so many walls. They concluded that "these walls separate foreign from domestic activities, foreign intelligence from law-enforcement operations, the FBI from the CIA, communications intelligence from other types of intelligence, the intelligence community from other types of federal agencies, and national-security information from other forms of evidence."

The most severe critic of the Wall was Senator Richard Shelby (R-AL). As a member of the Senate and House Joint Inquiry Committee on Intelligence, he accused the FBI of allowing the Foreign Intelligence Surveillance Act (FISA) Court to serve as a wall of "no coordination," leaving the United States open to attack. He further charged that the FBI "had, to suit its own institutional interests, created rules where they did not exist that allowed it to refuse to share the results of criminal investigations, specifically grand jury investigations, with the rest of the intelligence community." Shelby was uncertain whether the FBI could handle the task of coping with the intelligence needs of the country. He was no less critical of the CIA for its refusal to share intelligence with other government agencies.

The Wall and its variants endured until the events of September 11 made them obsolete. It was apparent that there was need for better communications, both within the FBI and among other government agencies. It took Congressional adoption of the USA PATRIOT Act in 2002 to dismantle the Wall.

See Also
Clinton Administration; Federal Bureau of Investigation; USA PATRIOT Act

See Document
Document #28

Suggested Reading
David Benjamin and Steven Simon, *The Age of Sacred Terror* (New York: Random House, 2002); Bill Gertz, *Breakdown: The Failure of American Intelligence to Defeat Global Terror*

(New York: Plume Books, 2003), rev. ed.; Bob Graham, *Intelligence Matters: The CIA, the FBI, Saudi Arabia, and the Failure of America's War on Terror* (New York: Random House, 2004); Thomas Kean, Lee Hamilton, and Benjamin Rhodes, *Without Precedent: The Inside Story of the 9/11 Commission* (New York: Random House, 2002); Richard Gid Powers, *Broken: The Troubled Past and Uncertain Future of the FBI* (New York: Free Press, 2004); John Yoo, *War by Other Means: An Insider's Account of the War on Terror* (New York: Atlantic Monthly Press, 2006).

Weldon, Curtis "Curt" (1947–)

Curt Weldon has been the leading champion of the Able Danger story about an agency of the U.S. government knowing of the presence of Mohamed Atta before September 11. Weldon used his position as a Republican congressman from the 7th Congressional District of Pennsylvania to charge that the government suppressed the fact that a special military intelligence program had identified Mohammad Atta as an al-Qaeda operative before September 11, 2001. His position as vice chair of the House Armed Services and Homeland Security Committees gave him a forum to express his views.

Weldon's early career was as an educator. He was born on July 22, 1947. His family lived in Marcus Hook, Pennsylvania. He was the youngest of nine children. After high school, he attended West Chester University of Pennsylvania. His major was Russian Studies. After graduation in 1969, he was subject to the military draft but failed the physical. He found a position as an educator in the Delaware County schools. His other interest was working with the volunteer Viscose Fire Company in Marcus Hook.

Weldon entered politics in 1977, running for Mayor of Marcus Hook. He served two terms as mayor, from 1977 to 1982. In 1984 Weldon ran for U.S. Congress on the Republican ticket but lost to incumbent Democrat Robert W. Edgar. When Edgar decided to run for the U.S. Senate, Weldon won Edgar's seat in 1986. Although his district leans Democratic, Weldon won election handily from 1986 until 2006. He was defeated in 2006, in part because of a scandal that arose based on reports that he sent lobbying contracts from foreign clients to a company operated by his daughter.

Weldon was one of the more conservative Republicans in the U.S. House, where he held a number of important assignments. Two issues he advanced were promotion of a national missile defense system and improvement of U.S.–Russian relations. He made several fact-finding trips to North Korea and Libya in furtherance of these concerns.

Soon after Weldon learned about Able Danger, he became its champion. Weldon was relentless, both in the House of Representatives and in public, in his attacks on the Clinton administration for having closed down the secret Able Danger program. Weldon did not acknowledge that the program was unauthorized or that it operated through the office of the Chairman of the Joint Chiefs of Staff. Although Able Danger was closed during the George W. Bush administration, Weldon did not publicly mention this fact.

Weldon was in full attack mode when his political career came to an abrupt halt in November 2006. Despite his conservative credentials, the district he represented was predominantly Democratic. This fact caught up with him when federal

Representative Curt Weldon (R-PA) testifies on "Able Danger" and the nature of intelligence sharing prior to the September 11 attacks before the Senate Judiciary Committee on Capitol Hill, September 21, 2005. James Smith (second from left) and Lt. Col. Anthony Shaffer (center) listen in the background. Both men were ordered by the Pentagon not to testify. A staff member holds an al-Qaeda organizational chart at right. (AP IMAGES/Dennis Cook.)

authorities began investigating his misconduct in directing consulting contracts to family members. In the November 2006 election, Weldon was decisively defeated by a Democratic candidate.

See Also
Able Danger; National Commission on Terrorist Attacks upon the United States

See Document
Document #38

Suggested Reading
Andrew C. McCarthy, "It's Time to Investigate Able Danger and the 9/11 Commission," *National Review* (December 8, 2005), p. 1; James Rosen, "A 9/11 Tip-Off—Fact or Fancy?: Debate Still Swirls around Claim That Secret Military Program ID'd Hijackers a Year before Attacks," *Sacramento Bee* (November 24, 2005), p. A1.

World Trade Center
The World Trade Center was one of the signature complexes in New York City. It was a complex of seven buildings on a sixteen-acre tract in the lower end of Manhattan on a superblock bounded by Vesey, Liberty, Church, and West Streets, and it was about three blocks north of the New York Stock Exchange. Nelson and David Rockefeller had proposed such a complex in the 1950s as a way to revitalize lower Manhattan. The Port Authority of New York and New Jersey (PANYNJ) constructed and operated the complex. The U.S. architect was Minoru Yamasaki,

assisted by Antonio Brittiochi and the architecture firm of Emery Roth and Sons, which handled the production work; the Worthington, Skilling, Helle, and Jackson firm served as project engineers. Yamasaki designed a complex with twin towers and three lower-rise structures. His design was selected over those of a dozen other American architects. The North Tower had a height of 1,368 feet and the South Tower 1,362 feet, making them the tallest buildings in the world—until Chicago's Sears Tower surpassed them both in 1974.

Construction of the World Trade Center complex took more than a decade to finish. The groundbreaking was on August 5, 1966. One World Trade Center (North Tower complex) was open to its first tenants late in 1970, although its top floors remained uncompleted until 1972. Two World Trade Center (the South Tower complex) was not finished until 1973. It cost an estimated $1.5 billion to construct the World Trade Center complex. Because the complex was built on six acres of landfill, the foundation for each tower had to be extended more than seventy feet below ground level, to rest on solid bedrock. The ribbon-cutting ceremony took place on April 4, 1973. It took two hundred thousand tons of steel, and controversy developed over the fireproofing of the steel.

The World Trade Center complex was immense. This complex was in the middle of New York City's financial district. Each of the towers had 110 stories. The complex contained 13.4 million square feet of office space—enough to house 50,000 office employees working for 438 companies from twenty-eight countries. It also had 21,800 windows. To provide access to the office space and other operations, each tower had 104 passenger elevators. In each tower were three staircases to be used in case of emergencies.

The World Trade Center complex was essentially a commercial site, but it was also a popular tourist destination. Around 140,000 tourists visited the World Trade Center complex daily to take advantage of its many amenities. In comparison, about 50,000 employees worked in the complex on any given workday. The four-star restaurant, Windows on the World, on the one hundred-and-seventh floor of the North Tower was popular, not only for its food but also because of the view. The twin towers were a major asset to the New York City skyline, but they were also a tempting target.

See Also
World Trade Center, September 11

Suggested Reading
Eric Darton, *Divided We Stand: A Biography of New York City's World Trade Center* (New York: Basic Books, 2001); James Glanz and Eric Lipton, *City in the Sky: The Rise and Fall of the World Trade Center* (New York: Times Books, 2004).

World Trade Center, September 11
On September 11, 2001, the day started normally in the World Trade Center. In the twin towers the number of employees was 14,154. Approximately 14,000 people were present at the time the first commercial aircraft hit the North Tower. American Airlines Flight 11 crashed into the North Tower at 8:46:40 a.m. The aircraft cut a swath through eight floors—from the ninety-third to the hundredth— as it hit at about 450 miles an hour.

Force of the impact and the resulting fire from aviation fuel destroyed most elevators and most staircases between the floors above the hundredth and below the ninety-third floors. Nearly one thousand people were trapped on the upper floors of the North Tower. A majority of them worked for Cantor Fitzgerald brokerage company. At least sixty people jumped from the North Tower rather than burn to death. One firefighter was killed after being hit by one of the jumpers.

An emergency call went out to the Fire Department of New York City (FDNY). More than a thousand firefighters from 225 units showed up at the World Trade complex. There were so many vehicles that parking became a problem. Immediately, FDNY commanders realized that they could not extinguish the growing fire in the North Tower, so they concentrated on evacuating people. Because of lack of water, only a few firefighters would engage in trying to put out the fire. Operators for the 911 system told people to stay put, and assured them that firefighters would be coming to rescue them. To those on the top floors of the North Tower the deteriorating conditions made it imperative that help come soon. Some tried to make it to the roof, but the FDNY had decided after the 1993 World Trade Center bombing to lock the heavy doors leading from the floors to the building's sole roof exit. This decision had been made because rooftop rescues by helicopters were a safety risk.

Events at the North Tower caused concern among those in the South Tower. Many of those in the South Tower decided to evacuate the building. Those who tried to evacuate the South Tower were told as they tried to leave the building to return to their offices. This was because the standard firefighting philosophy in high-rise fires was to "stay put, stand by." An announcement broadcast over the intercom at 8:55 a.m. stated that there was no need to evacuate the South Tower. This announcement directly contradicted a decision by Sergeant Al DeVona, ranking Port Authority police officer on the scene, who had ordered that both the North and South Towers be evacuated within minutes of the first crash. DeVona reordered the evacuations at 8:59 a.m. Captain Anthony Whitaker, commander of

---

Evaluation of the World Trade Center Disaster

To a large extent, the World Trade Center is a disaster that could be as much a result of its fundamental design as was the Titanic. The plane hit the South Tower and distributed the burning fuel throughout. The temperature of the fire was such that steel was stretched throughout. The steel trusses that held the weight of the corrugated steel and the 3 inches of concrete that formed the floor stretched. The weight of the floor was shifted to the interior columns, all 47 of them around the elevators and stairs, but those stretched and weakened columns could not withstand such a burden. The trusses on the fire floors separated from the exterior walls, almost all of them simultaneously, and the exterior walls buckled. Since the weight of the floor was no longer sustained by the exterior wall connections and no longer held by the interior columns, the floor collapsed. But it did not collapse partially; it collapsed fully in a pancaked layer to the floor below. The floor below could not sustain the dynamic weight of a uniform falling body, and it, too, collapsed, to the next floor, and to the next, and to the next, until moving at 120 miles per hour, the building fell in 12 seconds.

Dennis Smith, *Report from Ground Zero: The Story of the Rescue Efforts at the World Trade Center* (New York: Viking, 2002), p. 189.

Analysis of September 11 by First Deputy Police Commissioner Joe Dunne

No one made the right move. No one made the wrong move. No one made a critical mistake. No one made an ingenious decision. We were just in the Hands of God, or fate if you prefer, and those that got out of the place were fortunate and blessed and those that didn't are with God now. There's no rhyme or reason why people made it and why people didn't.

Quoted in Dennis Smith, *Report from Ground Zero* (New York: Viking, 2002), p. 69.

the Port Authority Police, confirmed this order shortly thereafter. Faulty communications equipment made these decisions difficult to implement. Because of the communication problems, the 911 operators could not be informed of the deteriorating situation and they continued to give outdated advice to people to stay where they were.

The difficulty in evacuating the twin towers was compounded by the structural defects of the towers. Decisions made during construction made it difficult for people to evacuate, there being only three staircases. Changes in building codes in 1968 had reduced both the number of staircases and the level of fire protection for high-rise buildings. These changes allowed more rentable space, but meant that the staircases were built for only a few hundred people at a time to walk three or four stories, not for mass evacuation. The location of the three staircases in the center of the building, rather than being dispersed, turned the upper floors of both towers into death traps because the plane crashes in both buildings cut off access to the staircases. With inferior fireproofing, there was nothing to prevent the spread of the fires. The New York City building codes were not an issue because the builder, the Port Authority of New York and New Jersey, as a regional entity was not required to follow building codes.

The twin towers had been able to sustain the impact of the two airliners, but it was the fire that endangered the structure. Later reports indicated that it was the high temperature of the fire, caused by the ignition of the aviation fuel and intensified by the burning office furniture and paper, that caused the worst damage. Another factor was that the World Trade Center complex buildings had been constructed with thirty-seven pounds of steel per square foot, in contrast to the normal high-rise buildings of that era, which were built with seventy-five pounds of steel per square feet. This type of construction saved millions of dollars during construction and increased the square footage of rental space, making the buildings more profitable. Since steel begins to degrade at 300 degrees and continues to degrade by 50 percent at 1,000 degrees, the high-temperature fire, combined with the reduced amount of steel supporting the buildings, led to weakening of the structure of the buildings.

Comments by Deputy Assistant Chief of FDNY on Those Rescued at the World Trade Center

That day we lost 2,752 people at the World Trade Center; 343 were firefighters. But we also saved 25,000 people. And that's what people should remember because firefighters and rescuers went in and they knew it was dangerous, but they went in to save people. And they saved many.

Quoted in Thomas H. Kean, Lee H. Hamilton, and Benjamin Rhodes, *Without Precedent: The Inside Story of the 9/11 Commission* (New York: Knopf, 2006).

The South Tower collapsed first. United Airlines Flight 175

Two firefighters hose down a hot spot as another looks on from above at the site of the destroyed World Trade Center, October 9, 2001. (AP IMAGES/Stuart Ramson.)

hit at higher speed than did American Airlines Flight 11. This higher speed and the resulting explosion and fire in the South Tower caused it to collapse in a heap.

Total deaths at the World Trade Center were 2,749. Of this total, 147 were passengers and crew of the two aircraft. Another 412 of the dead were rescue workers killed when the two towers collapsed. The remaining 2,190 dead succumbed to the plane crashes or in the collapse of the towers. Except for the actions of key individuals and the firefighters, the casualties could have been much higher. Except in the case of those trapped in the North and South Towers above where the planes hit, there was no discernable reason for some people to have died while others survived.

Besides attacking the physical structures of the twin towers, the hijackers also impacted the financial health of the United States. Many businesses simply went out of business in New York City. Many others struggled to regain financial viability. Layoffs in the period between September 12 and January 21, 2002, related to September 11 were calculated at 1,054,653. The attack on the airline industry was an indirect financial blow in that it accounted for about 9 percent of the total gross domestic product of the United States, and because around eleven million jobs are related directly to commercial aviation.

See Also

American Airlines Flight 11; Firefighters at Ground Zero; Giuliani, Rudolf William Louis "Rudy" III; United Airlines Flight 175

Suggested Reading

Richard Bernstein, *Out of the Blue: The Story of September 11, 2001, from Jihad to Ground Zero* (New York: Times Books, 2002); Jim Dwyer, "Errors and Lack of Information in New York's Response to Sept. 11," *New York Times* (May 19, 2004), p. B8; Jim Dwyer and Kevin Flynn, *102 Minutes: The Untold Story of the Fight to Survive Inside the Twin Towers* (New York: Times Books, 2005); Dennis Smith, *Report from Ground Zero* (New York: Viking, 2002).

World Trade Center (Movie)

Oliver Stone directed the movie *World Trade Center*, which tells the story of two of the survivors at the World Trade Center complex on September 11. The protagonists were two Port Authority of New York and New Jersey police officers, John McLaughlin and Will Jimeno. They had been trapped beneath falling rubble after the collapse of the twin towers. There were only six people rescued from beneath the debris. Stone became interested in the project after receiving a screenplay from Andrea Berloff.

Unlike in several of his other films, Stone avoided politics to tell a story. He let the drama build around the two main characters and their wives. To add authenticity Stone used input from McLoughlin and Jimeno. The stars of the film were Nicolas Cage, Michael Peña, Maria Bello, and Maggie Gyllenhaal. Most of the scenes were filmed at a soundstage in Playa Vista, California.

The movie opened on August 9, 2005. Most of the reviews by critics were positive. Paramount Pictures had released it as a mainstream film with a rating of PG-13. The Motion Picture Association of America decided on this rating because of the movie's emotional content and some of its disturbing images and language. On opening weekend it grossed over $18 million in the United States and Canada. Its total gross was over $70 million in North America. Worldwide the film grossed over $161 million.

Oliver Stone's Comment on Story Line

It's true—we don't cover the terrorist side in the film. It is concerned only with the survival of these two men. Politics doesn't enter into it—it's about courage and survival.

Quoted in Fiona Hudson, "Stone's Ode to Survival," *Sunday Herald Sun* [Australia] (September 24, 2006), p. E7.

Stone had a reputation for making politically controversial films. Among these films were *JFK*, *Platoon*, and *Natural Born Killers*. When news surfaced that Stone was going to make a movie about September 11, the assumption by many was that it would be an exposé or would outline a conspiracy theory. His right-wing critics were particularly vocal in expressing this fear. Once it became apparent that Stone was crafting a straightforward story line that showed the heroism of that day, conservative spokespersons embraced the movie and recommended it widely. The only segment of the American population disappointed in the movie were those in the 9/11 conspiracy movement. They expected him to outline elements of a U.S. government conspiracy, and when this did not happen, the conspiracy theorists rejected the movie.

See Also
World Trade Center, September 11

Suggested Reading
Sam Allis, "No Longer a Rolling Stone?" *Boston Globe* (August 6, 2006), p. N11; Paul Cullum, "After the Fall; Oliver Stone at Ground Zero," *LA Weekly* (August 10, 2006), p. 1; Ann Hornaday, "America's Character: In the Debris of 9/11, Bravery, Not Conspiracy, Stirred Oliver Stone," *Washington Post* (August 8, 2006), p. CO1; Carla Meyer, "Oliver Stone; Directing History," *Sacramento Bee* (August 6, 2006), p. TK24; Sara Stewart, "Patriot Games—Why Oliver Stone, Hollywood's Biggest Conspiracy Theorist, Put Politics Aside for 'WTC'," *New York Post* (August 6, 2006), p. 40; David Usborne, "How Stone Won Over the Right," *Independent* [London] (July 29, 2006), p. 33.

World Trade Center Bombing (1993)

The first attempt by terrorists to destroy the World Trade Center complex failed in 1993. Islamist terrorists exploded a bomb in the underground garage, level B-2, of One World Trade Center (North Tower) on Friday, February 26, 1993, at 12:18 p.m. They used a yellow Ford Econoline Ryder truck filled with 1,500 pounds of explosives. Their bomb was built from a mix of fuel oil and fertilizer with a nitroglycerin booster.

The conspirators were militant Islamists led by Ramzi Yousef. Yousef confessed to American authorities after his capture that they had selected the World Trade Center complex because it was "an overweening symbol of American arrogance." Other participants were Mohammed Salameh, Nidal Ayyad, Mahmud Abouhalima, and—to a lesser extent—Abdul Rahman. Beginning in January 1993, Yousef and his fellow conspirators began to locate and buy the ingredients for the bomb. They needed everything, ranging from a place to work to storage lockers, tools, chemicals, plastic tubs, fertilizer, and lengths of rubber tubing. It took about $20,000 to build the bomb. Yousef wanted more money so that he could build an even bigger bomb. Most of the funds were raised in the United States, but some money came from abroad. Yousef's uncle, Khalid Sheikh Mohammed, had sent him $600 dollars for the bomb.

It was Yousef's intention that the explosion bring down the North Tower of the World Trade Center complex, and that its impact on the South Tower would bring it down also. This expectation was too high. The North Tower shook in the explosion, but withstood its force.

Despite the force of the explosion, casualties were rela-

Timing of the Attack and Funding

Yousef told investigating agents that the date had been forced upon the conspirators because they could not afford to pay their rent for the next month. However, Yousef left New York on a first-class ticket, and the FBI discovered $2,615 in cash in the conspirators' apartments.

Simon Reeve, *The New Jackals: Ramzi Yousef, Osama bin Laden, and the Future of Terrorism* (Boston: Northeastern University Press, 1999), p. 246.

tively low. The bomb produced a crater twenty-two feet wide and five stories deep. The force of the explosion came close to breaching the so-called bathtub, a structure that prevented water from the Hudson River from pouring into the underground areas of the complex and into the subway system. If this breach had occurred, the resulting catastrophic loss of live would have eclipsed the losses from the attacks on September 11, 2001. Six people—John DiGiovanni, Bob Kirkpatrick, Steve Knapp, Bill Backo, Wilfredo Mercado, and Monica Rodriguez-Smith—were killed, and more than 1,000 were injured. The New York City Fire Department responded with 775 firefighters from 135 companies, but they arrived too late to do anything but tend to the wounded and carry away the dead. It took nearly ten hours to get everyone out because the elevators shorted out in the explosion and power to the staircases failed. Evacuations took place in the dark and in the midst of heavy smoke. The towers were repaired and the complex reopened in less than one month. It cost $510 million to repair the damage. The bombing was also significant for showing how vulnerable the World Trade Complex was to terrorist attacks.

At first investigators believed that a transformer had blown up, but once they started examining the site, it became obvious that a large bomb had detonated. Within five hours the FBI and the New York City Police Department had confirmed that the explosion had been caused by a bomb. The next question was who had done it. There had been twenty calls to the police claiming responsibility, but this was not unusual. The top candidate was Balkan extremists, but the investigation was just beginning.

Within weeks the investigating team of 700 agents had identified or arrested all of the World Trade Center bombers. What broke the case was the discovery of a unique vehicle identification number on the frame of the Ryder van. They learned that Salameh had rented the van. He had reported the van stolen and was trying to recover the $400 deposit. Salameh was arrested while trying to collect the deposit. Investigators then turned to identification of his fellow conspirators, and Yousef was finally identified as the leader of the plot.

By the time authorities had identified Yousef as the leader of the plot and maker of the bomb, he was already in Pakistan planning other operations. Ultimately, a CIA-and-FBI team captured him in Pakistan, but not before he had initiated several other plots. Yousef had always been a freelancer, but there is evidence that he had connections with al-Qaeda operatives before and after the World Trade Center bombing. After a series of trials, the participants in the bomb plot received life sentences. Yousef was sentenced to 240 years in solitary confinement.

See Also

Abouhalima, Mahmud; Mohammed, Khalid Sheikh; Yousef, Ramzi Ahmed

See Document

Document #1

Suggested Reading

J. Bowyer Bell, *Murders on the Nile: The World Trade Center and Global Terror* (San Francisco: Encounter Books, 2003); Peter Caram, *The 1993 World Trade Center Bombing: Foresight and Warning* (London: Janus Publishing, 2001); Mike Davis, *Duda's Wagon; A Brief History of the Car Bomb* (London: Verso, 2007); Peter Lance, *1000 Years for Revenge:*

International Terrorism and the FBI: The Untold Story (New York: ReganBooks, 2003); John Miller, Michael Stone, and Chris Mitchell, *The Cell: Inside the 9/11 Plot, and Why the FBI and CIA Failed to Stop It* (New York: Hyperion, 2002); Simon Reeve, *The New Jackals: Ramzi Yousef, Osama bin Laden, and the Future of Terrorism* (Boston: Northeastern University Press, 1999).

Y

Yousef, Ramzi Ahmed (1968–)

Ramzi Ahmed Yousef gained fame as the leader of the 1993 bombing of the World Trade Center complex in New York City. For a time Yousef was the most famous terrorist in the world. His exploit of bombing the World Trade Center complex made him a hero in Muslim extremist circles. He used his fame to recruit followers and plan other terrorist operations throughout South Asia, especially in the Philippines.

Yousef's political inclinations and strong scientific abilities prepared him to become a terrorist. He was born on April 27, 1968, in the small town of Fuhayhil, Kuwait, and was given the birth name of Abdul Basit Mahmud Abdul-Karim. His father was an engineer by training, from the Baluchistan region of Pakistan. He worked for Kuwaiti Airlines. Besides being a Baluchi nationalist, Yousef's father was a devotee of the theology of Wahhabism, a strict form of Muslim religious practice initiated by the conservative eighteenth-century cleric Muhammad ibn Abd al-Wahhab. (Wahhabism is the form of Sunni Islam practiced in Saudi Arabia.) His mother was a Kuwaiti of Palestinian origin. His uncle was Khalid Sheikh Mohammed of September 11 fame. Because of his non-Kuwait origin, Yousef and his family were treated as second-class citizens in Kuwait, causing him to resent the Kuwaiti regime. One of his childhood friends was Abdul Hakim Murad. After finishing his local schooling and showing promise in mathematics and science, he decided to study abroad. Beginning in 1986, Yousef took a twelve-week course in English at Oxford University. He then attended a small technical school in Wales—the West Glamogan Institute in Swansea, United Kingdom. In summer 1988 Yousef traveled to Afghanistan with the intention of fighting with the Afghans against the Soviets, but instead he spent his time in Peshawar at al-Qaeda training camps. It was at this camp that he first med Mahmud Abouhalima. Yousef obtained a Higher National Diploma in computer-aided electrical engineering in 1989. While still at the university, Yousef affiliated with a local cell of the Muslim Brotherhood. Hassan al-Banna (1906–49) had founded the Muslim Brotherhood in Egypt in 1928 to restore religious and political practices of the time of the Prophet Muhammad. Leaders of the Muslim Brotherhood form the opposition to most of the regimes in the Middle East.

Returning to Kuwait, Yousef landed a job with the Kuwaiti government, working as a communications engineer at the National Computer Center for the Ministry of Planning. This position lasted until Saddam Hussein invaded Kuwait in August 1990. The next year Yousef moved to Quetta, Pakistan, where he married a young Baluchistani woman.

Yousef committed himself to terrorism soon after he left Kuwait. Unlike other terrorists, Yousef was not particularly religious, and his motivation for taking up terrorism was the Palestinian cause. He identified with his Palestinian mother's family. While in Pakistan, Yousef participated in another al-Qaeda training camp, first as a trainee and later as an instructor in the making of bombs. His specialty in camp was making nitroglycerin bombs. At this camp Yousef made contact with terrorists in training from South Asia, particularly from the Philippines. One of his connections was with Abdurajak Janjalani, the future founder of the Abu Sayyaf group in the southern Philippines. Yousef briefly visited Basilian Island in the Philippines in 1991 to instruct at a Muslim guerrilla camp.

Yousef decided to turn his attention toward a terrorist act in the United States. He told a friend that he wanted to attack Israel, but because Israel was too tough a target he decided to attack the United States instead. This friend told him that a lot of Jews worked at the World Trade Center complex in New York City. Yousef was described by Terry McDermott as a "freelancer, the harbinger of a new type of independent, non–state-sponsored global terrorist." He entered the United States in 1992 with the goal of establishing contact with possible terrorist allies. Yousef lacked a valid visa so he filed a claim for political and religious asylum with the Immigration and Naturalization Service (INS) at the John F. Kennedy International Airport. Confronted by the choice of deportation or arrest, he chose arrest but authorities released him on his own recognizance with instructions to appear for an asylum hearing. His traveling companion, Ahmed Ajaj, was arrested and later deported. Yousef never showed up at the INS hearing scheduled for December 8, 1992, so after that date his stay in the country became technically illegal.

Yousef's first contacts in the United States were with the militant Islamists at the al-Kifah Refugee Center in Brooklyn. There he met with the Egyptian Islamist leader Sheikh Omar Abdel Rahman, formerly the spiritual leader of the Egyptian terrorist organization al-Gama'a al-Islamiyya (the Islamic Group). Although blind since infancy, Abdel Rahman had a considerable following in both the Middle East and United States. He had entered the United States in July 1990, and consolidated political control at the al-Kifah Refugee Center.

Yousef took advantage of the presence of these militants to plot a bombing attack of the World Trade Center complex. According to Terry McDermott, Yousef was able to recruit a team of "largely marginal, unaccomplished men" to build a bomb. His major accomplice was Mahmud Abouhalima. Yousef's intent was to build a bomb big enough to bring down the World Trade Center complex and kill 250,000 Americans.

A major problem for Yousef was his lack of funds to build the size bomb that he wanted. Yousef's uncle, Khalid Sheikh Mohammed, sent him $660 from Pakistan to help, but he needed much more money. The size of the bomb was determined by the amount of money he had available. Ultimately, Yousef had to limit the size of the bomb because he had only $20,000 available. Yousef and his small team of terrorists built a large bomb in an apartment at 40 Pamrapo Avenue in Jersey City, New Jersey. He was able to purchase fifteen hundred pounds of urea, 130 gallons of nitric acid, and a variety of other chemicals from City Chemical in New Jersey. These ingredients, one hundred pounds of aluminum powder, and hydrogen gas tanks made a 1,500-pound bomb.

On the morning of February 26, 1993, the conspirators loaded the bomb into a large, rented Ford Econoline Ryder van. After the van was parked in the underground garage of the World Trade Center under the North Tower, it was detonated at 12:18 p.m. on February 26, 1993. The explosion killed six and injured more than a thousand. It also produced $300 million in damage. Although the bomb produced a large crater, the World Trade Center complex remained standing. Yousef had hoped that by undermining one of the towers, it would fall and impact the other tower, achieving his goal of killing 250,000 people. By the time of the explosion Yousef was already en route back to Pakistan. Shortly after the detonation, Yousef had an associate send a letter to five American newspapers justifying the bombing. He was bitterly disappointed in the failure of the bomb to do more damage to the World Trade Center, but it did take six lives and caused thousands of injuries.

> **Intent of Yousef in Bombing the World Trade Center**
>
> Yousef did not aim to damage the World Trade Center: he set out to bring the towers down. Placed correctly, he thought, a large enough charge would cause one tower to topple into the other, killing everyone inside. . . . Ramzi's attack reversed the law of historical repetition— it was the farce that preceded the tragedy of September 11. For all his ingenuity, Yousef knew little about physics, civil engineering, or the structural safeguards built into the Twin Towers, so he underestimated the amount of explosives needed to destroy one building. He also did not understand that it was impossible to tip one tower over into the other. Gravity and the enormous inertial mass of the building meant that structural failure would result in pancaking.
>
> Quoted in Daniel Benjamin and Steven Simon, *The Age of Sacred Terror* (New York: Random House, 2002), p. 14.

After leaving the United States, Yousef returned to Quetta, Pakistan, where his family lived. Later he traveled to Karachi, where he had a fateful meeting with his uncle, Khalid Sheikh Mohammed. Yousef had several conversations with his good friend Abdul Hakim Murad, and they discussed ways to attack targets in the United States. Murad, who had a commercial pilot's license and had attended a commercial pilot school in the United States, proposed packing a small airplane full of explosives and dive-bombing into the Pentagon or the headquarters of the CIA. Yousef found this idea intriguing enough that he introduced Murad to his uncle. His uncle asked Murad about pilot training and the availability of aircraft. Nothing further happened with this idea at the time, but the idea had been planted in the mind of Khalid Sheikh Mohammed, and he presented a variation of it to Osama bin Laden in 1996.

Yousef kept busy planning terrorist operations in Pakistan. His next target was Pakistani politician Benazir Bhutto. Militant Islamists wanted her assassinated, and he was offered $68,000 to carry it out. His plan was to assassinate Bhutto with a bomb, but while he was planting the bomb detonator outside Bhutto's residence, it exploded in his face, injuring an eye. Prompt medical attention saved the eye, but the explosion attracted the attention of Pakistani authorities. Knowing that he was vulnerable to both American and Pakistani intelligence services, Yousef realized that he had to leave Pakistan. Before he left, however, Yousef traveled to Mashad, Iran, where he planted a C-4 bomb at a Shiite shrine that killed 26 people and injured another 200.

Yousef's next terrorist act was the bombing of the Israeli Embassy in Bangkok, Thailand, in early 1994. He built a bomb, and loaded it onto a truck. His designated driver became disoriented by Bangkok traffic and had an accident. Panicking, he abandoned the truck. The police had the truck towed to their headquarters. When they opened the truck, they found a huge bomb and the body of the truck's owner.

After this failure in Bangkok, Yousef decided to continue his career as a terrorist elsewhere, and he picked the Philippines as his new his area of operations. The Philippines was an obvious area of operations because it was home to a large cadre of militant Islamists, it was cheap, and Yousef already had contacts there. He moved to the Philippines, along with his uncle, Khalid Sheikh Mohammed, in spring 1994. After renewing his close ties with the Abu Sayyaf group, Yousef established his base of operations in Manila at the third-class Manor Hotel. By mid-1994 Yousef began planning several plots: one was to blow up eleven U.S. commercial airliners; another was to assassinate U.S. President William Clinton during a visit to the Philippines; and the final plot was to assassinate Pope John Paul II during a papal visit to Manila on January 15, 1995. Yousef and his uncle Khalid Sheikh Mohammed decided that the assassination of Pope John Paul II held the most promise. They settled on using remote-controlled pipe bombs planted along the route to and from the papal ambassador's home where the Pope would reside during his stay in Manila. Yousef experimented with a small nitroglycerine bomb that he tested first at a Manila movie theater on December 1, 1994, and then on an American commercial aircraft on December 8, 1994. Both tests were successful, with one of the bombs killing a passenger and almost causing the Boeing 747 to crash.

The bomb designed by Yousef was ingenious. He passed through Manila Airport carrying liquid nitroglycerin in a contact lens case and a nine-volt battery in the heel of each of his shoes. He assembled the bomb in the bathroom, using a Casio watch as a timer. On the first leg of the flight Yousef armed the bomb, and then he left the plane, headed for Cebu City in the southern Philippines. The bomb exploded two hours later, on the next leg of the flight. It tore a hole in the fuselage and damaged the aileron cables that controlled the plane's wing flaps. It took considerable skill for the plane's pilot to land the aircraft at Naha Airport in Okinawa. There was only one victim—a twenty-four-year-old Japanese engineer named Haruki Ikegami. Yousef has been described by FBI agents, after they studied his miniature bombs, as "a genius when it came to bomb building."

Yousef's next plan was the assassination of the Pope. This plan miscarried in a chemical mishap while Yousef was burning off extra chemicals in his Manila apartment on January 6, 1995. Yousef fled the scene and returned to Pakistan, but Philippine authorities found in his laptop computer the plans for his various plots. Among these plots was the one to fly commercial airliners into the Pentagon, White House, and other prominent targets. They also captured his associate and fellow bomb maker Murad. Under duress Murad identified Yousef and his role in the 1993 World Trade Center bombing. Murad also confessed that it was his idea for an aircraft to dive-bomb into CIA headquarters. This information enabled American and Philippine authorities to place Yousef on an international terrorist list. On the evening of February 7, 1995, Pakistani security forces arrested Yousef in Room 16 at the Su Casa Guest House in Islamabad, Pakistan, after being tipped to his location by former associate Istaique Parker. Parker turned him in because he did not want to participate in a suicide mission and because of the appeal of the $2 million reward that was offered. Pakistani Prime Minister Bhutto authorized turning Yousef over to American authorities, who transported him to the United States to stand trial for the World Trade Center bombing.

Yousef stood trial for both the World Trade Center bombing and for conspiracy to plant bombs on U.S. commercial airlines. His first trial was for the charge of conspiring to plant bombs on U.S. commercial airlines. After deciding to plead his case without a lawyer, Yousef was convicted by a jury on September 5, 1996, and was sentenced to life imprisonment in solitary confinement without possibility of parole. In the second and more publicized trial, for the World Trade Center bombing, Yousef was convicted on all charges on February 12, 1997. The judge sentenced him to 240 years in prison, fined him $4.5 million, and imposed restrictions on his visitors. The severity of the sentence resulted in part from witness testimony that Yousef intended to blow up the World Trade Center to let Americans know that they were at war with Islam and to punish their government for its support of Israel. Yousef has been serving his sentence at the federal "supermax" prison in Florence, Colorado.

There has been considerable conjecture about Yousef's relationship with Osama bin Laden and al-Qaeda. Yousef undoubtedly had connections with al-Qaeda—he had stayed at al-Qaeda safe houses and received training at al-Qaeda camps. There is even evidence that he was personally acquainted with bin Laden. Despite these connections, Yousef seems to have been operating outside of al-Qaeda. Most of his operations lacked the sophistication associated with al-Qaeda, and his money problems would have been solved if he had had al-Qaeda funding. Yousef has never provided valuable information about anything but his own exploits, so it remains difficult to determine his relationship with other terrorists and terrorist groups. His close relationship with his uncle, Khalid Sheikh Mohammed—future architect of the September 11 operation—does indicate that Yousef had a lasting impact among Islamist extremists.

See Also
Kifah Refugee Center, al-; Mohammed, Khalid Sheikh; Murad, Abdul Hakim Ali Hashim; World Trade Center Bombing (1993)

See Document
Document #1

Suggested Reading
J. Bowyer Bell, *Murders on the Nile: The World Trade Center and Global Terror* (San Francisco, CA: Encounter Books, 2003); Mike Davis, *Buda's Wagon: A Brief History of the Car Bomb* (London: Verso, 2007); Yosri Fouda and Nick Fielding, *Mastermind of Terror: The Truth Behind the Most Devastating Terrorist Attack the World Has Ever Seen* (New York: Arcade, 2003); Terry McDermott, *Perfect Soldiers: The 9/11 Hijackers: Who They Were, Why They Did It* (New York: HarperCollins, 2005); John Miller, Michael Stone, *The Cell: Inside the 9/11 Plot, and Why the FBI and CIA Failed to Stop It* (New York: Hyperion, 2002); Simon Reeve, *The New Jackals: Ramzi Yousef, Osama Bin Laden and the Future of Terrorism* (Boston: Northeastern University Press, 1999).

Z

Zadroga, James (1972–2006)

James Zadroga was a former New York City police detective who became a victim of the aftermath of the cleanup of the World Trade Center. At the time of his death he was on disability leave, suffering the effects of his work at Ground Zero. Zadroga was a thirteen-year veteran of the New York Police Department (NYPD).

Zadroga was inside Seven World Trade Center as the building collapsed on September 11. After surviving the collapse, Zadroga spent the next several weeks helping search for victims' remains, his work totaling more than 450 hours of digging through debris and inhaling noxious gases. Despite assurances from Environmental Protection Agency (EPA) officials that no health risks were associated with digging through the debris, Zadroga started exhibiting respiratory disorder symptoms. His health problems led the NYPD to grant him a tax-free disability pension of three-quarters pay in 2004. This settlement did not pay for his medical expenses. In the next two years Zadroga's health problems led to $50,000 in medical bills. Also in 2004, Zadroga's wife died of a brain tumor, leaving him alone to care for their young daughter. Zadroga expressed his anguish in a letter written soon after his illness began. Zadroga died on January 6, 2006, in Little Egg Harbor, New Jersey. He was thirty-four at the time of his death. An autopsy attributed his death to "foreign body granules in his lungs."

Life after Cleanup for NYPD Police Detective

Day after horrible day, I went back down surviving on two hours sleep a day for a three-week period away from home, away from my wife and unborn child. I can't pay my bills and work doesn't want to acknowledge that I'm sick, depressed and disgusted. I feel sorry and sympathize for those families that lost their loved ones, but I feel worse for those members of the service and their families that are going through what myself and family is going through. They remember the dead, but don't want to acknowledge the sick who are living. I'm not the only one out there. There are many suffering with similar, if not the same symptoms as myself.

Quoted in Robert F. Moore and Alison Gendar, "A Cop Dies & Kin Blame 9-11 Debris," *Daily News* (January 7, 2006), p. 5.

Linda and Joseph Zadroga, center top, parents of retired NYPD Officer James Zadroga, react as their son's casket is carried by New York police officers out of the Queen of Peace Church in North Arlington, New Jersey, on January 10, 2006. Zadroga was the first emergency responder to die as a result of exposure to dust and debris at the World Trade Center crash site. (AP IMAGES/Mike Derer.)

The controversy over Zadroga continued after his death. Although the medical examiner in Ocean County, New Jersey, determined that Zadroga's death was directly linked to his 500 hours of work at Ground Zero, the New York City officials refused to recognize his death as being in the line of duty. A statement by Christine Whitman, former governor of New Jersey and head of the EPA on September 11, implied that city officials, and even those working at Ground Zero, were to blame for not heeding warnings about contaminated air. Whitman's statement further inflamed the issue, and elicited the assertion from U.S. Senator Hillary Clinton (D-NY) that Whitman wanted "to wash her hands of this tragedy, but her EPA told New Yorkers that the air was safe to breathe." Charges and claims continue to cloud the issue while others who worked at Ground Zero continue to experience increasing health problems. The Zadroga family finally received some relief when New York Governor Pataki signed a bill in August 2006 that entitles Zadroga's daughter, Tylerann, to full line-of-duty death benefits until she reaches age nineteen. An effort by the family to have Zadroga listed among the victims of September 11 was opposed by the New York City Medical Examiner, who claimed in October 2007 that Zadroga died of ingested drugs rather than from the dust at Ground Zero. This opinion had been contradicted by previous examinations of the evidence.

See Also
Cleanup Operations at Ground Zero

Suggested Reading
Rosie DiManno, "Toll from 9/11 Climbs, Albeit Too Quietly," *Toronto Star* (January 13, 2006), p. A2; Kathleen Lucadamo, "Finally Some Good News for Family of 9-11 Hero," *Daily News* (August 15, 2006), p. 4; Robert F. Moore, "A Cop Dies & Kin Blame 9-11 Debris," *Daily News* (January 7, 2006), p. 5; Rich Schapiro, "WTC Air Doomed Ex-Cop," *Daily News* (April 12, 2006), p. 7; Paul H. B. Shin, David Saltonstall, and Paul D. Colford, "Dad Wants Christie Locked Up," *Daily News* (September 9, 2006), p. 4.

Zammar, Muhammad Heydar (1961–)

Muhammad Zammar was an al-Qaeda operative who recruited the key leader of the September 11 conspiracy. He was able to convince the members of the Hamburg Cell in the late 1990s to train in Afghanistan, rather than travel to Chechnya to fight with the Chechen rebels. Once they returned from the training camps Zammar kept track of them for al-Qaeda.

Zammar had extensive experience as a fighter for Islamist causes. He was born in 1961 in Aleppo, Syria. At age ten his family moved to West Germany. After high school, he attended a metalworking college and his goal was to work for Mercedes-Benz. Zammar traveled to Saudi Arabia, where he worked for a time as a translator. After returning to Germany, he found a job as a truck driver in Hamburg. His strong religious views led him to abandon truck driving in 1991 and travel to Afghanistan, where he underwent al-Qaeda training. Upon returning to Germany, Zammar spent all of his time as a freelance mechanic and traveled around Europe and the Middle East. He volunteered to fight in Bosnia in 1995. After leaving Bosnia in 1996, Zammar visited Afghanistan, where Osama bin Laden invited him to join al-Qaeda.

On his return to Hamburg, Germany, Zammar became a full-time recruiter for al-Qaeda. He spent so much time as a recruiter for al-Qaeda that he had no time to work as a mechanic. Zammar, his wife, and six children lived on state welfare. He traveled around Germany making speeches praising bin Laden and other jihadist leaders. His association with the Muslim missionary organization Tabligh afforded him some cover, but German police began watching him.

It was at the al-Quds Mosque in Hamburg that Zammar met the members of and then helped to form the Hamburg Cell. He first met and became friends with Mohamed Atta in 1998. He persuaded Atta, Marwan al-Shehhi, Ramzi bin al-Shibh, and Ziad Jarrah to train at al-Qaeda camps in Afghanistan for important missions. Zammar continued as the al-Qaeda contact person for the Hamburg Cell until its key leaders left for the United States.

Zammar continued to act as an al-Qaeda recruiter until his arrest. Many other Muslims in Germany were willing recruits for al-Qaeda, and Zammar was al-Qaeda's principal contact in Germany. German authorities left him alone, but they watched his activities with interest. American intelligence was also displaying concern about Zammar's connections with al-Qaeda. In July 2001 Zammar was briefly detained in Jordan, but was released after a short interrogation. After September 11, German police questioned Zammar, but released him because they believed they had too little evidence to charge him with a crime.

On October 27, 2001, Zammar traveled to Morocco to divorce his second wife; while there he was arrested by Moroccan security forces. The Moroccans sent Zammar to Syria, where he has undergone extensive interrogation at the notorious

Far Falastin Detention Center in Damascus. Zammar remains in Syrian custody, but American officials have learned much about the September 11 plot from him from answers to questions sent through the Syrians. There is evidence that Zammar has undergone torture at the hands of the Syrians, and this has led international organizations to protest. Regardless of how he is treated by the Syrians, Zammar knew the central players in the 9/11 attack and had a general knowledge of the plot, and so he has proven to be a valuable resource.

See Also
Atta, Mohamed el-Amir Awad el-Sayed; Hamburg Cell; Jarrah, Ziad Samir; Quds Mosque, al-; Shehhi, Marwan Yousef Muhammed Rashid Lekrab al-

Suggested Reading
Peter Finn, "German at Center of Sept. 11 Inquiry," *Washington Post* (June 12, 2002), p. A1; Peter Finn, "Al Qaeda Recruiter Reportedly Tortured," *Washington Post* (January 31, 2003), p. A14; Peter Finn, "Syria Interrogating Al Qaeda Recruiter," *Washington Post* (June 19, 2002), p. A1; Terry McDermott, *Perfect Soldiers: The 9/11 Hijackers: Who They Were, Why They Did It* (New York: HarperCollins, 2005); Steven Strasser (ed.), *The 9/11 Investigations: Staff Reports of the 9/11 Commission; Excerpts from the House-Senate Joint Inquiry Report on 9/11; Testimony from 14 Key Witnesses, Including Richard Clarke, George Tenet, and Condoleezza Rice* (New York: PublicAffairs, 2004).

Zawahiri, Ayman al- (1951–)

Ayman al-Zawahiri is the second most important leader of al-Qaeda, behind Osama bin Laden. As the former leader of the Egyptian terrorism group Islamic Jihad, he has considerable influence over bin Laden. Al-Zawahiri merged his group into al-Qaeda in the late 1990s, making his contingent of Egyptians influential in the operations of al-Qaeda.

Al-Zawahiri came from a prominent Egyptian family of medical doctors and religious leaders. He was born on June 9, 1951, in al-Sharquiyyah, Egypt. Both sides of his family have roots going back to Saudi Arabia, and his mother's family claims descent from the Prophet Muhammed. His father was a professor at Cairo University's medical school. At an early age, al-Zawahiri joined the Muslim Brotherhood; his first arrest by the Egyptian police was at age fifteen in 1966. After studying medicine at the University of Cairo, al-Zawahiri qualified as a physician in 1974, and then received a master's degree in surgical medicine in 1978.

Al-Zawahiri left medicine for political agitation against the Egyptian government of President Anwar Sadat. Inspiring his conversion to Islamic militancy were the writings of Sayyid Qutb, the ideological and spiritual leader of the Muslim Brotherhood. He was shocked by Qutb's execution in 1965 by the Nasser regime—enough so that he considered forming a clandestine Islamist group. While still in medical school, al-Zawahiri was instrumental in founding the terrorist group Islamic Jihad in 1973. This group's mission was to direct armed struggle against the Egyptian state. It did not take the Egyptian government long to ban activities of the Islamic Jihad.

In the aftermath of the 1981 assassination of President Anwar Sadat, Egyptian authorities arrested al-Zawahiri. He had learned of the plot against Sadat only a few hours before it went into operation. He had advised against proceeding because the plot was premature and destined to fail. Al-Zawahiri has claimed that prison authorities treated him brutally. After a trial and acquittal for his role in the assassination plot against Sadat, al-Zawahiri served a three-year prison sentence for illegal possession of arms. His stay in prison only increased his militancy. It was in prison that al-Zawahiri and Sheikh Omar Abdel Rahman shared their views. Under torture al-Zawahiri assisted the police in capturing some of his associates in the Islamic Jihad.

After his release from prison, al-Zawahiri resumed his anti-government activities. In 1984 he assumed the leadership of Islamic Jihad after its former head, Lieutenant-Colonel Abbud al-Zumar, was arrested by the Egyptian police. Al-Zawahiri fled Egypt for Jeddah, Saudi Arabia, in 1985 in the middle of President Hosni Mubarak's purge of Egyptian dissidents. There he worked in a medical dispensary. It was in Jeddah in 1986 that al-Zawahiri first met Osama bin Laden. The ongoing war against the Soviets in Afghanistan attracted al-Zawahiri, and he decided to move to Pakistan.

Soon after arriving in Pakistan, al-Zawahiri started coordinating plans between his Islamic Jihad and the Afghan Arabs fighting against Soviet forces in Afghanistan. It was in the late 1980s that al-Zawahiri became acquainted with and then allied with Osama bin Laden. He served as the chief advisor to bin Laden in the creation of the al-Qaeda network in 1988. Al-Zawahiri also engaged in a campaign to undermine bin Laden's relationship with Abdullah Azzam. Azzam's assassination benefited al-Zawahiri, but there is no concrete evidence that he played any role in it. The Pakistani security service concluded that six associates of al-Zawahiri carried out the assassination.

For the next several years in the early 1990s al-Zawahiri played a dual role as a member of al-Qaeda and as a leader of the Islamic Jihad. Al-Zawahiri left Pakistan and moved to Sudan with bin Laden in 1992. His closeness to Egypt allowed him to plot against the Egyptian government of President Mubarak. Al-Zawahiri's goal from the beginning was the

> **Friction between Azzam and al-Zawahiri as Seen by a Member of Egypt's Islamic Group**
>
> Ayman [al Zawahiri] had a severe conflict with Dr. Abdullah Azzam. He called him an agent of America, an agent of Saudi Arabia. I have spoken to Dr. al-Zawahiri many times. [He said to us] why do you have a good relationship with Dr. Azzam? Al Zawahiri [tried to maneuver] bin Laden away from Dr. Azzam. Two days before Dr. Azzam [was assassinated] I am in conversations with al Zawahiri [for] two hours and trying to change his mind, but he was very angry. I met al Zawahiri again at the funeral for Dr. Azzam. And Dr. al Zawahiri was very affected and sad. But before [Azzam was] dead he [was saying Azzam] is a spy.
>
> Quoted in Peter L. Bergen, *The Osama bin Laden I Know: An Oral History of al Qaeda's Leader* (New York: Free Press, 2006) p. 94.

> **Al-Zawahiri's Influence on Osama bin Laden**
>
> Zawahiri managed to introduce drastic changes to Osama bin Laden's philosophy after they first met in Afghanistan in the middle of 1986, mainly because of the friendship that developed between them. Zawahiri convinced bin Laden of his jihadi approach, turning him from a fundamentalist preacher whose main concern was relief work, into a jihadi fighter, clashing with despots and American troops in the Arab world. Zawahiri gave bin Laden some of his closest confidants to help him. They later became the main figures in bin Laden's Al-Qaeda.
>
> Montasser al-Zayyat, *The Road to Al-Qaeda: The Story of Bin Laden's Right-Hand Man* (London: Pluto Press, 2004), p. 68.

overthrow of the Egyptian government and replacement of it with an Islamic state. As head of the Islamic Jihad, he planned the unsuccessful assassination attempt on Egyptian President Mubarak during his visit to Addis Ababa on June 25, 1995. This failure led to the Sudanese government expelling him and his followers from Sudan.

His activities for al-Qaeda kept him traveling around the world. Bin Laden sent al-Zawahiri to Somalia to aid the opposition to American intervention there. Then he was active in building support for the Bosnian Muslims in their separatist war against Yugoslavia. Next he coordinated aid for Albanian Muslims in the Kosovo War. Finally, al-Zawahiri received the assignment to set up terrorist operations in Europe and the United States. He visited the United States in 1996 to inspect sites for possible terrorist operations there. His conclusion was that major terrorist activities could be undertaken against American targets in the United States.

Al-Zawahiri returned to Afghanistan to join bin Laden. He decided to merge his Egyptian Islamic Jihad group into al-Qaeda in 1998 for a combination of political, financial, and operational reasons. In 1997 al-Zawahiri had been implicated in his group's participation in the terrorist massacre of fifty-eight European tourists and four Egyptian security guards at Luxor, Egypt. This terrorist act was so brutal that it caused a backlash in both Egyptian public opinion and among the leadership of the Egyptian Islamic Jihad. It led to a schism within its leadership, with a significant number of the leaders concluding a ceasefire with the Egyptian government. Al-Zawahiri opposed the ceasefire with what he considered to be an apostate government. He led a much weakened Egyptian Islamic Jihad into an alliance with al-Qaeda.

> **Al-Zawahiri's Change of Heart**
>
> Zawahiri's alliance with Osama bin Laden changed his philosophy from one prioritizing combat with the near enemy (Egypt) to one confronting the far enemy: the United States and Israel. This development caused some confusion to Islamic Jihad members. Many were reluctant at first, but eventually agreed to be part of the Front in order to benefit from the many advantages it offered.
>
> Montasser al-Zayyat, *The Road to Al-Qaeda: The Story of Bin Laden's Right-Hand Man* (London: Pluto Press, 2004), p. 70.

Al-Zawahiri's influence over bin Laden has grown over the years. Bin Laden is neither as intellectual nor as militant as al-Zawahiri. Al-Zawahiri's views were expressed in the tract *Knights Under the Prophet's Banner*. In this work al-Zawahiri justified the use of violence as the only way to match the brute military force of the West led by the United States. For this reason it is necessary to target American targets, the tract posits, and the most effective way to do this is by the use of human bombs. The proposed strategy is to inflict enough damage to the United States that its citizens will demand that their government change policies toward Israel and the Arab world. This treatise was written before the September 11 attacks, but such attacks were obviously in its author's mind.

In his position as number two in al-Qaeda, al-Zawahiri serves as the chief advisor to bin Laden. Because of his more radical religious views, al-Zawahiri pushes bin Laden toward more radical positions. Al-Zawahiri was aware of the September 11 plot from the beginning, but stayed in the background. The subsequent loss of Afghanistan as a staging area for al-Qaeda made al-Zawahiri go into hiding along with bin Laden. Al-Zawahiri and bin Laden keep in contact, but they stay in

Osama bin Laden (second from left) and his top lieutenant, the Egyptian Ayman al-Zawahiri (second from right), are shown at an undisclosed location with two unidentified men in this image, which was broadcast by Al-Jazeera on Sunday, October 7, 2001. Bin Laden praised God for the 9/11 attacks and swore America "will never dream of security" until "the infidel's armies leave the land of Muhammad," in a videotaped statement aired after the strike launched by the United States and Britain in Afghanistan. (AP IMAGES/Al Jazeera.)

separate areas to avoid the possibility of al-Qaeda's chief leaders being wiped out in a single attack by the Americans and their allies. He continues to act as one of the chief spokesmen for al-Qaeda.

See Also
Atta, Mohamed el-Amir Awad el-Sayed; Bin Laden, Osama; Mohammed, Khalid Sheikh; Qaeda, al-

Suggested Reading
Abdel Bari Atwan, *The Secret History of al Qaeda* (Berkeley: University of California Press, 2006); J. Bowyer Bell, *Murders on the Nile: The World Trade Center and Global Terror* (San Francisco: Encounter books, 2003); Gilles Kepel, *The War for Muslim Minds: Islam and the West* (Cambridge, MA: Belknap Press, 2004); Lawrence Wright, *The Looming Tower: Al-Qaeda and the Road to 9/11* (New York: Knopf, 2006).

Zubaydah, Abu (1971–)
Abu Zubaydah was al-Qaeda chief of operations and number three in its hierarchy until his capture in March 2002. His position put him in charge of al-Qaeda training camps that selected the personnel for the September 11 plot. Zubaydah was originally a member of Ayman al-Zawahiri's Egyptian Islamic Jihad, but with al-Zawahiri he made the transition from that group to al-Qaeda in 1996.

Zubaydah has engaged in extremist Islamist activities since his youth. He was born on March 12, 1971, in Saudi Arabia. His original name was Zayn al-Abidin Mohamed Husayn, but he adopted the name Zubaydah early in his career as a radical Islamist. Although born a Saudi, he grew up among the Palestinians in a refugee camp in the Gaza Strip of Palestine. His first political association was with Hamas. Al-Zawahiri recruited him from Hamas to the Egyptian Islamic Jihad. When al-Zawahiri moved to Pakistan, Zubaydah went with him. As a teenager he fought with the Afghan Arabs in military operations against the Soviets. In one of these engagements in Afghanistan Zubaydah lost an eye. His abilities allowed him to move up in the hierarchy of al-Qaeda until he became al-Qaeda's chief of operations.

As chief of operations, Zubaydah played a role in all of al-Qaeda's military operations. Zubaydah selected Mohamed Atta for an important future martyr mission while Atta was in training at Khaldan camp in 1998. He was also active in planning the failed Millennium plots in Jordan and the United States. After the failed plots in Jordan and the United States, he became field commander for the attack on the USS *Cole* on October 12, 2000. Khalid Sheikh Mohammed was the operational chief for the September 11 attacks, but Zubaydah was a participant in the final draft of the plan, and was also active in post–September 11 plots. American authorities decided that Zubaydah was important enough to either capture or eliminate. What made Zubaydah important in al-Qaeda was his role in keeping all members' files, and in assigning individuals to specific tasks and operations.

A joint operation of Pakistani security, American Special Forces, and FBI Special Weapons and Tactics (SWAT) unit arrested Zubaydah in a suburb of Faisalabad, a town in western Pakistan, on March 28, 2002. From intercepted al-Qaeda communications, the National Security Agency learned that Zubaydah might be at a two-story house owned by a leader of the Pakistani militant extremist group Laskar-e-Toiba. In the subsequent assault thirty-five Pakistanis and twenty-seven Muslims from other countries were arrested. Among the captured was Zubaydah. He had been seriously wounded, with gunshots to the stomach, groin, and thigh. A medical unit determined that Zubaydah would survive, and he was taken into American custody.

Zubaydah has been held at an American interrogation camp since his capture. The Americans decided to interrogate him as if they were in Saudi Arabia. Instead of being frightened, Zubaydah asked his phony "Saudi" interrogators to contact a senior member of the Saudi royal family—Prince Ahmed bin Salman bin Abdul-Aziz—who would save him from the Americans. This claim stunned the interrogators. They returned later to confront him for lying. Zubaydah instead gave more details about agreements among al-Qaeda, Pakistani, and Saudi high-level government leaders. He went so far as to indicate that certain Pakistani and Saudi leaders knew about September 11 before the attack occurred. According to him, these officials did not have the details and did not want them, but they knew the general outlines of the plot. After Zubaydah learned that the "Saudi" interrogators were really Americans, he tried to commit suicide. This attempt failed, and Zubaydah no longer volunteered information and denied what he had said earlier.

American investigators quizzed the Saudi government about Zubaydah's comments. Representatives of the Saudi government called his information false and malicious. In a series of strange coincidences three of the Saudis named by

Zubaydah died in a series of incidents in the months after the inquiries—Prince Ahmed died of a heart attack at age forty-one; Prince Sultan bin Faisal bin Turki al-Said died in an automobile accident; and Prince Fahd bin Turki bin Saud al-Kabir died of thirst while traveling in the Saudi summer at age twenty-five. The supposed Pakistani contact, Air Marshal Ali Mir, was killed in an airplane crash on February 20, 2003, with his wife and fifteen senior officers.

Zubaydah remains in American custody at an unknown site, his eventual fate also unknown. Since American interrogators fooled him into talking, he has refused to provide further information about al-Qaeda or the September 11 plot. In September 2006 Zubaydah was transferred to the Guantánamo Bay Detention Center. Also in 2006, Ron Suskind produced the book *One Percent Doctrine*, which claimed Zubaydah was not nearly so important in al-Qaeda as had been thought. Suskind claimed that Zubaydah was mentally ill and only a minor figure in al-Qaeda. Suskind's assertions have been countered by numerous others, including former al-Qaeda operatives. Regardless of the controversy, Zubaydah appeared before a Combatant Status Review Tribunal in Guantánamo on March 27, 2007. There Zubaydah downplayed his role in al-Qaeda, but still claimed some authority. Zubaydah has also become part of another controversy: whether or not he was tortured by CIA operatives. Because the tapes of his interrogation have been destroyed, the nature of the torture is a matter of speculation.

See Also
al-Qaeda; Zawahiri, Ayman al-

Suggested Reading
Jane Corbin, *Al-Qaeda: The Terror Network That Threatens the World* (New York: Thunder's Mouth Press, 2002); Gerald Posner, *Why America Slept: The Failure to Prevent 9/11* (New York: Ballantine Books, 2003); Ron Suskind, *One Percent Doctrine* (New York: Simon and Schuster, 2006).